T0224585

R 4 Quick Syntax Reference

A Pocket Guide
to the Language, API's
and Library

Third Edition

Margot Tollefson

Apress®

R 4 Quick Syntax Reference: A Pocket Guide to the Language, API's and Library

Margot Tollefson
Vanward Statistics, PO Box 286, 612 Teneyck Avenue, Stratford, IA, 50249-0286, USA

ISBN-13 (pbk): 978-1-4842-7923-6
https://doi.org/10.1007/978-1-4842-7924-3

ISBN-13 (electronic): 978-1-4842-7924-3

Managing Director, Apress Media LLC: Welmoed Spahr
Acquisitions Editor: Steve Anglin
Development Editor: James Markham
Coordinating Editor: Mark Powers

Cover designed by eStudioCalamar

Cover image by Nkululeko Jonas on Unsplash (www.unsplash.com)

Distributed to the book trade worldwide by Apress Media, LLC, 1 New York Plaza, New York, NY 10004, U.S.A. Phone 1-800-SPRINGER, fax (201) 348-4505, e-mail orders-ny@springer-sbm.com, or visit www.springeronline.com. Apress Media, LLC is a California LLC and the sole member (owner) is Springer Science + Business Media Finance Inc (SSBM Finance Inc). SSBM Finance Inc is a **Delaware** corporation.

For information on translations, please e-mail booktranslations@springernature.com; for reprint, paperback, or audio rights, please e-mail bookpermissions@springernature.com.

Apress titles may be purchased in bulk for academic, corporate, or promotional use. eBook versions and licenses are also available for most titles. For more information, reference our Print and eBook Bulk Sales web page at http://www.apress.com/bulk-sales.

Any source code or other supplementary material referenced by the author in this book is available to readers on GitHub (https://github.com/Apress). For more detailed information, please visit http://www.apress.com/source-code.

Printed on acid-free paper

*This edition is dedicated to my parents,
Roy and Alice Marie, who stood by me.*

Table of Contents

About the Author

Margot Tollefson is a self-employed consulting statistician residing in the tiny town of Stratford in the corn and bean fields of central Iowa. Her business is Vanward Statistics. She started using the S-Plus language in the early 1990s and was happy to switch to R over 18 years ago. Margot enjoys writing her own functions in R–to do plots and simulations as well as to implement custom modeling and to use published statistical methods. She earned her graduate degrees in statistics from Iowa State University in Ames, Iowa.

About the Technical Reviewer

Matt Wiley leads institutional effectiveness, research, and assessment at Victoria College, facilitating strategic and unit planning, data-informed decision making, and state/regional/federal accountability. As a tenured, associate professor of mathematics, he won awards in both mathematics education (California) and student engagement (Texas). Matt earned degrees in computer science, business, and pure mathematics from the University of California and Texas A&M systems.

Outside academia, he coauthors books about the popular R programming language and was managing partner of a statistical consultancy for almost a decade. He has programming experience with R, SQL, C++, Ruby, Fortran, and JavaScript.

A programmer, a published author, a mathematician, and a transformational leader, Matt has always melded his passion for writing with his joy of logical problem solving and data science. From the boardroom to the classroom, he enjoys finding dynamic ways to partner with interdisciplinary and diverse teams to make complex ideas and projects understandable and solvable.

Acknowledgments

First, I would like to acknowledge the R Core Team at the R Foundation for Statistical Computing, Vienna, Austria. The team provides for the help pages in R, without which this book would not have been possible. The technical editor, Matt Wiley, gave many good suggestions and corrections, for which I would like to thank him. I would also like to acknowledge the editors, Mark Powers, Nirmal Selvaraj, and Steve Anglin, at Apress for their help. And, per usual, I would like to thank my husband, Clay Conard, for his patience as I spent days writing and for his support.

Introduction

In this third edition of *R Quick Syntax Reference*, there is more of an emphasis on RStudio and the conveniences that RStudio provides. The book continues to cover how to download and update R and RStudio, how to work with both programs, the types (and modes) and classes of R objects and expressions, using the S4 object system (at the introductory level), working with and creating scripts and functions, and importing from and exporting to external files. Also, working with objects that have dimensions, working with character objects, controlling the flow of a function or group of expressions, running some useful functions (in more and less detail), and working with some trickier parts of R.

This edition focuses on object and expression types rather than modes. The coverage of the S4 object system remains the same as in the second edition, but the Reference Class object system now has a couple of sections. In Chapter 5, the coverage of date and time classes has been expanded. The chapters on importing and exporting external files have been expanded, with detailed coverage of connection functions (for connecting to external locations, including URLs and URIs). Table 10-1, in Chapter 10, has been expanded to cover most of the importing and exporting functions that are in the default packages loaded by R.

In Chapter 11, there is one more apply function (for applying a function recursively). Also, some functions for working with character strings have been added. In Chapter 13, the last example has been substantially changed (but still codes the same process). The other examples in the chapter remain the same, although some argument names have been changed.

A few more functions are presented in Chapters 15 and 16. In Chapter 15, functions for finding derivatives and integrals are now included. Sections on parsing and deparsing text have been added. Also, the functions that return attributes are described, as well as the function to evaluate expressions. In Chapter 16, the functions are organized by subject matter more than in the first two editions.

Chapter 17 now has a section on functions that work with paths that go to external locations. Also, a section on entering and editing data objects at the console has been added, as has a section on some new changes in R. The information about getting results out of a function has been moved to Chapter 7.

My purpose in writing and revising this book has been to provide a useful reference for using the versatile R language. I feel the book achieves the purpose of the book. I hope the reader does too.

Source Code

All source code associated with this book can be accessed at `http://github.com/apress/r4-quick-syntax-reference`.

PART I

R Basics

CHAPTER 1

Downloading R and RStudio and Setting Up a File System

R is an open source statistical programming language based on the commercial programming language S. The S language was developed at Bell Laboratories in the 1970s and 1980s, mainly by John Chambers. The last version of S, called S4, came out in 1998. The R language was initially developed by Ross Ihaka and Robert Gentleman at the University of Auckland (in New Zealand) through "clean-room" methods. R was written to mimic S, but with its own code. The first official version of the R language was released in 1995 and version v1.0 in 2000. The current version of R is v4.1.1 (as of September 2021). R is a GNU package and is released under the GNU General Public License. The Comprehensive R Archive Network (CRAN) makes the language and packages available and is a network of mirrors at institutions. CRAN was first deployed in 1997. (The preceding information is from the Wikipedia pages **S (programming language)** and **R (programming language)**.) The citation for R is

> *R Core Team (2021). R: A language and environment for statistical computing. R Foundation for Statistical Computing, Vienna, Austria. URL* `https://www.R-project.org/`.

© Margot Tollefson 2022
M. Tollefson, *R 4 Quick Syntax Reference*, https://doi.org/10.1007/978-1-4842-7924-3_1

RStudio is an Integrated Development Environment for the R language. The citation for RStudio is

> *RStudio Team (2021). RStudio: Integrated Development Environment for R. RStudio, PBC, Boston, MA. URL* `http:// www.rstudio.com/`.

The first step in using R and RStudio is to download the two programs from the Internet. R must be downloaded first. R and RStudio can be downloaded for the modern operating systems: the Windows systems, the macOS systems, and the Linux distributions (and other UNIX-like systems). In this chapter, you will learn how to download and install R with the 30 basic packages of R, plus how to install RStudio. You will learn how to use R to install other R packages and how to update R. Updating packages using RStudio is covered in Chapter 2. Also, you will learn how to place R history and data files in individual folders within the file system of the computer.

Downloading R and RStudio

You can download R from the website of CRAN. CRAN updates the installation process from time to time; however, the instructions in this book are for the current steps at the time of publication. CRAN provides instructions on the website if the process has changed. (Solutions also exist for downloading R to a server or root system and linking the program to remote computers, e.g., using the open source program RStudio Server supplied by RStudio.)

Begin the download process by going to the website `www.r-project.org/`. At the website, in the left menu, click on the link labelled **CRAN** (below **Download**), which opens a list of CRAN mirrors. Choose a mirror near you. Links to the current versions of R for Windows systems, macOS systems, and Linux systems are listed in the first section of the window. Select the appropriate version.

The Windows Systems

On the page that opens with the Windows system link, select the link **base** (which is a link under **Subdirectories**). In the next window, click on the **download** link for the given Windows system version. (Currently, the link is **Download R 4.1.0 for Windows**.) R will begin to download.

When the program finishes downloading, find the downloaded file in your file system. Downloads are put in `C://Users/User_folder/Downloads`, where *User_folder* is the folder of the user. Click on the downloaded file, which is an `.exe` installation file (currently `R-4.1.0-win.exe`.) A question about whether to run the program may pop up. The installation program should be safe, so run the program (as an administrator). Choose which language to use.

The installation wizard will open. The installation process steps through several pages. On the first page, read the GNU GENERAL PUBLIC LICENSE; then, click **Next**. For the rest of the pages, accepting the defaults on each page is fine, so click **Next** on each page until the page of additional choices

At the page of additional choices, to place an icon on the desktop and/or the Quick Start menu, check one, or both, of the first two checkboxes. Then, click **Next**, and the program will begin to install. When the installation is finished, click **Finish** to complete the installation. The program and the 30 base packages are now installed. An icon for **R** will be on the computer desktop if placing an icon was chosen and in the Start menu. To run **R**, click on the icon or on the R entry in the Start menu.

The macOS Systems

On the page that opens from the macOS system link, **Download R for macOS**, first read the section under **R for macOS**. The R project gives the advice to check the files for viruses and other problems.

Under **Latest release**, the current package choices are R-4.1.0.pkg and R-4.1.0-arm64.pkg. R-4.1.0.pkg is for computers with a 64-bit Intel processor and macOS 10.13 or later. R-4.1.0-arm64.pkg is for computers with an Apple M1 or later processor and macOS 11 or later. (For earlier systems, there are links to earlier versions of R below on the page.) Selecting a version will download the package. When the packages have finished downloading, open the download folder in **Finder**.

Select the R version .pkg file in the download folder. Opening the version will open the installer. With the installer open, click **Continue** to go to the next page of the installer. Read the message from CRAN; then click **Continue**. Again, read the message from CRAN; then click **Continue**.

On the next page, you will find the license. After reading the license, click **Agree** to download **R**.

On the next page, select **Install**. The installation program will ask for a password. After you have entered the password (the password you use to get onto your computer), the installation will begin. When the installation is finished, click **Close**. You will next have the choice of keeping the .pkg file or discarding it. You can discard the file. **R** will be in the applications folder and on the launchpad, and the 30 base packages will be loaded. Start **R** by opening the launchpad and selecting the **R** icon or by clicking on **R** in the applications folder in **Finder**.

The Linux Systems

At the CRAN site, CRAN provides source code for R Linux distributions Debian, Fedora, Red Hat, openSUSE, and Ubuntu. The Debian and

Ubuntu distributions have been updated in 2021. The Fedora and Red Hat distributions date from 2020. The openSUSE distribution dates from 2016.

The developers state that R is available through the package management system for most distributions of Linux. Look under GNU R. If the command line version of R is not available using the package management system, installing R directly from the terminal is an option. For the Debian, Fedora, Red Hat, and Ubuntu distributions, instructions for installing R can be found by clicking one of the links in the parentheses after the **Download R for Linux** link. Instructions for openSUSE are found by clicking on the link **Download R for Linux** and on the **suse** link in the page that follows.

RStudio

At the RStudio site, RStudio provides free source code for RStudio, as well as versions that cost. RStudio is available for Windows systems, macOS systems, and most Linux distributions. To download the free version of RStudio, go to `www.rstudio.com/products/rstudio/download/`. Scroll down to the blue **Download** buttons and click on the left button (under **RStudio Desktop**, **Open Source License**, **Free**). The computer focus will go to a link for your operating system. Use the link to download and run the installer program.

For Windows systems, follow the directions of the installer. The instructions are like those for R.

On the macOS systems, the file `RStudio-version_number.dmg` is the installation file, where *version_number* is the RStudio version number. The current number is `1.4.1717`. RStudio must be installed by hand each time the computer is booted if RStudio is to be used during the session.

For Linux distributions, RStudio should be available in the package manager. Search under RStudio.

Installing and Updating Packages

When initially installed, by default, R comes with 30 packages. Often, the user will want to use the power of the many other packages available in R. Installing and updating a package is straightforward. The easiest way to install and update packages is to use RStudio. However, we cover installing and updating packages at the command line here and installing and updating packages using RStudio in Chapter 2, where we introduce the RStudio subwindows. Whether installed at the command line or by using RStudio (which just generates R commands and runs the R commands at command line), the packages are in the same folder and accessible to both programs.

Using the command line in R, for any of the operating systems, if the name of a package is known, typing

`install.packages("package name")`

at the R command prompt, where *package name* is the name of the package, will install the package. To update packages, typing

`update.packages()`

at the R command prompt will find those packages with updates and update the packages. To see which packages are already installed on the computer, enter

`installed.packages()`

at the R prompt.

If the name of the package is not known (also for known names), using the installer for the Windows operating systems and the macOS operating systems is easy. In Linux distributions, finding the name of a package is a bit harder. Instructions for Windows systems, macOS systems, and Linux systems are given in the following.

The Windows Systems

To install a package in a Windows system not using the command line, start by opening R. On the menu bar at the top of the screen, select **Packages**. A menu will drop down. **Select Install package(s)....** Either the CRAN mirror window or the Packages window will come up. If the CRAN mirror window comes up, select a close mirror and click **OK**, which will bring up the Packages window.

The Packages window consists of a list of all the available packages. Scroll down the list to find the package(s) you wish to install and select the package(s). Click **OK** to begin the installation. As the installation proceeds, the steps of the installation will scroll on the R console. When the R prompt returns to the screen, the installation is complete.

To update packages not using the command line, select **Packages** on the menu bar and then select **Update packages....** The **Packages to be updated** window will open, and it will have a list of all the installed packages with updates. If there are none, the window will be empty. Choose the packages for updating and click the **OK** button. If a question about using a personal library pops up, choose **Yes**. The packages will update. When the R prompt returns to the screen, the updates are complete.

The macOS Systems

To install packages in the macOS operating systems not using the command line, start by opening R. On the drop-down menu bar at the top of the screen, select **Packages & Data**. From the drop-down menu, select **Package Installer**, which brings up the R Package Installer. Choose the repository in which to look for the package. Click **Get List** for a full list of packages in the repository or use the **Package Search** option to search for a package. Under either option, select the package(s) to be installed from the list.

9

Below the list of packages are choices for the location to put the packages. Usually, one of the first two options will be correct. To the right of the location options are the **Install Selected** and **Update All** buttons. Before clicking on **Install Selected**, check the **Install Dependencies** box to make sure that any necessary packages are installed. Click **Install Selected** to start the installation process. The selected packages will install.

To update packages, select **Packages & Data** from the menu bar at the top of the screen. From the drop-down menu, select **Package Installer**, which opens the R Package Installer. At the bottom right of the Installer, select **Update All** and follow instructions.

The Linux Systems

For Linux distributions, use the command line method given at the start of this section to install and update packages. To access a list of package names, enter `available.packages()` at the R prompt. Since there are over 30,000 package names, the list should be assigned to an object and the object examined (e.g., entering `ap=available.packages(); ap[ which( substr( ap, 1, 3 )=="MAL" ) ]` at the R prompt will return all packages that begin with MAL).

Updating R

Since CRAN does not provide automatic updates for R, you must update it manually. For all the operating systems, the following instructions can be used. An alternative process for the macOS systems is easier and given separately below.

All Systems

The first step in updating R is to open R and install the package **installr** if the package has not already been previously installed. Next, use the function **library** to provide access to **installr**. Type

`library(installr)`

at the command prompt and press **enter**. Then, to update R, type

`updateR()`

at the command prompt and press **enter**. R will either do an update or give a message that the program is up-to-date and return **False**.

Once **installr** has been installed, **installr** does not need to be installed again. The library must be loaded if the library is to be used during an R session.

(Within an R session, a package must be loaded to be used. A package is loaded at the command line by entering **library(*package_name*)** where **package_name** is the name of the package. However, a package can only be loaded if the package has been installed at some time in the past. Once loaded, R has access to the objects in the package.)

The macOS Systems

The first step in the alternative version of updating R in the macOS systems is to open R and select **R** from the drop-down menu bar at the top of the page. To run the updater, select **Check for R Updates** in the drop-down menu under **R** and follow instructions.

Using R in Separate Folders

Separate workspace images for R can be maintained in separate folders for Windows systems, macOS systems, and Linux systems. This property of R is very handy for using R on separate projects. While the process of opening R in a given folder varies by the operating system, once in a folder, saving the workspace image is straightforward.

For all operating systems, the function `setwd()` can be used to set the working directory, for example, `setwd("Documents/Margot's MacBook/R stuff")` on my macOS system. (Entering `getwd()` at the R prompt returns the address of the current folder.) There are also operating system specific ways to open R in a folder (see below).

When an R session is closed, the program asks if the user would like to save the workspace image. If there are objects in the workspace and **Yes** is selected, then the `.RData` and `.Rhistory` (and `.Rapp.history` for macOS systems) files are saved in the current directory. (For macOS systems and Linux systems, the files are hidden, but the files are there.) If there are no objects in the workspace, only `.Rhistory` is saved.

The workspace of an R or RStudio session contains all the user-defined objects that have been created but not removed and that have been part of a saved workspace, starting with the first time the workspace was opened and saved.

The `.RData` file contains the objects that were in R at the beginning of the session plus any objects that were added during the session minus any objects that were erased during the session. The `.Rhistory` (`.Rapp. history` for macOS systems, if the file exists) file contains the history of the lines input at the R console. By default, all lines up to the last 512 lines are saved in Windows systems. For macOS systems and Linux systems, the default is 250 lines. Access to the lines carries over from session to session if the workspace image is saved.

As a note for the initial setup in a given folder, any objects in the desktop R will still be in R when the folder is changed. You can easily remove the objects. For the method to erase the workspace using the menus in RStudio, see Chapter 2. When using the command line, type `rm(list=ls())` at the R prompt. Also, removing old and no longer used objects from a workspace is a good idea since workspaces tend to get cluttered.

Projects in RStudio

One way to work with separate projects is to open new projects in RStudio. To open a project in a folder, first, the working directory in RStudio is set to the folder. A project can then be created using the menus in RStudio. The project can be saved in the usual way. After being saved, the project can be accessed by clicking on the name in the folder where the project was saved. Only one project can be created in a folder. The name for the project is the folder name followed by `.Rproj`. (The `.RData` and `.Rhistory` files are also saved when the project is saved.) A more complete description of setting up an RStudio project is described in Chapter 2.

The Windows Systems

To initially set up R in a folder, open R at the desktop. (Click on the **R** icon on the desktop or click **R** in the Start menu.) Select **File** on the menu bar at the top of the screen. From the drop-down menu, select **Change dir...**. The **Browse to Folder** window will open. Navigate to the folder of choice.

When exiting **R**, save the workspace image and R will create `.RData` (if objects are present) and `.Rhistory` files in the folder. The `.RData` file will have a blue **R** icon associated with the file. In the future, going to the folder and clicking on the **R** icon will open R, and the history and objects saved within the folder will be present. Otherwise, if there is no `.Rdata` file, navigate to the folder within R and load the history by hand (click **Load History...** under the **File** choice in the top menu or enter `loadhistory()` at the R prompt).

The macOS Systems

For working within different folders in the macOS systems, the first time you use the folder, change the working directory to the folder before closing and saving R. To change the working directory, you can press **Command** and **D** together on the computer keyboard and select the folder. Or click **Misc** in the top menu on the computer screen, and then choose **Change Working Directory...** and select the folder.

To open R after the workspace and history have been initially saved, go to the folder in the terminal and enter `open -a R` at the prompt. Or go to the folder on the computer and click on the hidden file `.Rdata`. (Press the **shift**, **command**, and `>/.` keys simultaneously to toggle the hidden files in Finder–the hidden file names are gray rather than black.) Or open the terminal and type

```
open -a R "folder_location"
```

where *folder_location* is the location of the folder. Be sure to quote the location. R will open in the folder using the `.RData` and `.Rapp.history` files for that folder.

The Linux Systems

To open R in a folder in the Linux systems, you can use the terminal. In the terminal, change the directory to the folder and type **R** at the command prompt. If an `.Rhistory` is present in the folder, the history will be present in the R session. If an `.RData` file is present in the folder, objects that were in the workspace will be present.

CHAPTER 2

The R Prompt and the RStudio Main Menus and Subwindows

This chapter covers the R prompt and the RStudio main menus and subwindows. It starts with descriptions of the three parts of R: objects, operators, and assignments. It continues with a discussion of working with the R prompt, followed by an example of doing a calculation at the R prompt. Afterward, it describes the RStudio main menus and the four RStudio subwindows. One nice thing about RStudio is that when you type, it provides autocompletion for object names. But RStudio can be slow to load and run.

In Windows systems and macOS systems, R runs in GUIs: *RGUI* in Windows systems and *R.app GUI* in macOS systems. Both RGUI and R.app GUI open an R Console and run from the R prompt in the R Console. GUIs are available in Linux systems, but this book only covers running R from the terminal window R prompt. RStudio, for the three operating systems, is also covered.

© Margot Tollefson 2022
M. Tollefson, *R 4 Quick Syntax Reference*, https://doi.org/10.1007/978-1-4842-7924-3_2

The Three Parts of R: Objects, Operators, and Assignments

There are basically three parts of R: objects, operators, and assignments. (Numbers, character strings, and logical values are implicitly included here.)

> *Objects* contain information and can be, among other things, data, functions, or the results of functions. Objects always have a name. Users create some objects, which are automatically saved on creation. Other objects are constants, functions, and datasets contained in the packages of R.

> *Operators* manipulate objects, numbers, strings, and/or logical variables. For example, entering **a = 2*b** at the R prompt would multiply **b** by two and assign the result to **a**. The objects **a** and **b** are numeric objects, and * is the multiplication operator. The equal sign makes an assignment of two times **b** to **a**. Operators are a type of function.

> *Assignments* assign an expression to an object. *Expressions* can consist of objects, numbers, logical variables, strings, lists, other expressions, and/or functions, which can be operated on by operators.

Expressions can be evaluated from the R prompt or be evaluated when assigned to an object. (The other places where assignments and operations occur are within functions and within flow control.)

The R Prompt

All of R flows from the R prompt. R is essentially the running of functions and the doing of calculations. Functions and calculations can be run at the R prompt with or without an assignment to an object. Functions and calculations can also be run as part of another function, but everything starts at the R prompt.

Using R from the R prompt may seem daunting at first. R opens with some text and then a lonely little greater-than sign (>), which is the R prompt. The opening text gives the R version number and some other information about the program, including the fact that the program runs with no warranty.

R remembers every line that is entered into the program, up to a set number of lines. A very handy side of R is that the up and down arrows on the keyboard will step through the lines. You only need to enter an expression once. Corrections to expressions are easy to do without typing the entire expression again.

To close R, enter **q()** at the R prompt or, for Windows systems and macOS systems, close the window. R will close with the option to save the workspace. In Linux systems, if the terminal window is closed without using **q()**, the current workspace will be lost.

The workspace consists of any objects present in R at the time the program is closed and the current history. Closing R without saving the workspace will result in reverting to the workspace present at the time the R session started.

An Example of a Calculation

The simplest use of R is as a calculator. The following calculation was done from the R prompt. There is no assignment in the calculation, so the result is returned on the screen.

```
> (1 + 3 + 7)/5
[1] 2.2
>
```

The first line gives the expression to be evaluated, and the second line gives the result. The **[1]** in the second line is a label that tells the user that the result is the first value returned from the expression. Many expressions return more than one value. At the third line, the R prompt comes back, and R is ready for another task.

The Main Menus and the Four Subwindows in RStudio

On opening the program for the first time, RStudio presents you with three subwindows. On the left side of the main RStudio window is a single subwindow. On the right are two vertically aligned subwindows. Across the top, above the three subwindows, are two menus that provide several options for working with RStudio. Both menus extend the full width of the main window.

The Main Menus

In Windows systems and Linux systems, the upper menu is in the main RStudio window, while in macOS systems, the upper menu is on the main macOS system menu bar. In macOS systems, if RStudio is expanded to the full screen, you must hover over the top of the page to see the upper menu.

The upper menu has the buttons **File**, **Edit**, **Code**, **View**, **Plots**, **Session**, **Build**, **Debug**, **Profile**, **Tools**, **Window** (the Windows system does not have the **Window** tab), and **Help**. Each button opens a drop-down menu. The drop-down menus are somewhat self-explanatory. Here, we cover **File**, **Session**, and **Tools**.

The first menu item under **File** is **New File**. Hovering over **New File** brings up a menu of the types of files that can be opened. The choice of a type opens the fourth subwindow (which is placed above the first subwindow). The available types are an R Script, an R Notebook, an R Markdown document, a Shiny Web App, a Plumber API, a C file, a C++ file, a Header file, a Markdown file, an HTML file, a CSS file, a JavaScript file, a D3 file, a Python script, a shell script, an SQL script, a Stan file, a text file, an R Sweave document, an R HTML document, an R Presentation file, or an R Documentation file. (Some of the choices under New File require more packages to be installed, which is straightforward to do.)

R scripts are lines of R code. R Notebook creates HTML documents. R Markdown creates documents in HTML, PDF, or WORD format; presentations in HTML, PDF, and PowerPoint formats; documents and presentations in Shiny format; and documents from templates. Both R Notebook and R Markdown can contain code chunks that are run when the document or presentation is created. Shiny Web apps are apps that can be used on the web and that are interactive. Plumber APIs are application programming interfaces for R. The default interface is `openapi.json`. The next several choices for **New File** are for specific programming languages.

There are four more choices below the languages. R Sweave creates documents in LATEX format. R code can be included in the document. R HTML creates an HTML document with chunks of R code. R Presentation creates slides that can contain R code. Both the code and the output from the code can be displayed in one slide for each code chunk. R Documentation provides a template for creating documentation for an R package.

The **New Project** choice under **File** sets up a new RStudio project. The project can be put in a new folder or in an existing folder. Or a project can be imported from a repository. Below **New File** and **New Project** are options for opening existing files and projects, importing datasets, saving or closing files and projects, knitting and compiling documents and presentations, and printing or publishing documents or presentations. Knitting a document or presentation creates a file that can be rendered. Rendering creates the final document by running the code in the knit document.

Under the **Session** tab in the upper main menu are choices to open a new session, interrupt a running script, terminate the current session, restart a session, change the working directory, load or save a workspace, clear a workspace (clearing a workspace removes the objects in the workspace), and close the session in an orderly way. Under the **Tools** tab are options to install packages and check for updates, to set up and use a version control system, to open a terminal shell, to work with terminals, to manage jobs, to use add-ins, and to manage memory. Also, in the drop-down menu, there are links to lists of keyboard shortcuts, project options, and global options, along with an option to change keyboard shortcuts.

The menu below the upper main menu contains icons for (from left to right) opening new files (listing most of the types under **File**/**New File**, but not all of the programming languages), opening a new project, opening a file on the computer, saving the contents of the **Source** subwindow to the computer (see the section on the fourth subwindow), saving the contents under all of the **Source** subwindow tabs, printing the contents of the **Source** subwindow, searching for and opening files in the working directory, adjusting the look and positions of the subwindows, and adding add-ins. On the right of the lower main menu, the name of the RStudio project is displayed. The drop-down menu below the name gives options for working with the project and for changing the project. The menu also lists all the RStudio projects present on the computer. Many of the options in the lower menu duplicate options in the upper menu.

The First Subwindow

The subwindow on the left opens to the standard R console, under a tab labeled **Console**. Commands are entered at the R prompt in the same way as in R. At the top of the subwindow, the version of R and the working directory is given. The console can be cleared by clicking on the broom in the upper right corner of the subwindow. (Entering CTRL+L or `cat("\014")` works too.)

To the right of the **Console** tab is a tab labeled **Terminal**, which gives access to the terminal of the computer. Under the **Terminal** tab, the tab **Terminal 1** has a drop-down menu for opening, working with, and closing terminals. To the left of **Terminal 1** are arrows that step through any open terminals.

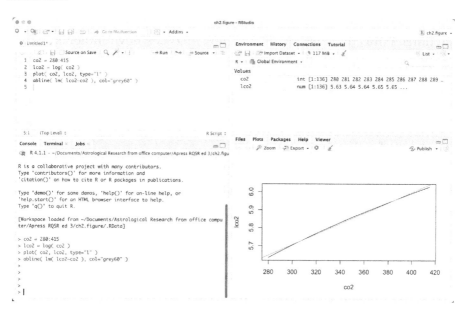

Figure 2-1. *A screenshot of the four subwindows in RStudio, from my MacBook Air computer (the range of the carbon dioxide levels sources from the Mauna Loa Observatory CO2 data found at* `https://gml.noaa.gov/ccgg/trends/` *for the upper level and from estimates of CO2 levels using the ice core from the Law Dome in Antarctica found at* `https://cdiac.ess-dive.lbl.gov/trends/co2/lawdome.html` *for the lower level)*

To the right of the **Terminal** tab is the tab labelled **Jobs**. The **Jobs** subwindow shows the messages returned when a job is run. Jobs are scripts that are stored in the Source subwindow or outside of R and that are run in R. At the top left of the subwindow is a button **Start Local Job**. A menu drops down from the button asking for the location of the script, whether to access the global environment, and what to do with the output from the script.

The Second Subwindow

The upper subwindow on the right contains the tabs **Environment**, **History**, **Connections**, and **Tutorial**. Under the **Environment** tab, RStudio lists the objects in the workspace, classified as **Data**, **Values**, and **Functions**. **Data** contains lists, data frames, matrices, environments, and S4 objects (all to be described later). **Values** contains objects that are not lists, data frames, matrices, environments, S4 objects, or user-defined functions. **Functions** contains user-defined functions. Various properties of the objects are given in **Environment**, such as the type of the object and the number of dimensions of the object.

Under the **Environment** tab are two menus. The upper menu lets you open a workspace, save a workspace, import a dataset, monitor memory usage, clear the workspace, choose to display objects as a list or as a grid, and choose options to refresh the subwindow. The lower menu lets you choose whether to use R or Python and the location of the displayed environment. A search box is to the right on the lower menu.

Under the **History** tab are the lines of code that have been entered at the console. Only a set number of lines are retained. There is a menu below the tab. The menu provides for loading a history, saving a history, moving highlighted code to the **Console** (first) or **Source** (fourth) subwindows, removing highlighted lines of history, and removing the full history. On the right side of the menu is a search function for searching the history.

Under the **Connections** tab is a list of connections. Initially, there are none. Connections are links to files, URLs, pipes, or sockets outside of R. Connections provide for the interactive reading of outside data and are often used in data mining. Clicking on the **New Connection** button under the **Connections** tab gives a list of the possible connections that RStudio sees as available. To the right of the button is a search box.

To the right of the **Connections** tab is the **Tutorial** tab, which provides links to several tutorials. The tutorials are in the learnr package.

The Third Subwindow

The lower right subwindow has the tabs **Files**, **Plots**, **Packages**, **Help**, and **Viewer**. Under the **Files** tab is a list of the files and folders in the working directory of the computer. Options exist to add a folder, delete a file, rename a file, copy a file, or move a file, and to go to or set a working a directory, as well as other tasks. Clicking on a file displayed in the subwindow opens the file in the **Source** subwindow. You can move the displayed folder to the folder containing it by clicking on the two dots just below **Name**. To open a folder in the current folder, click on the folder. The folders and files are sorted alphabetically, either ascending or descending, using the triangle to the left of **Name**.

Under the **Plots** tab are any plots that have been created. In the menu below the tab, you can use the left and right arrow icons to move through the plots. The **Zoom** button opens the plot in a stand-alone, larger window. Plots can be exported to image or PDF files or to the clipboard by using the drop-down menu below the **Export** button. Individual plots can be deleted by clicking on the white cross in the red circle. All plots can be deleted by clicking on the broom. A plot can be published by clicking on the **Publish** button. Clicking on the triangle to the right of the Publish button brings up a menu from which you can set up places to publish. RStudio provides RPubs (a free service) and RStudio Connect as locations to publish the plot.

The **Packages** tab gives a list of installed packages. Each package is listed with the package name, the description, the version number, and, for some, a link to the source of the package and a button to delete the package. Checking the box to the left of a package opens the library in the **Console** subwindow, and unchecking the box detaches the library.

In the menu below the **Packages** tab, clicking on the **Install** link opens a search box to find packages to install. Entering characters into the search box brings up all packages beginning with the characters, making it easier to find the package to be installed. Clicking on the **Update** link gives a list of those installed packages with updates and offers a choice to update them. There is a search box, on the far right on the menu below the **Packages** tab, for searching the installed packages.

The **Help** tab provides a link to the help pages. Below the tab is a menu in which there are (from left to right) arrows to scroll through the open help pages, a link to the RStudio help page home, a button to open the help page in a stand-alone window, a search box, and a button to refresh the page. Entering characters into the search box on the menu bar brings up function, dataset, and topic names that contain the characters (in the order of the characters and not necessarily contiguous). The search is case sensitive. Below the menu, on a second menu bar, there is a link to a drop-down menu containing the help page search history and a search box for searching within the help page.

The **Viewer** tab is for viewing content on the local web. The RStudio website has helpful information on using **Viewer**.

The Fourth Subwindow

The fourth subwindow is the **Source** subwindow. When open, the **Source** subwindow is in the upper left corner of the main window. The subwindow can contain plain text or code in the languages and formats available in RStudio. Or the subwindow can contain objects from the **Data** and **Function** sections under the **Environment** tab. The subwindow opens when a new file is opened or an existing file is loaded (by using **File** in the upper main menu or the left buttons in the lower main menu). Or the subwindow opens when a data object or function is clicked in the **Environment** subwindow. If a data object or function is opened, the object appears in the subwindow for inspection but cannot be edited.

When opening a new file, for the languages R (you open an R Script), C, C++, Markdown, HTML, CSS, JavaScript, and Python, and for the shell commands and the Header and text files, the subwindow opens a blank space in which to type the code or other text. (The language name is displayed in the lower right corner of the subwindow.) For the **R Notebook**, **R Markdown…**, **Shiny Web App…**, **Plumber API…**, **D3 Script**, **SQL Script**, **Stan File**, **R Sweave**, **R HTML**, **R Presentation**, and **R Documentation…** buttons, the subwindow opens with skeleton code and, for some files, instructions. (The format is displayed in the lower right corner.)

If a source file (a file with an extension for an available programming language) is in the working directory, the file can be loaded into the Source subwindow. For example, a file with an .R extension is called a script and, when loaded, is editable and executable. The files of most of the other available languages are editable but not executable. A text file with no code extension is not executable but is editable. All the aforementioned types of files can be saved.

More than one page can be opened in the **Source** subwindow, but only one is displayed at a given time. Each open page in the subwindow has a tab above the subwindow containing the name of the source file or a label **Untitled***n*, where *n* is a number indicating which untitled object is under the tab. The source files can be displayed by clicking on the tab and closed by clicking on the small **x** on the right side of the tab.

For all the types of files, the menu below the subwindow tab contains (from the left) arrows to go back to the previous tab or forward to the next one and an icon to open the subwindow in a stand-alone window. For R scripts, to the right of the first icons are an icon to save the current object, a checkbox to source (run) the script when saving, a wand icon to use specialized editing tools, an icon to run highlighted text, an icon to rerun text, and an icon to source (run) the entire contents of the subwindow.

If the object is a text file, the tab menu contains the first two icons. The menu also contains an icon to save the current object, a spellchecker icon, and a find and replace icon. If the object is an R Script, R Notebook, R Markdown, Shiny Web App..., Plumber API..., C++, Markdown, Python, Shell, R Sweave, R HTML, R Presentation, or R Documentation file, the code can be run within the subwindow. For R Notebook, R Markdown..., Shiny Web App..., Plumber API..., and Markdown files, the output can be published to the web. For R Notebook, Markdown, HTML, D3, SQL, R Presentation, and R Documentation files, the result can be previewed. R Markdown and R HTML files can be knit. Stan files can be checked.

If the object is an R Notebook, R Markdown, R Sweave, R HTML, or R Presentation file, there is a green circle containing a C on the menu that can be clicked to enter a chunk of executable code in one of the following languages: R, Bash, D3, Python, Rcpp, SQL, or Stan.

If the object is a data frame or matrix, the menu contains the first two icons, plus a filter option to filter the columns by range values and, on the far right, a search box to search the data. For lists, environments, and S4 objects, to the right of the first two icons are a checkbox, for showing attributes, and a search box. If the object is a function, the menu contains the following extra icons: an icon to print the function, a search function, a wand icon for code tools or to open help functions for highlighted text, and, on the right side of the menu, run and rerun icons for running all or a selected part of the function. Below the menu is a second menu bar where there is one button for a drop-down menu labeled **Method**. The drop-down menu contains function names from under the **Environment** tab and relevant functions within R. Clicking on a function name opens the function in the subwindow.

For data frames and matrices, the contents of the data frame or matrix is displayed below the menu by row and column. For lists, at the levels of the list, the name of the level, the type of the content of the level, and some of the values of the level content are displayed. If the object is an environment, the Names, Types, and some of the values of the objects in the environment are displayed. For S4 objects, the Names, Types, and some of the values for the variables in the class are displayed. If the object is a function, the function is displayed.

CHAPTER 3

Assignments and Operators

R works with objects. Objects can include vectors, matrices, functions, the results from a function, or other kinds of objects. Objects make working with information easier. This chapter covers assigning names to objects, listing and removing objects, and object operations. Part II (Chapters 4 and 5) covers the possible forms of objects.

Objects exist in an object system. Three main object systems (S3, S4, and Reference Class) are used in R. S3, S4, and Reference Class systems are discussed throughout the book. The S4 system is described in the PDF at `www.r-project.org/conferences/useR-2004/Keynotes/Leisch.pdf`. Reference Classes are described at `https://search.r-project.org/R/refmans/methods/html/refClass.html`.)

Some objects come with the packages in R. Other objects are user-created. User-created objects have names that are assigned by the user. Knowing how to create, list, and remove user-created objects is basic to R.

Types of Assignment

Names in R must begin with a letter or a period (or be contained within backquotes). The name cannot have breaks (unless the name is within backquotes) and can contain letters, numeric digits, periods, and underscores (except names within backquotes, which can have other

© Margot Tollefson 2022
M. Tollefson, *R 4 Quick Syntax Reference*, https://doi.org/10.1007/978-1-4842-7924-3_3

characters). The names that begin with a period are hidden and are used by R for startup defaults, the random seed, and other such things. The indexing symbols **[ ]**, **[[ ]]**, **$**, and **@** have special meanings with regard to R names, as explained in the "Subscripting Operators" section of this chapter.

Some examples of names are

```
ex123
ex_123
`12 3`
`12-3`
```

R originally used five types of assignment, four of which are still current. The four types are

```
a <- b,
```

which assigns **b** to **a**,

```
a -> b,
```

which assigns **a** to **b**,

```
a <<- b,
```

which assigns **b** to **a** and can be used inside a function to bring the assignment down to the lower levels, including the workspace level, and

```
a ->> b,
```

which assigns **a** to **b** and brings an assignment in a function down to the lower levels, including the workspace level.

The developers at R have also included the more standard

```
a = b,
```

which assigns **b** to **a**. Using the equal sign for assignment is considered poor practice in R, but we have almost never had a problem using it. While any of the types of assignment can be used, the use of the equal sign is easiest to type.

When R makes an assignment, the name is automatically saved in the workspace. Note that no warning is given if the assigned name already exists. The assignment will overwrite the object in the workspace with the assigned object.

R is interesting in that a function of an object can be assigned to the original object. For example:

```
a = 2*a,
```

where the object **a** is replaced by the original **a** times two.

For more information about assignment operators, use the Help tab in RStudio or enter `?assignOps` at the R prompt.

Example of Three Types of Assignment

An example of some of the types of assignment follows. Three objects are created: **abc**, **bcd**, and **cde**. You create the objects by assigning sequences to the objects. The sequences are generated when you put a colon between two integers, which creates a sequence of integers starting with the first integer and ending with the second integer.

To show that the objects contain the assigned sequence, the contents of the three objects are displayed as follows. Note that entering the name of an object at the R prompt will always display the contents of the object. The **[1]** refers to the first element of the objects.

```
> abc  =  1:10
> abc
 [1]  1  2  3  4  5  6  7  8  9 10

> bcd  <-  11:20
> bcd
 [1] 11 12 13 14 15 16 17 18 19 20
```

```
> 21:30  ->  cde
> cde
 [1] 21 22 23 24 25 26 27 28 29 30
```

As you can see, the assignment operators <- and = give the same result. The assignment operator -> works in the opposite direction.

Listing and Removing Objects in RStudio and R

To see the objects present in the workspace, it is easier to use RStudio rather than R. In RStudio, the objects in the workspace are listed under the **Environment** tab (in the right upper subwindow). Also, the environment can be searched in RStudio.

R has the function ls() to list the workspace objects. Entering ls() at the R prompt for the preceding example gives

```
> ls()
[1] "abc" "bcd" "cde"
>,
```

which are the three objects created previously.

Although functions are covered in detail in Part III, one interesting property of functions to note here is they can have arguments that the user enters. Two of the possible arguments for ls() are **pattern** and **all.names**.

The first argument is entered as **pattern** = *"a_string"*, where *"a_string"* is any part of an object name. For example, in the preceding workspace, searching for those objects containing **bc** in the name gives **abc** and **bcd**, that is

```
> ls( pattern="bc" )
[1] "abc" "bcd"
```

The argument **pattern** can be reduced to **pat**, as in ls(pat="bc"). The shortening of arguments of functions is a property of R. Most arguments in R can be reduced to the shortest unique form, but they are usually given in the full form in manuals.

The second argument is **all.names**, which can equal **TRUE** or **FALSE**. If set to **TRUE**, the **all.names** argument instructs R to list all of the files in the workspace, including those that begin with a period. **FALSE** is the default value and does not need to be entered. For the previous example workspace, setting **all.names** equal to **TRUE** gives

```
> ls(  all.n=TRUE  )
[1] ".commander.done" ".First"    ".Random.seed"    ".Traceback"
[5] "abc"                "bcd"       "cde"
.
```

The **[1]** refers to ".commander.done" since ".commander.done" is the first element of the vector, and the **[5]** refers to "abc" since "abc" is the fifth element of the vector. (In R, if the elements of a vector have not been given a name, the convention for listing the elements is to show the index of the first element in each line of the lines of listed elements.)

In RStudio, objects can be removed under the grid option for listing the environmental objects. To the right side of the menu under the **Environment** tab is an icon that says **List**. Click on the icon and choose **Grid** instead of **List**. In the resulting grid, check the boxes to the left of the objects to be removed. Then, click on the little broom in the middle of the menu. You will be asked if you really want to delete the checked objects.

From the R prompt, the function rm() can be used to remove objects from the workspace. For rm(), the names of the objects to be deleted are separated by commas. For example:

```
rm( a, b, c )
```

will remove the objects **a**, **b**, and **c**. You remove S4 classes by using removeClass().

For more information about ls() or rm(), use the RStudio Help tab or enter ?ls or ?remove at the R prompt.

Operators

Operators operate on objects. Operators can be logical, arithmetic, matrix, relational, or subscripting, or they may have a special meaning. Each of the types of operators is described here.

For operators, *elementwise* refers to performing the operation on each element of an object or paired elements for two objects. If two objects do not have the same dimensions, the operator will often cycle the smaller object against the larger object. The cycling proceeds through each dimension. For example, for matrices, the first dimension is the rows and the second dimension is the columns, so the cycling is down rows starting with the first column.

The letters **NA** are used to indicate that an element is missing data. Most operators have rules for dealing with missing data and may return an **NA** if data is missing.

CRAN gives a help page of information about operation precedence. To access the help page, use the Help tab in RStudio or enter ?Syntax at the R prompt.

Logical Operators and Functions

Logical operators and functions return the value **TRUE**, **FALSE**, or **NA**, where **NA** refers to a missing value. The logical operators are the **not** operator, two **or** operators, two **and** operators, and an **in** operator. The functions xor(), isTRUE(), isFALSE(), any(), and all() (which are functions that operate on logical objects) also return logical values. For all the logical operators except **%in%**, if the two objects do not have the same dimensions, the number of elements in the larger object must be a multiple of the number of elements in the smaller object for cycling to occur. For **%in%**, the two objects can be any length. The logical operators and five logical functions are listed in Table 3-1.

Table 3-1. *The Logical Operators and Functions*

Operator	Operation	Description
!	not	Negation operator—e.g., !a
I	or	Elementwise **or** operator—e.g., a I b
II	or	**or** operator, just evaluates the first elements in the objects—e.g., a II b
&	and	Elementwise **and** operator—e.g., a & b
&&	and	**and** operator, just evaluates the first elements in the objects—e.g., a && b
%in%	logical tests	**in** operator—e.g., a %in% b
xor( )	exclusive or	**exclusive or** function—e.g., xor(a , b)
isTRUE( )	logical test	Returns **TRUE** if the argument contains only one value and the value is true, otherwise returns **FALSE**—e.g., isTRUE(a)
isFALSE( )	logical test	Returns **TRUE** if the argument contains only one value and the value is false, otherwise returns **FALSE**—e.g., isFALSE(a)
any( )	logical test	Returns **TRUE** if **TRUE** is present in a logical object—e.g., any(a)
all( )	logical test	Returns **TRUE** if **TRUE** is the only value in a logical object—e.g., all(a)

The logical operators, except for the **%in%** operator, operate on objects that are logical, numeric, or raw. When a numeric object is coerced to logical, the nonzero values are set to **TRUE,** and the zero values are set to **FALSE**. For raw vectors, the operators are applied bitwise.

The negation operator changes **TRUE** to **FALSE** and **FALSE** to **TRUE** in a logical object. An **NA** remains an **NA**.

The | operator compares the two objects elementwise and, for each pair of elements, returns **TRUE** if **TRUE** is present, **FALSE** if no **TRUE** or **NA** is present, and **NA** if any **NA** is present. The || operator compares the first element of the first object to the first element of the second object and returns **TRUE** if either element is **TRUE**, **FALSE** if both are **FALSE**, and **NA** if either element is **NA**.

The **&** operator compares two objects elementwise and, for each pair of elements, returns **TRUE** if both elements are **TRUE**, **FALSE** if **FALSE** is present, and **NA** if both elements are **NA**. The **&&** operator compares the first element of the first object to the first element of the second object and returns **TRUE** if the first elements are both **TRUE**, **FALSE** if **FALSE** is present, and **NA** if both elements are **NA**.

The **%in%** operator returns **TRUE** for the values in the object to the left of **%in%** that are in the object to the right and **FALSE** for those values on the left that are not in the object on the right. The length of the result is the length of the first object. If the first object has more than one dimension, the object is converted to a vector.

The xor() function compares objects elementwise and returns **TRUE** if the paired elements are different and **FALSE** if the paired elements are the same, unless an **NA** is present. If an **NA** is present, the test returns **NA**.

For a logical vector or a vector that can be coerced to logical, the function any() will return **TRUE** if any of the elements are **TRUE**, **FALSE** if no **TRUE** or **NA** is present, and **NA** if no **TRUE** is present but an **NA** is.

For a logical vector or a vector that can be coerced to logical, the function all() will return **TRUE** if all of the elements are **TRUE,** otherwise **FALSE** if a **FALSE** is present and **NA** if not.

The functions **isTRUE()** and **isFALSE()** only evaluate single element objects or expressions. If more than one element is present, the function will give an error. The function **isTRUE()** returns **TRUE** if the value is **TRUE** and **FALSE** if otherwise. The function **isFALSE()** returns **TRUE** if the value is **FALSE** and **FALSE** otherwise.

For more information about the logical operators, except for **%in%**, and the functions xor(), isTRUE(), and isFALSE(), the CRAN help pages for logical operators can be found by using the Help tab in RStudio or by entering **?Logic** at the R prompt and clicking on **Logical Operators**. The help page for **%in%**, any(), and all() can be accessed by using the Help tab in RStudio or by entering **?"%in%"**, **?any,** or **?all** at the R prompt.

Arithmetic Operators

Arithmetic operators can have numeric operands or operands that can be coerced to numeric. For example, for logical objects, **TRUE** coerces to **1** and **FALSE** coerces to **0**. For some types of objects, specific operators have a different meaning, but those types of objects will not be covered in this chapter.

Arithmetic expressions are evaluated elementwise. If the number of elements is not the same between the objects in an expression, the smaller object cycles through the larger one until the end of the larger one. The numbers of elements in the larger object do not have to be a multiple of the smaller object for cycling. Expressions are evaluated from left to right, under the rules of precedence (see the help page for **Syntax**).

The arithmetic operators are the standard * for multiplication, / for division, + for addition, and - for negation and subtraction. The exponentiation symbol is ^. The operator **%%** gives the modulus of the first argument with respect to the second argument. The operator **%/%** performs integer division. Expressions can be grouped using parentheses, for example, **(a+b)/c**. Table 3-2 lists the arithmetic operators.

Table 3-2. *Arithmetic Operators*

Operator	Operation	Example
*	Multiplication	a * b
/	Division	a / b
+	Addition	a + b
-	Negation or subtraction	-a, a - b
^	Exponentiation	a^b
%%	Modulus	a %% b
%/%	Integer division	a %/% b

For more information, the CRAN help pages for arithmetic operators can be found by using the Help tab in RStudio or by entering **?Arithmetic** at the R prompt.

Matrix Operators and Functions

R provides operators and functions to manipulate matrices. A list of some matrix operators and functions can be found in Table 3-3.

Table 3-3. *Matrix Operators and Functions*

Operator/function	Operation	Example
%*%	Matrix multiplication	a %*% b
%o% or **outer( )**	Outer product of two vectors, matrices, or arrays	a %*% b, outer(a, b)
%x% or **kronecker( )**	Kronecker product of two matrices (or arrays)	a %x% b, kronecker(a, b)
t( )	Transpose of a matrix	t(a)
crossprod( ) or **tcrossprod( )**	Crossproduct of a matrix or two matrices	crossprod(a) or crossprod(a, b) or tcrossprod(a) or tcrossprod(a, b)
diag( )	Diagonal of a matrix or a diagonal matrix	diag(a), **a** is a matrix or diag(a), **a** is a vector
solve( )	Inverse of a matrix or solution to **Xa=b**	solve(a), solve(X, b)
det( )	Determinant of a square matrix	det(a)

The matrix multiplication operator is **%*%**. R will return an error if the two matrices do not conform.

For two arrays (arrays include vectors and matrices), **%o%**, or outer( ), gives the outer product of the arrays.

For two arrays, **%x%**, or kronecker( ), gives the Kronecker product of the arrays.

To transpose a matrix, use the function t( ), for example, t(a).

For the cross product of one matrix with another (or the original matrix), use either the function crossprod( ) or the function tcrossprod( ). If **a** and **b** are conforming matrices, then

```
crossprod( a ) = t( a ) %*% a,
tcrossprod( a ) = a %*% t( a ),
crossprod( a, b ) = t( a ) %*% b,
tcrossprod( a, b ) = a %*% t( b ).
```

To find the inverse of a nonsingular square matrix, use the function solve(), for example, solve(a). The function solve() also can solve the linear equation

Xa=b,

for **a**, where **X** is a nonsingular square matrix and **b** has the same number of rows as **X**. The syntax is solve(X,b).

To find the determinant of a square matrix, use det(X), where **X** is a square matrix.

To create a diagonal matrix or obtain the diagonal of a matrix, use the function diag(). If **a** is a vector, diag(a) will return a diagonal matrix with the diagonal equal to the **a**. For example:

```
> a = 1:2
> a
[1] 1 2
> diag( a )
      [,1] [,2]
[1,]    1    0
[2,]    0    2
```

If **a** is a matrix, diag(a) will return the diagonal elements of the matrix, even if the matrix is not square. For example:

```
> a = matrix( 1:6, 2, 3 )
> a
      [,1] [,2] [,3]
[1,]    1    3    5
```

```
[2,]    2    4    6
> diag( a )
[1] 1 4
```

For more information on the preceding operators and functions, you can use the RStudio Help tab. Or the CRAN help page for matrix multiplication can be found by entering **?matmult** at the R prompt and, for the eight functions, by entering **?*name***, where *name* is the name of the function, at the R prompt.

Relational Operators

Relational operators are used in logical tests. The tests are evaluated elementwise. For vectors, if the lengths of the vectors are not the same, the shorter vector cycles against the longer one. If the length of the longer vector is not a multiple of the shorter one, a warning is given but the tests are performed. A logical vector of the length of the longer vector is returned.

For a vector and a matrix or array, the vector will cycle down the columns of the matrix or dimensions of the array. If the length of the vector is not a multiple of the number of elements in the matrix or array, a warning is given but the tests are performed–unless the vector is longer than the matrix or array, in which case an error is returned.

Only conformable matrices or arrays (i.e., matrices or arrays with the same dimensions) can be compared. The test returns a logical matrix or array with the same dimensions as the matrices or arrays that were tested.

The six relational operators are == for equal to, != for not equal to, < for less than, <= for less than or equal to, > for greater than, and >= for greater than or equal to. The list of logical operators can be found in Table 3-4.

Table 3-4. *Logical Operators*

Operator	Operation	Example
==	Equal to	a == 9
!=	Not equal to	a != 9
>	Greater than	a > 9
>=	Greater than or equal to	a >= 9
<	Less than	a < 9
<=	Less than or equal to	a <= 9

Note that the **equal to** relational operator is ==, not =. A common mistake is to enter = for == in a logical expression. R will return an error for =.

As with arithmetic operators, logical expressions can be grouped using parentheses. For example, if **a** and **b** are numeric vectors,

```
( ( a>0 & b>0 ) & ( a<5 & b<5 ) )
```

is a logical expression and can be used in an expression or assigned a name.

The CRAN help page for relational operators can be found by using the Help tab in RStudio or by entering **?Comparison** at the R prompt.

Subscripting Operators

Many objects in R have more than one element. Subscripting is used to access specific elements of an object. Vectors, matrices, arrays, lists, and slots can be subscripted. In S3, single square brackets ([ ]), double square brackets ([[ ]]), and dollar signs ($) are used. For S4 objects, the *at* symbol (@) is used for subscripting. None are used elsewhere.

Vectors

For vectors, using single square brackets is usually appropriate. Double square brackets can also be used, but they can only access a single element of the vector at a time. Within single square brackets, there may be a logical expression or a set of indices. For example:

```
a[ 3:7 ]   or   a[ a>3 ]
```

The first expression results in the third through seventh elements of **a**. The second expression results in those elements of **a** that are greater than three.

If indices are given a negative sign, those indices are not included. For example:

```
a[ -2:-6 ]
```

would return the object **a** with elements two through six removed.

An object can be subsetted in one set of square brackets and subsetted again in another set of square brackets. For example:

```
a[ 1:10 ][ b>3 ],
```

where the length of **a** is greater than or equal to ten and **b** is of length ten. The expression would return those elements of the first ten elements of **a** for which the corresponding element of **b** is greater than three. The subsetting can be continued with more sets of square brackets. Each set will operate on the result of all previous subsetting.

Assignments can be done to subsets of a vector. For example, let **a** be a vector, and let the user want to change those values in **a** that are greater than 100 to 100. Then, the statement

```
a[ a>100 ] = 100
```

will do the replacement and leave the rest of the vector intact.

Elements can be added to a vector by assigning a value to the name of the vector subscripted by [i], where i is the index of the value to be added. For example:

```
> a = 1:4
> a[ 6 ] = 7
> a
[1]  1  2  3  4 NA  7
```

Matrices

For matrices, both kinds of square brackets are also used. For single square brackets, the selection instructions for the rows are separated from the selection instructions for the columns by a comma. Or, by not using the comma, the matrix is treated like a vector, going down the rows starting with the first column. Like the subsetting for vectors, for single square brackets, indices or a logical expression may be used to subset a matrix. To reference all rows of a matrix, put nothing to the left of the comma inside the brackets. To reference all columns of a matrix, put nothing to the right of the comma inside the brackets.

Double square brackets return just one value. If subsetted with a row and a column index separated by a comma, the value in the cell is returned. If just one index value is entered within double square brackets, R treats the matrix as a vector—going down rows—and returns the indexed element of the vector.

An example of matrix subscripting is

```
a[ a[ , 1 ]>3 , 1:4 ],
```

where **a** is a matrix with at least four columns. The expression would return the first four columns of those rows for which the elements of the first column are bigger than three. Notice that **a[,1]** consists of one column and contains all of the rows.

A matrix can also be subsetted using a matrix with two columns. The two-column matrix would contain row and column indices and would pick out individual cells in the matrix based on the indices in each row. For example, if **b** is a matrix with [1 2] in the first row and [2 3] in the second row, then a[b] would return the two elements: a[1,2] and a[2,3].

Assignments can be done to subsets of a matrix. For example, let **a** be a matrix, and let the user want to change the values in the first four columns of **a** to 3 when values in the first column are greater than three. Then, the statement

```
a[ a[ , 1 ]>3 , 1:4 ] = 3
```

will do the replacement and leave the rest of the matrix intact. To replace all elements of the matrix that are greater than three with three, the following code

```
a[ a>3 ] = 3
```

works.

Arrays

Arrays are like matrices but can have more than two dimensions. Note that a matrix is an array with two dimensions and a vector is an array with one dimension. Subscripting arrays with more than two dimensions is just like subscripting matrices except that for single square brackets, there are more commas in the brackets. An example is

```
a[ 1:3, , 2:7 ],
```

where **a** is a three-dimensional array with at least three levels in the first dimension and at least seven levels in the third dimension. The result of the subsetting would be all the elements in the second dimension for which the index in the first dimension is one, two, or three and the indices in the third dimension are between two and seven, inclusive. Assignments are done in the same way as vectors and matrices.

Like matrices, arrays can be subsetted using a matrix that has the same number of columns as the number of dimensions of the array, the rows of which would consist of indices for individual cells of the array. Single square brackets with no comma and double square brackets work the same as with vectors and matrices.

Lists

Lists are collections of R objects (and a kind of vector). The objects in a list can be any kind of object and do not have to be of the same kind within a list. The objects are indexed in the list. To look at objects in a list, single square brackets are used. For example:

```
blist[ 1:5 ]
```

would return the first five objects in **blist** and would also be a list.

To access an object in a list, double square brackets or a dollar sign is required. For example:

```
blist[[ 2 ]]
```

would return the second object in the list **blist** and

```
blist$b1
```

would return the object in **blist** with name **b1**. Objects in a list can only be accessed one at a time.

If a list is created from objects that do not have names associated with the objects, names will be given to the objects when the list is created. The names can be changed at any time.

Data frames are a special kind of list. Data frames have the same number of elements for every object in the list and are of the data.frame class (classes are covered in Chapter 5). Each object in the list is of one atomic type (to be described in Chapter 4), though the different objects need not be of the same type. Data frames can be subsetted like a matrix or like a list. If subsetted like a matrix, the resulting object will be a list. If subsetted like a list, the resulting object will be raw, complex, numeric, logical, or character depending on whether the list object is raw, logical, numeric, complex, or character. Individual cells in a data frame can be accessed using indices in the double square brackets. For example:

```
dframe[[ 1, 2 ]]
```

would return the element in the first row and second column of the data frame **dframe**.

Many functions return output in lists. Dollar sign subscripting is usually used to access the output, although square bracket indexing can be used. For example, for the linear model function lm(), entering

```
lm( y~x )$resid
```

or

```
lm( y~x )[[ 2 ]]
```

will return the residuals from a simple linear regression of y on x, as will the two sets of statements:

```
a = lm( y~x )
a$resid
```

or

```
a = lm( y~x )
a[[ 2 ]].
```

Elements of a list can be changed or replaced by assigning new values. For example:

```
> a = list( 1:2, 3:4 )
```

47

```
> a
[[1]]
[1] 1 2

[[2]]
[1] 3 4

> a[[ 1 ]] = 1:5

> a[[ 1 ]][ 2 ] = 3

> a
[[1]]
[1] 1 3 3 4 5

[[2]]
[1] 3 4
```

Unlike with matrices and arrays, elements can be added to a list (since a list is a vector) by assigning a value to the name of the list subscripted by [[i]], where i is the index of the value to be added. For example:

```
> a = list( 5:10 )

> a
[[1]]
[1]   5   6   7   8   9 10

> a[[ 3 ]] = 1:3

> a
[[1]]
[1]   5   6   7   8   9 10
```

```
[[2]]
NULL

[[3]]
[1] 1 2 3
```

Other Types

Other types of objects can be subsetted, for example, factors and slots. Objects that are factors are vectors and can be subsetted like vectors. Slots are S4 objects and are subsetted using **@**. (Slots should never be subsetted except in a method statement, which will be described in Chapter 7.) More information about subsetting both can be found by using the RStudio Help tab or by entering **?Extract** at the R prompt.

Odds and Ends

The colon is used in four ways in R. Of interest here is the use of a single colon to define a sequence and the double colon to refer to package objects by package and name.

If **a** and **b** are two numbers, the expression **a:b** will give the sequence of integers between **a** rounded down to an integer and **b** rounded down to an integer. Note that the number **a** can be larger than the number **b**.

Double colons are used in referring to objects in packages. The functions, data sets, and topic descriptions that come with R are all part of a package. If a package is not loaded, a search using just the function name will return nothing. The full name of a function, package.name::function. name, where package.name is the name of the package and function. name *is the name of the function,* opens the help page for the function if the package is installed. If the package is not installed, an error message is returned. For more information on colons, enter **:** under the Help tab in RStudio or **?Colon** at the R prompt.

The operator ~ is used in model formulas to separate the left and right sides of a model. For more information, enter ~ under the Help tab in RStudio or type **?tilde** at the R prompt.

The symbol # is used for comments. When writing functions, anything found to the right of a # on a line of the code is ignored.

In RStudio, the help pages are easy to access and have their own subwindow. The search engine in RStudio is more sophisticated than the engine used when R is searched directly. When using the RStudio search box, RStudio opens a drop-down list containing matches to the characters entered in the box. Clicking on a match opens the help page. For a function, say, lm( ); data set, say, volcano; or topic, say, Colon, both RStudio and R return the same help page.

At the R prompt, the **?** and **??** operators open the help pages. For known function, data set, and topic names, **?*name*** (or **help(*name*)**) will return the help page for the function, data set, or topic, where *name* is the name of the function, data set, or topic. To search for functions related to techniques or methods, the operator **??** is used. Entering **?? *"keywords"*** (or **help.search(*"keywords"*)**), where *keywords* consists of keywords about the technique or method, may give a list of functions in packages related to the topic. Sometimes, the search comes up blank. Try again with different keywords.

PART II

Kinds of Objects

## CHAPTER 4

Types and Modes of Objects

R objects exist within an object system. R currently uses three object systems: S3, S4, and Reference Class. S3, S4, and Reference Class are all object-oriented systems. S3 is the simplest with informal classes. S4 is a newer system and uses formal classes that are associated with methods. Reference Class uses formal classes that are associated with both methods and environments. The three versions run concurrently in R. The writers at CRAN say that Reference Class is easier to code than S4, but both require a solid knowledge of S3 to work with. This book includes some Reference Class and S4 syntax but focuses on S3 syntax.

Overview of the Types and Modes

Types and modes describe the information an object contains and how the information is stored. The type of an object can be found using the typeof() function, and the mode can be found by using the mode() function. With a few exceptions, the types and the modes are the same. The differences can be found at the help page for mode(). Currently, the differences are the following: the typeof() function returns either integer or double where mode() returns numeric; typeof() returns closure, special, or builtin where mode() returns function; typeof() returns symbol where mode() returns name; and typeof() returns language where mode()

returns (or call (objects of the (and call modes are the objects that make up the language of R). From the help page for typeof(), R objects fall into one of the following types: NULL, raw, logical, integer, double, complex, character, list, closure, special, builtin, environment, S4, symbol, pairlist, promise, language, char, ..., expression, externalptr, weakref, bytecode, and any. Since R is constantly changing, the list of types may change.

Commonly Used Types

Most users will only use some of the types. The commonly used types are NULL, raw, logical, integer, double, complex, character, list, closure, special, builtin, environment, and S4. According to the help page for typeof(), the symbol, pairlist, promise, language, char, ..., expression, externalptr, weakref, bytecode, and any types are not used by the average person working with R.

The NULL type is the type of an otherwise typeless empty object. Objects of the raw type are made up of bytes. **NA**s are converted to **00**, with a warning. Objects of the logical type contain elements that can take on the value **TRUE**, **FALSE**, or **NA**. Objects of the integer type can take on integer values or **NA**s. Objects of the double type can take on double-precision values, **NA**s, **NaN**s, **Inf**s, and -**Inf**s. Objects of the complex type can take on complex numbers or **NA**s. The real and imaginary parts of complex numbers can take double-precision values, **NA**s, **NaN**s, **Inf**s, and -**Inf**s.

NA s are missing values, and the type of an **NA** depends on where the **NA** is used. **NaN**s are values that are not a number but are of the double type. **NaN**s result from calculations that are undefined, such as 0/0. **Inf** and -**Inf** are plus and minus infinity and are of the double type.

Objects of the character type are made up of character strings or **NA**s. The elements of character objects are quoted, except for **NA**s. Objects of the list type are lists of other objects–which can be of any type. Objects of the closure, special, and builtin types are functions. Objects of the environment type are R environments, such as the environment of a package. Objects of the S4 type are those S4 objects that are complex (referring to the structure of the object, not to complex numbers). S4 uses more specialized structures than S3.

The sources for the preceding information are the help pages for typeof(), mode(), **NA**, and **NaN**.

Atomic, Recursive, Language, and S4 Kinds

Most types come in one or two of four kinds: atomic, recursive, language, or S4. The types of the atomic kind are NULL, raw, logical, integer, double, complex, and character. *Atomic* refers to the elements of the objects being atomlike. For the atomic kind, all the elements within an object are of the same type.

Recursive kinds are collections of objects and can contain objects of different types. According to the help page for is.recursive(), the recursive kinds include all types except the atomic kind of types, symbols, S4 objects that contain slots, external pointers, weak references, and byte code. (External pointers, weak references, and byte codes are generally used only in interactions with C code, internally. R references do not say what kind they are.) The most common types of the recursive kind used by the R user are list and the types that have the function mode. Sometimes, objects of the environment type are used.

The types of the *language* kind are symbol, language, and expression and, according to the writers at the R project, contain objects that make up the language of R.

The *S4* kind refers to S4 data objects. Objects can be of both the recursive and language kinds or recursive and S4 kinds.

More information about the kinds of types can be found under the help pages for the functions that test for the kind of type of an object: `is.atomic()`, `is.recursive()`, `is.language()`, and `isS4()`. Also, you can see Chapter 2 of `https://cran.r-project.org/doc/manuals/r-devel/R-lang.pdf`.

Some Functions for the Atomic Kind of Types

For atomic objects, the type and mode are the same, except for the integer and double types, which are the numeric mode. Each of the atomic kind of types, except NULL, has three functions associated with the type. If we let *name* be the name of the type, the three functions are the function named for the type, *name*(); an `as.`*name*`()` function; and an `is.`*name*`()` function. The *name*() function creates a vector of the length given by the argument or arguments, if the argument(s) are of the correct type and permissible value(s).

The `as.`*name*`()` function attempts to coerce the argument of the function to the named type. If the coercion is not possible, the `as.`*name*`()` function returns a vector of **NA**s or gives an error. Note that if the argument is a matrix or array, a vector of the elements of the matrix or array will be returned, where the conversion to a vector proceeds down each dimension of the matrix or array in turn (in the case of a matrix, going down the rows of the first column, then the second column, and so on).

The `is.`*name*`()` function tests whether the argument of the function is of the named type and returns **TRUE** or **FALSE**, depending on whether the argument is or is not.

The NULL Type

NULL is a reserved object in R and is also a type. While there is no NULL() function in R, as.null() and is.null() are functions. The as.null() function takes two arguments: **x** and **....** According to the help page for NULL, **...** is ignored. With any object assigned to the **x** argument or with no argument, as.null() returns just one NULL. The is.null() function takes one argument **x** and returns **TRUE** if the argument is equal to **NULL**; **FALSE** otherwise. For example:

```
> a = 1:3
> as.null( a )
NULL

> is.null( a )
[1] FALSE

> is.null( as.null( a ) )
[1] TRUE
```

There are no default values for **x** for either function.

The Raw Type

The raw type is for bytewise analysis. The numbers in a raw object are in hexadecimal format, with each element consisting of two digits, either of which can take on any of the values zero through nine or **a** through **f**. Raw elements cannot have a decimal equivalent of greater than 255 (i.e., be a hexadecimal number with more than two digits) or be negative.

The raw() function has the (single) argument **length** and returns a vector of **00**s of length specified by the argument. If no argument or an argument of zero is given, raw() returns raw(0), a raw empty set with length zero. If a single number or number enclosed in quotes is entered as the argument, raw() returns a vector of length equal to the number rounded down to an integer. If any other kind of object is entered as the argument, raw() gives an error. For example:

```
> raw( 0 )
raw(0)
```

```
> raw( 2 )
[1] 00 00
```

```
> raw( "3" )
[1] 00 00 00
```

```
> raw( 1:2 )
Error in raw(1:2) : invalid 'length' argument
```

```
> raw( "a" )
Error in raw("a") : vector size cannot be NA/NaN
In addition: Warning message:
In raw("a") : NAs introduced by coercion
```

The default value of **length** is zero.

The as.raw() function takes the (single) argument **x** and attempts to coerce the argument to raw. If an atomic object can be coerced to numeric, and the resulting numbers are greater than or equal to zero and less than 256, as.raw() returns the hexadecimal values of the coerced elements. Double-precision numbers are rounded down to integers. For NULL, as. raw() returns raw(0). For logical type objects, **FALSE**s are set to **00** and **TRUE**s are set to **01**. For integer and double type objects, for values less than zero and greater than or equal to 256, R returns **00** and a warning. For objects of complex type, the real portion is treated in the same way as double-precision objects, and the imaginary portion is discarded. A warning is given that the conversion to a real number has occurred. Objects of the character type give **00** unless a string contains a valid number within quotes. Objects of types other than the atomic kind, except for lists with only one level consisting of single legal values, give an error. For example:

```
> as.raw( NULL )
raw(0)

> as.raw( 0 )
[1] 00

> as.raw( c( TRUE, FALSE ) )
[1] 01 00

> as.raw( c( 1, 2 ) + 0.1 )
[1] 01 02

> as.raw( c( 1, 2 ) + 0.1i )
[1] 01 02
Warning message:
imaginary parts discarded in coercion

> as.raw( c( "1", "2" ) )
[1] 01 02

> as.raw( list( "1.1", "2.1" ) )
[1] 01 02

> as.raw( -30 )
[1] 00
Warning message:
out-of-range values treated as 0 in coercion to raw

> as.raw( c( "-1", "200", "a" ) )
[1] 00 c8 00
Warning messages:
1: NAs introduced by coercion
```

```
2: out-of-range values treated as 0 in coercion to raw
```

```
> as.raw( list( c( "-1", "200" ), 1:3 ) )
Error: (list) object cannot be coerced to type 'raw'
```

There is no default value for **x**.

The is.raw() function takes the (single) argument **x** and tests if an object assigned to **x** is of the raw type. The function returns **TRUE** if the object is of the raw type and **FALSE** otherwise. Any object can be used as the argument to is.raw(). There is no default value for **x**.

More information about the raw type can be found by using the Help tab in RStudio or by entering **?raw** at the R prompt.

The Logical Type

The logical() function takes a (single) argument **length**. With no argument or with zero for an argument, the function returns logical(0), which is the logical empty set and has length zero. The logical() function with an integer greater than zero as an argument returns a vector of **FALSE**s of length equal to the integer. If the argument is a single double-precision element, the element is rounded down, and a vector of **FALSE**s of the length equal to the resulting integer is created. If the argument is a numeric object other than a single number, the function gives an error. If the argument is of the NULL, logical, character, complex, or raw type or a nonatomic kind, then logical() gives an error. For example:

```
> logical()
logical(0)
```

```
> logical( 0 )
logical(0)
```

```
> logical( 2 )
[1] FALSE FALSE
```

```
> logical( 2.7 )
[1] FALSE FALSE
```

```
> logical( 1, 2 )
Error in logical(1, 2) : unused argument (2)
```

As noted before, running `logical()` with no argument returns logical(0), so the default value of **length** is zero.

The `as.logical()` function takes two arguments: **x** and **....** The **x** argument is a single object. (The second argument **...** allows for passing arguments between methods.) The `as.logical()` function coerces the **x** argument to logical, if possible, and returns a vector containing **TRUE**s, **FALSE**s, and/or **NA**s. If there is no argument or the argument is **NULL**, `as.logical()` returns logical(0). If the argument is of the integer or double type, zeroes will be returned as **FALSE**s, and all other numbers will be returned as **TRUE**s.

If the argument is a complex object, the function gives **FALSE** for 0+0i and **TRUE** otherwise. If the type is raw, 00s will return **FALSE**, and any other value will return **TRUE**. If the argument is of the character type, the function returns a vector of **NA**s of length equal to the length of the argument. If the argument contains **NA**s, for any of the types except raw, **NA**s will be returned for the elements containing **NA**s. For the raw type, there are no **NA**s since **NA**s are coerced to 00s for the type. For the list type, for lists made up of elements with just a single atomic value each, if the type of the elements will coerce to logical, the coercion takes place. Otherwise, list objects give an error. For any other type, `as.logical()` gives an error. For example:

```
> as.logical()
logical(0)
```

```
> as.logical( 0, 2 )
[1] FALSE
```

```
> as.logical( c( 0, 2 ) )
[1] FALSE   TRUE

> as.logical( list( 0, 2.5, 0+1i, as.raw( NA ), NA, "2" ) )
[1] FALSE   TRUE   TRUE   FALSE      NA      NA
Warning message:
out-of-range values treated as 0 in coercion to raw

> as.logical( list( c( TRUE, TRUE ), 0:3 ) )
Error: (list) object cannot be coerced to type 'logical'
```

Neither **x** nor **...** have default values.

The is.logical() function returns **TRUE** if the (single) argument **x** is a logical object and **FALSE** otherwise. The result of is.logical(logical(0)) is **TRUE**. There is no default value for **x**.

For more information about the logical type, use the Help tab in RStudio or enter **?logical** at the R prompt.

The Integer or Double Types and the Numeric Mode

For the integer and double types and the numeric mode, things get a bit complicated. Originally in S, numeric objects could be integer, real, or double (for double precision). In R, the real option is deprecated and should not be used. In S3, the integer and double types are both under the numeric mode. In S4, each has a separate type. For convenience, the double(), as.double(), and is.double() functions are covered here. With two exceptions, the integer(), as.integer(), and is.integer() functions behave similarly.

The double() function takes the (single) argument **length**. If the argument equals zero or there is no argument, double() returns numeric(0) (integer(0) for integer()), an empty object of the double type (integer type for integer()) and zero length. Given a single positive numeric value for the argument, where double-precision numbers are rounded down to an integer, the function returns a vector of double-precision zeroes of length equal to the value of the argument. For negative arguments and arguments of modes other than numeric or of length greater than one, R returns an error—except for a character string containing a single positive number, which behaves like a positive number. For example:

```
> double()
numeric(0)
```

```
> double( 3 )
[1] 0 0 0
```

```
> double( 3.7 )
[1] 0 0 0
```

```
> double( "3.7" )
[1] 0 0 0
```

```
> double( -3 )
Error in double(-3) : invalid 'length' argument
```

```
> double( 3:4 )
Error in double(3:4) : invalid 'length' argument
```

The default value of **length** is zero.

The as.double() function attempts to coerce an object to double precision. The function takes the same two arguments as as.logical(). The **x** argument can be any atomic kind of object. If the argument is NULL or no argument is given, numeric(0) (integer(0) for as.integer()) is returned, where numeric(0) is an empty object of the double type (integer type for as.integer()) and of zero length. If the object is the logical type, **TRUE**s are set to one and **FALSE**s are set to zero in the object. If the object is of the integer or double types, the values of the elements are returned as double precision. If the object is of the complex type, only the real parts are returned, as double-precision numbers, and a warning is given. If the object is of the raw type, as.double() converts the hexadecimal values to double precision. If the object is of the character type, the function returns **NA**s for the elements of the object unless an element is a number enclosed in quotes, in which case the number is returned. A warning is given if **NA**s are created. If the argument is not atomic, but a single level list with each element of the list equal to a single element atomic object that is not of the raw type, as.double() returns the elements coerced to double precision. Otherwise, R gives an error. Elements with a value of **NA** are returned as **NA**. (The second argument **...** allows passing arguments between methods.) For example:

```
> as.double()
numeric(0)

> as.double( NULL )
numeric(0)

> as.double( c( FALSE, TRUE, NA ) )
[1]  0  1 NA

> as.double( 1:3 + 0.2 )
[1] 1.2 2.2 3.2

> as.double( 1:3 + 2+3i )
[1] 3 4 5
Warning message:
imaginary parts discarded in coercion

> as.double( c( "1", "a", "3" ) )
[1]  1 NA  3
Warning message:
NAs introduced by coercion
```

```
> as.double( as.raw( 2 ) )
[1] 2

> as.double( list( as.raw( 2 ) ) )
Error: unimplemented type 'raw' in 'asReal'

> as.double( list( 1:3 ) )
Error: 'list' object cannot be coerced to type 'double'

> as.double( list( 1:3 )[[1]] )
[1] 1 2 3
```

Neither argument has a default value.

The is.double() function takes one argument **x**. The argument can be an object of any type. The value **TRUE** is returned if **x** is of the double type and **FALSE** otherwise.

When entering numbers, integer type values can be denoted differently. Integers can be just entered or can be defined by using integer() and as.integer() or by putting an **L** after an integer; for example:

```
> typeof( 1:3 )
[1] "integer"

> typeof( 1L:3L )
[1] "integer"

> typeof( 1:3 + 0.1 - 0.1 )
[1] "double"
```

Double-precision numbers are not entered with a suffix.

More information about integer and double types of objects can be found by using the RStudio Help tab or by entering **?integer** or **?double** at the R prompt. For information about the numeric mode, search under **numeric**.

The Complex Type

The complex type is the type of complex numbers. In R, complex numbers can be created using complex() or by simply typing in the numbers at the R prompt. For example:

```
> complex( real=1:2, imaginary=6:7 )
[1] 1+6i 2+7i

> 1:2 + 6:7*1i
[1] 1+6i 2+7i
```

Note that for complex numbers, there is always a number with no operator in front of the **i**, which lets R know that the **i** is the imaginary root of minus one.

For the complex() function, if the first argument **length.out** is zero and no other argument is given or there is no argument, the function returns complex(0), an empty set of the complex type and zero length. If the argument is a single positive number or a string containing a single positive number, complex() returns a vector of complex zeroes of the length of the number rounded down to an integer. If the argument consists of a numeric object with more than one element, a multielement character object with the first element containing a positive number in quotes, or if the argument is logical either with one element or more than one element, only the first element of the argument is used, where for logical objects **FALSE** is coerced to zero and **TRUE** to one. Any other argument gives an error. For example:

```
> complex()
complex(0)

> complex( 0 )
complex(0)

> complex( 3 )
```

```
[1] 0+0i 0+0i 0+0i

> complex( "3" )
[1] 0+0i 0+0i 0+0i

> complex( 1:3 )
[1] 0+0i

> complex( c( "1", "2", "3" ) )
[1] 0+0i

> complex( c( TRUE, FALSE ) )
[1] 0+0i

> complex( list( TRUE, FALSE ) )
Error in complex(list(TRUE, FALSE)) : invalid length
```

The default value of **length.out** is zero.

The complex() function also takes the **real** and **imaginary** or **modulus** and **argument** arguments. The **real** and **imaginary** or **modulus** and **argument** arguments can be set equal to any numeric object, any character object containing numbers in quotes, or any logical object. Character and logical objects are coerced to double-precision numbers. The **real** and **imaginary** arguments are the real and imaginary parts of the numbers, while the **modulus** and **argument** arguments are the polar coordinates of the numbers, with **modulus** equal to the lengths of the numbers and **argument** equal to the angles above the x axis of the numbers (in radians). The objects do not have to be the same length and will cycle.

For the **real** and **imaginary** pair, either one can be omitted, and the omitted argument will be set to zero. For the **modulus** and **argument** pair, if **modulus** is omitted, the value for **modulus** will be set to one, and if **argument** is omitted, the value for **argument** will be set to zero. Some examples of complex() include the following:

```
> complex( real=3:5 )
[1] 3+0i 4+0i 5+0i

> complex( im=3:5 )
[1] 0+3i 0+4i 0+5i

> complex( mod=3:5 )
[1] 3+0i 4+0i 5+0i

> complex( arg=45/180*pi )
[1] 0.7071068+0.7071068i

> complex( modulus=1:2, argument=45/180*pi )
[1] 0.7071068+0.7071068i 1.4142136+1.4142136i
```

The default values of **real** and **imaginary** are numeric(0), and those of **modulus** and **argument** are one and zero.

The as.complex() function will try to coerce an object to the complex type. The function takes the same arguments as as.logical() and as.double(). If the **x** can be coerced to numeric (objects of the atomic kind and one level lists containing single element elements of the atomic kind—except the raw type) but is not complex, then the result is a complex object with the coerced argument as the real part and with zeros for the imaginary part, except for **NA**s, which are returned simply as **NA**s. For nonatomic kinds of types, except for single value one level lists not containing raw types, as.complex() returns an error. (The second argument **...** allows passing arguments between methods.) Some examples are

```
> as.complex( NULL )
complex(0)

> as.complex( list( NA, FALSE, 2, 2i, "2" ) )
[1]    NA 0+0i 2+0i 0+2i 2+0i
```

```
> as.complex( as.raw( 2 ) )
[1] 2+0i

> as.complex( list( as.raw( 2 ) ) )
Error: unimplemented type 'raw' in 'asComplex'
```

The is.complex() function tests whether the (single) argument to the function **x** is of the complex type. The function returns **TRUE** if the argument is of the complex type and **FALSE** otherwise.

More information about the complex type can be found by using the Help tab in RStudio or by entering **?complex** at the R prompt.

The Character Type

The character type objects are made up of quoted character strings. The three usual functions for the other atomic kind of objects also apply to the character type.

The character() function creates a vector of empty strings and only takes numeric mode objects or character type objects containing a number in quotes for the (single) argument **length**. The object must contain only one element. The default value is zero. If the argument is greater than or equal to one, the argument is rounded down to an integer, and the function returns a vector of ""s of length equal to the integer. If the argument is less than one and greater than minus one, the character empty set of zero length, character(0), is returned. Other arguments return an error. For example:

```
> character()
character(0)

> character( -0.5 )
character(0)
```

```
> character( -3 )
Error in character(-3) : invalid 'length' argument

> character( 3 )
[1] "" "" ""

> character( "3" )
[1] "" "" ""

> character( c( 3, 4 ) )
Error in character(c(3, 4)) : invalid 'length' argument
```

The as.character() function has the same arguments as as.logical(), as.double(), and as.complex(). The function tries to convert the first argument **x** to character strings. If **x** is not given or set equal to **NULL**, character(0), the empty object of the character type, is returned. For the atomic kind of objects, the conversion is literal, but the elements are returned within quotes. For double-precision numbers, up to 15 significant digits are used. (The second argument ... allows passing arguments between methods.) For example:

```
> as.character()
character(0)

> as.character( NULL )
character(0)

> as.character( c( TRUE, FALSE ) )
[1] "TRUE"  "FALSE"

> as.character( 1:4 )
[1] "1" "2" "3" "4"

> as.character( 1:4 + 2i )
[1] "1+2i" "2+2i" "3+2i" "4+2i"
```

```
> as.character( as.raw( 100 ) )
[1] "64"
```

```
> as.character( pi )
[1] "3.14159265358979"
```

Unlike the other atomic kinds—except NULL—the `as.character()` function also returns results for some of the recursive kinds. According to the help page for `character()`, if an object is of the language type, a line feed is inserted at each 500 characters for objects of more than 500 characters. Objects of the list type are described under the next section. However, lists can be arguments to as.character().

With an object of the list type as an argument, `as.character()` may return some strange things depending on the list. The function may return something different from what is returned if the argument is entered at the R prompt. Examples follow:

```
> a.list
[[1]]
     [,1] [,2]
[1,]   1    3
[2,]   2    4
[[2]]
[1] 1 2 3 4
[[3]]
[1] "a" "b"
```

```
> as.character( a.list )
[1] "1:4"                "1:4"              "c(\"a\", \"b\")"
```

The `lm()` function used in the succeeding example fits a linear regression model, with the value to the left of the tilde being the dependent variable and the value to the right the independent variable. The output from `lm()` is a list.

```
> a.lm
Call:
lm(formula = y ~ x)
Coefficients:
(Intercept)                 x
          1                 1
> as.character( a.lm )
 [1] "c(0.999999999999999, 1)"
 [2] "c(0, 0, 0)"
 [3] "c(-5.19615242270663, -1.41421356237309, 0)"
 [4] "2"
 [5] "c(2, 3, 4)"
 [6] "0:1"
 [7] "list(qr = c(-1.73205080756888, 0.577350269189626,
     0.577350269189626, -3.46410161513776, -1.41421356237309,
     0.965925826289068), qraux = c(1.57735026918963,
     1.25881904510252), pivot = 1:2, tol = 1e-07, rank = 2)"
 [8] "1"
 [9] "list()"
[10] "lm(formula = y ~ x)"
[11] "y ~ x"
[12] "list(y = 2:4, x = 1:3)"
```

Play around with different kinds of lists to see how as.character() performs.

Objects of the language and expression types can also be coerced to character. Objects of the closure, special, builtin, environment, and S4 types cannot.

The is.character() function takes one argument **x** and tests to see if **x** is of the character type. The function returns **TRUE** if **x** is of the character type and **FALSE** otherwise. Any object can be used as the argument.

For more information about the character type, use the Help tab in RStudio or enter **?character** at the R prompt.

The Common Recursive Kind of Types

The common recursive kinds are covered in this section. The list, closure, special, builtin, and environment types (and some S4 types) are the common recursive kinds. The recursive kinds of types that are not used by the usual R user are described in the next section, along with the language kinds.

The List Type

Lists are collections of objects, which may be of any type and which do not have to be of the same type within the list. The list type has the same three functions as the atomic kind of objects; however, there are a few more.

The list() function takes the (single) argument **...** and creates a list out of the values entered for the argument. Within the parentheses, the values are separated by commas. The values can be any kind of object or statements. To create an empty list with a given number of objects (where the objects are **NULL**s), use

```
vector( "list", n ),
```

where **n** is the number of objects to be in the list. The variable **n** must be numeric and greater than minus one, is rounded down to an integer if positive and up if negative, and can only contain one element. If **n** equals zero, is negative, or is omitted, a list of zero length is created. An empty list can also be created by running list() with no argument. Some examples are

```
> list()
list()
```

```
> vector( "list", -0.5 )
list()

> vector( "list", 2 )
[[1]]
NULL

[[2]]
NULL

> list( 1:2 )
[[1]]
[1] 1 2

> list( 1, 2 )
[[1]]
[1] 1
[[2]]
[1] 2

> list( -0.5 )
[[1]]
[1] -0.5
```

The as.list() function attempts to coerce the first argument **x** to the list type. The other argument is .... If more than one argument is supplied, only the first argument is coerced. The other arguments are ignored unless applicable. The NULL argument returns a list of length zero. For example:

```
> as.list( NULL )
list()

> as.list( 1:2, 3:4 )
[[1]]
[1] 1
```

```
[[2]]
[1] 2

> as.list( x = c( sinpi, 0:1/2 ) )
[[1]]
function (x)  .Primitive("sinpi")

[[2]]
[1] 0

[[3]]
[1] 0.5

> as.list( x = sinpi( 0:1/2 ) )
[[1]]
[1] 0

[[2]]
[1] 1
```

(Note that sinpi(x) equals sin(pi*x) and that pi in radians equals 180 in degrees. The pi object is a reserved word in R.)

The is.list() function takes the (one) argument **x** and tests if **x** is a list (or a pairwise list, which is covered below). If the **x** is of the list type, **TRUE** is returned. Otherwise, **FALSE** is returned.

The unlist() function removes the list property for lists of elements and returns a vector of the elements of the objects in the list. For example:

```
> list( 1:2, 3:4 )
[[1]]
[1] 1 2
[[2]]
[1] 3 4

> unlist( list( 1:2, 3:4 ) )
[1] 1 2 3 4
```

The function takes three arguments: **x**, **recursive**, and **use.names**. The first argument **x** is the object to be coerced and has no default value. If the list is more than one level deep, the **recursive** argument can be used to just recurse the first level. The **use.names** argument tell R whether to keep the names of the list values, if the list values have names. For example:

```
> a.list = list( list( a=1:3, 2:4 ) )
> a.list
[[1]]
[[1]]$a
[1] 1 2 3

[[1]][[2]]
[1] 2 3 4

> unlist( a.list, rec=0 , use=1 )
$a
[1] 1 2 3

[[2]]
[1] 2 3 4

> unlist( a.list, rec=1, use=1 )
a1 a2 a3
 1  2  3  2  3  4

> unlist( a.list, rec=1, use=0 )
[1] 1 2 3 2 3 4
```

The default values of **recursive** and **use.names** are **TRUE**.

The alist() function creates a list where the values of variables in the list do not have to be specified. The alist() function is most often used in evaluating functions, where some variables can be prespecified and others are assigned at each running of the function.

More information can be found by using the Help tab in RStudio or by entering **?list** at the R prompt, which brings up the help pages for list(), as.list(), is.list(), and alist(). The help page for the unlist() function is separate.

The Closure, Special, and Builtin Types

Functions in R are of the closure, special, or builtin types. Functions of the closure type are written in the R language and have an argument list, a body, and an environment in which they run. Functions of special and builtin types are *primitive* functions and are written in C. Primitive functions are only found in the base package, and the two kinds differ on how the arguments are evaluated. According to the help page for is_ function(), functions that are the special type are evaluated lazily, and those that are the builtin type are evaluated eagerly.

Objects of the closure type are created by the function() function. Of the three functions listed for the atomic kind of types, only function() and is.function() exist for the function mode. The structure of functions is different from the structures of the atomic kind of types and the list type, and the help page for function() is different from the help page for is. function(). We will cover the creation of functions using function() in Chapter 7. The is.function() function returns **TRUE** if the argument is a function and **FALSE** otherwise. Also, the is.primitive() function, on the same help page, tests if a function is a primitive function, returning **TRUE** if the function is primitive and **FALSE** otherwise. Both is.function() and is.primitive() take the one argument **x**.

The help page under is_function(), which is in the **rlang** package, is more useful than that for is.function(). The help page covers is_ function(), is_closure(), is_primitive(), is_primitive_eager(), and is_primitive_lazy(). The is_closure() function tests if a function is a closure. The is_primitive() function tests if a function is a primitive function. The is_primitive_lazy() and is_primitive_eager()

functions distinguish between the special and builtin types. All take just one argument **x** and return **TRUE** or **FALSE** depending on whether the condition is true or false. The argument of the testing functions need not be a function.

As examples of different types of functions, the seq() function is an object of the closure type, the log() function is an object of the special type, and the cos() function is an object of the builtin type.

More information about is.function() and is.primitive() can be found by using the Help tab in RStudio or by entering **?is.function** at the R prompt. More information about the three types of functions can be found by loading the rlang package and then using the Help tab in RStudio or entering **?is_function** at the R prompt.

The Environment Type

Environments are the structures within which R works. The following is from the help pages for the environment() and sys.parent() functions. Environments consist of objects (the group of objects is called a *frame*), and a pointer to the environment where that which is run executes (called the *enclosing environment*). When R calls a function, the stack keeps track of how many functions deep the call is. The numbering of the stack goes from 0 to the depth of the calls. The sys.frame() function has a single argument **which**, for the stack number, and returns the environment of the stack number entered into the function, for example:

```
> sys.frame( 0 )
<environment: R_GlobalEnv>
> sys.frame( 1 )
Error in sys.frame(1) : not that many frames on the stack

> ( function() sys.frame( 0 ) )()
<environment: R_GlobalEnv>
```

```
> ( function() sys.frame( 1 ) )()
<environment: 0x127aa2600>
> ( function() sys.frame( 2 ) )()
Error in sys.frame(2) : not that many frames on the stack

> ( function() ( function() sys.frame( 0 ) )() )()
<environment: R_GlobalEnv>
> ( function() ( function() sys.frame( 1 ) )() )()
<environment: 0x127ac13c8>
> ( function() ( function() sys.frame( 2 ) )() )()
<environment: 0x127ac7400>
> ( function() ( function() sys.frame( 3 ) )() )()
 Error in sys.frame(3) : not that many frames on the stack
```

Note that the environment name changes for the functions from call to call. When a function runs, it creates its own environment, which disappears when the function finishes, unless the function has been assigned a name.

The opening environment in R is the global environment, named R_GlobalEnv, and is listed as **.GlobalEnv in the namespace**. (Running the globalenv() function and entering **.GlobalEnv** at the R prompt give the same result.) The global environment contains the workspace of the opening R session and is assigned the stack number 0 when R executes code at the R prompt.

Each package in R that is loaded has its own environment. A session in R usually has several environments loaded. The search() function returns the loaded environments in the workspace, in the order of the position of each environment–starting with position 1. Environments exist within other environments, and the lowest level environment is the empty environment (returned by emptyenv()). The parent environment of an environment is the enclosing environment for the given environment.

The parent.env() function gives the parent environment of the (single) argument to the function **env**–which must be of the environment type. For example:

```
> search()
 [1] ".GlobalEnv"        "tools:rstudio"      "package:stats"
 [4] "package:graphics"  "package:grDevices" "package:utils"
 [7] "package:datasets"  "package:methods"    "Autoloads"
[10] "package:base"

> a=.GlobalEnv; for( i in 2:20 ) { a=parent.env( a ); cat( "\
npos =", i, " " ); print( a ) }

pos = 2   <environment: 0x1323744c8>
attr(,"name")
[1] "tools:rstudio"

pos = 3   <environment: package:stats>
attr(,"name")
[1] "package:stats"
attr(,"path")
[1] "/Library/Frameworks/R.framework/Versions/4.1-arm64/
Resources/library/stats"

pos = 4   <environment: package:graphics>
attr(,"name")
[1] "package:graphics"
attr(,"path")
[1] "/Library/Frameworks/R.framework/Versions/4.1-arm64/
Resources/library/graphics"

pos = 5   <environment: package:grDevices>
attr(,"name")
[1] "package:grDevices"
```

```
attr(,"path")
[1] "/Library/Frameworks/R.framework/Versions/4.1-arm64/
Resources/library/grDevices"

pos = 6   <environment: package:utils>
attr(,"name")
[1] "package:utils"
attr(,"path")
[1] "/Library/Frameworks/R.framework/Versions/4.1-arm64/
Resources/library/utils"

pos = 7   <environment: package:datasets>
attr(,"name")
[1] "package:datasets"
attr(,"path")
[1] "/Library/Frameworks/R.framework/Versions/4.1-arm64/
Resources/library/datasets"

pos = 8   <environment: package:methods>
attr(,"name")
[1] "package:methods"
attr(,"path")
[1] "/Library/Frameworks/R.framework/Versions/4.1-arm64/
Resources/library/methods"

pos = 9   <environment: 0x152aaa918>
attr(,"name")
[1] "Autoloads"

pos = 10   <environment: base>

pos = 11   <environment: R_EmptyEnv>
Error in parent.env(a) : the empty environment has no parent
```

The parent frame can be found using the `parent.frame()` function. In an R session, the parent frame refers to the environment at the level of the R prompt. Note that the parent environment and the parent frame are two different concepts and should not be confused.

There are several functions associated with environments. The `attach()`, `library()`, and `require()` functions can take a package name as the first argument and the **pos** argument as another argument. The **pos** argument gives the position of the package environment in the search list. For `attach()`, `library()`, and `require()`, the default value of **pos** is 2 or 2L. The `attach()` function can have values other than package names for the first argument, so it can be used to attach user-created environments; `library()` and `require()` cannot. The `library()` function is usually used at the R prompt and the `require()` function within a function.

When an environment is loaded, by default, the environment is loaded in position two, and the position of other environments increases by one–except for the global environment, which stays at position one. The `detach()` function can take an environment as the first argument, takes the **pos** argument, and takes some other arguments. The default value of **pos** equals 2 in `detach()`. The function removes an environment from the search list.

The `new.env()` function is used to assign a name to a new environment. The function takes the **hash**, **parent**, and **size** arguments. The **hash** argument is logical. If set to **TRUE**, a hash table is created. Otherwise, none is created. The default value of hash is **TRUE**. The **parent** argument takes an object of the environment type. The default value of **parent** is `parent.frame()`. The **size** argument takes an integer and gives the initial size of the hash table. The default value of **size** is 29L. An example using `new.env()` is

```
> ne=new.env()
> ne
<environment: 0x110cce870>
```

The environment() function takes a function, a formula, or NULL for the (single) argument **fun** and either returns the environment of the argument or assigns an environment to the argument. The default value of **fun** is NULL. For example:

```
> environment( lm )=ne
> environment( lm )
<environment: 0x110cce870>
```

Note that the environment number remains the same between the two examples before since the environment was assigned a name.

The is.environment() function only takes one argument **x** and tests if the argument is of the environment type. The function returns **TRUE** if the argument is an environment and **FALSE** otherwise.

You can create an environment, attach the environment, assign objects to the environment, and run a function in the environment within an R session. Using the environment created before, an example follows.

First, **ne** is attached to the global environment and search() is run. The **ne** environment is in the second position.

```
> attach( ne )
> search()
 [1] ".GlobalEnv"       "ne"                "tools:rstudio"
 [4] "package:stats"    "package:graphics"  "package:grDevices"
 [7] "package:utils"    "package:datasets"  "package:methods"\
[10] "Autoloads"        "package:base"
```

Next, the variables **x** and **y** are assigned values at the level of the global environment. Then, **x** and **y** are assigned values at the level of the **ne** environment by using the assign() function. The ls.str() function displays the contents of **ne**.

```
> x=1:10
> y=2:11
```

```
> assign( "x", 0:9, pos=2 )
> assign( "y", 2:11, pos=2 )

> ls.str( "ne" )
x :   int [1:10] 0 1 2 3 4 5 6 7 8 9
y :   int [1:10] 2 3 4 5 6 7 8 9 10 11
```

Then, lm() is run. The lm() function finds **x** and **y** in the global environment and runs the regression. Then, the variables are removed from the global environment, and lm() is run again. In the second regression, R does not find **x** and **y** in the global environment, so the function searches the **ne** environment and finds the variables and runs the regression. Last, **ne** is detached and removed.

```
> lm( y~x )
Call:
lm(formula = y ~ x)
Coefficients:
(Intercept)              x
          1              1

> rm( y )
> rm( x )

> lm( y~x )
Call:
lm(formula = y ~ x)
Coefficients:
(Intercept)              x
          2              1

> detach( ne )
> rm( ne )
```

Note that **x** in the second environment is equal to **x** in the first environment plus one, so the intercept increases by one for the regression run using the second environment. The variable **y** is the same in both environments.

In the preceding example, the type of **ne** is environment. User-created environments are found in the **Data** section under the **Environment** tab in RStudio. When an environment has been loaded, the contents of an environment can be found by opening the drop-down menu under **Global Environment** (below the **Environment** tab) in RStudio and choosing the name of the environment.

More information about environments and functions that operate on environments can be found using the Help tab in RStudio or by entering **?environment** at the R prompt. Another useful help page is found under **?sys.parent**. The attach() and detach() functions each have a help page. The library() and require() functions share a help page.

The S4 Type

The S4 type identifies objects that contain data and are assigned an S4 class. S4 classes contain the structure of data to be used by S4 methods. The data for an S4 class are put into an object that identifies the class. The data are entered as slots—referred to by name. An S4 method is a function associated with the class(es). The typeof() function returns **S4** if the argument is of the *S4* type. The isS4() function returns **TRUE** if an argument is an S4 object and **FALSE** otherwise.

For example:

```
> setClass( "linearmodel", slots=c(x="numeric", y="numeric" ) )
> lm.data=new( "linearmodel", x=1:10, y=2:11 )
> typeof( lm.data )
[1] "S4"
```

```
> setGeneric( "lm.fun", function( object ) { standardGeneric(
"lm.fun" ) } )
[1] "lm.fun"
> setMethod( "lm.fun", "linearmodel", function( object ) { lm(
object@y~object@x ) } )
> typeof( lm.fun )
[1] "closure"

> lm.fun( lm.data )
Call:
lm(formula = object@y ~ object@x)
Coefficients:
(Intercept)       object@x
1                 1
```

First, the S4 class is set. Then, an S4 data object is entered. The data object, **lm.data**, is found to be of the S4 type. Next, an S4 method is created, and the method, **lm.fun**, is found to be of the closure type. The method is run on the data object. Both **lm.data** and **lm.fun** return **TRUE** when entered in isS4().

S4 functions are under **Values** below the **Environment** tab in RStudio. S4 data objects are under **Data**. More information about S4 classes is given in Chapter 5 and about S4 methods in Chapter 7.

You can find more information by using the Help tab in RStudio or by entering **?S4** at the R prompt.

The Less Common Types

The less common types of objects are used when code is running in R and are not usually manipulated by the person running R. The less common types are the symbol, pairlist, promise, language, char, ..., expression, externalptr, weakref, bytecode, and any types. Some of the less common types of objects fall in one or both of two groups: the recursive kinds and the language kinds. Some types do not belong to a group. Some are strictly internal.

According to the help page for `is.atomic()`, the recursive kinds not listed in the **Common Recursive Kinds of Types** section are pairlist, promise, language, char, …, and expression. The language kinds are the symbol, language, and expression types. They make up the language of R. (Note that the language and expression types are in both groups.) The externalptr and weakref types are external pointers and weak references and are used in the interaction between R and C routines. The bytecode type refers to objects that are compiled to byte code. The any type is a descriptor when no specific type is to be used. According the R project writers, no actual objects have the any type.

From the R project writers, the pairlist, char, …, and bytecode types are mostly or exclusively used internally. Also, objects of the pairlist type are like lists and are accessed like lists but are deprecated. The char type consists of character scalars. The … type is used in function calls to indicate an unspecified set of arguments.

The symbol, language, and expression types are the object names, the calls, and the expressions that make up the R language. The promise types are the unevaluated objects in functions and not accessible to the user. (The promise type is not related to the promises that are part of the **promises** package.)

The Language Kind of Objects

The names that R uses to access R objects are objects of the symbol type. Objects of the symbol type can be generated with the `as.symbol()` or `as.name()` functions–both of which give the same result. The functions take one argument **x** and usually return the first element of **x** in backquotes. The result is limited to 10,000 bytes. The `is.symbol()` and `is.name()` functions also exist, take the **x** argument, and return **TRUE** or **FALSE** depending on whether **x** is of the symbol type or not. More information about the functions can be found by using the Help tab in RStudio or by entering **?name** at the R prompt.

Objects of the language type are unevaluated functions, with arguments (if the function takes arguments). The objects are generated by the call() function. The as.call() and is.call() functions also exist.

The first argument of call() is **name**–the name of the function in quotes. The other argument **...** gives the arguments to the function assigned to **name**. The arguments are separated by commas. The eval() function can be used to evaluate the call. For example:

```
> call( "+", a=1, b=2 )
1 + 2

> eval( call( "+", a=1, b=2 ) )
[1] 3

> typeof( call( "+", a=1, b=2 ) )
[1] "language"
```

The as.call() function tries to coerce the single argument **x** to an object of the language type. If the argument is a list, then the conversion takes place; otherwise, an error is returned. However, if the list does not consist of the name of a function followed by the arguments to that function, the object cannot be evaluated. For example:

```
> as.call( list( `+`, 1, 2 ) )
.Primitive("+")(1, 2)
> eval( as.call( list( `+`, 1, 2 ) ) )
[1] 3

> typeof( as.call( list( `+`, 1, 2 ) ) )
[1] "language"
```

Note that the function name must be in backquotes (rather than regular quotes) in the list.

The is.call() function takes one argument **x**. The function tests the argument and returns **TRUE** if the argument is a call and **FALSE** otherwise.

Further information about the call() functions can be found by using the Help tab in RStudio or by entering **?call** at the R prompt.

Objects of the expression type contain a group of statements (statements that are legal at the R prompt), where the statements are separated by commas. Note that for the statements, if assignments are used in the statement, the assignments must be done with <- or ->. The objects can be subsetted like lists and are not evaluated when created.

The expression type uses the three functions that the atomic kind of objects use: expression(), as.expression(), and is.expression(). The expression() function takes one argument **...**, for the statements to be entered, and creates a listing of the entered statements. In the function, the statements are separated by commas and can be of any type. The eval() function can be used to evaluate the expression. All the statements are evaluated, but only the result of the last statement is returned. Values assigned in a statement are also assigned in the workspace. An example follows:

```
> expression( a <- 3:5, b <- 2, 2*( a + b ) )
expression(a <- 3:5, b <- 2, 2 * (a + b))

> eval( expression( a <- 3:5, b <- 2, 2*( a + b ) ) )
[1] 10 12 14

> typeof( expression( a <- 3:5, b <- 2, 2*( a + b ) ) )
[1] "expression"
```

The as.expression() function takes the **x** and **...** arguments and attempts to coerce the **x** argument to the expression type. Unlike in expression(), the variables in the statement assigned to **x** are evaluated before the expression object is generated. The **...** argument contains

89

arguments passed to methods (currently, there is only one). According to
the help page for expression(), the NULL, language, symbol, and pairlist
types are coerced to a single element expression. Atomic kind of types
other than NULL is coerced elementwise. The list types are coerced with
no changes except to the type. Other types of objects will give an error if
coercion is attempted. Some examples are

```
> as.expression( call( "+", a=1, b=2 ) )
expression(1 + 2)
> eval( as.expression( call( "+", a=1, b=2 ) ) )
[1] 3
> typeof( as.expression( call( "+", a=1, b=2 ) ) )o
[1] "expression"

> as.expression( 1:4 )
expression(1L, 2L, 3L, 4L)
> eval( as.expression( 1:4 ) )
[1] 4

> as.expression( list( 1:4 ) )
expression(1:4)
> eval( as.expression( list( 1:4 ) ) )
[1] 1 2 3 4

> as.expression( lm )
Error in as.vector(x, "expression") :
  cannot coerce type 'closure' to vector of type 'expression'
```

The is.expression() function takes the (single) argument **x** and
tests the argument. The function returns **TRUE** if the argument is of the
expression type and **FALSE** otherwise.

More information about the expression type can be found by using
the Help tab in RStudio or by entering **?expression** at the R prompt.

Notes

Much of the information in this chapter can be found at `https://cran.r-project.org/doc/manuals/r-devel/R-lang.pdf` and `https://cran.r-project.org/doc/manuals/r-release/R-exts.html`, as well as the help pages for the individual functions. Most of the types are described in Chapter 2 of the document at the first link. Weak references and external pointers can be found in Chapter 5 at the second link.

CHAPTER 5

Classes of Objects

In R, objects belong to classes as well as types and modes. Classes tell something about what the object contains. All objects belong to at least one class. The S3, S4, and Reference Class object systems differ regarding classes. In S3, there are specific classes into which an R object falls. In S4, the user defines a class for an S4 object. Classes in S3 are called informal classes, whereas classes in S4 are called formal classes. In both systems, classes are functional classes. In Reference Class, the classes are formal and referential. (For functional classes, an object is only changed when assigned a new value–locally. For referential classes, when an object changes, the value of the object changes everywhere the object is present.) Reference Class classes are usually defined for packages. This chapter covers the three kinds of classes.

Some Basics on Classes

S3 classes are attributes of S3 objects and are not usually assigned by the user but can be. Given an object, the class of the object can be found by using the class() function. If an object has not been given a class in the package to which the object belongs, then the class of the object is just the type or mode of the object. For example, an object of the function mode is also of the function class.

The output from many functions will have a class attribute specific to the function. For example, the class of the output from a linear model fit with the lm() function is lm. Also, objects can belong to more than

© Margot Tollefson 2022
M. Tollefson, *R 4 Quick Syntax Reference*, https://doi.org/10.1007/978-1-4842-7924-3_5

one class. An example is a model fit using the generalized linear model function (`glm()`). The classes of the output are `glm` and `lm`.

On a more technical side, according to the help page for `class()`, the classes of an object are the classes from which an object inherits. So the output of `lm()` inherits from `lm,` and the output from `glm()` inherits from both `lm` and `glm`.

One useful function for classes is the function `methods()`. Entering **methods(class=*name*)**, where *name* is the name of a class, will show functions specifically written to be applied to objects of the class. For example:

```
> methods( class=lm )
 [1] add1           alias          anova         case.names   coerce
 [6] confint        cooks.distance deviance      dfbeta       dfbetas
[11] drop1          dummy.coef     effects       extractAIC   family
[16] formula        hatvalues      influence     initialize   kappa
[21] labels         logLik                       model.frame model.matrix nobs
[26] plot           predict        print         proj         qr
[31] residuals      rstandard      rstudent      show         simulate
[36] slotsFromS3 summary          variable.names vcov
see '?methods' for accessing help and source code
```

S4 (formal) classes are the starting point for S4 methods. An S4 class contains a user-defined name for the class and the variables to be used by methods associated with the class, along with the classes of the variables. Many S3 classes are also S4 classes. The Reference Class object system uses S4 classes in a specialized way.

Using the RStudio Help tab or entering **?class** at the R prompt gives more information about S3 and S4 classes and inheritance. The help page for reference classes can be accessed under the Help tab in RStudio or by entering **?ReferenceClasses** at the R prompt.

Vectors

Although there is no vector class, the vector merits discussion as one of the most basic kinds of objects. For vectors containing objects of just one atomic type or mode (atomic vectors), the vector is a collection of elements and has one dimension (unlike matrices, which have two dimensions, or arrays, which can have more than two dimensions). For atomic vectors, the class of the vector is the type of the vector, except for double-precision vectors, which are of the numeric class. Also, for the as.*name*() functions, where *name* is the *name* of an atomic type or mode (except for the type NULL), as.*name*() returns a vector for any legal argument.

The functions vector(), as.vector(), and is.vector() exist and operate somewhat like the similar functions for the types and modes. The function vector() takes the arguments **mode** and **length** and creates a vector of the given type or mode and length. The acceptable types and modes are the atomic types and modes (except NULL), the list type, and the expression type. Other types and modes give an error.

For the atomic types and modes:

```
vector( mode="name", length=n )
```

behaves the same way as

```
name( length=n ),
```

where **name** is the name of the type or mode and **n** is the length argument. Note that **name** must be in quotes in the call to vector(). For the list type, vector() returns a list of **NULL**s of length given by the length argument. With the mode set equal to **expression**, vector() gives an expression with **NULL**s for elements, where the number of **NULL**s is given by the length argument.

The function as.vector() tries to coerce an object to a vector. For some objects, as.vector() just passes the object through and does not create a vector. For some other objects, an error is returned if the function as.vector() is run.

For matrices and arrays, dimensional information is removed by as.vector() (e.g., names of columns in a matrix and the number of rows and columns), and a vector of the elements of the matrix or array is returned. The elements of the vector are ordered starting with the first dimension of the matrix or array and continuing through the dimensions. For example:

```
> a=array( 1:8, c( 2, 2, 2 ) )
> dimnames( a )=list( c( "a", "b" ), c( "m", "n" ), c(
"y", "z" ) )
> a
, , y
  m n
a 1 3
b 2 4
, , z
  m n
a 5 7
b 6 8
> as.vector( a )
[1] 1 2 3 4 5 6 7 8
```

Here, the collection function c() is used to create the vector of the dimensions for the 2x2x2 array() and to create names for the three dimensions of the array.

For objects of the list type, as.vector() passes the list through–since lists are vectors.

For objects of the expression type, as.vector() passes the expression through, and the result gives **TRUE** for is.vector(). The type does not change.

For objects of the function mode, environment type, and S4 type, as.vector() returns an error.

For objects of the `language` type, `as.vector()` passes the object through but does not create a vector. The type does not change.

The function `is.vector()` returns **TRUE** if the object is a vector and **FALSE** otherwise, although some objects that do not look like vectors return **TRUE**.

More information about `vector()`, `as.vector()`, and `is.vector()` can be found by using the RStudio Help tab or by entering **?vector** at the R prompt.

Some Common S3 Classes

Some common S3 classes are `integer`, `numeric`, `matrix`, and `array`. Objects of class `integer` and `numeric` are vectors. Matrices are objects made up of elements in rows and columns, with the type of the elements the same for all elements. Matrices have two dimensions: the rows and columns. Arrays are like matrices, but they can have more than two dimensions.

Some other common S3 classes are `ts` and `mts`, for time series; `factor`, for factors; `Date`, for dates; and `POSIXct`, for dates with times, all of which are of the `numeric` type.

Some common classes of the `list` type are `data.frame`, for data frames; `POSTXlt`, for dates and times; and most output from higher-level functions, such as **lm** and **glm**.

The `formula` class contains formulas and is of the `language` type.

The Matrix Class: matrix

Objects of `matrix` class are matrices made up of elements of one of the atomic types (except `NULL`) or of the `list` or `expression` types. The functions `matrix()`, `as.matrix()`, and `is.matrix()` exist and behave similarly to the functions for atomic modes.

The function matrix() creates a matrix. The function takes five possible arguments. The first argument **data** is an object of an atomic, list, or expression type. The second argument is **nrow**, the number of rows in the matrix. The third argument is **ncol**, the number of columns. The fourth argument is **byrow**, which tells R to create the matrix going across rows rather than down columns. The **byrow** argument is useful for scanning tabular atomic data into a matrix. The fifth argument is **dimnames**, which assigns names to the rows and columns within the call to matrix().

Using the **a** array from the section on vectors, two examples of creating a matrix follow:

```
> matrix( a, 3, 3 )
      [,1] [,2] [,3]
[1,]    1    4    7
[2,]    2    5    8
[3,]    3    6    1
Warning message:
In matrix(a, 3, 3) :
  data length [8] is not a sub-multiple or multiple of the
number of rows [3]
```

and

```
> matrix( a, 3, 3, byrow=TRUE, dimnames=list( NULL, c( "c1",
"c2", "c3" ) ) )
      c1 c2 c3
[1,]   1  2  3
[2,]   4  5  6
[3,]   7  8  1
Warning message:
```

```
In matrix(a, 3, 3, byrow = TRUE, dimnames = list(NULL, c("c1",
"c2",  :
  data length [8] is not a sub-multiple or multiple of the
  number of rows [3]
```

Note that R gives a warning if the product of the number of rows and columns is not a multiple of the number of elements in the first argument. The warning message does not affect the result.

For the atomic types, if just **data** is given, R creates a matrix with the number of rows equal to the number of elements in the object and the number of columns equal to one. The default value of **data** is **NA**.

If just **nrow** or **ncol** is given, R creates a matrix out of the object in the first argument with the given number of rows or columns, filling out as many of the columns or rows that it takes to use up the elements in the first argument—cycling if necessary. If both **nrow** and **ncol** are present, R will go through the elements of the first argument until the matrix is full, cycling as necessary. The default value of both is one.

The **byrow** argument takes a logical value and can be used to cycle the first argument across rows rather than down columns. The default value of **byrow** is **FALSE**.

The argument **dimnames** takes a list of character vectors or **NULL**s or a single **NULL**. The default value for **dimnames** is **NULL** and if supplied should be a list of two vectors of names, with a name for each row and/or column. The row names are in the first element of the list and the column names in the second. **NULL** can be substituted for either vector.

For objects of the list type, matrix() creates a matrix that describes the contents of each of the lowest level elements of the list. The elements of the list are not necessarily of the same type. The description gives the type of the element and the size of the element. Sometimes, an **?** is placed in the cell of the matrix. Referencing cells in the matrix returns the contents of the list for the cell. The following code gives an example:

```
> a.list = list( matrix( 1:4, 2, 2 ), c( "abc", "cde" ), 1:3,
function(){ print( 1:3 ) } )
> a.list
[[1]]
     [,1] [,2]
[1,]    1    3
[2,]    2    4
[[2]]
[1] "abc" "cde"
[[3]]
[1] 1 2 3
[[4]]
function ()
{
    print(1:3)
}
> matrix( a.list, 2, 2 )
     [,1]          [,2]
[1,] Integer,4    Integer,3
[2,] Character,2 ?
> matrix( a.list, 2, 2 )[2, 2]
[[1]]
function ()
{
    print(1:3)
}
```

Objects of the expression type are legal for matrix(). The result of matrix() is to return the contents of the expression, where the contents cycle to fill in the size of the matrix and are enclosed within an expression function statement. The result is of the expression type and of the matrix class.

The function as.matrix() attempts to coerce an object to the matrix class and is mainly used with data frames (see below). The function takes three arguments: **x**, for the object to be coerced; **rownames.force**, for how to handle row names; and **...**, for exchanging arguments between methods. If the argument **x** can be coerced to a vector and is not a matrix or data frame, then as.matrix() creates a single column matrix of the coerced elements. The class is matrix. If **x** is a matrix, as.matrix() returns the matrix and maintains row and column names.

If **x** is a data frame (data frames have their own section below), then as.matrix() coerces the data frame to a matrix. (A data frame is a special kind of list for which the elements of the list all have the same length and the elements in a column of the list are of the same atomic type, but the types are not necessarily the same between columns.) If there is a column in the data frame that contains character data or raw data, then the entire data frame is coerced to character. Otherwise, the data frame is coerced to a logical matrix if all the columns are logical, to an integer matrix if an integer column is present but no numeric or complex columns are present, to a numeric matrix if a numeric column is present and no complex columns are present, and to a complex matrix if a complex column is present. There is no default value for **x**.

The argument **rownames.force** takes a logical value. The argument affects data frames with automatically generated numeric row names and data frames row names consisting of numbers made into character strings. If **TRUE**, the row names are used; if **FALSE**, no row names are used; and if **NA**, automatically generated row names are not used but manually generated row names are. The default value of **rownames.force** is **NA**.

Data frames can also be converted to a matrix using the data.matrix() function. The function data.matrix() converts a data frame to a matrix by coercing all of the elements in the data frame to numeric, using as.numeric() (see Chapter 4). Character columns are converted to numeric factor levels.

The following example shows the results for as.matrix() and data. matrix(), using a data frame called **a.df**:

```
> a.df = data.frame( c( T, F ), 1:2, 1:2+.5, 1:2+1i, c( as.raw(
1 ), as.raw( 10 ) ), c( "a", "b" ) )
> dimnames( a.df )=list( 1:2, c( "logical",  "integer",
"double", "complex", "raw", "character" ) )
> a.df
  logical integer double complex raw character
1    TRUE       1    1.5    1+1i  01         a
2   FALSE       2    2.5    2+1i  0a         b
> as.matrix( a.df )
  logical integer double complex raw    character
1 " TRUE" "1"      "1.5"  "1+1i"  "01" "a"
2 "FALSE" "2"      "2.5"  "2+1i"  "0a" "b"
> as.matrix( a.df[,1:5] )
  logical integer double complex raw
1 " TRUE" "1"      "1.5"  "1+1i"  "01"
2 "FALSE" "2"      "2.5"  "2+1i"  "0a"
> as.matrix( a.df[,1:4] )
  logical integer double complex
1    1+0i    1+0i 1.5+0i    1+1i
2    0+0i    2+0i 2.5+0i    2+1i
> as.matrix( a.df[,1:3] )
  logical integer double
1       1       1    1.5
2       0       2    2.5
> as.matrix( a.df[,1:2] )
  logical integer
1       1       1
2       0       2
> as.matrix( a.df[,1] )
```

102

```
        [,1]
[1,]   TRUE
[2,] FALSE
> data.matrix( a.df )
  logical integer double complex raw character
1     1       1    1.5       1   1         1
2     0       2    2.5       2  10         2
Warning message:
In data.matrix(a.df) : imaginary parts discarded in coercion
```

The function is.matrix() tests whether an object is of the matrix class. The function returns **TRUE** if the class of the argument is matrix and **FALSE** otherwise. (If an object of the expression type and class is used in a matrix() or in as.matrix(), the result will have class matrix, even though the structure of the result is not matrixlike.)

More information on matrix(), as.matrix(), and is.matrix() can be found by using the Help tab in RStudio or by entering **?matrix** at the R prompt. More information about data.matrix() can be found by using the Help tab in RStudio or by entering **?data.matrix** at the R prompt.

The Array Class: array

The array class is a class of data that is organized using dimensions, such as a multidimensional contingency table. Matrices are two-dimensional arrays. Vectors can be set up as one-dimensional arrays. (A vector created by array() will be of the array class; a two-dimensional array will be of both the matrix and array classes.)

The function array() creates an array out of an object. The function takes three arguments. The first argument **data** is any object that can be coerced to a vector by using as.vector(). The default value of **data** is **NA**. The second argument **dim** is a numeric vector that contains the size of each dimension and is of length equal to the number of dimensions of the array. The default value of **dim** is the length of **data**. The third argument **dimnames** is a list of character vectors containing names for each of the dimensions and can be omitted. The default value for **dimnames** is **NULL**.

The following is an example of setting up an array:

```
> array( 1:12, c(  2, 3, 2 ), dimnames=list( c( "", "" ), c(
"a", "b", "c" ), NULL )  )
, , 1
  a b c
  1 3 5
  2 4 6
, , 2
  a  b  c
  7  9 11
  8 10 12
```

Other than there being more than two dimensions, array() behaves the same as matrix() (except regarding matrix operations such as matrix multiplication).

The function as.array() attempts to coerce an object to the array class. The function takes two arguments: **x**, for the object to be coerced, and **...**, to exchange arguments between methods. The object **x** must be of the atomic types (except for the NULL type) or of the list or expression types. Otherwise, as.array() returns an error. For the legal types, as. array() behaves like as.matrix().

The function is.array() tests the single argument **x** to see if a class of **x** is array. The function returns **TRUE** if a class is array and **FALSE** otherwise. Matrices return **TRUE**, independently of how the matrix was created.

More information about array(), as.array(), and is.array() can be found under the Help tab in RStudio or by entering **?array** at the R prompt.

Names for Vectors, Matrices, Arrays, and Lists

A chapter on objects would not be complete without information on how to set names for vectors, matrices, arrays, and lists. Dimension names are always of the character type. For objects of more than one dimension, the name objects are put together in a list.

To see what names a vector has or to assign names to a vector, the names() function is used. The function just has one argument, **x**–the object. For example:

```
> cde
 [1] 21 22 23 24 25 26 27 28 29 30
> names( cde )
NULL
> names( cde ) = paste( "v", 1:10, sep="" )
> cde
 v1  v2  v3  v4  v5  v6  v7  v8  v9 v10
 21  22  23  24  25  26  27  28  29  30
> names( cde )
 [1] "v1"  "v2"  "v3"  "v4"  "v5"  "v6"  "v7"  "v8"  "v9"  "v10"
> typeof( names( cde ) )
[1] "character"
> class( names( cde ) )
[1] "character"
```

You can also assign names directly to vectors at the time the vector is created. For example:

```
> a.vec = c( a=1, b=2, c=3 )
> a.vec
a b c
1 2 3
```

Objects of the `list` type are vectors. For lists, assigning names to the lowest level of the list is done with `names()` or by direct assignment.

For matrices, there are three possible functions used to see the names or to assign names: `rownames()`, `colnames()`, and `dimnames()`. The functions `rownames()` and `colnames()` have three arguments: **x**, the R object; **do.NULL**; and **prefix**. The argument **do.NULL** is logical with default value **TRUE**, which tells the function to do nothing if the row or column names are NULL. If **do.NULL** is **FALSE**, the row or column names are indexed with the prefix equal to the value of the argument **prefix**. For example:

```
> mat
      [,1] [,2]
[1,]    1    3
[2,]    2    4
> colnames( mat )
NULL
> colnames( mat ) = colnames( mat, do.NULL=FALSE, prefix="cl" )
> mat
     cl1 cl2
[1,]   1   3
[2,]   2   4
```

Note that the right-hand side of the third expression only returns the names of the columns and does not do the assignment.

The function `dimnames()` can be used to see or assign names to matrices and arrays. If `dimnames()` operates on an object, then the names of the dimensions in the object are returned as a list. If names are assigned using `dimnames()`, the object on the right side of the assignment must be a list with the same number of lowest level elements as there are dimensions in the object and with each lowest level element either being **NULL** or of the same length as there are elements in each dimension of the matrix or array. For example:

```
> a
, , d31
     d21 d22
d11   1   3
d12   2   4
, , d32
     d21 d22
d11   5   7
d12   6   8
>
> dimnames( a )
[[1]]
[1] "d11" "d12"
[[2]]
[1] "d21" "d22"
[[3]]
[1] "d31" "d32"
>
> dimnames( a ) = list( c( "11", "12") ,c( "21", "22" ),
c( "31", "32" ) )
>
> a
, , 31
   21 22
11  1  3
12  2  4
, , 32
   21 22
11  5  7
12  6  8
```

More information about names can be found by using the Help tab in RStudio or by entering **?names**, **?rownames**, or **?dimnames** at the R prompt.

The Data Frame Class: data.frame

The `data.frame` class is a matrixlike class of the `list` type. Data frames and how to use them are important. Many of the data sets that are available for R are data frames. When data is read from external sources, many of the functions that do the reading create data frames. Learning how to work with and create data frames pays high dividends.

Data frames contain atomic data in rows and columns. Within a column, the data must be of the same type. Across columns, the type can change. Because data frames do not have to be of just one type, data frames are a special kind of list.

Accessing elements of the data frame can be done like matrices or like lists, which makes data frames more versatile than the usual list. By default, the columns take names that reflect what is or is not in the original objects making up the data frame.

The functions `data.frame()`, `as.data.frame()`, and `is.data.frame()` all exist in R. In `data.frame()`, the first argument is ..., so the objects to be included in the data frame are listed first, separated by commas. The objects can be any object of an atomic type or lists made up of atomic columns. If an object is made up of more than one column, like some matrices and lists, then each column in the original object becomes a column in the data frame. Otherwise, each object becomes a column. If the columns had names in the original objects, the names are brought into the data frame by default.

The objects used to make up the data frame do not have to be of the same length (or number of rows for matrices) but must be multiples of each other in length. The number of rows in the data frame will equal the length of the longest column. The data in the other columns will cycle until the column has the right number of rows. For example:

```
> a.list
[[1]]
     a1 a2
[1,]  1  7
[2,]  2  8
[3,]  3  9
[4,]  4 10
[5,]  5 11
[6,]  6 12
[[2]]
[1] "abc" "cde"
>
> data.frame( a.list, 1:3 )
  a1 a2 c..abc....cde.. X1.3
1  1  7            abc    1
2  2  8            cde    2
3  3  9            abc    3
4  4 10            cde    1
5  5 11            abc    2
6  6 12            cde    3
```

Note that R has created names for the third and fourth columns and that the third and fourth columns both cycle.

The function data.frame() has four arguments in addition to the objects that will make up the data frame. The first argument is **row. names**, which assigns names to the rows and by default is **NULL**; that is, no names are assigned. The second argument is **check.rows**, which is a logical argument and will check for consistency of row lengths and row names if set to **TRUE**. The default value is **FALSE**. The third argument is

check.names, which is also logical and which checks that column names are syntactically correct and corrects names that are not. The default for **check.names** is **TRUE**.

The last argument is **stringsAsFactors**. By default, previously data.frame() converted any column containing character data to the factor class (see below). Currently, the default is that character class columns remain of the character class. The argument **stringsAsFactors** is a logical variable. If set to **TRUE**, factors are created. If set to **FALSE**, character columns remain columns of the character type. The actual default value of stringsAsFactors is generated by the function default.stingsAsFactors(). The value from default.stringsAsFactors() is set in options() (Chapter 15) by the stringsAsFactors option and by default is **FALSE** but can be changed in options() (or be set in the call to data.frame()).

The function I() can be used in the setting up of data frames. I() ensures that for a matrix, the column structure is maintained in the data frame. An object in the data.frame() call enclosed in I() will be treated as one element of the data frame, even if the object contains more than one column. Objects enclosed in I() do not cycle. For example:

```
> mat
      one two
row1   1   3
row2   2   4
> a.char
[1] "a1" "a2" "a3" "a4"

> a.df1 = data.frame( mat, a.char )
Warning message:
In data.frame(mat, a.char) :
  row names were found from a short variable and have been
  discarded
> a.df1
```

```
    one two a.char
1   1   3      a1
2   2   4      a2
3   1   3      a3
4   2   4      a4
> a.df1[[3]]
[1] "a1" "a2" "a3" "a4"

> a.df2 = data.frame( I( mat ), I( a.char[ 1:2 ] )  )
> a.df2
        mat.one mat.two a.char.1.2.
row1          1       3          a1
row2          2       4          a2
> a.df2[[1]]
        one two
row1      1   3
row2      2   4
> a.df2[[2]]
[1] "a1" "a2"
```

If row names are not entered in the call to data.frame(), row names are taken from the first column if the first column has row labels and does not cycle. Otherwise, row names are set to **1**, **2**, **3**, and so forth. See the preceding example.

The function as.data.frame() attempts to coerce an object to a data frame. If the object is a list made up of atomic elements of lengths that are multiples of each other or is an object of an atomic type (vector, matrix, or array), then as.data.frame() creates a data frame out of the object. (For lists, the atomic elements need not be at the lowest level of the list.) Otherwise, as.data.frame() gives an error.

The function takes up to nine arguments—with the number differing for character vectors, lists, and matrices (and arrays). The first argument in the three cases is the object to be coerced, **x**. If **x** is a character

vector, the second argument is **...**, and the third (and last) argument is
stringsAsFactors. If **x** is a list, the second through ninth arguments are
**row.names, optional, ..., cut.names, col.names, fix.empty.names,
check.names**, and **stringsAsFactors**. If **x** is a matrix, the second through
sixth arguments are **row.names, optional, make.names, ...,** and
stringsAsFactors.

The argument **...** allows for the exchange of variables between
methods. The arguments **row.names** and **stringsAsFactors** behave the
same way as in data.frame() and take the same default values. The
argument **optional** is a logical variable that, if set to **TRUE**, tells as.data.
frame() that setting column names is optional. If set to **TRUE** and no
column names have been set in the original object, column names are not
present in the result. The default value for **optional** is **FALSE**.

For lists, the arguments **cut.names, col.names, fix.empty.names**, and
check.names affect column names. The argument **cut.names** indicates
whether to cut long column names if the names exist in the list or if the
names are assigned by **col.names**. The argument can take a logical value
or an integer that gives the maximum number of characters for the column
name. According to the help page for as.data.frame(), by default, the
maximum number of characters is 256 if **cut.names** is **TRUE**. If cutting is
done, the last six characters before the CUT are replaced with six periods
(......). On my MacBook Air computer, the last two periods are removed. If
cut.names equals **FALSE** (the default), no cutting is done. For example:

```
> z = paste0( rep( "z", 301 ), collapse="" )
> nchar( z )
[1] 301
> names( as.data.frame( list( 1:12 ), col.names=z ) )
[1] "zzzzzzzzzzzzzzzzzzzzzzzzzzzzzzzzzzzzzzzzzzzzzzzzzzzzzzzzzzz
zzzzzzzzzzzzzzzzzzzzzzzzzzzzzzzzzzzzzzzzzzzzzzzzzzzzzzzzzzzzzzzzz
zzzzzzzzzzzzzzzzzzzzzzzzzzzzzzzzzzzzzzzzzzzzzzzzzzzzzzzzzzzzzzzzz
```

```
zzzzzzzzzzzzzzzzzzzzzzzzzzzzzzzzzzzzzzzzzzzzzzzzzzzzzzzzzzzzzzzzzzzzzzzz
zzzzzzzzzzzzzzzzzzzzzzzzzzzzzzzzzzzzzzzzzzzzzzzzzzzzzzzz"
> nchar( names( as.data.frame( list( 1:12 ), col.names=z ) ) )
[1] 301

> names( as.data.frame( list( 1:12 ), col.names=z, cut.
names=TRUE ) )
[1] "zzzzzzzzzzzzzzzzzzzzzzzzzzzzzzzzzzzzzzzzzzzzzzzzzzzzzzzzzzzz
zzzzzzzzzzzzzzzzzzzzzzzzzzzzzzzzzzzzzzzzzzzzzzzzzzzzzzzzzzzzzzzzz
zzzzzzzzzzzzzzzzzzzzzzzzzzzzzzzzzzzzzzzzzzzzzzzzzzzzzzzzzzzzzzzzz
zzzzzzzzzzzzzzzzzzzzzzzzzzzzzzzzzzzzzzzzzzzzzzzzzzzzzzzzzzzzzzzzz
zzzzz...."
> nchar( names( as.data.frame( list( 1:12 ), col.names=z, cut.
names=TRUE ) ) )
[1] 254
> names( as.data.frame( list( 1:12 ), col.names=z, cut.
names=10 ) )
[1] "zzzz...."
> nchar( names( as.data.frame( list( 1:12 ), col.names=z, cut.
names=10 ) ) )
[1] 8
```

Note that the function nchar() counts the number of characters in a character string.

The argument **cut.names** does not affect names generated by R when column names are missing.

The **col.names** argument takes a character vector of the same length as the list. If the list has more than one level, R generates column names based on the names that are given at the lowest level. The default value of **col.names** is **names(x)**.

113

The **fix.empty.names** argument is a logical variable that indicates whether to create column names if names are missing. The default value of **fix.empty.names** is **TRUE**. For example:

```
> as.data.frame( list( 1:2, "a" ) )
  X1.2 X.a.
1    1    a
2    2    a

> as.data.frame( list( 1:2, "a" ), fix.empty.names=FALSE )

1 1 a
2 2 a
```

The **check.names** argument is a logical variable that behaves like the same argument in data.frame(). The default value of **check.names** in as.data.frame() is **!optional**, where **optional** is the argument to as.data.frame() given before.

If **x** is a matrix (or array), the argument **make.names** is a logical variable that applies to row names. If there are duplicate row names and **make.names** is **TRUE**, then the names are made into different names. If FALSE, and an error is returned. The default value of **make.names** is **TRUE**. For example:

```
> a.mat
    one two
one   1   3
one   2   4

> as.data.frame( a.mat )
      one two
one     1   3
one.1   2   4

> as.data.frame( a.mat, make.names=FALSE )
```

```
Error in `.rowNamesDF<-`(`*tmp*`, make.names = make.names,
value = row.names) :
  duplicate 'row.names' are not allowed
In addition: Warning message:
 Error in `.rowNamesDF<-`(`*tmp*`, make.names = make.names,
 value = row.names) :
  duplicate 'row.names' are not allowed
4.
stop("duplicate 'row.names' are not allowed")
3.
`.rowNamesDF<-`(`*tmp*`, make.names = make.names, value =
row.names)
2.
as.data.frame.matrix(a.mat, make.names = FALSE)
1.
as.data.frame(a.mat, make.names = FALSE)
```

For arrays, a data frame with the same number of rows as the first dimension in the array is created out of the array. The elements go down through the dimensions. For example:

```
> as.data.frame( array( data=1:24, dim=c( 2, 3, 2, 2 ) ) )
  V1 V2 V3 V4 V5 V6 V7 V8 V9 V10 V11 V12
1  1  3  5  7  9 11 13 15 17  19  21  23
2  2  4  6  8 10 12 14 16 18  20  22  24
```

The is.data.frame() function takes one argument **x** and tests if **x** is of the data.frame class and, if so, returns **TRUE**. Otherwise, is.data.frame() returns **FALSE**.

The as.matrix() and data.matrix() functions can be used to convert a data frame to a matrix. See the section on the matrix class for more information about the two kinds of conversions.

For more information, use the Help tab in RStudio to access the help pages. Or for more information about data.frame(), enter **?data.frame** at the R prompt; for as.data.frame() and is.data.frame(), enter **?as.data. frame** at the R prompt; for I(), enter **?I** at the R prompt.

The Time Series Classes: ts and mts

Classes ts and mts refer to objects that have a starting point, an end point, and a frequency or period defined and for which observations are assumed to be sampled at equal intervals. The default class for a vector of time series observations is ts. For a matrix of concurrent time series observations, the default classes are mts, ts, and matrix. The class of the time series can be changed when the time series object is created.

Time series objects can be created out of vector, matrix, some list, and expression objects, as well as some other classes of objects (such as factor and Date) using the function ts(). Objects of the array class give an error. All of the atomic types are legal as arguments for the function ts() (except the NULL type). For list objects, depending on the contents and structure of the list, the ts() function will create a, sometimes strange, time series object. Similarly, operating on an object of mode expression with ts() does not give an error but does give strange results.

If the argument to ts() is a data frame, then the data frame is coerced to a matrix by the function data.matrix(). For matrix arguments, the different time series are indexed across the columns and time is indexed down the rows.

The function ts() takes eight arguments. The first argument **data** is the object to be changed into a time series. The second argument is **start** and gives a value for the start of the series. The third argument is **end** and gives a value for the end of the series. The fourth argument is **frequency**, which gives the periodic frequency for the series. The fifth argument is **deltat**, which is the inverse of the frequency. Either **frequency** or **deltat** is supplied, not both.

The sixth argument is **ts.eps**, which gives the acceptable tolerance for comparing frequencies between different time series. The seventh argument is **class**, which tells R what class to assign to the time series object. The eighth argument is **names** and gives names to the time series for time series matrices. If no names are given, R assigns the names **Series 1**, **Series 2**, and so forth.

The second, third, fourth, and fifth arguments can be confusing. R treats monthly or quarterly data as a special case regarding printing and plotting. Other types of periodic data have to be treated specially. For monthly data, setting **start** equal to

```
start = c( 'year', 'month number' )
```

and **frequency** equal to

```
frequency = 12
```

or **deltat** equal to

```
deltat = 1/12,
```

where **year** is the starting year and **month number** is the number of the starting month (**1** for January, **2** for February, and so on), assigns months and years to the points in the object being converted to a time series.

To generate a monthly time series, include **end** with

```
end = c( 'year', 'month number' ),
```

where **year** is the ending year and **month number** is the number of the ending month. The function **ts()** will cycle the first argument until the time series is filled out. (For any time series, supplying start, end, and frequency will create a time series out of the first argument by cycling. If the first argument is a matrix, each column cycles independently.)

For quarterly data, follow the same steps but use a frequency of four. For example:

```
> ts( 1:12, start=c( 2019, 2 ), freq=12 )
     Jan Feb Mar Apr May Jun Jul Aug Sep Oct Nov Dec
2019       1   2   3   4   5   6   7   8   9  10  11
2020  12
> ts( 1:12, start=c( 2019, 2 ), freq=4 )
     Qtr1 Qtr2 Qtr3 Qtr4
2019         1    2    3
2020    4    5    6    7
2021    8    9   10   11
2022   12
```

On a more general level, say there is daily data for 1 week and 3 days and the starting week is number 32. Let **d.data** be the data. Then, the time series can be created as follows:

```
> ts( 1:12, start=c( 3, 2 ), freq=7 )
Time Series:
Start = c(3, 2)
End = c(4, 6)
Frequency = 7
 [1]  1  2  3  4  5  6  7  8  9 10 11 12
> print( ts( 1:12, start=c( 3, 2 ), freq=7 ), calendar=T )
  p1 p2 p3 p4 p5 p6 p7
3     1  2  3  4  5  6
4  7  8  9 10 11 12
```

Note that the default for printing the time series is not in periods— except for frequencies of 4 and 12, for which R assumes that the data is monthly or quarterly. The printing of periods can be turned on and off with the **calendar** argument to print().

If one number, instead of two, is used for each of **start** and **end**, then only the quantities (n+i/f) can be used as the starting and end points, where **n** is the integer of the first or last period, **f** is the frequency, and **i** can take integer values between zero and (f-1). For example:

```
> ts( data=1:5, start=2+2/3, end=4+1/3, deltat=1/3)
Time Series:
Start = c(2, 3)
End = c(4, 2)
Frequency = 3
[1] 1 2 3 4 5 1

> print( ts( 1:5, 2+2/3, 4+1/3, deltat=1/3), calendar=TRUE )
  p1 p2 p3
2        1
3  2  3  4
4  5  1
```

The quantity (n+i/f) must be taken out to at least five decimal places if entered manually unless the argument **ts.eps** is changed from the default value of 1.0E-5. The value of **ts.eps** is set in options() (see Chapter 15). R is very picky here.

The default values of **start** and **end** are 1 and numeric(), the empty numeric vector. The default values of **frequency** and **deltat** are both 1. The default value of **ts.eps** is getOption("ts.eps"), which on my computer is 1e-05. The arguments **class** and **name** do not have default values that are set in the call to the function.

The function as.ts() takes the argument **x** and attempts to coerce an object to class ts. Objects that are vector—or matrixlike—will coerce. Arrays will not, functions will not, calls will not, and environments will not; expressions and lists will. The function as.ts() also takes the argument **...** for exchanging arguments between methods and which, according to the help page, is not used for the default method.

The function is.ts() takes the argument **x** and tests if **x** is of class ts and returns **TRUE** if so and **FALSE** otherwise.

More information about ts(), as.ts(), and is.ts() can be found by using the Help tab in RStudio or by entering **?ts** at the R prompt.

The Factor Classes: factor and ordered

The factor class is the class of objects that are factor levels. Factors with ordered factor levels belong to two classes: factor and ordered. Factors and ordered factors are used in modeling for which at least some categorical data is present. The type of factors and ordered factors is integer, and the levels are associated with integers that increase in value from one. However, when printed, the nominal levels are given.

The factor levels are ordered alphabetically or numerically by default, depending on the type of the argument, but can be assigned a different order.

The functions factor(), as.factor(), and is.factor() exist, as well as ordered(), as.ordered(), and is.ordered(). According to the help page for factor(), the second set of functions is included for backward compatibility with S, since ordered factors can be set using the first set of functions. We only discuss the first set of functions here.

The function factor() creates a vector of factor levels and an associated list of levels. The function takes six arguments. The first argument is **x**, the object from which the factors will be generated. The argument must be of an atomic mode or a list. (Not all lists will form factors.) The default value of **x** is character(), the null character vector.

The second argument is **levels** and sets the order of the factor levels. The **levels** argument is optional and has no default value assigned in the call to the function.

The third argument is **labels** and assigns labels to the levels. The third argument is optional and defaults to the value of **levels**.

The fourth argument is **exclude** and gives any levels to be excluded in the result. Excluded levels are set to **<NA>**. The argument is optional and defaults to **NA**.

The fifth argument is **ordered**. The argument is a **logical variable** and tells factor() whether to create a factor with ordered levels. (The function factor() with **ordered** set to **TRUE** gives the same result as the function ordered()). The default value of **ordered** is is.ordered(x).

The sixth argument is **nmax** and is described as the maximum number of levels to use, where many values are present in the object to be made into a factor. The argument does not appear to work on my computer. The default value of **nmax** is **NA**.

Converting between factors and the original data is sometimes of interest. If labels have not been assigned in factor():

as.*type*(levels(*fac.obj*))[*fac.obj*],

returns the original values of the object, where *type* is the type of the original object and *fac.obj* is the factor object. Note that the function,

as.integer(*fac.obj*),

returns the integers associated with the levels, even if the original object was not of the integer type. If labels have been assigned, then usually the original data cannot be extracted.

An example follows:

```
> a.log = c( TRUE, TRUE, FALSE, TRUE )
> a.log
[1]  TRUE  TRUE FALSE  TRUE

> af1 = factor( a.log )
> af1
[1] TRUE   TRUE   FALSE TRUE
Levels: FALSE TRUE
> as.logical( levels( af1 ) )[ af1 ]
```

```
[1]   TRUE   TRUE FALSE   TRUE
> as.integer( af1 )
[1] 2 2 1 2

> af2 = factor( a.log, levels=c( TRUE, FALSE ) )
> af2
[1] TRUE   TRUE   FALSE TRUE
Levels: TRUE FALSE
> as.logical( levels( af2 ) )[ af2 ]
[1]   TRUE   TRUE FALSE   TRUE
> as.integer( af2 )
[1] 1 1 2 1

> af3 =factor( a.log, labels=c( "flab", "tlab" ) )
> af3
[1] tlab tlab flab tlab
Levels: flab tlab
> as.logical( levels( af3 ) )[ af3 ]
[1] NA NA NA NA
> as.integer( af3 )
[1] 2 2 1 2
> as.character( levels( af3 ) ) [ af3 ]
[1] "tlab" "tlab" "flab" "tlab"
```

The as.factor() function takes one argument **x** and operates the same way as factor(). The argument **x** can be any object that is legal for a factor, and **x** has no default value.

The is.factor() function takes one argument **x** and tests if **x** is a factor. The function returns **TRUE** if **x** is a factor and **FALSE** otherwise.

There is also a related function, addNA(). The function creates a factor object with a level for missing data (NAs). The function has two arguments. The first argument **x** is an object from which an object of class factor can be created. The second argument is **ifany**. The **ifany** argument is logical and takes on the value **TRUE** if the extra level is only added when **NA**s are present and the value **FALSE** if the extra level is to always be included. The default value is **FALSE**.

More information about the seven functions can be found by using the Help tab in RStudio or by entering **?factor** at the R prompt.

The Date and Time Classes: Date, POSIXct, POSIXlt, and difftime

Sometimes, working with dates and times is useful, as when printing and plotting against time. R provides classes for dates and for dates and times. The classes are Date, POSIXct, POSIXlt, and difftime. (There is also a virtual class POSIXt that contains both POSIXct and POSIXlt.) Date is the date class, and POSIXlt and POSIXct are the date and time classes. The difftime class contains objects formed by taking the differences between two date objects and/or date and time objects. Objects of the Date, POSIXct, or difftime class are of the double type, and objects of the POSIXlt class are of the list type. Of the three kinds of functions usual for the classes given in the preceding sections, only the functions as.Date(), as.POSIXct(), and as.POSIXlt() exist for date and date and time objects. Both difftime() and as.difftime() exist.

POSIX stands for Portable Operating System Interface and is a family of standards used by the IEEE Computer Society. The formats used in the Date, POSIXct, and POSIXlt classes are based on the POSIX standards, but according to the writers at CRAN, the standards are not universal across platforms.

The functions as.Date(), as.POSIXct(), and as.POSIXlt() take character strings, numeric objects, date objects, or date and time objects and convert the objects to the Date, POSIXct, and POSIXlt classes,

respectively. By default, dates are read and returned in the format
"Year-Month-Day," and times are read and returned in the format
"Hour:Minute:Second." For example:

```
> as.Date( "2021-8-13" )
[1] "2021-08-13"
> class( as.Date( "2021-8-13" ) )
[1] "Date"

> as.POSIXct( "2021-8-13 15:24:00" )
[1] "2021-08-13 15:24:00 CDT"
> class( as.POSIXct( "2021-8-13 15:24:00" ) )
[1] "POSIXct" "POSIXt"
```

To get a date and time stamp in R, enter **date()** at the R prompt—
which returns the day of the week, date, and time. The result is of the
`character` type and class. The system date function `Sys.Date()`
returns the system date and is of the `double` type and `Date` class.
The system date and time function is `Sys.time()` and returns the
system date, time, and time zone and is of the `double` type and the
`POSIXct` and `POSIXt` classes. The functions `Sys.timezone()` and
`Sys.getlocale()` return the time zone and locale of the computer
system. The returned objects are of the `character` type.

The function as.Date() creates an object of the Date class. The
arguments to as.Date() are **x,** the object to be converted to a date(s);
format, which gives the format(s) of **x** in terms of year, month, and day;
tryFormats, which is a character vector of formats to try if **format** is not
given; **optional**, which is logical and, when set to **TRUE,** causes as.Date()
to return an **NA** if format matching returns an error; **origin**, which is an
origin for **x**; and **tz** for the time zone name.

The argument **x** is one of the following: a character object that can be converted to dates, a numeric object, or a **POSIXct** object. There is no default value for **x**.

If **x** contains character strings containing dates and the dates are not in the POSIX standard format or in one of the formats in **tryFormats** (see below), then the format of the dates must be given. The **format** argument gives the format(s) of the character string(s) in **x**. The following example uses the POSIX standard character variables for the year (**%Y**), the day (**%d**), and the month (**%m**). (A list of the available POSIX standard character variables is shown in Table 5-1 and at the `strptime` help page. There are 36 POSIX standard character variables listed.) The **format** argument takes a character vector with elements such as **"%m/%d/%Y"**.

Table 5-1. *Standard Character Variables for Dates and Times*

%a	%A	%b	%B
short weekday name, for locale	full weekday name, for locale	short month name, for locale	full month name, for locale
%c	%C	%d	%D
`date and time,` `%a %b %e %H:%M:%S` `%Y`	century, first 2 digits, (00-99)	day of month, (01-31)	date, %m/%d/%y
%e	%F	%g	%G
day of month, 2 spaces, no leading 0, (1-31)	date, %Y-%m-%d, (ISO 8601 standard)	year, (00-99, see %V)	year, (0000-9999, see %V)
%h	%H	%I	%j
same as %b	hour, (00-23)	hour, (01-12)	day of year, (001-366)

(*continued*)

Table 5-1. (*continued*)

%m month, (01-12)	%M minutes, (00-59)	%n new line (output), white space (input)	%p AM or PM, (as in locale)
%r time, AM/PM format if exists in locale (output), %I:%M:%S %p (input)	%R time, %H:%M	%S seconds, (00-61)	%t tab (output), white space (input)
%T time, %H:%M:%S	%u day of week, (1-7, Mon-Sun)	%U week of year, (00-53, Sun starts week, US standard)	%V week of year, (01-53, Mon starts week, ISO 8601 standard)
%w day of week, (0-6, Sun-Sat)	%W week of year, (00-53, Mon starts week, UK standard)	%x date, %y/%m/%d (input), locale specific (output)	%X time, %H:%M:%S (input), locale specific (output)
%y year, last 2 digits, (00-99)	%Y year, (0-9999 gives limits for input)	%z time offset from UT, negative west, (-1400 to +1400)	%Z time zone name, (if exists, for output only)

Based on the help page for strptime in the base package of R.

If **x** is longer than **format**, **format** cycles out to the length of **x**. If **format** is longer, **x** cycles out. Note that the format is the format of the object to be converted, not the format of the result. There is no default value for **format**.

The **tryFormats** argument takes a collection of character strings containing possible formats for dates. The default value of **tryFormats** is **c("%Y-%m-%d", "%Y/%m/%d")**.

The **tryFormats** and **format** arguments are only used with character data.

The **optional** argument, for returning **NA**s, takes a logical value. If set to **TRUE**, **NA**s are returned if the conversion cannot be done; if **FALSE**, an error occurs. The **optional** argument only applies for character vectors, and the default value of **optional** is **FALSE**.

The **origin** argument takes an object of the Date or POSIXct class or a character vector of dates in the POSIX standard format. If **origin** is given, **x** can be any numeric object. The function adds or subtracts the value(s) of **x** to or from the date(s) given by the **origin** argument and converts the result to a date(s). The **origin** argument is only used with numeric data. The **origin** argument cycles if the length of **origin** is shorter than the length of **x**. If **x** is shorter, **x** cycles out to the length of **format**. If the length of the longer vector is not a multiple of the shorter vector, a warning is given, but the conversion takes place. An example of weekly spacing is

```
> as.Date( 0:2*7, origin="2021-8-13" )
[1] "2021-08-13" "2021-08-20" "2021-08-27"
```

There is no default value for **origin**.

The **tz** argument takes a character string containing the time zone name. According to the writers at CRAN, some time zones are recognized, and some are not. (A list of–not always legal for all systems–time zone names is returned by entering OlsonNames() at the R prompt.) Only **x** values that are of the POSIXct class use **tz**. The default value of **tz** is "UTC", which is Coordinated Universal Time.

The functions as.POSIXct() and as.POSIXlt() take the same arguments as as.Date() except that the dates also contain times and the **tz** argument is the second argument rather than the last. Also, **tz** is used for all legal classes for the value of **x**. The default values are the same except that **tz** takes the default value of "" and **tryFormats** takes the default value **c("%Y-%m-%d %H:%M:%OS", "%Y/%m/%d %H:%M:%OS", "%Y/%m/%d %H:%M", "%Y-%m-%d", "%Y/%m/%d")**.

The POSIX standard format for time is **%H:%M:%S** (for hours, minutes, and seconds). In the POSIX standard format for date and time objects, time is part of the character string that contains the date. The time is after the date and separated from the date by one character space. For example:

```
> as.POSIXct( "1/13/2000 00:30:00", format="%m/%d/%Y
%H:%M:%S" )
[1] "2000-01-13 00:30:00 CST"
```

Note that the result is in the POSIX standard format.

Dates and dates and times can be operated on by addition and subtraction. Decimals for times are converted correctly. Dates in the as.Date() function are incremented by days; times in the two date and time functions are incremented by seconds. Examples follow:

```
> as.Date( "2021-8-13" ) + 1:2
[1] "2021-08-14" "2021-08-15"
> typeof( as.Date( "2021-8-13" ) + 1:2 )
[1] "double"

> as.POSIXct( "2021-8-13 00:00:00" ) + 1:2*3600
[1] "2021-08-13 01:00:00 CDT" "2021-08-13 02:00:00 CDT"
> typeof( as.POSIXct( "2021-8-13 00:00:00" ) + 1:2*3600 )
[1] "double"
```

```
> as.POSIXlt( as.POSIXct( "2021-8-13 00:00:00" ) + 1:2*3600 )
[1] "2021-08-13 01:00:00 CDT" "2021-08-13 02:00:00 CDT"
> typeof( as.POSIXlt( as.POSIXct( "2021-8-13 00:00:00" ) +
1:2*3600 ) )
[1] "list"

> as.POSIXlt( "2021-8-13 00:00:00" ) + 1:2*3600
[1] "2021-08-13 01:00:00 CDT" "2021-08-13 02:00:00 CDT"
> typeof( as.POSIXlt( "2021-8-13 00:00:00" ) + 1:2*3600 )
[1] "double"
```

The function `difftime()` takes two numeric date and/or date and time objects and finds the difference in time elementwise between the two objects. The objects must be of the same length. For objects of the `Date` class and the `POSIXct` class, the difference between the dates and/or the dates and times is measured in units chosen by R by default. The units can be set in the call to the function.

The function `as.difftime()` takes a character object giving a date or time and finds the elapsed time from a base date or base time in one of several possible units of time.

The `difftime()` function takes four arguments: **time1**, for the first time; **time2**, for the second time; **tz**, for the time zone; and **units**, for the units in which to return the result. The arguments **time1** and **time2** are the objects to be subtracted. The value of **time2** is subtracted from the value of **time1**. Either argument can be of the `Date` or `POSIXct` classes. There is no default value for either argument.

The argument **tz** takes a time zone name (see the description of `as.Date()` for time zone information). There is no default value for **tz**.

The argument **units** takes a character string containing the name of the units to be used for the result. The default value of **units** is **c("auto", "secs", "mins", "hours", "days", "weeks")**. The **"auto"** value lets R choose the time units to use. The other values give which time unit to use. The default value of **units** is **"auto"**.

If the subtraction is done with the formula **time1-time2** instead of with `difftime()`, both times must be of the Date class or of the POSIXct class. Both **time1-time2** and **difftime(time1,time2)** give a result that is in the difftime class.

An example of a date difference is

```
> as.Date( "2021-8-13" ) - as.Date( "2000-1-1" )
Time difference of 7895 days
> typeof( as.Date( "2021-8-13" ) - as.Date( "2000-1-1" ) )
[1] "double"
> class( as.Date( "2021-8-13" ) - as.Date( "2000-1-1" ) )
[1] "difftime"
```

An example of a time difference is

```
> t1 = as.POSIXct( "2021-8-13 12:00:00" )
> t2 = as.POSIXct( "2021-8-13 11:00:00" )
> difftime( t1, t2 )
Time difference of 1 hours
> difftime( t1, t2, units="mins" )
Time difference of 60 mins
> as.numeric( difftime( t1, t2, units="mins" ) )
[1] 60
```

The `as.difftime()` function converts a time interval into a number of units of time (e.g., converting 1 hour and 20 minutes to 80 minutes). The function takes four arguments: **tim**, for a time interval or the beginning of the time interval for dates; **format**, for the format of **tim** using POSIX standard character variables; **units**, for the units to which **tim** is to be converted; and **tz**, for the time zone.

The argument **tim** takes a character vector containing time interval(s), with the time format(s) of the interval(s) given by the argument **format**. There is no default value for **tim**.

The argument **format** takes a character vector containing the time format(s) formatted by using the POSIX standard character variables (the formats are found on the `strptime()` help page). The formats cycle out to the length of **x** if the **format** is shorter than **x**. If **x** is shorter, **x** cycles out to the length of **format**. The default value of **format** is **"%X"** (which is shorthand for **"%H:%M:%S"**).

The argument **units** takes a character string containing the units to be used for the result (which can be **"auto"**, **"secs"**, **"mins"**, **"hours"**, **"days"**, or **"weeks"**). The default value of **units** is **"auto"**.

The argument **tz** takes a character string containing the name of the time zone (see the description of `as.Date()` for information about time zone names). The default value of **tz** for date and time objects is the time zone of the computer system (for my computer, Central Time) and for date objects is Coordinated Universal Time (UTC).

An example of using `as.difftime()` is

```
> as.difftime( c( "20:15", "2021-1-1" ), format=c( "%H:%M",
"%Y-%m-%d" ), units="weeks" )
Time differences in weeks
[1]    0.1205357 -32.1428571
> class( as.difftime( c( "20:15", "2021-1-1" ), format=c(
"%H:%M", "%Y-%m-%d" ), units="weeks" ) )
[1] "difftime"
```

Note that the difference for the date is from the current date (today is 2021-8-14) while the difference for the time is from zero time. (Date differences are measured from zero hours midnight of the second date to zero hours midnight of the first date.) The result is in the `difftime` class.

Some other functions for dates and/or dates and times follow. The functions `strftime()` and `strptime()` format character objects containing dates or dates and times that are not formatted in the POSIX standard format from and to the POSIX standard format, respectively.

The strftime() function returns an object of the character class, while strptime() returns an object of the POSIXlt and POSIXt classes.

The strftime() function converts a character vector of times in the POSIX standard format to another format. The function takes five arguments: **x**, for the object to be converted; **format**, for the formats to which **x** is to be converted; **tz**, for the time zone to use; **usetz**, for whether to print the time zone; and **...**, for any arguments to be passed between methods.

The argument **x** takes a vector of the Date, POSIXct, or POSIXlt class or a character vector containing the dates or dates and times in the POSIX standard format. There is no default value for **x**.

The argument **format** takes a character vector containing the formats to which the values in **x** are to be converted. The argument cycles if the length of **format** is less than the length of **x**. The elements of **x** cycle if the length of **format** is longer than **x**. The default value of **format** is "".

The argument **tz** takes a character string containing the name of the time zone for the values in **x**. The default value of **tz** is "". (See the description of as.Date() for more information about time zone names.)

The argument **usetz** takes a logical value. If set to **TRUE**, the time zone is printed; if **FALSE**, the time zone is not printed. The default value of **usetz** is **FALSE**.

Two examples of using strftime are

```
> strftime( c( "2021-08-13" ), format=c( "%m/%d/%Y", "%d/%m/%Y" ), tz="America/Chicago", usetz=TRUE )
[1] "08/13/2021 CDT" "13/08/2021 CDT"
```

and

```
> strftime( x="2021-08-13 12:00:00", format="%m/%d/%Y %I:%M %p" )
[1] "08/13/2021 12:00 PM"
```

Note that in the first example, the first date uses the standard used in the United States while the second uses the standard used in Europe. In the second example, the POSIX standard character variable **%I** gives the hour in 12-hour increments, and the POSIX standard character variable **%p** returns AM or PM depending on whether the time is before noon or not. Only one time zone is permitted.

The strptime() function converts dates or dates and times that are not in POSIX standard format to objects of the POSIXlt and POSIXt classes. The function takes three arguments: **x**, for the object to be converted; **format**, for the formats of the elements of **x**; and **tz**, for the time zone to use.

The argument **x** takes a character vector of dates or dates and times that are not in the POSIX standard format. There is no default value for **x**.

The argument **format** takes a character vector of formats for the elements of **x**, where the formats use the POSIX standard character variables (from the help page for **strptime**). Just one format can be used if all the elements of **x** have the same format. The formats cycle if the length of **format** is shorter than the length of **x**. If **format** is longer, **x** cycles. There is no default value for **format**.

The argument **tz** takes a single character string containing the time zone name to be used. The default value of tz is "". (See the description of as.Date() for more information about time zone names.)

Two examples of using strptime() are

```
> strptime( "8/13/2021", format="%m/%d/%Y", tz="UTC" )
[1] "2021-08-13 UTC"
> class( strptime( "8/13/2021", format="%m/%d/%Y", tz="UTC" ) )
[1] "POSIXlt" "POSIXt"

> strptime(c( "8/13/2021 12:00 AM", "8/13/2021 12:00 pm" ) ,
format=c( "%m/%d/%Y %I:%M %p" ) )
[1] "2021-08-13 00:00:00 CDT" "2021-08-13 12:00:00 CDT"
```

```
> class( strptime( c( "8/13/2021 12:00 AM", "8/13/2021 12:00
pm" ), format=c( "%m/%d/%Y %I:%M %p" ) ) )
[1] "POSIXlt" "POSIXt"
```

Note that if the time zone is not set, R uses the system time zone, which in my case is Central Time in the United States.

There are a number of functions that operate on the date and time classes, including weekdays(), months(), quarters(), and julian()– which return the day of the week, the month, the quarter, and the Julian date for objects of Date, POSIXlt, and POSIXct classes.

The weekdays(), months(), and quarters() functions take two arguments: **x**, for the object from which to extract the day of the week, the month, or the quarter; and **abbreviate**, for whether to abbreviate the result.

The argument **x** takes an object of the Date, POSIXct, or POSIXlt class. There is no default value for **x**.

The argument **abbreviate** takes a logical vector. If **TRUE**, the result is abbreviated; if **FALSE**, the result is not abbreviated. The default value of abbreviate is **FALSE**.

Both **x** and **abbreviate** cycle out to the longer of the two. An example of using the three functions is

```
> c( t1, t2 )
[1] "2021-08-13 12:00:00 CDT" "2021-08-13 11:00:00 CDT"
> weekdays( x=c( t1, t2 ), abb=c( TRUE, FALSE ) )
[1] "Fri"     "Friday"
> months( x=c( t1, t2 ), abb=c( TRUE, FALSE ) )
[1] "Aug"     "August"
> quarters( x=c( t1, t2 ), abb=c( TRUE, FALSE ) )
[1] "Q3" "Q3"
```

Note that quarters are already abbreviated. (The Friday the 13th was unintentional.)

The function `julian()` returns the the number of days from a reference date–referenced, by default, from January 1, 1970, at zero hours midnight GMT (GMT and UTC are equivalent). Hours, minutes, and seconds are converted into portions of a day. (In astronomy and astrology, the Julian date is the time in days from noon Universal Time on January 1, 4713 BC, using the Julian calendar.)

The function `julian()` takes three arguments: **x**, for the dates or dates and times from which to find the number of days; **origin**, for the reference date or date and time; and **...**, for exchanging variables between methods.

The **x** argument takes an object of the `Date,` `POSIXct,` or `POSIXlt` class. There is no default value for **x**.

The **origin** argument also takes an object of the `Date,` `POSIXct,` or `POSIXlt` class. For objects of the `Date` class, **origin** has the default value of **as.Date("1970-1-1")**. The default value of **origin** is **as.POSIXct("1970-1-1 00:00:00", tz="GMT")** for objects of the `POSIXct` or `POSIXlt` classes. Three examples of using `julian()` are

```
> julian( as.Date( "1971-1-1" ) )
[1] 365
attr(,"origin")
[1] "1970-01-01"
> julian( as.POSIXct( "1971-1-1 12:00:00" ) )
Time difference of 365.75 days
> julian( as.POSIXlt( "1971-1-1 12:00:00" ) )
Time difference of 365.75 days
```

Note that the date version returns the origin while the date and time version does not. Also, for date and time objects, **origin** is in Universal Time, while (by default) **x** is in the time zone used by the computer system. In January, Central Time (my system time standard) is 6 hours behind Coordinated Universal Time, so the number of days that is calculated is 0.25 (6 hours divided by 24 hours) days longer than if the time zone of **x** had been Greenwich Mean Time.

The `format()`, `print()`, `summary()`, `cut()`, `seq()`, `round()`, and `trunc()` functions have methods for the Date, POSIXct, and POSIXlt classes—see Chapter 15. (To see all the methods of objects of the Date class, enter **methods(class="Date")** at the R prompt; for the POSIXt classes, enter **methods(class="POSIXt")**.)

More information about the date and time classes and the related methods for `print()` and `summary()` can be found at the help page for `DateTimeClasses` by using the Help tab in RStudio or by entering **?DateTimeClasses** at the R prompt.

More information about the date and time functions can be found by using the Help tab in RStudio or by entering **?as.Date**, **?as.POSIXlt**, or **?difftime** at the R prompt.

For the `strftime()`, `strptime()`, and `format()` functions, use the Help tab in RStudio or enter **?strptime** at the R prompt.

For the `weekdays()`, `months()`, `quarters()`, and `julian()` functions, use the help page in RStudio or enter **?weekdays** at the R prompt.

For the `cut()`, `seq()`, `round()`, and `trunc()` functions, use the Help tab in RStudio or enter **?*name*.Date** at the R prompt for dates and **?*name*. POSIXt** at the R prompt for dates and time, where *name* is the name of the function (e.g., **?cut.Date** and **?cut.POSIXt**).

The Formula Class: formula

Formulas are used by various functions in R; for example, the functions `lm()`, `glm()`, `nls()`, `plot()`, `coplot()`, and `boxplot()` use formulas. Formulas have their own class and are created by either setting an object equal to a formula, by using the function `formula()`, or by using the function `as.formula()`. Formulas are of the `language` type.

The formulas use some specialized notation. The symbol ~ separates the left side of the formula from the right side. The symbol + tells R to include the variables on either side of the + in the model. The symbol − tells R not to use the variable to the right of the –. (Use **-1** to not use an intercept.) The symbol **:** tells R to use the interaction between the variables on either side of **:**. The symbol ***** tells R to use all the levels of interaction between the variables on either side of *****. If a data frame is present in the call, the symbol **.** on the right side tells R to use all the variables in the data frame not already in the model. The symbol **^** tells R to use all interactions up to the level of the **^**. The operator **%in%** can be used to nest variables. Functions of variables can be used within the formula, but functions involving arithmetic expressions need to be enclosed in an I() function to avoid confusing R–since many symbols have special meanings inside of the formula statement.

The `formula()` function takes two arguments: **x**, for the formula, and **...**, for exchanging arguments between methods. Neither have a default value.

The `as.formula()` function takes two arguments: **object**, for the object to be transformed to a formula, and **env**, for the environment in which to look for the variables in the formula. There is no default value for **object**. The default value of **env** is **parent.frame()**.

If a data frame is specified in the function using the formula, then the function looks first in the data frame for the variables in the formula. If there is no data frame assigned or if the variable is not in the data frame, where to look depends on the function used to create the formula. There are three possibilities. The difference between the three possibilities is in which environment R searches for the variables in the formula. Formulas that are just entered are evaluated in the environment within which the formula is used. Formulas created using `formula()` are evaluated in the environment in which the formula was created. Formulas created by `as.formula()` have an environment assigned by the **env** argument, which by default is the parent frame. For each of the functions, the formula must be quoted for the environment assignment to occur. The following is an example of a function that demonstrates the above. First, the function `a.fun()` is listed.

```
> a.fun
function() {
# at the first function level
# formulas defined using the expression and formula()
  cat( "\nlevel a \n\n" )
  print( parent.frame() )
  print( environment() )
    x=1:10
    y=11:20
  cat( "\nx=", x )
  cat( "\ny=", y, "\n" )
    a.formula="y~x"
    b.formula=formula("y~x")
  b.fun=function() {
# at the second function level
# lm() is run for the formulas defined at the first level
    cat( "\nlevel b \n\n" )
      x=1:10
      y=21:30
    print( parent.frame() )
    print( environment() )
    print( lm( a.formula ) )
    cat( "\nx=", x )
    cat( "\ny=", y, "\n" )
    print( lm( b.formula ) )
# the cc environment is defined at the second level
# the formula from as.formula() is run
    cat( "\nenvironment cc \n\n" )
      cc=new.env()
        assign( "x", 1:10, env=cc )
        assign( "y", 31:40, env=cc )
```

```
    c.formula=as.formula( "y~x", env=cc )
    cat( "\nx=", cc$x )
    cat( "\ny=", cc$y, "\n" )
    print( lm( c.formula ) )
  }
 # the second function is run at the first level
  b.fun()
}
<bytecode: 0x10a767448>
```

Second, the function a.fun() is run.

```
> a.fun()
level a
<environment: R_GlobalEnv>
<environment: 0x10d3d28c8>
x= 1 2 3 4 5 6 7 8 9 10
y= 11 12 13 14 15 16 17 18 19 20
level b
<environment: 0x10d3d28c8>
<environment: 0x10d39e388>
Call:
lm(formula = a.formula)
Coefficients:
(Intercept)             x
         20             1
x= 1 2 3 4 5 6 7 8 9 10
y= 21 22 23 24 25 26 27 28 29 30
Call:
lm(formula = b.formula)
Coefficients:
(Intercept)             x
```

```
        10                    1
environment cc
x= 1 2 3 4 5 6 7 8 9 10
y= 31 32 33 34 35 36 37 38 39 40
Call:
lm(formula = c.formula)
Coefficients:
(Intercept)              x
        30                    1
```

The formula object **formula.a** uses the data at level b, where it is run. The formula object **formula.b** uses the data from level a, where it was created. The formula object **formula.c** uses the data in the environment cc, which was created for this example.

For more information on formulas, use the Help tab in RStudio or enter **?formula** at the R prompt.

The S4 Class

In S4, data objects have a user-defined S4 (formal) class. (Note that many S3 classes are also S4 classes.) There are several functions associated with S4 classes, including setClass(), removeClass(), getClass(), getClasses(), and isClass(). S4 classes are used with S4 methods (to be covered in Chapter 7).

The function setClass() sets up a class and takes the arguments **Class, representation, prototype, contains, validity, access, where, version, sealed, package, S3methods,** and **slots**. The argument **Class** is a character string containing the class name. There should be no blank spaces in the string. The most important argument after the name is **slots**, which is the only extra argument that must be included. The argument

slots is a vector with each element of the vector taking on a name and an S4 class. For example:

```
> setClass( "example", slots=c( x="numeric",
y="numeric",  z="matrix" ) )
> getClass( "example" )
Class "example" [in ".GlobalEnv"]
Slots:
Name:        x        y        z
Class: numeric numeric  matrix
```

The second important argument is **contains**. The argument consists of the names of other classes to be included in the class being defined. The slots in the classes listed in the **contains** argument are included in the new class. The names are a vector of character strings. For example:

```
> setClass( "example.2", slots=c( xx="numeric", yy="numeric",
zz="matrix" ), contains="example" )
> getClass( "example.2" )
Class "example.2" [in ".GlobalEnv"]
Slots:
Name:        xx        yy        zz
Class: numeric numeric  matrix
Name:        x         y         z
Class: numeric numeric  matrix
Extends: "example"
```

According to the authors at CRAN, the arguments **where**, **sealed**, and **package** are redundant and need not be included. Also from the authors, the argument **prototype**, which gives default values for the slots, is better implemented using the function initialize(), and the argument **validity,** which sets restrictions on the values in the slots, is better implemented using the function setValidity().

141

According to the authors at CRAN, the arguments **representation, access, version,** and **S3methods** are deprecated and should not be used.

The function removeClass() removes a class. It takes two arguments. The first argument **Class** is the name of the class to be removed, in quotes. The second argument is **where**, the environment in which to start looking for the class. The default value is the environment where removeClass() is run. (Note that to make changes to a class, remove the class and redefine it.)

The function getClass() returns the contents of a class. The function takes three arguments: the name of the class **Class** in quotes, **.Force**, and **where**. The argument **.Force** is a logical variable. If set to **TRUE**, a NULL rather than an error is returned if the class does not exist. The default value is **FALSE.** The argument **where** is as described in the last paragraph. The two examples given before use getClass().

The function getClasses() gets the S4 classes in an environment. The function takes two arguments: **where** and **inherits**. The argument **where** tells R the specific environment to search. The argument **inherits** is a logical variable that, when set to **TRUE**, tells the function to look in all of the parent environments. By default, **inherits** equals **TRUE** if **where** is not used and **FALSE** otherwise. An example:

```
> getClasses( .GlobalEnv )
[1] "example.2" "example"
```

Running getClasses() without an argument returns every class in the parent environments, which can be many.

The function isClass() tests if a class is an S4 (formal) class. The function takes on three arguments: **Class, formal**, and **where**. The argument **Class** is the name of the class, enclosed in quotes. The argument **formal** is always set to **TRUE**, indicating that the test is for S4 (formal) classes. The argument **where** tells R in which environment to look for the class. By default, the level of the calling environment is used. For example:

```
> isClass( "example" )
[1] TRUE
> isClass( "numeric" )
[1] TRUE
```

Here, **numeric** is both an S3 and an S4 class.

More information about S4 (formal) classes can be found by using the Help tab in RStudio or by entering **?setClass, ?getClass**, and **?getClasses** at the R prompt.

Reference Classes

According to the writers at CRAN, reference classes implement a form of object-oriented programming (OOP) in R that is like object-oriented programming in other computer languages. With reference classes, the classes are formal classes, and methods (methods are functions but functions are not necessarily methods) are defined within a class. Also, objects within a class are referential rather than functional. With referential classes, if a change is made in an object, the change occurs in all references to the object. (Note that if an object in the class is the result from a method in the class, the function must be run before the changes occur in the result. See the example below.) In functional classes, changes are only made in the current copy of the object. According to the writers at CRAN, R reference classes are mainly used when creating packages, and the reference class approach is easier to program than the S4 approach.

Reference classes are created with the function setRefClass(). The function takes seven arguments: **Class**, for the name to be assigned to the class; **fields**, for the objects in the class; **contains**, for superclasses from which the class inherits; **methods**, for the functions that are defined for the class; **where**, for the environment in which to put the class; **inheritPackage**, for whether to inherit the environment of the packages within which the classes listed in **contain** exist; and **...**, for other arguments to be used by the methods.

The **Class** argument takes a single character string that contains the name to be given to the class. The name must be legal for an R object. There is no default value for **Class**.

The **fields** argument gives names to the objects to be associated with the class other than the methods. The argument takes one of the following: a character vector of field names; a list of named objects, where the name is set equal to the class of the field in quotes (the class can be any S4 or Reference Class class); or an accessor function (not recommended by CRAN). If **fields** is a character vector, the fields can have the ANY class (a virtual class containing all classes). There is no default value for **fields**, and **fields** must be set. Fields cannot be added after the class is set.

The **contains** argument gives the names of the classes from which the class inherits and takes a character vector of class names. All reference classes except the superclass **envRefClass** inherit from other classes. There is no default value set in the call to the function but **contains** does not need to be set.

The **methods** argument gives a list of user-defined functions to be associated with the class. The functions are regular R functions of the closure class. Each function is one element of the list and is given a name. Methods can be added after the class is defined, so while there is no value assigned by default in the call, the argument need not be set.

The **where** argument gives the name of the environment in which to put the class and takes an unquoted name of an environment. According to help page for setRefClass(), if the definition is in the source code for a package, the argument should not be assigned a value. There is no default value set in the call to the function, and as noted, the argument need not be assigned a value.

The **inheritPackage** argument takes a logical variable. If set to **TRUE**, the class uses the namespace of the superclass(es) listed in **contains**. If not, the namespace is the namespace of the class. The default value of **inheritPackage** is **FALSE**.

An example of setting a reference class is

```
RCE = setRefClass( "RCE", fields=list( x="numeric",
y="numeric", rs="lm" ), method=list( rg=function() { rs <<- lm(
y~x ) } ) )
```

Note that the name of the class is **RCE**. The object named **RCE** is called the generator function of the class. (In RStudio, generator functions are found in Values under the Environment tab.) The generator function has both fields and methods associated with the function. The fields and methods are accessed with the **$** operator (like an object of the list or expression class). The <<- operator (rather than the = operator) must be used for assignments within the definitions of the methods.

The fields and methods of the class are listed by entering the class name at the R prompt or by using the getRefClass() function. Both give the same result if the default value for **where** (see below) is used in getRefClass(). An example of what is returned is

```
> RCE
Generator for class "Reference Class":

Class fields:

Name:        x        y        rs
Class: numeric numeric      lm

Class Methods:
     "rg", "field", "trace", "getRefClass", "initFields",
     "copy", "callSuper",
     ".objectPackage", "export", "untrace", "getClass", "show",
     "usingMethods",
```

```
".objectParent", "import"
```

Reference Superclasses:
```
    "envRefClass"
```

Note that the rg() method defined in the call to setRefClass() is the first method that is listed. The other methods are methods included for any reference class.

The function getRefClass() takes two arguments: **Class**, the name of the class for which to get information, and **where**, the environment in which to look for the class. The **Class** argument takes a single character string containing the name of a class and must be supplied; the **where** argument takes the unquoted name of an environment and does not need to be supplied. The argument defaults to the environment in which the class was created.

The generator function is an S4 object, for example:

```
> isS4( RCE )
[1] TRUE
```

There are also methods that are not methods of the class, but methods of generator function objects. The methods can be accessed by appending a dollar sign to the class name followed by the method name (e.g., RCE$new()).

The generator function methods are currently new(), to enter information (usually data) for the fields; help(), for a simple help page on a topic; methods(), for the methods in the class; fields(), for the fields of the class; lock(), to lock specific fields so that the fields cannot be changed; trace(), for tracing the computing process; and accessors(), for accessing specific fields of a class. Only new() is covered here. (See the help page **ReferenceClasses** for a full discussion of class fields and methods as well as the methods of generating function objects.)

When a class is created, the fields (e.g., data) are given names and a class, but nothing else. To create an object with data (or other information) for the methods in the class, a name for the object is set equal to the function ***class_name*$new(*field_name1*=stuff,*field_name2*=stuff,etc.)**, where *class_name* is the name of the class and *field_name*s are the field names.

An example of using a reference class is as follows:

First, the values for **x** and **y** in the workspace are printed out. Then a new data object **RCE.p1** is created:

```
> x
[1] 0 1 2
> y
[1] 1 2 3

> RCE.p1 = RCE$new( x=1:6, y=3:8 + rnorm( 6 ), rs=lm( y~x ) )
> RCE.p1
Reference class object of class "RCE"
Field "x":
[1] 1 2 3 4 5 6
Field "y":
[1] 3.586657 6.675763 3.855253 7.173745 6.072426 8.417201
Field "rs":

Call:
lm(formula = y ~ x)

Coefficients:
(Intercept)          x
          1          1
```

Note that the values for **x** and **y** are new but the regression coefficients are based on **x** and **y** in the workspace, not in the class.

The fields and methods can be accessed by appending a dollar sign to the object name followed by the field name or the method name (e.g., RCE. p1$rs or RCE.p1$rg()).

Next, the function rg() is run with the data.

```
> RCE.p1$rg()
> RCE.p1
Reference class object of class "RCE"
Field "x":
[1] 1 2 3 4 5 6
Field "y":
[1] 3.586657 6.675763 3.855253 7.173745 6.072426 8.417201
Field "rs":

Call:
lm(formula = y ~ x)

Coefficients:
(Intercept)              x
     3.3974         0.7332
```

Note that the values of **x** and **y** in the class have not changed, but the regression coefficients are now based on the class fields, not the fields in the workspace.

Next, a change is made to **RCE.p1**; that is, the value one is added to **x** and the regression is rerun.

```
> RCE.p1$x = RCE.p1$x + 1
> RCE.p1$rg()
> RCE.p1
Reference class object of class "RCE"
Field "x":
[1] 2 3 4 5 6 7
Field "y":
```

```
[1] 3.586657 6.675763 3.855253 7.173745 6.072426 8.417201
Field "rs":

Call:
lm(formula = y ~ x)

Coefficients:
(Intercept)                 x
     2.6642          0.7332
```

Note that the value of **x** is changed before the regression is run. After the regression, the regression coefficients reflect the change in the data.

For Reference Class objects, the classes are relational rather than functional. So if a data object is directly copied to another variable, changes in the new variable also change the original variable. An example of the relational property of Reference Classes is

```
> RCE.pc = RCE.p1
> RCE.pc$x
[1] 2 3 4 5 6 7
> RCE.pc$x = 15:20
> RCE.pc$x
[1] 15 16 17 18 19 20
> RCE.p1$x
[1] 15 16 17 18 19 20
```

Note that **x** changes in both **RCE.pc** and **RCE.p1** when **x** is changed in **RCE.pc** because the **RCE** class is relational rather than functional.

To create another independent data object out of an object, use the class method copy(). Changes to the copied object do not affect the original object. See the following example.

```
> RCE.p2 = RCE.p1$copy()
> RCE.p2
Reference class object of class "RCE"
```

```
Field "x":
[1] 15 16 17 18 19 20
Field "y":
[1] 3.586657 6.675763 3.855253 7.173745 6.072426 8.417201
Field "rs":

Call:
lm(formula = y ~ x)

Coefficients:
(Intercept)              x
     2.6642        0.7332
```

Note that **RCE.p2** has the same values as **RCE.p1** for the fields. Next, the value of **y** is changed in **RCE.p2**.

```
> RCE.p2$y = 3:8 + rnorm( 6 )
> RCE.p2$y
[1] 3.035117 3.826674 6.413020 6.371358 8.681975 9.796374
> RCE.p1$y
[1] 3.586657 6.675763 3.855253 7.173745 6.072426 8.417201
```

Note that the value of **y** in **RCE.p2** has changed but **y** in **RCE.p1** has not.

The class of a generator function is refObjectGenerator. The class of an object generated by the generator function is the class defined when the generator function is generated. The fields of the reference class object have the class assigned in the definition of the class. The methods of a reference class object are of the refMethodDef class. The class of a method appended with () is the class of what the method returns when run. The classes and types of some of the preceding objects are

```
> class( RCE )
[1] "refObjectGenerator"
> typeof( RCE )
```

```
[1] "closure"
> class( RCE.p1 )
[1] "RCE"
attr(,"package")
[1] ".GlobalEnv"
> typeof( RCE.p1 )
[1] "S4"

> class( RCE.p1$y )
[1] "numeric"
> typeof( RCE.p1$y )
[1] "double"

> class( RCE.p1$rg )
[1] "refMethodDef"
attr(,"package")
[1] "methods"
> typeof( RCE.p1$rg )
[1] "closure"

> class( RCE.p1$rg() )
[1] "lm"
> typeof( RCE.p1$rg() )
[1] "list"
attr(,"package")
[1] "methods"
```

More information about reference classes, setRefClass(), and getRefClass() can be found through the Help tab in RStudio or by entering **?ReferenceClasses** at the R prompt. Reference class methods are further covered in Chapter 7.

PART III

Functions

CHAPTER 6

Packaged Functions

R has over 18,000 packages, most of which contain functions. Functions are at the heart of R and provide R with R's great versatility. Functions are R objects, and they are of the `closure`, `builtin`, or `special` type, the `function` mode, and the `function` class. Packaged functions are functions that have been created as a part of an R package. On the computer, packages are stored in a library (i.e., in a folder) and are placed in the library (folder) when installed.

The Libraries

When R is initially installed, the base packages `base`, `compiler`, `datasets`, `graphics`, `grDevices`, `grid`, `methods`, `parallel`, `splines`, `stats`, `stats4`, `tcltk`, `translations`, `tools`, and `utils` are installed in a folder on the hard drive. The packages are always installed and cannot be deleted from under the Packages tab in RStudio (other packages can be deleted from the computer folder where the packages are stored by using options under the Packages tab). Currently, by default, the recommended packages `boot`, `class`, `cluster`, `codetools`, `foreign`, `KernSmooth`, `lattice`, `MASS`, `Matrix`, `mgcv`, `nlme`, `nnet`, `rpart`, `spatial`, and `survival` are also installed in the folder.

In Windows systems, any packages installed after the initial installation can be installed in a different library (i.e., in another folder). The folder is created when R is installed. In macOS systems, all installed packages are in the same library (folder). In Linux systems, any packages installed after the initial installation are installed in a different library (another folder). The folder is created when the first extra package is installed.

© Margot Tollefson 2022
M. Tollefson, *R 4 Quick Syntax Reference*, https://doi.org/10.1007/978-1-4842-7924-3_6

Loading and Removing Packages

When R is running a function, only functions in the workspace and functions in those packages that have been loaded into the current session are accessible to the function. R gives an error if an attempt is made to run a function when a necessary package(s) has not been loaded.

In RStudio, the installed packages can be accessed under the Packages tab in the lower right subwindow. The packages that are in the library folder(s) are listed alphabetically in the subwindow. To the left of a package name is a square box. Clicking on the box enters a check mark in the box and loads the package into the R session. (Unchecking a box detaches the package from the search stream of the R session.) To the right of the package name is a description of the package. To the right of the description is the version number of the package. For most packages, to the right of the version number are two circles. The circle on the left links to the website of the developer of the package. The circle on the right can be used to delete the package. As noted before, the base packages cannot be deleted here, so base packages have no circles.

In R, to see a listing of the installed packages, enter **.packages(TRUE)** at the R prompt. To view much more information about the packages, enter *installed.packages()* at the R prompt. To uninstall a package from the library folder on the computer, enter **remove.packages(“*package_name*”)** at the R prompt, where *package_name* is the name of the package. (The “*package_name*” argument can be replaced with a vector of names of packages to be removed.) Note that all packages can be removed at the R prompt.

In R, you can load a package by entering *library(package_name)* at the R prompt. To remove a loaded package from the search stream, enter **detach(“package:*package_name*”, unload=TRUE)** at the R prompt. Here, *package_name* is the name of the package.

Most R functions contain other R functions, which must be accessible if the function is to run. A package containing the function must be loaded into the R session for the function to be accessible. If the package containing the function that is not accessible exists in one of the libraries on the computer, the package can be loaded in RStudio or at the R console as described before. If the package is not in the library(ies), installing new packages is straightforward (see Chapter 1). Once installed, the package can then be loaded (see above).

To see the functions (and datasets) in a package, click on the package name under the Packages tab in RStudio or enter **help(package=*package_name*)** at the R prompt, where *package_name* is the name of the package. Note that the package must be installed for **help(package=*package_name*)** to return the contents of the package. Some of the objects in a package may be datasets, but for most packages, the objects are all or mostly functions.

Functions can be written to load a package from inside the function. The `require()` function should be used instead of the `library()` function to load the package within a function (see the library help page for more information).

At any given time, you can look under the Packages tab in RStudio for which packages are checked to see the packages that are loaded in the workspace. Or you can enter **search()** at the R prompt to get a list of the packages that are loaded.

Default Packages and Primitive Functions

When a user starts an R session, the packages `base`, `datasets`, `utils`, `grDevices`, `graphics`, `stats`, and `methods` are loaded into the workspace by default. (Which default packages are loaded can be changed by changing **defaultPackages** in the `options()` function. See Chapter 15.) Often, depending on the computing needs of the user, no more packages are needed.

Functions that are written in C and compiled at the time R is compiled are called **primitive** functions. According to the help page for **primitive**, all primitive functions are in the base package, which is always loaded. The advantage of primitive functions is that the functions are already compiled, so the functions run faster. Primitive functions include the operators and most of the mathematical functions as well as functions basic to the running and structure of R. The functions are described at `http://cran.r-project.org/doc/manuals/R-ints.html#g_t_002eInternal-vs-_002ePrimitive`. Depending on how the argument(s) is handled, primitive functions are of the `builtin` or `special` type. (Functions that are written in the R language are of the `closure` type.) The `is.primitive()` function tests whether an object is a primitive function. (Types and modes are the subject of Chapter 4.)

Using the Help Pages

Each packaged function in R has a help page, and each help page has essentially the same structure. Like much else in R, the help pages can be daunting at first. However, the help pages often contain a wealth of information.

Given the name of a function, if the package containing the function has been installed, entering the name of the function in the main search box under the Help tab in RStudio (lower right subwindow) will bring up the help page or a list of help pages containing the function name (see the "The Third Subwindow" section in Chapter 2 for a description of the Help tab subwindow). If the package containing the function has been loaded, entering **?*function*** or **help(*function*)** at the R prompt, where *function* is the name of the function, brings up the help page for the function. (If the package has been installed but not loaded, entering **?*package::function***, where *package* is the name of the package and *function* is the name of the function, brings up the help page.)

Some help pages cover more than one function. The help page can be brought up using any of the function names. In RStudio, the help pages open in the lower right window. In R, for Windows systems and macOS systems, the help pages open in a separate window. For Linux systems, the help pages display in the terminal.

Identifier

The first line of the help page for a function lists the function name, followed by the function package name in curly brackets (e.g., lm{stats}), then on the far right the text R Documentation.

Title

Below the identifier is a title that says something about the function(s). For example, for the lm() function, the title is

Fitting Linear Models.

Help page for lm() in R

Description

Below the title is a description of how the function(s) is used, headed by the word "Description." The description can be long or short, depending on the complexity of the function(s). For the lm() function, you will find the following description:

lm is used to fit linear models. It can be used to carry out regression, single stratum analysis of variance and analysis of covariance (although aov may provide a more convenient interface for these).

Help page for lm() in R

Usage

The section "Usage" is found below the description. In the Usage section, the function(s) is listed with all the possible arguments to the function(s). Usually, for arguments with default values, the default values are given.

The Usage section lists the S4 usage. For many functions, S3 usages are also listed.

For the lm() function, the Usage section contains the following:

```
lm(formula, data, subset, weights, na.action,

method = "qr", model = TRUE, x = FALSE, y = FALSE,
qr = TRUE, singular.ok = TRUE, contrasts = NULL,
offset, ...)
```

Help page for lm() in R

The arguments with default values are the arguments for which the arguments have been set equal to a value.

Arguments

Below the Usage section is a section entitled "Arguments." In the Arguments section, the arguments found in the Usage section are listed with a description of each argument. The description includes the legal values for the argument.

For example, from the lm() help page, the first two arguments listed are as follows:

formula	an object of class "formula" (or one that can be coerced to that class): a symbolic description of the model to be fitted. The details of model specification are given under "Details."
data	an optional data frame, list, or environment (or object coercible by as.data.frame to a data frame) containing the variables in the model. If not found in data, the variables are taken from environment(formula), typically the environment from which lm is called.

Help page for lm() in R

So for the lm() function, the first argument is an argument of the formula class, and the second argument can be an argument of the data. frame class, but the second argument is optional.

Details

Sometimes, there is a section entitled "Details," which gives details related to the arguments. In the lm() function example, the section on details gives the rules for setting up a formula and how the function behaves for differing inputs to the formula.

Value

The next section is entitled "Value." The Value section gives a description of what is returned from the function(s). For some functions, what functions can operate on the output and what components can be subsetted from the output are relevant and listed in this section.

The first few lines of the Value section for the lm() function are as follows:

> lm returns an object of class "lm" or for multiple responses of class c("mlm", "lm").

> The functions *summary and anova* are used to obtain and print a summary and analysis of variance table of the results. The generic accessor functions*coefficients, effects, fitted.values, and residuals*extract various useful features of the value returned by *lm*.

> An object of class "lm" is a list containing at least the following components:

> coefficients a named vector of coefficients

> residuals the residuals, that is response minus fitted values.

> Help page for lm() in R

161

Some Other Optional Sections

Following the Value section, there may be other sections giving more information. For the lm( ) function, there are three other sections: "Using time series," "Note," and "Author(s)." Some sections for other functions might be "Warning," "Source," or other headings.

References

The next section is called "References." The References section gives references to books and articles related to the method, both for more information and for how the method was derived.

For the lm( ) function, the References section contains

> Chambers, J. M. (1992) Linear models. Chapter 4 of Statistical Models in S eds J. M. Chambers and T. J. Hastie, Wadsworth & Brooks/Cole.

> Wilkinson, G. N. and Rogers, C. E. (1973). Symbolic descriptions of factorial models for analysis of variance. Applied Statistics, 22, 392–399. doi: 10.2307/2346786.

> Help page for lm( ) in R

See Also

The section "See Also" follows the References section. The See Also section gives information about other functions related to the help page function(s). For the lm() function, the first three lines of the See Also section are the following:

> *summary.lm for summaries and anova.lm for the ANOVA table; aov for a different interface.*
>
> *The generic functions coef, effects, residuals, fitted, vcov.*
>
> *predict.lm (via predict) for prediction, including confidence and prediction intervals; confint for confidence intervals of parameters.*
>
> Help page for lm() in R

The See Also section is a good source for clues to functions related to the method the user is applying.

Examples

The final section, which most pages have, is "Examples." The Examples section gives examples of the use of the function(s). Seeing actual examples of usage can be very helpful. From the help page of the lm() function, part of the example includes the following:

```
require(graphics)

## Annette Dobson (1990) "An Introduction to
Generalized Linear Models".

## Page 9: Plant Weight Data.

ctl <- c(4.17,5.58,5.18,6.11,4.50,4.61,5.17,4.53,
5.33,5.14)

trt <- c(4.81,4.17,4.41,3.59,5.87,3.83,6.03,4.89,
4.32,4.69)

group <- gl(2, 10, 20, labels = c("Ctl","Trt"))
```

```
weight <- c(ctl, trt)
lm.D9 <- lm(weight ~ group)
lm.D90 <- lm(weight ~ group - 1) # omitting intercept
anova(lm.D9)
summary(lm.D90)
```

Help page for lm( ) in R

In this example, the structure of a formula is shown rather than explained. Some of the functions that operate on objects of the lm class are also shown. (Since the graphics package is loaded by default, the call to **require(graphics)** would not normally be necessary.) Note that the output that results from running the examples in a help page is not shown in the help page. The examples can be copied, pasted into the R console, and run to see the output.

CHAPTER 7

Scripts, User-Created Functions, and S4 and Reference Class Methods

Scripts and user-created functions often make the life of an R user easier. If a repetitive task involves several different lines of code, creating a script or function to do the task saves time. In the S4 object system, methods for generic S4 functions are the functional side of S4 and require special treatment. For Reference Class methods, the methods are regular user-defined functions but are defined within a reference class.

Designing plots is one example of when a script or user-created function makes sense. Plots often take several lines of code, and the design of a plot is usually an interactive process. From command line R, creating a function to do the plot and making changes to the function are often much easier than using the up arrow and changing lines.

Another example of when a script or user-created function is useful is when a user wants to try out a statistical technique that is not available in the R packages. Often, the user can create a function or script for the technique using functions that are available in the packages.

In RStudio, the Source subwindow (the upper left subwindow) provides a place to create and run code, which can then be saved as an R script, externally, or as a function, internally. The Source subwindow is also a place into which to load R scripts or other text files.

Scripts

Scripts are code that is written in the R language and stored outside of the R program. Storing a script outside of R tends to be safer than creating a function within R, because overwriting an object is very easy in R and because R sometimes crashes with work being lost. Functions can be defined in R scripts. A file containing an R script is a text file and has the extension .R.

In RStudio, there is no need to edit a script externally. If the script already exists outside of R, the script can be loaded into the Source subwindow. Click on the icon of a manila folder with a green arrow on the first menu just above the subwindows. Then, browse to the location of the script and click on the file. The file will open in the Source subwindow. To run the file, click on the Source button on the right side of the Source subwindow menu bar. To run a portion of the file, highlight the portion and click on the Run button. The script can be easily edited and the changes saved. To save to the original file, click on the blue icon of a floppy disk above the Source window (or on Save in the drop-down menu under File in the main menu). To save to another file, select Save As... in the drop-down menu under File in the main RStudio menu.

From command line R, a script is run using the source() function. For example, let lm.example.R be a file in the working directory that contains

```
x=1:3; y=2:4
print( x ); print( y )
print( lm(y~x) )
```

Then, running source() on the file gives

```
> source( "lm.example.R" )
[1] 1 2 3
[1] 2 3 4

Call:
lm(formula = y ~ x)

Coefficients:
(Intercept)              x
          1              1
```

Note that only the results from the calls to the functions in lm. example.R are printed. To see the calls to the functions, set the argument **echo** to **TRUE** in source(), for example:

```
> source( "lm.example.R", echo=TRUE )

> x=1:3; y=2:4

> print( x ); print( y )
[1] 1 2 3
[1] 2 3 4

> print( lm(y~x) )

Call:
lm(formula = y ~ x)

Coefficients:
(Intercept)              x
          1              1
```

To enter a new script in RStudio, open the far-left icon in the menu bar above the upper subwindows and choose the first option, "R Script." The Source subwindow will open to a blank page. Just enter the lines of code.

Run the code or sections of the code to debug the script (using the Run or Source buttons as described before).

RStudio helps with debugging, by flagging syntax errors and by doing other helpful things (e.g., highlighting the matching parenthesis or bracket for parentheses and brackets). When done, you can save the script. Click on the floppy disk icon (the single blue square containing two different sized white rectangles) in the menu of the Source subwindow and enter a name for the file (or use the menu under File in the main RStudio window). RStudio automatically gives the file an .R extension. To run the code when saving the code, check the "Source on Save" box.

The Structure of a Function

Functions that are not primitive functions all have the same structure. On the first line of the function is the word **function (or \, a shorter version of function)**, followed by open and close parentheses, which may or may not contain arguments. In most cases, an open bracket follows the parentheses. Usually, the body of the function is placed below the first line, and the last line is a blank line after the close bracket, which bracket is usually on its own line. Normally, functions are assigned to a name (which can be considered a verb since functions are used to perform an action). For example:

```
> c.fun = function() {
+ print( 1:5 )
+ }

> c.fun
function() {
print( 1:5 )
}
> c.fun()
[1] 1 2 3 4 5
```

In this example, first, the function is assigned to **c.fun**; next, the content of c.fun() is listed; and, last, the function c.fun() is run.

The brackets are not necessary if the function consists of just one statement—which can be entered on the same line as the function statement or on the following line(s). For example:

```
> d.fun = \() print( 1:5 )
> d.fun
\() print( 1:5 )
> d.fun()
[1] 1 2 3 4 5
```

Again, the function is assigned a name, the function is listed, and the function is run. Note that \ is substituted for the word **function** in the function definition. (On the help page for function(), the writers at CRAN say the \ form may be changed at a later time.)

Arguments are objects that are used by the function and that must be input to the function at the time the function is run—unless a default value exists for the argument or the function missing() is used in the function to handle specific missing argument values. Arguments are placed within the parentheses when the function is defined and are separated by commas. A default value for an argument is supplied within the parentheses by setting the argument equal to a value. Arguments with default values or that are handled with missing() within the function need not be specified when the function is run. If the value is not specified, the function uses the default value.

An example follows of a function with two arguments, where **a** does not have a default value and must be specified and **b** has the default value of 3:

```
> e.fun = function( a, b=3 ){
+ print( a:b )
+ }
```

```
> e.fun
function( a, b=3 ){
print( a:b )
}
> e.fun( 10 )
[1] 10  9  8  7  6  5  4  3
> e.fun()
Error in a:b : 'a' is missing
```

Again, the function is assigned a name, listed, and run. Note that since **a** is the first argument, **a** can be supplied without a name. In the second attempt to run e.fun(), no argument is supplied for **a**, so e.fun() returns an error.

If an argument can be missing, but no default value should be assigned in the call, then the missing() function can be used to handle the missing value. The missing() function takes one argument, **x**, the argument name, and returns a logical value. The function returns **TRUE** if **x** is not set to a value in the call to the function and does not have a default value; otherwise, missing() returns **FALSE**. In the case of an argument that is an argument to both the defined function and to missing(), where missing() is used within the defined function, the argument can be set to an equal sign in a call to the defined function.

An example of missing() follows:

```
> k.fun = function( x, y ) {
+      if ( missing( y ) ) y=10
+      x+y
+ }

> k.fun
function( x, y ) {
    if ( missing( y ) ) y=10
    x+y
}
```

```
> k.fun( 9 )
[1] 19
> k.fun( x=9, y= )
[1] 19
```

The second kind of call in the preceding example contains **y=**, with no value set for **y**. This technique is sometimes used in the Usage section of a help page (where the name of the function and the list of arguments of a function are given, e.g., see the help page for setRefClass()).

The value ... can be used as an argument. The value ... specifies an arbitrary number of objects, which are entered, separated by commas. The value ..**n** is used within the function to specify the **n**th argument in .... (If named arguments follow ... in the function definition, the named arguments must be specified by their full name in the call to the function. Normally, argument names can be truncated to a unique version.) An example follows:

```
> g.fun = function( a=3, ... ) c( a + c( ... ) )
> g.fun
function( a=3, ... ) c( a + c( ... ) )
> g.fun( 1, 5, 4, 5 )
[1] 6 5 6
> g.fun( , 5, 4, 5 )
[1] 8 7 8
> g.fun()
numeric(0)

> h.fun = function( a=3, ... ) c( a + ..1 + ..2 )
> h.fun( , 5, 4, 5 )
[1] 12
```

The g.fun() function adds the value of **a** to the numbers entered with the ... argument. In the first call to g.fun(), 1 is added to 5, 4, and

5. In the second call, the default value of **a** (equal to 3) is added. In the h.fun() function, **a** is added to the first and second numbers input for the ... argument. Note that in the second call to g.fun() and in the call to h.fun(), **a** is not supplied (the default value is used), but a comma is added to tell R to count the argument in the order of arguments (see Chapter 8).

The functions ...elt(), ...length(), and ...names() are functions that operate on the argument .... The ...elt() function returns individual values of the arguments entered through .... The function takes one argument, **n**, the index of the element to be returned. There is no default value for **n**, so **n** must be supplied. The ...length() function returns the number of arguments entered through the ... argument. The ...names() function returns a vector of the names of the arguments entered through the ... argument. The ...length() and ...names() functions do not take arguments.

An example follows:

```
> i.fun = function( a=3, ... ) {
+    for( i in 1:...length() ) {
+      print( c( a, ...elt( i ) ) )
+    }
+ }
> i.fun( 1, 5, 4, 5 )
[1] 1 5
[1] 1 4
[1] 1 5
> i.fun( , 5, 4, 5 )
[1] 3 5
[1] 3 4
[1] 3 5

> j.fun = function( a=3, ... ) {
```

```
+    for( i in 1:...length() ) {
+       print( c( a, ...names()[ i ], ...elt( i ) ) )
+    }
+ }
> j.fun( 1, b=5, c=4,  5 )
[1] "1" "b" "5"
[1] "1" "c" "4"
[1] "1" NA  "5"
```

(For those not familiar with for loops, also called do loops in some computer languages, for loops are used to loop an index over a set of statements. The `for()` function in R is covered in Chapter 12.)

Note that in the second call to `i.fun()`, **a** is not supplied, so **a** equals the default value of three. Also, `...names()` returns a vector, while `...elt()` returns a single value, the index of which must be specified. In the call to `j.fun()`, the fourth argument does not have a name, so **NA** is returned for the name.

If the last line before the closing bracket in a function contains the name of a single object (or expression), the value of the object is returned by the function. The `print()` and `return()` functions can also be used to return the value of a single object in a user-defined function. The function `print()` prints the value of a single object to the output device. The function `return()` returns the value of a single object and exits the function without continuing to any following lines of code.

Using four versions of the function `f.fun()` (which finds a quantile of the normal distribution), several ways returning the value of the object q_value or q_value+1 are given.

The first example uses `return()`:

```
> f.fun
function(  mu, se=1, alpha=.034 ){
    q_value = qnorm( 1-alpha/2, mu, se )
```

```
    return( q_value )
    q_value + 1
}
> f=f.fun(0)
> f
[1] 2.120072
```

Note that within a function, if `return()` is called, the function returns the value of the (single) argument to `return()` and then exits the function.

The second example just uses `print()`:

```
> f.fun
function(  mu, se=1, alpha=.034 ){
    q_value = qnorm( 1-alpha/2, mu, se )
    print( q_value )
}
> f=f.fun(0)
[1] 2.120072
> f
[1] 2.120072
```

Note that when `f.fun()` is run, the value of q_value is printed at the console as well as being assigned to f.

The third example uses first `print()` and then `return()`. One is added to q_value in `return()`:

```
> f.fun
function(  mu, se=1, alpha=.034 ){
    q_value = qnorm( 1-alpha/2, mu, se )
    print( q_value )
    return( q_value + 1 )
}
> f=f.fun(0)
```

```
[1] 2.120072
> f
[1] 3.120072
```

Note that **q_value** is printed to the console when f.fun() is run, but **q_value+1** is returned by f.fun(), so **q_value+1** is the value given to **f**.

In the last example, print() is called first, and then the name of the object plus one is the last line before the closing bracket:

```
> f.fun
function(  mu, se=1, alpha=.034 ){
    q_value = qnorm( 1-alpha/2, mu, se )
    print( q_value )
    q_value + 1
}
> f=f.fun(0)
[1] 2.120072
> f
[1] 3.120072
```

Note that the result is the same as in the third example.

Often, the user uses brackets within a function to enclose groups of statements, such as when writing **if**, **else**, **for**, **while**, and **repeat** groups. There must be the same number of opening brackets as closing brackets in a function; otherwise, the function will not save. Mismatched brackets are a common source of errors in R code and are flagged in RStudio. The return() and print() functions can be used in groups of statements, too, and behave in a similar way.

Lines of code in R (both in a function and at the R prompt) can be broken and continued on the next line. R looks for things such as a closing parenthesis, bracket, or quotation mark to designate the end of a statement or a part of a statement.

Empty lines are legal in R functions. Also, any text can be commented out by placing a pound sign (#) in front of the text. On a line, anything entered after a pound sign is ignored. A piece of advice for writing functions is to write a little chunk at a time, debug at each step, and use plenty of comments.

I created a function to plot the airmiles dataset in the datasets package. The airmiles dataset contains a single time series of total airmiles flown for the years 1937 to 1960. The function could be used with any time series vector. The color of some elements of the plot is set in the call to the function. The function is

```
> airmiles.plot
function( ts=airmiles, col="grey55",
          tt="Airmiles Flown over Time",  yl="Airmiles",
          tx="Source: Airmiles dataset in\nthe datasets package
          of R" ) {
    plot( x=ts, col=col, axes=FALSE , ylab="" )
    axis( side=1, col=col )
    axis( side=2, col=col, yaxp=c( 0, 30000, 3 ) )
    box( col=col )
    title( tt, font.main=2, col.main=col, ylab=yl )
    mtext( side=1, line=3.6, , adj=1, cex=0.75, text=tx  )
}
```

By splitting the plotting process into several steps, plotting a nice-looking plot is easier. In the airmiles.plot() function, the plot() function does not plot the axes. The x and y axes are added using the axis() function, and the box around the plot is added with the box() function. The title and y axis label are added with the title() function (the default x axis label is acceptable). The mtext() function adds source text to the lower right corner of the margin. The function could be used with any time series vector, not just the airmiles time series vector. The plot that is generated by the function is in Figure 7-1.

176

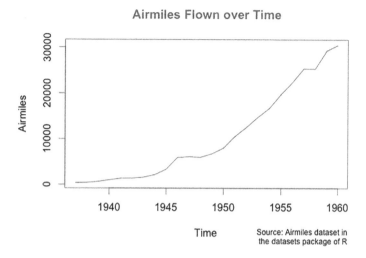

Figure 7-1. *A time series plot generated in several steps within the user-generated function airmiles.plot( )*

For more information about function(), use the Help tab in RStudio or enter **?function** at the R prompt. For more information about missing(), use the Help tab in RStudio or enter **?missing** at the R prompt. For more information about **...**, use the Help tab in RStudio or enter **?dots** at the R prompt.

How to Enter a Function into R

This section describes one way to get a function into R using RStudio and four ways using the command line. Using RStudio involves using the RStudio Source subwindow. At the command line, the first way involves using an editor. The second involves inline entry, as shown in the preceding section. The third involves creating a function outside of R and using dget() to get the function into R. The fourth is a variation on the second and third and involves copying and pasting from a source that can be outside of R.

In RStudio

In RStudio, to create a new function, open a new R script (far left icon). Use an R script rather than a text file so that you can run the code from the Source subwindow while debugging. Do not enter the function statement or the enclosing brackets. Enter variables to be entered as arguments first, assigning them values. When the lines of code run and run correctly, click on the wand icon above the Source subwindow and choose "Extract Function." RStudio will cue you for a name and create the function in the Source subwindow with the name assignment. The arguments should be in the correct place, but you may need to do some editing on the result. Running the resulting script assigns the function to the name within the workspace.

Clicking on the name of an existing function under the Environment tab (in the upper right subwindow in RStudio) opens the function in its own tab in the Source subwindow. You cannot edit or run the code, but you can copy it, open a new R script, and paste the code into the R script for editing.

Using an Editor

For the Windows operating systems and macOS operating systems, there is a function, edit(), in the utils package that works well for creating new functions. The purpose of the edit() function is to call an editing function.

In Windows systems, the default editing function is the **internal** editor. The possible other choices for editor are xedit(), emacs(), xemacs(), vi(), and pica(), where the choice is available only if the editor is present on the system. The default editor is listed in options() and can be changed at any time (see Chapter 15).

For macOS systems, the default editor is the **vi** editor, but the other editors are available and the default editor can be changed in options().

For Linux operating systems, calling edit() from the terminal window does not give a good result. A better editor is emacs(), which is available for Linux systems.

Most of the preceding information is from the help page for edit().

To create an object that is a function by using an editor, the function is first assigned to a name. For example, let the name be **f.fun**. To create the function **f.fun()**, start by entering **f.fun = function(){}** at the R prompt. The object **f.fun** then contains a function with no arguments and no statements.

The next step is to edit the function. For simplicity, only the function edit() is shown in the example here. The other editors behave similarly. Enter **f.fun = edit(f.fun)** at the R prompt. An editing window opens up for editing (Figure 7-2).

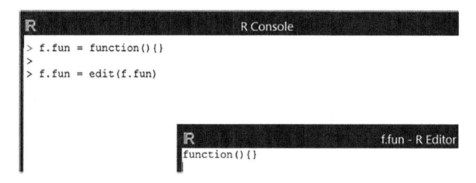

Figure 7-2. *Creating a function: the first and second steps*

For the third step, the arguments are entered within the parentheses, and the statements of the function are entered within the brackets (Figure 7-3).

179

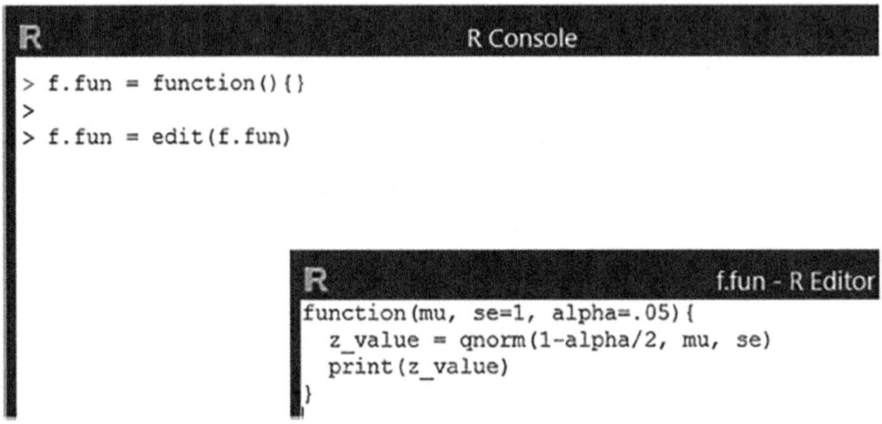

Figure 7-3. *Creating a function: the third step*

The fourth step is to exit the editor. To exit the editor, click the **x** at the top right-hand corner of the editing window. A window will appear with options to save the file, to exit without saving, or to cancel the request and go back to editing. (If no changes were made to the file, the options screen does not appear.) Click **Yes** to save the changes, **No** to revert to the earlier version, or **Cancel** to go back to editing.

If the function is syntactically correct, the function will save. Otherwise, edit() returns an error, such as the following:

```
Error in .External2(C_edit, name, file, title, editor) :
  unexpected '}' occurred on line 4
 use a command like
 x <- edit()
 to recover
```

To recover the work already done, enter **f.fun = edit()**. Using parentheses with no content is very important. If the name of the function is entered within the parentheses, the editing changes are lost, and the function reverts to the version before the edit. Note that the error message gives information about the problem with the R code.

The following shows the input and output at the R console when creating the function f.fun() with the editor, followed by the listing of the function and the running of the function with the first argument set to zero.

```
> f.fun = function(){}
> f.fun = edit( f.fun )
> f.fun
function(mu, se=1, alpha=.05){
  z_value = qnorm(1-alpha/2, mu, se)
  print( z_value )
}
> f.fun( 0 )
[1] 1.959964.
```

Use the Help tab in RStudio or enter **?edit** at the R prompt for more information about the editing functions.

Inline Entry

As shown in the first section of this chapter, a function can be entered inline. Let b.fun be the name of a new function created to list the digits three through six. Then, the steps to create the function, to list the code, and to run the function are as follows:

```
> b.fun = function(){
+ print( 3:6 )
+ }
> b.fun
function(){
print( 3:6 )
}
> b.fun()
[1] 3 4 5 6
```

If a syntactical error is made in the process of entering a function inline, R will give an error and return to the R prompt. For example:

```
> b.fun = function(){
+ print( 3:6
+ }
Error: unexpected '}' in:
"print( 3:6
}"
```

For longer functions, using an R editor or an external editor tends to be less frustrating.

An Outside Editor: dget( ) and Copying and Pasting

An outside editor can be used to create a function. Any editor that produces text files, such as **Notepad**, **TextEdit**, or **gedit**, can be used to create an R function. The rules for creating a function are the same as those described in the first section. Once the function is created, the function can be imported into the workspace by using the dget() function or by copying and pasting. (The dget() function and the corresponding dput() function are one way to import and export functions in R. See Chapters 9 and 10.)

Say that a function is in a file called **function.txt** in the same folder as the R workspace and that the function is syntactically correct. Then, the following line imports the function into the object k.fun:

```
k.fun = dget( "function.txt" )
```

(Note that R accepts more complex file paths for files, including absolute addresses on the hard drive and URLs. See Chapter 9.)

If the text file is not syntactically correct, R returns an error with information about the syntactical problem in the file.

If the file does not contain a function or contains more than a function, R will attempt to run the code.

The file can also be copied and pasted from an outside source (or from elsewhere in the R session) into an object in R. Start by copying the function onto the clipboard of the computer. Next, enter the name that the object is to be called, followed by an equal sign, at the R prompt. The cursor should then be to the right of the equal sign. Next, paste.

If the function is syntactically correct, the cursor stops to the right of the close bracket. Press the **Return** key to complete the process. If the function is not syntactically correct, copying and pasting will give an error containing information about the problem with the syntax.

More information about dget() can be found in Chapter 9, by using the Help tab in RStudio, or by entering **?dget** at the R prompt.

S4 Methods

S4 methods are functions based on specific S4 classes and a given S4 generic function. An S4 method includes a name for the function being created, the S4 class(es) of the data to be used by the function, and the function definition. The method can also specify where to store the method, if different from the workspace in which the method is created, as well as whether to seal the definition (not allow future changes).

S4 methods depend on the existence of a generic function that has the same name as the method. In the S3 object system, generic functions are functions for which the way the function behaves depends on the class of an argument. For S4 functions, all functions are generic. When developing S4 methods, a generic function is either created or exists, and methods are created for the generic function.

The setGeneric() function creates an S4 generic function. (An S4 method is created by the setMethod() function. The help page for setMethod() says that setMethod() usually does the creation of the generic function automatically when setMethod() is run for functions that are S3 generics, but it must be done manually for new functions.)

There are ten arguments to setGeneric(), two of which are usually assigned. The first is **name**, which is a character string containing the name to be assigned to the function. The standard for S4 function names is **lowercasefirstUpperCaseAfter** (see section "Types of Assignment" in Chapter 3 for what constitutes a legal name in R). The second argument is **def**, which is a function definition and is optional in some cases. For new generic functions, the argument **def** is set equal to the function standardGeneric(), which normally has one argument, **f**. In standardGeneric(), **f** is set equal to the name given to the generic function, in quotes. The rest of the arguments to setGeneric() are optional or have a default value that should be used.

The function setMethod() is similar to setGeneric() but also includes the class(s) associated with the method. The first argument is **f** and is a character string of the name to be assigned to the method. (For a method with a newly defined generic function, you must create the generic function with the desired name before creating the method. See the succeeding example.) If the generic function already exists, the names must match between the generic function and the method. The second argument is **signature** that is a character vector and gives the names of class(s) associated with the data objects used by the method.

The third argument, **definition**, defines the function of the method. The function definition is usually a mixture of S3 and S4 objects; however, variables entered through the signature class(s) are subscripted using **@** or the function slots() rather than **$** or **[[**. But, if—say—there is a slot **mat** in class **mats**, where **mat** is a matrix, then **mat** could be subscripted with a combination of S3 and S4 methods; for example, mats@mat[1:3, 4].

The last three arguments to setMethod() are usually left as their default values. The argument **where** tells R where to store the method, by default, the namespace of the package for which the function is being defined. The argument **valueClass** is obsolete and by default is set to **NULL**. The argument **sealed** lets you freeze changes to the method and by default is set to **FALSE**. (This information is from the help page for setMethod().)

Say you have two equally sized matched sets of numbers and you want to estimate the linear relationship between the two sets. In R, the function lm(), which does ordinary least squares regression, can estimate a linear relationship. Below, a method that estimates the relationship between two numeric vectors is defined and run. The example of creating and running a method (there is also one in Chapter 5) follows (first with no generic function defined, which gives an error, and second with a generic function defined):

```
> setClass( Class="xyz", slots=c( x="numeric", y="numeric" ) )

> setMethod( f="lmFunction", signature="xyz",
+                          definition=function( x="xyz",
                           y="missing", ... )
+                          { print( lm( x@y ~ x@x ) ) }
+                          )
Error in setMethod(f = "lmFunction", signature = "xyz",
definition = function(x = "xyz",   :
  no existing definition for function 'lmFunction'

> setGeneric( name="lmFunction",
+                function( x, y, ... )
+                { standardGeneric( "lmFunction" ) }
+                )
[1] "lmFunction"
> setMethod( f="lmFunction", signature="xyz",
+                definition=function( x="xyz", y="missing", ... )
+                { print( lm( x@y ~ x@x ) ) }
+                )
```

```
> xyz.p1 = new( "xyz", x=1:10, y=21:30 )
> lmFunction( xyz.p1 )

Call:
lm(formula = x@y ~ x@x)

Coefficients:
(Intercept)            x@x
         20              1
```

First, the xyz class is defined with two slots that are both numeric. Then the lmFunction() method is defined. (The method is written to return the regression coefficients for a regression on two equal length numeric vectors.) You can see that the method cannot be defined until the generic function has been defined.

Once the lmFunction() method is defined, the new() function creates the object **xyz.p1** to be used to enter data of the xyz class into the lmFunction() method. The new() function takes the arguments **Class**, for the class of the method, and **...**, for the arguments of the method. The values of the arguments are set in new() by assigning the values to the names of the arguments, which are separated by commas.

Last, the method is run with the data object and returns the regression coefficients of **y** on **x**. So for **x** equal to 1 through 10 and **y** equal to 21 through 30, the relationship between **x** and **y** is that **y** equals 20 plus **x** (i.e., the first regression coefficient is 20 and the second regression coefficient is 1).

Note that **x** in the definition of the xyz class contains both the **x** and the **y** as defined in setMethod() and that **y** from the xyz class is set to **missing** in setMethod(). A variable set to **missing** in setMethod() is not used. Also note that the function is a new function, i.e., not in any of the loaded packages.

There are some testing functions to determine qualities of an object. The functions isGeneric(), isS4(), isS3method(), and isS3stdGeneric() can help determine if an S4 method can be defined for a function name.

For example:

```
> isGeneric( "lm" )
[1] FALSE

> isS4( "lm" )
[1] FALSE

> isS3method( "lm" )
[1] FALSE

> isS3stdGeneric( "lm" )
[1] FALSE

> setClass( "lm", slots=c( fo="formula", df="data.frame" ) )
Error in setClass("lm", slots = c(fo = "formula", df = "data.
frame")) :
  "lm" has a sealed class definition and cannot be redefined
```

Here, lm() has a sealed class definition, so a new method cannot be defined for the function.

For some S3 functions, methods can be defined. For example:

```
> isGeneric( "plot" )
[1] FALSE

> isS4( "plot" )
[1] FALSE

> isS3method( "plot" )
[1] FALSE
```

```
> isS3stdGeneric( "plot" )
plot
TRUE

> setClass( "plot", slots=c( x="numeric", y="numeric" ) )
> setMethod( "plot", signature="plot", definition=function( x,
y ,... ){ plot( x@x, x@y ) } )
> tester=new( "plot", x=1:10, y=21:30 )
> plot ( tester )

> isGeneric( "plot" )
[1] TRUE
> isS4( "plot" )
[1] FALSE
> isS3method( "plot" )
[1] FALSE
> isS3stdGeneric( "plot" )
[1] FALSE
```

Note that after creating the S4 method for plot(), the function becomes an S4 generic function rather than an S3 standard generic function, at least in the workspace environment.

The plot() function is a generic function in the S3 object system since the kind of plot that is output by plot() depends on the class of the object(s) being plotted. For example, when plotting a time series object, to get information about the arguments to the function, you would look at the help page for plot.ts, rather than that for plot. However, you would call plot() to plot the time series. The plot.ts form of plot() is an S3 method of plot().

The results of calling isS3method() for plot() and plot.ts when R has been opened in a new session are

```
> isS3method( "plot" )
[1] FALSE
> isS3method( "plot.ts" )
[1] TRUE
```

So plot.ts is a method of plot(). For example, to plot the airmiles dataset in the datasets package, which is a time series of the ts class, you would enter **plot(airmiles)** at the R prompt. You would get a line plot with time on the x (horizontal) axis and the number of airmiles on the y (vertical) axis.

The function showMethods() shows the methods for an S4 generic function(s). The function takes eight arguments. The first is **f**, the name(s) of the function(s). The argument is optional. If not used, the function returns all S4 generic functions in the environment(s) given by the **where** argument (see the next sentence). The second argument is **where**, which sets the environment(s) in which to look for the function(s). By default, **where** is set to the top environment of the parent frame of the workspace, which is usually **.GlobalEnv** (see the help page for the topenv() function).

The third argument is **classes** and is a list of the classes to be used to restrict the search. The argument is optional. The fourth argument is **includeDefs**, a logical variable. If **TRUE**, the function definitions are printed out. The default value is **FALSE**. The fifth argument is **inherited**, a logical variable. If **TRUE**, the inherited methods that have been used during the session are included in the list of methods. The default value is the reverse of the value of **includeDefs** (**TRUE** if **FALSE** and **FALSE** if **TRUE**).

The sixth argument is **showEmpty**, a logical variable. See the help page for more information. The seventh argument is **printTo**, which tells R where to print the result of the call to the function. By default, the function prints to the standard output, usually the terminal. The last argument is **fdef**, which allows you the option of choosing which generic function definition to use. The argument is optional.

There are other functions associated with S4 methods. The functions selectMethod(), findMethod(), getMethod(), existsMethod(), and hasMethod() are all grouped together in one help page. The functions selectMethod() and getMethod() return the function and the class of the method. The functions existsMethod() and hasMethod() return a logical value of **TRUE** or **FALSE** depending on whether the method is found or not. The functions differ as to whether they allow inheritance. The functions selectMethod() and existsMethod() do. The functions getMethod() and hasMethod() do not. The function findMethod() returns the location of a method.

The first argument to all of the functions is **f**, the name of a generic function. The second argument is **signature**, a character vector of class name(s) consisting of the class(s) (for which the method is defined) that is of interest. The functions selectMethod() and getMethod() behave similarly, except that selectMethod() has three arguments that getMethod() does not have, **useInherited**, **verbose**, and **doCache**, none of which are normally used (the writers at CRAN recommend to not use the arguments).

All of the functions except selectMethod() have the argument **where**, which is an optional character variable giving the environment in which to look for the method. Both selectMethod() and getMethod() have the arguments **optional, mlist**, and **fdef**. The argument **optional**, if set to **TRUE**, tells R to return **NULL** rather than an error if selectMethod() (or getMethod()) does not find a method. The default value is **FALSE** for both functions. According to the help page for these functions, the other arguments are rarely used, and the writers at CRAN recommend against using them.

The function removeMethod() removes a method. The function takes the **f, signature**, and **where** arguments, which are as described previously.

Generic functions are removed by using `removeGeneric()`. The arguments to `removeGeneric()` are **f** and **signature**, which are as described previously. Some of the other functions listed on the same help page are `isGeneric()`, already described; `findFunction()`, which finds the locations of a function; `removeMethods()`, which removes all methods associated with an S4 generic function; and `getGenerics()`, which lists all generic functions in an environment. For the last two functions, the location can be specified with the argument **where** (use **.GobalEnv** for the R workspace.)

For more information about `setGeneric()`, `standardGeneric()`, `setMethod()`, `new()`, `isS4()`, `isS3Method()`, `isS3stdGeneric()`, `showMethods()`, or `removeMethod()`, use the Help tab in RStudio or enter **?setGeneric**, **?standardGeneric**, **?setMethod**, **?isS3Method**, **?new**, **?isS4**, **?isS3stdGeneric**, **?showMethods,** or **?removeMethod** at the R prompt, respectively.

The help page for `getMethod()`, `selectMethod()`, `findMethod()`, `existsMethod()`, and `hasMethod()` can be found by using the RStudio help tab or by entering **?getMethod** at the R prompt.

The help page for `isGeneric()`, `removeGeneric()`, `signature()`, `findFunction()`, `removeMethods()`, and `getGenerics()` can be found by using the Help tab in RStudio or by entering **?GenericFunctions** at the R prompt. (All six functions are on the help page titled the "Tools for Managing Generic Functions"–which also contains other functions.)

CRAN's introduction to S4 methods can be found by using the Help tab in RStudio or by entering **?methods::Introduction** at the R prompt.

Reference Class Methods

The Reference Class object system treats objects that are not methods in the same way that the S4 object system does. Internally, the class structure of the Reference Class classes is the S4 structure (i.e., the classes are formal). Unlike S4 classes, with Reference Class classes, methods are defined as part of the class. Classes are defined with *fields* and *methods* (as covered in Chapter 5). However, the fields and methods of a Reference Class class are accessed with the **$** operator rather than the **@** operator.

Creating a Reference Class class creates a generator function. The generator function can be used to create the two types of objects associated with the class–data objects and method objects. Data objects (and one example of a method object) are covered in Chapter 5. Here, we cover method objects in more detail.

A generator function is an object of the refObjGenerator class. Given an object of the refObjGenerator class, finding the methods in the object can, or adding a new method to the object does, involve appending $methods() to the name of the generator function. For example, say that the name of the generator function is rOG, then the function to see the methods in or to add methods to the rOG class is rOG$methods(). The function takes the single argument **...**, which can be empty, can contain a collection of method names, or can contain named function definitions that are separated by commas. The function definitions should be standard function definitions as written in the R language. If no arguments are entered in the function call, the function returns the methods in the generator function object.

An example (where RCE is the generator function defined in Chapter 5) is

```
> RCE$methods()
 [1] ".objectPackage" ".objectParent"  "callSuper"    "copy"
     "export"
 [6] "field"          "getClass"       "getRefClass" "import"
     "initFields"
[11] "rg"             "show"           "trace"       "untrace"
     "usingMethods"
```

If a method name is entered into the function call with no function definition, the function definition with the given name is returned. The name must be a character string or object.

An example is

```
> RCE$methods( "rg" )
Class method definition for method rg()
function () {
    rs <<- lm(y ~ x)
}
```

(Note that RCE$rg() was defined in an example in Chapter 5.) A collection of function names can be entered also (e.g., c("pl","rg")). A collection returns a list of function definitions.

For the Reference Class object system, the objects of the refObjGenerator class (e.g., RCE in the preceding example) create the parent frame within which the methods run, so the fields in the refObjGenerator class (e.g., **x**, **y**, and **rs** in the RCE class) need not be specified in the argument list of the function in a method definition (see the RCE$rg() method in the preceding example).

Methods are added to an object of the refObjGenerator class (a generator function) by setting function definitions equal to names within a call to *generator_function*$methods(). (Here, substitute the name of the generator function for *generator_function* in the call.)

An example is

```
> RCE$methods(
+    li=function( xx=x ) print( xx ),
+    qu=function( xx=x ) print( xx^2 )
+ )
> RCE.p1 = RCE$new( x=1:6, y=3:8, rs=lm( y~x ) )
> RCE.p1$li()
[1] 1 2 3 4 5 6
```

```
> RCE.p1$qu()
[1]  1   4   9 16 25 36
> RCE.p1$qu( 3:4 )
[1]  9 16
```

The methods $li() and $qu() are defined first. (The $li() method returns the value of **x**. The $qu() method returns the value of **x** raised to the power of two.) Then, the $new() generator function method is used to create the data object RCE.p1 (to contain data for the fields in the Reference Class). The call to RCE$new(), which generates RCE.p1, sets **x** equal to 1 through 6, **y** equal to 3 through 8, and **rs** equal to lm(y~x). (The $new() generator function method is covered in the last section of Chapter 5.)

Note that the two methods, $li() and $qu(), are called by appending the method to the data object RCE.p1. In the example, the call to RCE.p1$li() returns the values in **x**; the first call to RCE.p1$qu() returns the values in **x** raised to the power of two; and the second call to RCE.p1$qu() returns the values entered into the call raised to the power of two. Entering values into the call to RCE.p1$qu() does not give an error because **xx** is an argument that can be set in the call (and is set to **x** by default).

The **...** argument can be used to enter arguments to a function (which are used when the function is run) without specifically entering the argument names within the function definition.

An example is

```
> RCE$methods(
+     sa=function( xx=x, ... ) sample( xx, ... )
+ )
> RCE.p1$sa()
[1] 1 4 3 6 2 5
> RCE.p1$sa( size=3 )
[1] 4 2 6
```

```
> RCE.p1$sa( 1:3, size=10, replace=TRUE )
 [1] 1 3 3 3 2 3 3 3 3 2
```

In the preceding example, the RCE.p1$sa() function takes a sample of the elements in **xx** (by default, **xx** equals **x**). In the first call to RCE.p1$sa(), a permutation of **x** is returned (a permutation returns the same numbers usually in a different order). In the second call, a sample of size three, sampled without replacement from **x**, is returned. In the third call, a sample of size ten, sampled with replacement from integers 1 through 3, is returned. In the examples, the **size** and **replace** arguments to sample() are entered through the **...** argument of RCE.p1$sa(). (The sample() function, which the RCE.p1$sa() function applies, is covered in Chapter 9.)

Another way to get data into the fields of a generator function involves using the $methods() method of the generator function to create a method with the **initialize** name. The method sets values for the fields. Before the $initialize() method is initially set, the fields in the class are of zero length. After the $initialize() method is set and the generator function is run without arguments, the fields contain the values that are set.

Note that you can use the $new() generator function method or use the $initialize() class method, but not both. If the $initialize() method has been set, the $new() method gives an error. To go back to using the $new() method, the generator function must be removed and redefined.

An example of using the $initialize() method is

```
> rm( RCE )
> RCE = setRefClass( "RCE",
+                                         fields=list( x="numeric",
                                        y="numeric", rs="lm" )
+ )
> RCE
Generator for class "RCE":

Class fields:
```

```
Name:        x        y       rs
Class: numeric numeric        lm

Class Methods:
     "field", "trace", "getRefClass", "initFields", "copy",
     "callSuper",
     ".objectPackage", "export", "untrace", "getClass", "show",
     "usingMethods", ".objectParent", "import"

Reference Superclasses:
     "envRefClass"
> RCE()
Reference class object of class "RCE"
Field "x":
numeric(0)
Field "y":
numeric(0)
Field "rs":
NULL
> RCE.p1 = RCE$new( x=1:6, y=4:9, rs=lm( y~x ) ) #initialize
has not been set
> RCE$methods( initialize=function() {
+        x <<- as.numeric( 1:4 );
+        y <<- as.numeric( 5:8 );
+        rs <<- lm( y~x )
+   }
+   )
> RCE()
Reference class object of class "RCE"
Field "x":
[1] 1 2 3 4
Field "y":
```

```
[1] 5 6 7 8
Field "rs":

Call:
lm(formula = y ~ x)

Coefficients:
(Intercept)            x
          4            1
> RCE.p1 = RCE$new( x=1:6, y=4:9, rs=lm( y~x ) )
 Error in .Object$initialize(...) :
  unused arguments (x = 1:6, y = 4:9, rs =
list(c(-7.771561e-16, 1), c(5.516712e-16, -9.260952e-16,
1.494686e-16, 2.517161e-16, -5.813201e-18, -2.094752e-17),
c(-8.573214, 4.1833, -5.968337e-17, -1.764561e-16,
-6.530055e-16, -8.8716e-16), 2, c(1, 2, 3, 4, 5, 6), 0:1,
list(c(-2.44949, 0.4082483, 0.4082483, 0.4082483, 0.4082483,
0.4082483, -8.573214, 4.1833, -0.0537243, -0.29277, -0.5318157,
-0.7708615), c(1.408248, 1.185321), 1:2, 1e-07, 2), 4, list(),
lm(formula = y ~ x), y ~ x, list(1:6, 1:6)))
4.
initialize(value, ...)
3.
initialize(value, ...)
2.
methods::new(def, ...)
1.
RCE$new(x = 1:6, y = 4:9, rs = lm(y ~ x))
```

First, the RCE generator function is deleted, and a new RCE generator function is set. The new RCE has no initialize method, as can be seen from the listing of the generator function. Also, the values for **x**, **y**, and **rs** have been initialized with vectors of zero length. Then, the RCE$new() method is run; the method does not give an error but has no effect on the generator function.

Next, an initialize method is set. The **x** field is set to 1 through 4; the **y** field is set to 5 through 8; and the **rs** field is set to lm(y~x). (Note that the <<- operator must be used when assigning values to objects in the $initialize() method.) Then, the generator function is run with no arguments. The three fields are returned with the correct values for **x**, **y**, and **rs** (which returns the result of the lm() function operating on y~x). An attempt is made to run the RCE$new() method. The method returns an error since the RCE class contains an initializer method. (Note that the RCE$rg() method is not set in this example. The regression in RCE$rg() is run when RCE() is run.)

Trying to run the new method to set new values now gives an error. To run a new value, you redefine the initializer with new data.

An example is

```
> RCE$methods( initialize=function() {
+       x <<- as.numeric( 1:3 );
+       y <<- as.numeric( 3:5 );
+       rs <<- lm( y~x )
+ }
+ )

> RCE()
Reference class object of class "RCE"
Field "x":
[1] 1 2 3
Field "y":
[1] 3 4 5
Field "rs":

Call:
lm(formula = y ~ x)
```

198

```
Coefficients:
(Intercept)              x
          2              1
```

Note that the RCE() generator function is run after the new $initialize() method is defined. The data returned are the data set in the initializer method. The result in **rs** gives the regression coefficients of regressing 3 through 5 on 1 through 3.

The Reference Class approach to objects is usually only used in the code for a package. However, there is no restriction on Reference Class objects to be in the source code of a package, as can be seen in the preceding examples. The writers at CRAN recommend that Reference Class methods be kept simple—that more complex tasks be written in functions outside of the class and accessed from simpler methods.

More information about Reference Class objects and how to work with the objects can be found under the Help tab in RStudio or by entering **?ReferenceClasses** at the R prompt.

CHAPTER 8

How to Use a Script or Function

While scripts are just listings of code stored outside of R, functions are objects of the function mode and are stored in the workspace. Most functions require specific kinds of arguments, which must be input into the function correctly. For example, if a function calls for a matrix and a data frame is input, the function will return an error. Since external tables are often read into the R workspace as data frames, using a data frame for a matrix is quite a common error. This chapter covers an example of using a script to do a simple mining of Twitter tweets, as well as how to call a function, use arguments in a function, and access the output of a function.

Example of a Script: Mining Twitter

This example demonstrates a way to mine Twitter and gives a result from the mining call. The example is a script in the Source subwindow of an RStudio session and is not a function. A mixture of S3 and S4 objects is used in the script. Most of the objects in twitteR, the Twitter mining package used here, are S4 objects and are methods.

To mine Twitter, you must sign up for a developer account on Twitter and create an app. To sign up for a developer account, you must have a Twitter account. If you have a Twitter account, sign up for a developer

© Margot Tollefson 2022
M. Tollefson, *R 4 Quick Syntax Reference*, https://doi.org/10.1007/978-1-4842-7924-3_8

account at `https://apps.twitter.com`. Otherwise, open a Twitter account and then sign up for a developer account.

To sign up for a developer account, follow the instructions at `https://apps.twitter.com`. When the account is approved, the "Developer Portal" will be on the left of the computer screen. Open the menu below "Projects & Apps" and choose "New Project." On the window to the right of the Developer Portal, you will be requested to name the project and to answer questions about how you will use the project. When the project is approved, scroll down to the "+ Create App" button in the window to the right of the Developer Portal and click on the button.

Follow the instructions to create the app. First you will be asked to name the app. After naming the app, you will be given the API key, API secret key, and the Bearer token. Copy the keys and token and save them, since you will only have access to the codes one more time. There is a button to copy the key (or token) to the right of the displayed key (or token). (You can regenerate the keys and token with new values at any time.)

Below the keys and token is the "Next, setup your App." section. Select the "App settings" button to generate access tokens. To the right of the Developer Portal, a new window will open with the app name at the top. Below the name, select "Keys and tokens." Scroll down to the "Access Token and Secret" line and click on the "Generate" button on the right. If this is the first time the button has been clicked for the new app, the full set of keys and tokens will appear (this is the last time you have access to the API keys). Copy and save the access token and access token secret.

Go back to the settings for the app by selecting "Settings" under the name of the app. Note that the access is given either as "Read," "Read and Write," or "Read and Write and Direct Messages." The access setting can be edited.

The keys and tokens can be revoked or regenerated at any time. The keys and tokens are used by the twitteR package in R to connect to the Twitter API. In twitteR, the API keys are called the customer keys, and the access tokens are as named.

The script follows. The libraries of twitteR and tm (for text mining) are loaded first in the script. The script is as follows:

```
library( twitteR )
library( tm )
ck = "########################"
cs = "##################################################"
at = "##################################################"
as = "#############################################"
setup_twitter_oauth( consumer_key=ck, consumer_secret=cs,
access_token=at, access_secret=as )

# Below, in the call to searchTwitter(),  Biden is the
search topic,
# 200 is the number of tweets to collect,
# English is the language for which to search,
# 42.27 is the geographic latitude, -93.9 is the geographic
longitude,
# 200 miles is the radius of the circle around the latitude
# and longitude within which to search,
# only recent tweets are collected,
# and 120 retries are blocked before trying again
# if Twitter encounters a tweet limit.

sr.1 = searchTwitter(
  "Biden",
  n=200,
  lang="en",
  geocode="42.27,-93.9,200mi",
  resultType="recent",
  retryOnRateLimit=120
)
```

```
sr.1.df = twListToDF( sr.1 )
tf = termFreq( sr.1.df$text,
                control=list(
                    tolower=TRUE,
                    stopwords=TRUE,
                    removePunctuation=TRUE,
                    stemming=TRUE
                )
            )
```

Note that the actual keys and tokens have been replaced with # signs in the script. The actual codes must be used. The function setup_twitter_oauth() is in the twitteR package and creates a file on the computer that R uses to connect R to the Twitter API. The searchTwitter() function, also in the twitteR package, retrieves the tweets from Twitter. The search was for 200 recent tweets that were tweeted within 200 miles of Stratford, Iowa, and that were written in English and related to the word "Biden."

The twListToDF() function converts the output from searchTwitter(), which is an S4 object, to a data frame, which is an S3 object. The twListToDF() function is also in the twitteR package.

The termFreq() function counts the frequency of the words in the text of the 200 tweets retrieved by searchTwitter(). The arguments to the function were set to make all letters lowercase, to not include the words returned by the stopwords() function, to remove punctuation marks, and to stem the words. (The stopwords() function returns the words to be excluded from the words to be counted. There are 174 conjunctions, contractions, prepositions, or pronouns returned by stopwords().) The termFreq() and stopwords() functions are in the tm package.

The termFreq() function returns an integer vector with the number of times each word occurs within the 200 tweets, excluding the words returned by stopwords(). There is one element for each word, and the name for the element is the word.

The result of running the script on Sunday afternoon of September 5, 2021, was

```
> sort( tf[ tf>11 ], decreasing=TRUE )
     biden          joe      presid afghanistan        trump
       139           27          27          16           13
```

Only words that occurred more than 11 times were printed. Also, "Biden" only shows up 139 times in the tweets. Many of the tweets were truncated; however, the tweets also include some tweets related to Biden as well as tweets including the word "Biden."

(The rtweet package also has functions to mine Twitter. One difference between the twitteR and rtweet packages is the following: for twitteR, long tweets are truncated in searchTwitter() but are not in the search_tweets() function of the rtweet package. Both functions collect tweets. Also, either the setup_twitter_oauth() function from the twitteR package or the create_token() function from the rtweet package can set up a credential file for R. Once set up by either function, the file need not be set up again and can be accessed by functions in both packages. R uses the file to get access to Twitter.)

More information about the preceding functions can be found by using the Help tab in R Studio or by entering **??tm::tm**, **??twitteR::twitterR**, or **??tweet::tweet** at the R prompt (the tm, twitter, and tweet packages must have been installed).

Calling a Function

Calling a function is straightforward. The name of the function is entered at the R prompt followed by a set of parentheses that may or may not contain arguments, depending on the function. If the function does require arguments, the arguments are separated by commas within the parentheses.

Sometimes, the argument name must be used, but not always. For values that are entered without names, R assigns the values to the arguments that are unnamed in the call, starting with the first unnamed variable and continuing in order until the unnamed arguments are exhausted. The order of the arguments is the order of the arguments within the parentheses of the function definition.

To illustrate the use of arguments, an example follows using a version of the function **f.fun( )**, introduced in the last chapter. This version of the function **f.fun( )** calculates a quantile of the normal distribution given the mean, the standard deviation, and alpha. The function returns the **(1-alpha/2) × 100**th percentile of the distribution. The arguments **se** and **alpha** are given default values and **mu** is not.

The example starts with listing the definition of the function, which is followed by five different calls to the function:

```
> f.fun
function(  mu, se=1, alpha=.034 ){
    q_value = qnorm( 1-alpha/2, mu, se )
    q_value
}
```

Note the last line before the closing bracket in f.fun() just contains **q_value**, so the value of **q_value** is returned.

In the first call, each of the arguments is specified by name. In R, arguments can be in any order if specified by name.

```
> f.fun( se=1, mu=0, alpha=0.034 )
[1] 2.120072
```

In the second call, the values for the arguments are entered without names. Since the arguments are entered in order, the function knows which argument to assign to which value. The argument **mu** takes on the value of **0**, **se** the value of **1**, and **alpha** the value of **0.067**, which is the order of the arguments within the parentheses in the function definition.

```
> f.fun( 0, 1, 0.067 )
[1] 1.831674
```

In the third call, the first argument is entered without a name, and the third argument is entered with a name. The second argument takes on the default value. The argument **mu** takes on the value of **0**, **se** the value of **1**, and **alpha** the value of **0.129**.

```
> f.fun( 0, alpha=0.129 )
[1] 1.518057
```

In the fourth call, values for the first two arguments are entered without names, and the third argument takes on the default value. The argument **mu** takes on the value of **4**, as does **se**. The argument **alpha** takes on the default value of **0.034**.

```
> f.fun( 4, 4 )
[1] 12.48029
```

In the fifth call, the second argument is named, and the first and third are not, so **mu** takes on the value **0** and **alpha** takes on the value **0.129**, while **se** takes on the value **1**.

```
> f.fun( se=1, 0, 0.129 )
[1] 1.518057
```

Note that the named arguments can be placed anywhere in the list (Also, as is true of any argument that appears before an **...** in the argument list of a function, argument names can be shortened to a unique version of the name, i.e., **al** for **alpha** in the f.fun() function.)

Arguments

Given a function, a listing of the arguments to the function can be found at the help page for the function. Most help pages distinguish between the S3 and S4 versions of the functions. The S3 versions give the arguments for the S3 form of the function. The S4 versions give only those arguments that must be included, plus the **...** argument. In S4, each method for a generic function is different, so the arguments may vary by the method.

For some functions, the user must know something about the theory behind the function to understand the arguments, but for many functions, the arguments are straightforward. As noted in the last chapter, arguments with default values or that can be handled with the `missing()` function within the function need not be given a value when the function is called.

Arguments to a function must be of the correct type and class. On the help page of a function, descriptions of the arguments are listed in the "Arguments" section, sometimes giving the type and/or class, but not always. Sometimes, the type and/or class is obvious. Sometimes, more information can be found in the "Details" section. Sometimes, looking in the "Examples" section is enough to clear up the form of an argument.

One argument that needs a little explaining is the **...** argument. The **...** argument tells the user that there are more arguments that may be entered. The arguments would usually be arguments to a lower-level function called by the higher-level function. An example follows.

The example starts by listing two vectors, **x** and **y**, and then continues with two calls to the function `lm()` with two different values for the argument **tol**. (The function `lm()` fits an ordinary least squares linear regression.) On the help page for `lm()`, there is no argument **tol**. However, there is the argument **...**, indicating that `lm()` calls another function for which an argument can be entered.

The `lm.fit()` function is a lower-level function that `lm()` calls, and `lm.fit()` has the **tol** argument. (The **tol** argument gives the tolerance for the QR decomposition as to whether a matrix is singular.) In the first call to lm(), the default value for **tol** is used, since **tol** is not specified. In the second call, lm() passes the value for **tol** to lm.fit().

```
> x
[1] 2.001 2.000 2.000
> y
[1] 4.03 4.00 4.01
> lm( y~x )
Call:
lm(formula = y ~ x)
Coefficients:
(Intercept)              x
     -45.99          25.00
> lm( y~x, tol=.001 )
Call:
lm(formula = y ~ x, tol = 0.001)
Coefficients:
(Intercept)              x
      4.013             NA
```

In the first call, the default value for **tol** is 1.0e-7, so lm.fit() does not find a linear dependency in the matrix consisting of a column of ones and **x**. As a result, two coefficients are fit.

In the second call, **tol** is set to 1.0e-3, and lm() determines that there is a linear dependency in the matrix consisting of a column of ones and **x**, so only one coefficient is fit.

For a different example of the use of the ... argument and more discussion of the arguments of functions, see the "The Structure of a Function" section in Chapter 7.

The Output from a Function

The output from a function will vary with the function. Functions that plot mainly give plots. Summary functions give summarized results. Functions that test a hypothesis give the results from the test.

Most packaged functions print some results directly to the screen, but many packaged functions also have output that is a list and that can be accessed through subscripting. For example, looking at the help page of the function lm(), under the "Value" section, coefficients, residuals, fitted. values, rank, weights, df.residual, call, terms, contrasts, xlevels, offset, y, x, model, and na.action are all values that can be accessed from a call to the function.

Since, for most functions, the output is of the list type, the most common method used to access the elements is with the **$** operator, although index subscripting can be used, too. (The elements of the list can be of any type.).

For the first simple regression model fit in the last section, the accessible 15 values are as follows:

```
> a.lm = lm( y~x )
> a.lm$coef
(Intercept)           x
    -45.995      25.000
> a.lm$res
            1              2              3
-4.336809e-19 -5.000000e-03  5.000000e-03
> a.lm$fit
    1     2     3
4.030 4.005 4.005
> a.lm$rank
[1] 2
> a.lm$weights
```

```
NULL
> a.lm$df
[1] 1
> a.lm$call
lm(formula = y ~ x)
> a.lm$terms
y ~ x
attr(,"variables")
list(y, x)
attr(,"factors")
  x
y 0
x 1
attr(,"term.labels")
[1] "x"
attr(,"order")
[1] 1
attr(,"intercept")
[1] 1
attr(,"response")
[1] 1
attr(,".Environment")
<environment: R_GlobalEnv>
attr(,"predvars")
list(y, x)
attr(,"dataClasses")
        y         x
"numeric" "numeric"
> a.lm$contrasts
NULL
> a.lm$xlevels
```

```
named list()
> a.lm$offset
NULL
> a.lm$y
NULL
> a.lm$x
named list()
> a.lm$model
     y     x
1 4.03 2.001
2 4.00 2.000
3 4.01 2.000
> a.lm$na.action
NULL
```

In the example, the call to lm() was assigned a name, but lm() could have been subscripted directly. An example is **lm(y~x)$coef**. Values accessed from a call to a function are often used in another function.

Running an R function takes a little care, but with some experimentation and determination, the results can be very useful.

PART IV

I/O and Manipulating Objects

CHAPTER 9

Importing and Creating Data

When you are loading data into RStudio or R, you have options. R reads external objects using connection functions. The connections can be to files, Uniform Resource Locator (URL) addresses, pipes, or socket connections and can be an internal part of a function that reads from the connection, an argument to a function that reads from the connection, or a stand-alone function that opens a connection for reading (and, sometimes, writing). Some functions read textual data, some binary data, and some both kinds of data.

In RStudio, many datasets can be read using the Import Dataset button under the Environment tab (in the upper right subwindow). Other types of files can be loaded into the Source (upper left) subwindow, as described in Chapter 2. R also comes with canned datasets, which can be loaded.

There are format specific functions (e.g., files with the extension .csv) that read external files in a specific format. For information that is not in files, but accessible through pipes or sockets, there are functions that read from the pipes and sockets. There are two functions within the seven core packages that read from the console.

Many of the functions that read data have corresponding functions that write data. Writing data is the subject of Chapter 10. Table 10-1, at the end of Chapter 10, lists the functions that read and write data, matching functions where appropriate.

© Margot Tollefson 2022
M. Tollefson, *R 4 Quick Syntax Reference*, https://doi.org/10.1007/978-1-4842-7924-3_9

Sometimes, the user wants to create data. R has a multitude of random number generators for data creation. Data can also be entered manually using c() or by using various other functions for creating data with patterns.

The first section of this chapter covers connection functions, reading data into RStudio and R, and loading R datasets. The second section covers probability distributions, including random number generators and the sample() function. The third section covers manual data entry and creating data with patterns.

Reading Data into RStudio and R, Including R Datasets

External objects are read into an RStudio or R workspace through connection functions. In the seven core packages of R, there are 12 connection functions that read from external locations. The functions can be used as stand-alone functions or from within other functions–usually functions that read external files or other kinds of information.

In RStudio, importing datasets is simple for some specific kinds of datasets. RStudio takes care of the connections, so not much effort is required to load datasets into the R workspace–if the datasets are in the correct format.

At the R console, there are functions that read textual data into R. In the seven core packages, the functions are scan(), to read textual data of a given type or mode; read.table(), read.csv() or read.csv2(), and read. delim() or read.delim2(), to read data from a spreadsheet structured table where the structure is given by an argument, comma-separated variables, or tab-delineated variables; read.fortran(), to read data coded in the FORTRAN format; read.fwf(), for reading tables in a fixed width format; read.DIF(), for files in the Data Interchange Format; read. dcf(), for files in the Debian Control File format; and read.ftable(), for files in the flat table format used with contingency tables in R. (There are functions for reading Excel files and other kinds of files in packages other than the seven core packages.)

The `readLines()`, `read.socket()`, `readClipboard()`, and `readline()` functions read textual data and have their own subsection in this section, as do the `dget()` and `source()` functions and the `loadhistory()` function. The `readCitationFile()`, `readEnviron()`, and `readRegistry()` functions are briefly described in a subsection of this section.

For binary data, the `load()`, `attach()`, and sometimes `data()` functions load objects saved with the `save()` function. The `readRDS()` function loads an object that has been saved with `saveRDS()`. (These functions are recommended by the R Project for transferring R objects between R workspaces.) The `readBin()` function reads binary data from an open connection. The `readChar()` reads binary and raw data. The `unserialize()` function reads through a connection from files created by the `serialize()` function.

For a complete listing and a lengthy discussion of importing into R, see `http://cran.r-project.org/doc/manuals/r-release/R-data.html`.

Connections

There are 12 connection functions in the base package of R. The functions are `file()`, `url()`, `gzfile()`, `bzfile()`, `xzfile()`, `unz()`, `pipe()`, `fifo()`, `socketConnection()`, `serverSocket()`, `socketAccept()`, and `stdin()`. The `file()` and `url()` functions are usually used with textual input—for files on the computer or files at URLs. The `gzfile()`, `bzfile()`, `xzfile()`, and `unz()` functions open files compressed with gzip, lzma, bzip2, xz, and zip. The `pipe()` and `fifo()` functions are used with pipes and named pipes, respectively. The `socketConnection()`, `serverSocket()`, and `socketAccept()` functions are used with sockets. There is also the `stdin()` function for reading data from the console.

According to the help page for connections, from which the information on connections comes, the intention of the developers at the R project is that file() be used for textual input and gzfile() for binary input, but either can be used for either.

The first eight functions take the same first two arguments: **description**, for the description of the object to which to connect, and **open**, for the kind of connection to open (to read from, write to, append, and/or truncate the connection).

The possible values for **open** are ""; **"r"** or **"rt"**, for textual input; **"w"** or **"wt"**, for textual output; **"a"** or **"at"**, to append a file with textual output; **"rb"**, for binary input; **"wb"**, for binary output; **"ab"**, for appending binary files; **"r+"** and **"r+b"**, for inputting from and outputting to text and binary files, respectively; **"w+"** and **"w+b"**, for inputting from and outputting to a file after truncating the file, for textual and binary files, respectively; and **"a+"** and **"a+b"**, for inputting from and appending textual and binary files, respectively.

file( )

For file(), **description** is a character string that can contain an address on the computer or a URL (see below) or "clipboard" or "stdin" or "". The **open** argument takes a single character string and can be one of the choices given in the note above or "". The legal choices depend on the value of **description**. According to the help page for connections, usually if the choice is not legal, R will substitute a legal choice without a warning.

According to the help page for connections, the "stdin" choice opens the input of the process being run at the level of the C code and may not go anywhere. My computer tends to hang if **file("stdin")** is entered at the R prompt or as an argument to a function that reads data.

The "clipboard" choice is misleading. The value of **description** for reading the clipboard varies by operating system. For Windows systems, the value should be "clipboard". For macOS systems, the `pipe()` connection function is used instead of `file()`, and the **description** argument is "pbpaste". For Linux systems, **pipe( )** is used, and **description** is "xsel -b" (which only works if the xsel software has been loaded into the Linux system).

If **description** is a URL, `file()` and `url()` perform in the same way. See the following for the description of how `url()` behaves.

Some examples of the use of `file()` for reading are given in the following example. In the first part of the example, the object **ch9.fex1** (which equals "" whether contained in a `file()` function or not) lets you enter data at the console and returns the entered data when the data entry is exited. (Note that the **ch9.fex1** is the argument to `scan()`, not **ch9.fexcon**.) Data entry is exited by entering a blank line or by entering Ctrl-D. To quit the data entry without returning the data, press the Esc key. The first part of the example follows:

```
ch9.fex1 = ""
ch9.fexcon = file(
  ch9.fex1,
  "w+"
)
showConnections()
scan( ch9.fex1 )
1
2
5
```

```
close( ch9.fexcon )
showConnections()

scan( ch9.fex1 )
1
4
```

In the second part of the example, **ch9.fex2** equals "ch9.df.txt" (and does not contain the file:// prefix). The scan() function reads the ch9.df.txt file (which is in the folder of the computer from which the R session was run) and outputs a numeric vector of the numbers that were entered by the cat() function. Note that the **file** argument in cat() was set equal to ch9. fexcon. The second part of the example follows:

```
> ch9.fex2 = "ch9.df.txt"
ch9.fexcon = file(
  ch9.fex2,
  "w+"
)
cat(
  1:3,
  "\n",
  1:2,
  file=ch9.fexcon
)
close( ch9.fexcon )
scan( ch9.fex2 )
```

In the third part of the example, the file:// prefix is included in the value of **description**. The file on the computer is the same file used in the second part. The readLines() function reads numeric data and creates a character vector for which each element contains some of the numbers entered—where the different groups of numbers in the elements are separated by "\n" when entered into cat().

Then the example shows that when a connection with **open** set equal to **"r+", "a+"**, or **"w+"** is opened, the file can be written over, appended, or emptied (truncated), respectively. In the example, the showConnections() and close() functions provide information and close connections. The third part of the example follows:

```
ch9.fex2 = "ch9.df.txt"
ch9.fexcon = file(
  ch9.fex2,
  "w+"
)
cat(
  1:3,
  "\n",
  1:2,
  file=ch9.fexcon
)
close( ch9.fexcon )
scan( ch9.fex2 )

ch9.fex3 = "file://ch9.df.txt"
ch9.fexcon = file(
  ch9.fex3,
  "r+"
)
cat(
  1:2,
  "\n",
  3:4,
  "\n",
  file=ch9.fexcon
)
```

```
close( ch9.fexcon )
readLines( ch9.fex3 )

ch9.fexcon = file(
  ch9.fex3,
  "a+"
)
cat(
  2:3,
  "\n",
  4:5,
  "\n",
  file=ch9.fexcon
)
close( ch9.fexcon )
readLines( ch9.fex3 )

ch9.fexcon = file(
  ch9.fex3,
  "w+"
)
readLines( ch9.fex3 )
```

This example is based on the examples at the connections help page. Note that in the preceding examples, the connection is set equal to a name and accessed through the name. Otherwise, R opens a new connection each time file() is called.

url()

For url(), **description** is a character string that contains a URL, including the prefix. According to the help page for connections, the possible prefixes include **http://**, **https://**, **ftp://**, and **file://** (the last to open a file on the computer). Other than those mentioned, the prefixes that work are operating system dependent. Note that URLs can only be opened for reading.

Most websites that provide datasets have links to download the datasets. There is no address for the actual dataset. Trying to directly read the dataset returns HTML code. An example of a government dataset that is accessible is

```
ch9.uex1 = "http://berkeleyearth.lbl.gov/auto/Global/Land_and_
Ocean_complete.txt"
ch9.uexcon = url(
  ch9.uex1
)
readLines(
  ch9.uexcon,
  n=3
)
close(
  ch9.uexcon
)
```

Note that the first three lines of the file are returned, since **n** equals 3.

gzfile(), bzfile(), and xzfile()

The gzfile(), bzfile(), and xzfile() functions read (and write to) compressed files. The three take the same arguments but differ as to the compression method and level. The functions cannot read a file at a URL. (The function download.file() will download a file to the computer, which file can then be read.) The gzfile() function can read from (and write to) files compressed by gzip, bzip2, xz, and lzma and files that have not been compressed. The bzfile() function reads (and writes to) files compressed with bzip2. The xzfile() function reads (and writes to) files compressed with xz and (just) reads files compressed with lzma.

The **description** argument takes a character string containing an address on the computer. The **open** argument can be a read string, a write string, or an append string. The value of **open** will not open a file for both reading and writing, even if set to "r+b", "w+b", or "a+b". (The writers at the R project warn that for appending, the new data is not connected to the data there before and may not be read correctly.) An example of gzfile() is

```
ch9.gzex1 = "ch9.bin"
ch9.gzexcon = gzfile(
  ch9.gzex1,
  "wb"
)
cat(
  "binary file\n",
  file=ch9.gzexcon
)
close(
  ch9.gzexcon
)
ch9.gzexcon = gzfile(
  ch9.gzex1,
  "rb"
)
readBin(
  ch9.gzex1,
  what=character()
)
```

```
readLines(
  ch9.gzex1
)
close(
  ch9.gzexcon
)
```

Note that first the ch9.bin file is opened for writing, written to, and then closed. Next, the ch9.bin file is opened for reading. The readBin() and readLines() functions read the file. The readBin() function returns binary code, while the readLines() function returns what was entered. Last, the connection to the ch9.bin is closed.

unz()

The unz() function reads single files from a file compressed in the zip format (i.e., has the extension .zip). The function cannot unzip a file at a URL. The function takes the same arguments as gzfile() plus the **filename** argument. For unz(), the **description** argument takes the address to a file with the .zip extension on the computer. The function only opens in the read and binary mode, so the **open** argument should be "rb" or "". An example of using unz() is

```
ch9.zex1 = "ia090121-exempt.zip"
ch9.zexcon = unz(
  ch9.zex1,
  "ia090121-exempt.csv"
)
readLines(
  ch9.zexcon
)[[ 982 ]][ 1 ]
close(
  ch9.zexcon
)
```

Note that the zip file was downloaded from the website of the US Securities and Exchange Commission. The address of the file is www.sec.gov/files/investment/data/information-about-registered-investment-advisers-and-exempt-reporting-advisers/ia090121-exempt.zip.

pipe()

The pipe() function sends commands to the operating system and returns the result of the commands. The **description** argument takes a character string containing the commands. The **open** argument should be left as the default value. An example of using pipe() to read the clipboard on my MacBook computer is

```
ch9.pex4 = "pbpaste"
ch9.pexcon = pipe(
  ch9.pex4,
  ""
)
scan(
  ch9.pexcon,
  what=character()
)
readLines(
  ch9.pexcon
)
readChar(
  ch9.pexcon,
  105
)
close(
  ch9.pexcon
)
```

The clipboard contained the first line of the help page for connections. Note that scan(), readLines(), and readChar() give different results.

fifo()

The fifo() function opens a buffer, allowing data to be read into and out of the buffer. Data is read by the first in, first out method. Once read out, the data is no longer in the buffer. When the connection is closed, nothing is saved. Not all systems support FIFO connections. If your computer supports fifo(), then entering **capabilities("fifo")** at the R prompt returns TRUE.

For fifo(), the **description** argument takes a character string that must end in **fifo** and that contains an address on the computer (including a file name that need not exist before fifo() is run). On my MacBook computer, the **open** argument must be **"w+"** or **"a+"** for text data or **"w+b"** or **"a+b"** for binary data, unless the file location is opened more than once. For **open** equal to a single mode, the read mode connection must be opened before the write or append mode connection.

An example of using fifo() is

```
ch9.ffex1 = tempfile(
   fileext="-fifo"
)
ch9.ffex1
ch9.ffexcon = fifo(
   ch9.ffex1,
   "a+"
)
writeLines(
   paste( 10:12 ),
   con=ch9.ffexcon
)
```

```
cat(
   20:22,
   file=ch9.ffexcon
)
readLines(
   ch9.ffexcon
)
scan(
   ch9.ffexcon
)
scan(
   ch9.ffexcon
)
close(
   ch9.ffexcon
)
unlink(
   ch9.ffex1
)
```

Note that a temporary file is created by the tempfile() function and given the extension "**-fifo**" (as shown in the examples on the connections help page). The file is removed (deleted) from the computer with the unlink() function.

In the first part of the example, the temporary file address is created and assigned the name ch9.ffex1. The address is printed out, and the connection is created and assigned the name ch9.ffexcon.

In the second part of the example, two groups of data are put into the buffer, the first group being of the character type and written by writeLines() and the second group being of the integer type and written by cat(). In the third part, readLines() reads the first group. When read, the data is no longer in the buffer. The scan() function then reads the second group of data. (The readLines() and writeLines() functions only read or write data of the character type. The scan() function reads data of the numeric type by default but can read any atomic type.) A second call to scan() returns numeric(0) (i.e., the numeric NULL vector) since all of the data in the buffer has been read. In the last part of the example, the connection is closed, and the temporary file is deleted.

socketConnection( ), serverSocket( ), and serverAccess( )

The last three connection functions create sockets to form connections. Sockets provide a connection between R and a port on the computer. The socket connects a server, which reads or writes data, to a client, which reads or receives data. Usually, the R connection function is the server, and the port is the client.

The socketConnection() function creates a connection that automatically closes if a new connection is made to the port. The first five arguments of socketConnection() are **host**, for the name of the host of the port; **port**, for the number of the port; **server**, for whether the port is a server or client; **blocking** (see below); and **open**, for how to open the client.

The **host** argument takes a character string containing the name of the host of the port. The default value for **host** is "localhost".

The **port** argument takes the integer number of the port. The argument has no default value.

The **server** argument takes a logical variable; if TRUE, the port is the server, and if FALSE, the port is the client. The default value of **server** is FALSE.

The **blocking** argument is covered below.

The **open** argument is as described previously. The argument takes the value "a+" by default.

The serverSocket() function opens a port for listening. Multiple connections can be made to the port (using socketAccess(); see below). The function takes one argument, **port**, the integer number of the port–which has no default value. The port is closed by a call to the close() function.

The serverAccess() function connects to a socket and is used with the serverSocket() function. The first three arguments are **socket**, for the name of the socket (as assigned to the result of the serversocket() function); **blocking** (see below); and **open**, for how to open the connection.

There is no default value for **socket**, but the argument takes a value of both the servsockconn and connection classes. The default value of **blocking** is FALSE. The default value of **open** is "a+".

The Other Arguments to the Connection Functions

The **blocking** argument is found in the argument lists of file(), url(), socketConnection(), and socketAccess(). The argument tells a function whether to use connection blocks when reading or writing to a location. According to the help page for connections, with **blocking** set to TRUE, the process does not return to the computer until the reading or writing is completed. With **blocking** set to FALSE, the process returns as soon as the process can. (See the help page for a detailed explanation of blocking.) The default value of blocking is TRUE for file() and url() and FALSE for socketConnection() and socketAccess().

All the connection functions except serverSocket() have the **encoding** argument. The argument gives the encoding of what is read or written and takes a character string. Enter iconvlist() at the R prompt for a (long) list of possible encoding names. Many are not used by all systems. (See the help page for connections for more detailed information.) The default value of encoding for the ten functions for which encoding is an argument is getOption("encoding"), which returns "native.enc" on my macOS system, my Windows 10 system, and my Linux Mint system.

The **raw** argument only appears in the argument list of `file()`. The **raw** argument takes a logical value. If set to TRUE, the connection reads the data as raw data. (See the help page for connections for more details.) The default value of **raw** is FALSE.

The `file()` and `url()` connection functions have the **method** argument. The **method** argument tells R the prefixes that are legal for the **description** argument. The **method** argument takes a character string, and the possible values of the character string are "default", "internal", "wininet", or "libcurl". The value "wininet" is only used with Windows systems, while the value "libcurl" can always be used on Linux systems and is optional on Windows systems. The values "default" and "internal" can be used for all systems. The default value of **method** for both `file()` and `url()` is getOption("url.method", "default")–which returns "default" on my macOS system, my Windows 10 system, and my Linux Mint system.

The **headers** argument is used by the `url()` connection function. The argument lets you set values for HTTP headers that are used when R opens and reads the website. The **headers** argument takes a character vector where the elements of the vector are named. The default value for **headers** is NULL.

The **compression** argument appears in the argument list of `gzfile()`, `bzfile()`, and `xzfile()`. The argument can take integer values from 0 to 9, and the value gives the amount of compression used by the connection function. The default values of **compression** for `gzfile()`, `bzfile()`, and `xzfile()` are 6, 9, and 6, respectively.

The **filename** argument appears in the `unz()` function and gives the name of the file in the zipped file (the zipped file name is given by the **description** argument) that is to be extracted. The argument takes a character string containing the name of the file to be extracted. There is no default value for **description**.

The **timeout** argument appears in the socketConnection() and socketAccess() functions and gives the number of seconds to wait until timing out the process. The argument takes a numeric value. The default value of **timeout** is getOption("timeout"), which equals 60 on my macOS system, my Windows 10 system, and my Linux Mint system.

The **options** argument appears in the socketConnection() and serverSocket() functions and gives options for the socket. The argument is optional and, when used, takes a character vector of option names in quotes. (According to the help page for connections, only one option is currently available.) The default value for options is getOption("socketOptions"), which equals NULL on my macOS system, my Windows 10 system, and my Linux Mint system.

open( ), close( ), isOpen( ), isIncomplete( ), and socketTimeout0( )

There are five functions included on the connections help page that work with connections that read: open(), close(), isOpen(), isIncomplete(), and socketTimeout(). The open() function opens a connection for reading (and/or writing). The close() function closes a connection. The isOpen() function checks if a connection is open. The isIncomplete() function checks if the data to be read from a connection has been read. The socketTimeout() function either sets the number of seconds until the connection times out when attempting to read or returns the time-out value of the socket connection.

The first four functions take the argument **con**, for the connection object. The argument takes a single value of the connection class. The open() function also takes the **open**, **blocking**, and **...** arguments. The **open** and **blocking** arguments are as described before. The **...** argument allows for arguments of other methods to be entered. The default value of **open** is "r", and the default value of **blocking** is TRUE.

The close() function takes the **con**, **type**, and ... arguments. According to the help page for connections, **type** is currently ignored. The **con** and **...** arguments are as described before.

The isOpen() function takes the **con** and **rw** arguments. The **rw** argument indicates if the connection is open for reading or writing and takes a character string that can be "", "read", or "write" (where the letters within the quotes can be shortened, say, to "r" and "w"). The default value of **rw** is "". If the connection is open for the kind of interaction described by **rw**, isOpen() returns TRUE. Otherwise, the function returns FALSE.

The isIncomplete() function takes no other argument than **con**. If an attempt to read the connection is blocked, the function returns TRUE. Otherwise, the function returns FALSE.

The socketTimeout() function takes two arguments: **socket**, for a socket connection to a port, and **timeout**, for the number of seconds to wait before the socket connection times out when reading from (or writing to) the port. The value assigned to the **socket** argument must be a socket connection. The **socket** argument has no default value. The value assigned to **timeout** must be a numeric value giving the number of seconds to wait until timing out or, if negative, the current value of **timeout** for the socket. The preceding functions are described at the connections help page.

showConnections(), getConnections(), and closeAllConnections()

The showConnections help page covers six more functions that create or work with connections open for reading. The functions are showConnections(), getConnection(), closeAllConnections(), stdin(), nullfile(), and isatty().

The showConnections() function shows which connections are open and closes connections that are no longer active–with a warning. The function returns a matrix of descriptive attributes of the open connections. If no connections are open, then just the headings for the columns of the matrix are returned. The function takes one argument, **all**, for whether to list all open connections or only those connections that were opened by the user. If set to TRUE, all open connections are returned. If set to FALSE, only those connections opened by the user are returned. The default value of **all** is FALSE.

The getConnection() function returns the connection function in a given row of the showConnections() matrix. The function has one argument, **what**, for the row of the connection function to be returned. The **what** argument takes a single positive integer and returns NULL or the connection function of that number in the list of connections. There is no default value for **what**.

The closeAllConnections() function closes all user opened connections. The function has no arguments.

An example of using the three functions is

```
> ch9.scex1 = file()
> showConnections()
  description class  mode text   isopen    can read can write
3 ""           "file" "w+" "text" "opened" "yes"     "yes"
> ch9.scex2 = getConnection(
+   3
+ )
> showConnections()
  description class  mode text   isopen    can read can write
3 ""           "file" "w+" "text" "opened" "yes"     "yes"
> ch9.scex1
A connection with
description ""
class       "file"
mode        "w+"
text        "text"
opened      "opened"
```

```
can read    "yes"
can write   "yes"
> ch9.scex2
A connection with
description ""
class       "file"
mode        "w+"
text        "text"
opened      "opened"
can read    "yes"
can write   "yes"
> closeAllConnections()
> showConnections()
      description class mode text isopen can read can write
```

Note that even though the connection was assigned to two names, there is only one connection.

stdin( ), nullfile( ), and isatt( )

The stdin() function opens a connection to the R console (in the lower left subwindow of RStudio). The stdin() function does not open a user opened connection and cannot be closed with closeAllConnections(). See the following example:

```
> stdin()
A connection with
description "stdin"
class       "terminal"
mode        "r"
text        "text"
opened      "opened"
can read    "yes"
can write   "no"
```

```
> showConnections()
     description class mode text isopen can read can write
```

```
> showConnections( all=TRUE )
   description class       mode text   isopen   can read can write
0 "stdin"     "terminal" "r"  "text" "opened" "yes"    "no"
1 "stdout"    "terminal" "w"  "text" "opened" "no"     "yes"
2 "stderr"    "terminal" "w"  "text" "opened" "no"     "yes"
```

```
> closeAllConnections()
```

```
> showConnections( all=TRUE )
   description class       mode text   isopen   can read can write
0 "stdin"     "terminal" "r"  "text" "opened" "yes"    "no"
1 "stdout"    "terminal" "w"  "text" "opened" "no"     "yes"
2 "stderr"    "terminal" "w"  "text" "opened" "no"     "yes"
```

Note that the result from entering stdin() at the R prompt is a connection and is not closed by closeAllConnections().

The stdin() function takes no arguments and accepts values one at a time at the console. An example of setting **file** to stdin() in the scan() function is

```
showConnections()
showConnections( all=TRUE )
closeAllConnections()
showConnections( all=TRUE )

scan( stdin() )
2
4
1
```

Note that scan() returned a numeric vector of the numbers that were entered.

The `nullfile()` function returns the location of the null file on the computer. On macOS and Linux systems, the null file address is "/dev/null". On Windows systems, the address is "nul:".

The last function associated with reading from connections is `isatty()`, which should determine whether a connection is a terminal. The function takes one argument, **con**, for the connection to be checked. The **con** argument is as described before. According to the help page for `showConnections()`, the result that is returned is not reliable–as is the case on my macOS system, my Windows 10 system, and my Linux Mint system. An example of an unreliable value is

```
> isatty( stdin() )
[1] FALSE
```

Note that, as can be seen in an earlier example, the `stdin()` function returns an object of the `terminal` class but `isatty()` returns FALSE.

make.socket( ), gzcon( ), and pushback( )

There are three more functions used in reading from connections: `make.socket()`, `gzcon()`, and `pushback()`. The `make.socket()` function opens a socket connection or makes a socket connection a server; `gzcon()` reads from (and writes to) an open connect through a decompression (or compression) program; and `pushBack()` pushes text that has been read back into the connection for functions that do not return to the beginning on after reading from a connection.

seek( ), isSeekable( ), and truncate( )

The `seek()`, `isSeekable()`, and `truncate()` functions also work with connections. The `seek()` function returns how far into the file the reading has gone and can set a new starting point. The `isSeekable()` function returns whether the connection is seekable (according to the help page for `seek()`, currently, only compressed files compressed with gz-compression are seekable). The truncate() function truncates a connection at the point the reading has reached. The function is not always supported and only works on computer files, according to the help page for seek().

For more information about connections, use the Help tab in RStudio or enter **?connections** at the R prompt for the first 11 functions; **?showConnections** for the next seven functions; **?make.socket**, **?gzcon**, or **?pushBack** for make.socket(), gzcon(), and pushBack(), respectively; and **?seek** for seek(), isSeekable(), and truncate().

Reading Data Using RStudio

To load datasets into RStudio, go to the **Environment** tab in the upper right subwindow. Select **Import Dataset**. You are given six possible choices for importing a dataset: from a text file using functions in the base package, from a text file using functions from the readr package, from an Excel dataset, from an SPSS dataset, from an SAS dataset, or from a Stata dataset.

If the data is in a text file in columns (e.g., a **.csv**, **.txt**, or **.dat** file with the same number of data points in each line), **From Text (base)** is appropriate. By selecting this choice, you are taken to the directory of files on your computer. Select the file containing the data to be loaded. A form opens with an **Input File** subwindow. Below the subwindow, on the left, there are choices to be used in reading the data on and on the right a **Data Frame** subwindow. The **Input File** subwindow shows how RStudio sees the input file given the default choices on the left, and the **Data Frame** subwindow shows the data frame that would be created given the choices.

RStudio automatically chooses values for the choices based on the data in the file; however, the choices can be changed. The first choice on the left is the name to be supplied to the data frame that will be output to the workspace. The default name is based on the file name. Spaces in the file name are replaced by underscores. The name can be changed. The second choice is the encoding of the text in the file. Normally, the default value of **Automatic** will read the file. The drop-down menu lists many different encodings. The third choice is **Header**. If there is a header in the data file, **Header** should be **Yes**. Otherwise, **Header** should be **No**.

The fourth choice is **Row names**, giving the choices for row names of **Automatic**, **Use first column**, or **Use numbers**. The fifth choice is **Separator**. Depending on the type of separator used in the data file, the separator can be **Whitespace**, **Comma**, **Semicolon**, or **Tab**. The sixth choice is the form of the decimal point in the data. The choices are **Period** and **Comma**. The seventh choice is **Quote** for the type of quoting used in the data file. The choices are **Double quote (")**, **Single quote (')**, and **None**.

The eighth choice is the symbol used to indicate that a line in the file is a comment. The choices are **None**, **#**, **!**, **%**, **@**, **/**, and **~**. The ninth choice is the value to use for missing data. Any text can be entered. The default value is **NA**. The last choice is **Strings as factors**. Check the box if strings should be read in as factors rather than as character strings. The default value is not to check the box, (i.e., not to read strings as factors).

When the data in the **Data Frame** subwindow is in the desired form, select the **Import** button to the right below the subwindow. RStudio will import the dataset.

With the import choice, **From Text (readr)**, you can read from a file or a URL. The **readr** package must have been installed to import with this choice. Enter the file or URL address in the **File/URL** box. After entering the address, select the **Update** button to the right of the **File/URL** box. The data, based on the default import options, appears in the **Data Preview** box under the **File/URL** box. The **Import Options** box is below the **Data Preview** box. Choose the appropriate options for the data. The choices are like those for **From Text (base)** but a little more flexible.

The option **Name** defaults to a name based on the name of the file from which the dataset is read. **Skip** tells RStudio how many lines to skip before beginning reading. If there is no header row, uncheck **First Row**

as Names (the first row is the row after any skipped lines.) Uncheck **Trim Spaces** to not trim white space in the data file. Uncheck **Open Data Viewer** to not open the dataset in the **Source** subwindow after loading.

The **Delimiter** choices include **Comma, Semicolon, Tab, Whitespace**, and **Other...** (for the choice of a user-specified one-character delimiter.) The **Other...** choice provides more flexibility than the choices with **Read Text (base)**. **Quotes** gives the method of quoting if quotes are present. **Locale** gives choices for the format to be used for the data in the file, where the format is assumed to be that which is normal in the locale (country or language) in which the data was written. **Escape** gives the escape character for the data, if present. The possible values for indicating a comment are **Default**, #, %, //, ', !, ;, —, *, ||, ", *, \, and *>. (If there are comment lines in the dataset that are commented out and the comment lines begin with one of the indicators, the lines should not be marked to be skipped, as the lines will be ignored.) The **NA** choices are **Default, NA, null, 0**, and **empty**.

Make any necessary changes to the import options, based on the data displayed in the **Data Frame** subwindow. The data preview will update as changes are made. The **Code Preview** box is to the right of the **Import Options** box. The code in the box will be used by RStudio to import the dataset (which occurs in the R console subwindow). When ready, select the **Import** button below the **Code Preview** box. The dataset will load. Or select **Cancel** to leave the subwindow without loading the data.

The options **From Excel, From SPSS, From SAS**, and **From Stata** are like **For Text (readr)** and are not covered here—except to say that **From Excel** uses the **readxl** package and the **From SPSS, From SAS**, and **From Stata** use the **haven** package.

The scan() Function

The scan() function imports data from a file, a connection, or directly from the console. The function reads data of the atomic types (except the NULL type), that is, the raw, logical, integer, double, complex, and character types. The scan() function also reads data of the numeric mode and the list type.

The function takes 22 arguments. The arguments are **file**, for the location of file or the name of the connection to be read; **what**, for the type or mode of what is to be read; **nmax**, for the maximum number of values or records to be read; **n**, for the maximum number of values to be read; **sep**, for the separator between values in the data being input; **quote**, for the style of quoting; **dec**, for the style of the decimal point; **skip**, for the number of lines to skip; **nlines**, for the number of lines to read; **na.strings**, for the character(s) to which to set missing values; **flush**, for whether to flush to the end of a line in the file being read; **fill**, for whether to fill out elements if values are expected but not present; **strip.white**, for whether to strip white space in character strings; **quiet**, for whether to return the number of values read; **blank.lines.skip**, for whether to skip blank lines; **multi.line**, for whether a record can be on multiple lines if the **what** argument is a list; **comment.char**, for the character used to start comment lines; **allowEscapes**, for whether to interpret escape codes or treat escape codes as characters; **fileEncoding**, for how a file is encoded (and will be written if output); **encoding**, for the encoding of characters being input; **text**, for a character string of text to be input; and **skipNul**, for whether to skip nuls if **what** is set to character( ).

For a value, the **file** argument takes a character string, a single-element object of the character type, or a connection function. If **file** is a character value, **the value** contains the location of the dataset to be read. Otherwise, **file** can be set to a connection connected to what is to be read. If **file** equals "" (the default value), R reads data from the console (or from the value of stdin() if that value is different from the console).

An example of calling scan is

```
scan()
4
6
2
```

Here, R cues for a data point with the point number followed by a colon. To stop entering data, enter Ctrl-D or enter a blank line. To exit without returning the entered values, press the Esc key on the keyboard. Only one value can be entered at a time.

The **what** argument takes the *name*() function for an argument, where *name* is list or is the name of an atomic type or mode (e.g., raw()). For all types except list, the data being read must be interpretable as the type given by **what**. For objects of the list type, each second-level object must be interpretable as a single atomic type. The type of each element of the list is given by entering one value of the correct type within the list parentheses, separated by commas (see the following example). Those values are not returned by the function.

The scan() function reads the data row by row and creates a vector of what is read. If a list is read, the function fills out the list by filling first the first element of each of the first level elements, then the second element, and so forth. Also, for importing from a file or the console, the rows need not be the same length. An example of reading a list is

```
scan(
  text="1 a 3 b 2 c 4 d",
  what=list( 0, "" )
)
```

Note that here the **text** argument lets us enter data in a character string contained in the call to scan(). Also, types are mixed in the character string.

The scan() function is most often used to read an external file or connection, such as a file on the computer or a URL address. A file reference may be relative to the location of the workspace or an absolute location. An example is

```
> cat( "#junk\nnone, two, three, four
+ 1, 2, 3, 4\n2, 3, 4, 5 ",
+       file="ch9.tb2.txt"
+     )
> system( "cat ch9.tb2.txt" )
#junk
one, two, three, four
1, 2, 3, 4
2, 3, 4, 5

> scan(
+    file="ch9.tb2.txt",
+    skip=2,
+    sep=","
+ )
Read 8 items
[1] 1 2 3 4 2 3 4 5
```

The file ch9.tb2.txt is written to the working directory on the computer by the cat() function. The system() function sends a command to the operating system and returns the result to the console. In scan(), to browse for a file, enter **file.choose()** for the **file** argument (i.e., **scan(file. choose())**). The **skip** and **sep** arguments are described before, with specifics below.

If the type of the data being entered is not numeric, the **what** argument must be included in the call to scan(). For example:

```
> scan(
+   text="1 2 4+1i",
+   what=complex()
+ )
Read 3 items
[1] 1+0i 2+0i 4+1i
> scan(
+   text="1 2 4+1i",
+   what=character()
+ )
Read 3 items
[1] "1"     "2"     "4+1i"
```

The scan() function will convert values to a higher type and will not convert values to a lower type, where the order of types, from lowest to highest, is raw(), logical(), integer(), double() (or numeric()), complex(), and character(). If some of the data in the file is not readable as the given type, scan() returns an error.

The **nmax** argument gives a limit to the number of records read when a list is being input or the number of values read if an atomic vector is being input. (For lists, the argument does not always work as described on the scan() help page.) The argument takes any value that can be coerced to integer. If the value is zero, negative, or larger than the number of values or records being read, all the values or records are read. The **n** argument is like the **nmax** argument, except lists can give different results. The default value of **nmax** and **n** is -1; that is, the full file, text, or connection is read.

Some examples of setting **nmax** and **n** are

```
> scan(
+   file="ch9.tb2.txt",
+   skip=2,
+   sep=",",
+   nmax=5
+ )
Read 5 items
[1] 1 2 3 4 2
> scan(
+   file="ch9.tb2.txt",
+   what=list( 1, 1 ),
+   skip=2,
+   sep=",",
+   nmax=3
+ )
Read 4 records
[[1]]
[1] 1 3 2 4

[[2]]
[1] 2 4 3 5

> scan(
+   file="ch9.tb2.txt",
+   skip=2,
+   sep=",",
+   n=5
+ )
Read 5 items
[1] 1 2 3 4 2
```

```
> scan(
+    file="ch9.tb2.txt",
+    what=list(1,1),
+    skip=2,
+    sep=",",
+    n=3
+ )
Read 2 records
[[1]]
[1] 1 3

[[2]]
[1] 2 4
```

The scan() function also has the **sep** argument, which tells scan() the separator between values in either an external file or in the value of **text**. By default, the separator is a white space. The **sep** argument can be set to any single-character value that R can read. In the call to scan(), the value for **sep** is placed within quotation marks. See the examples using the ch9. tb file. There, a comma is used as the separator between data values.

If two separating symbols in the call to scan() do not have a value between the two, then by default, the value is set to **NA**. For example:

```
> scan(
+    text="1, 2, 3,, 4",
+    sep=","
+ )
Read 5 items
[1]  1  2  3 NA  4
```

The **quote** argument can change the characters for quoting if there is encoding for more than one locale present. The argument takes NULL or a single character string for a value. The default value of **quote** is if(identical(sep, "\n")) "", else "\"".

The **dec** argument takes a single one-character string containing the character to use for the decimal point. The default value of **dec** is ".".

For data with header lines, the **skip** argument tells scan() to skip lines before reading data. The value of **skip** tells scan() how many lines to skip and can be set to any value or object. The first element of the value or object is coerced to a positive integer if possible or else interpreted as zero. If **skip** equals zero, no lines are skipped. The default value of **skip** is zero.

The **nlines** argument tells scan() to read lines up to and including the value of **nlines** and can be used to read a header. The **nlines** argument behaves like **skip** regarding acceptable values. If **nlines** is set to zero, all lines are read. The default value of **nlines** is zero.

The **na.strings** argument takes a character string containing the value to assign if a data point is missing. The default value of **na.strings** is "NA".

The **flush** argument takes a single logical value. If set to TRUE, R will flush to the end of a line after the reading of the first value in a line. If set to FALSE, R will read as many values as are requested. The default value of **flush** is FALSE. Two examples with **flush** set to TRUE are

```
> cat(
+    "1 7 3 4 5 #flush\n2 3 4 5 6",
+    file="ch9.tb3.txt"
+ )
> system( "cat ch9.tb3.txt" )
1 7 3 4 5 #flush
2 3 4 5 6

> scan(
+    file="ch9.tb3.txt",
+    flush=TRUE
+ )
Read 2 items
[1] 1 2
```

```
> scan(
+    text="1 a 3 b 2 c 4 d",
+    what=list( 0, "" ),
+    flush=TRUE
+ )
Read 1 record
[[1]]
[1] 1

[[2]]
[1] "a"
```

Note that the computer file, ch9.tb3.txt, contains the data in the first part of the example. The first values of the two rows in ch9.tb3.txt are returned. In the second part of the example, a list of two elements is generated from the text string. Only the first record in the text string is returned.

The **fill** argument takes a single logical value. If set to TRUE, and **what** is a call to list(), R will read a field in each row of the data and will fill in any records that are missing. Also, the correct number of fields is returned, based on the call to list(). If **fill** is set to FALSE, R fills out the records as simply as possible and prints a warning if the number of data points does not fill out the records based on the call to list(). The default value of **fill** is FALSE. An example is

```
> cat(
+    "1 2 3\n4 5\n6",
+    file="ch9.tb4.txt"
+ )
> system(
+    "cat ch9.tb4.txt"
+ )
```

```
1 2 3
4 5
6
> scan(
+   file="ch9.tb4.txt",
+   list( 1, 1, 1, 1 ),
+   fill=FALSE
+ )
Read 2 records
[[1]]
[1] 1 5

[[2]]
[1] 2 6

[[3]]
[1]   3 NA

[[4]]
[1]   4 NA

Warning message:
In scan(file = "ch9.tb4.txt", list(1, 1, 1, 1), fill = FALSE) :
  number of items read is not a multiple of the number
  of columns

> scan(
+   file="ch9.tb4.txt",
+   list( 1, 1, 1, 1 ),
+   fill=TRUE
+ )
```

```
Read 3 records
[[1]]
[1] 1 4 6

[[2]]
[1]  2  5 NA

[[3]]
[1]  3 NA NA

[[4]]
[1] NA NA NA
```

Note that the ch9.tb4.txt computer file has three rows of data, but not the same number of data points in each row. The value to which the call to **what** is set in the call to scan() in both parts of the example (list(1,1,1,1)) creates four (fields) elements out of the data. With **fill** equal to FALSE, the data is split as evenly as possible into the four elements and a warning is given, since there are six data points and four elements. With **fill** equal to TRUE, each element has three records (for the three rows in the dataset). In both parts of the example, missing values are set to NA.

The **strip.white** argument applies to character fields. The argument takes a logical vector with the length of the vector equal to either one or the number of fields (if **what** is not equal to a call to list(), the number of fields is one). If **strip.white** is set to TRUE, white space is removed when the data in the computer file is converted to the character type. If FALSE, then the white space is not removed. The default value of **strip.white** is FALSE. An example of the effect of **strip.white** is

```
> scan(
+    "ch9.tb2.txt",
+    what=character(),
+    sep=",",
+    skip=2
```

```
+ )
Read 8 items
[1] "1"     " 2"   " 3"   " 4"   "2"     " 3"   " 4"   " 5 "
> scan(
+    "ch9.tb2.txt",
+    what=character(),
+    sep=",",
+    strip.white=TRUE,
+    skip=2
+ )
Read 8 items
[1] "1" "2" "3" "4" "2" "3" "4" "5"
```

Note that the computer file is ch9.tb2.txt, the first file referred to in this section. Without **strip.white** set to TRUE, the conversion to character can give strange results.

The **quiet** argument takes a logical value. If set to TRUE, scan() does not return the number of items or records read. If set to FALSE, the number is returned. The default value of **quiet** is FALSE.

The **blank.lines.skip** argument takes a logical value. If set to TRUE, blank lines are skipped when reading from a file or connection. If set to FALSE, R inserts an NA for each blank line. The default value of **blank. lines.skip** is TRUE.

An example is

```
cat(
+    "1 7 3 4 5\n\n2 3 4 5 6",
+    file="ch9.tb5.txt"
+ )
> system(
+    "cat ch9.tb5.txt"
+ )
```

```
1 7 3 4 5

2 3 4 5 6

> scan(
+    file="ch9.tb5.txt"
+ )
Read 10 items
 [1] 1 7 3 4 5 2 3 4 5 6

> scan(
+    file="ch9.tb5.txt",
+    blank.lines.skip=FALSE
+ )
Read 11 items
 [1]   1   7   3   4   5 NA   2   3   4   5   6

> scan(
+    file="ch9.tb5.txt",
+    list( 1, 1 ),
+    blank.lines.skip=FALSE
+ )
Read 6 records
[[1]]
[1] 1 3 5 2 4 6

[[2]]
[1]   7   4 NA   3   5 NA

Warning message:
In scan(file = "ch9.tb5.txt", list(1, 1), blank.lines.skip =
FALSE) :
  number of items read is not a multiple of the number
  of columns
```

Note that the computer file, ch9.tb5.txt, has three lines and the second line is blank. In the third call to scan(), the second NA is supplied because the number of items that are read has increased to 11, so to fill out the list, a 12th item is necessary.

The **multi.line** argument takes a logical value and only applies when the value of **what** is a call to list(). If set to TRUE, records can be on multiple lines. If set to FALSE, each line must contain an entire record; that is, the number of elements set in list() must be the number of items in a line of the data being read. The default value of **multi.line** is TRUE.

An example of setting **multi.line** is

```
> cat(
+    "1 7 3\n2 3 4",
+    file="ch9.tb6.txt"
+ )
> system(
+    "cat ch9.tb6.txt"
+ )
1 7 3
2 3 4
>scan(
+ file="ch9.tb6.txt",
+ list( 1, 1 ),
+ multi.line=FALSE
+ )
Error in scan(file = "ch9.tb6.txt", list(1, 1), multi.line = FALSE) :
line 1 did not have 2 elements
> scan(
+ file="ch9.tb6.txt",
+ list( 1, 1, 1 ),
+ multi.line=TRUE
+ )
```

```
Read 2 records
[[1]]
[1] 1 2

[[2]]
[1] 7 3

[[3]]
[1] 3 4
> scan(
+    file="ch9.tb6.txt",
+    list( 1, 1 ),
+    multi.line=TRUE
+ )
Read 3 records
[[1]]
[1] 1 3 3

[[2]]
[1] 7 2 4
```

Note that the computer file, ch9.tb6.txt, has two lines with three data points in each line. The call to list() generates two fields. The first call to scan() has **multi.line** set to TRUE, so scan() has no problem reading the file. In the second call to scan(), **multi.line** is set to FALSE, so scan() is expecting two items in each line and returns an error since there are three items on each line. In the third call to scan(), **multi.line** is set to TRUE and the number of fields is three, so the file is read correctly.

The **comment.char** argument takes a single character string containing one character. If the character appears in a data file or connection, R ignores anything after the character until a line feed is encountered. The default value of **comment.char** is ""; that is, no character is set. An example of not setting and setting **comment.char** is

```
> system(
+   "cat ch9.tb3.txt"
+ )
1 7 3 4 5 #flush
2 3 4 5 6

> scan(
+   file="ch9.tb3.txt"
+ )
Error in scan(file = "ch9.tb3.txt") :
  scan() expected 'a real', got '#flush'

> scan(
+   file="ch9.tb3.txt",
+   comment.char="#"
+ )
Read 10 items
 [1] 1 7 3 4 5 2 3 4 5 6
```

Note that the computer file ch9.tb3.txt contains a comment indicated with the character #. Without setting **comment.char** to "#", the file cannot be read. With the value set correctly, scan() reads the file.

The **allowEscapes** argument takes a single logical value. If set to TRUE, some C escape codes are returned as escape codes, so the codes control the output if the output is entered into the cat() function (and some other functions in R). If FALSE, the escape codes are treated as text. The default value of **allowEscapes** is FALSE. An example of setting **allowEscapes** is

```
> system(
+   "cat ch9.tb7.txt"
+ )
1 "\b\b" 2  # two backspaces
# 3 "\f" 4    one form feed (not run)
```

```
5 "\n" 6     # one line feed
7 "\r" 8     # one carriage return
9 "\t" 10    # one horizontal tab
11 "\v" 12  # one vertical tab

> scan(
+    file="ch9.tb7.txt",
+    what=character(),
+    allowEscapes=TRUE,
+    comment.char="#"
+ )
Read 15 items
 [1] "1"      "\b\b"
"2"      "5"     "\n"     "6"     "7"      "\r"     "8"
[10] "9"      "\t"    "10"     "11"    "\v"     "12"
> cat(
+    scan(
+      file="ch9.tb7.txt",
+      what=character(),
+      allowEscapes=TRUE,
+      comment.char="#"
+    )
+ )
Read 15 items
 2 5
 8 9     10 11     12
> scan(
+    file="ch9.tb7.txt",
+    what=character(),
+    allowEscapes=FALSE,
+    comment.char="#"
+ )
```

```
Read 15 items
 [1] "1"        "\\b\\b" "2"        "5"        "\\n"      "6"        "7"
 [8] "\\r"      "8"        "9"        "\\t"      "10"
"11"        "\\v"
[15] "12"
> cat(
+   scan(
+     file="ch9.tb7.txt",
+     what=character(),
+     allowEscapes=FALSE,
+     comment.char="#"
+   )
+ )
Read 15 items
1 \b\b 2 5 \n 6 7 \r 8 9 \t 10 11 \v 12
```

Note that the computer file, ch9.tb7.txt, contains all the escape codes that scan() recognizes. The escape codes must be within quotes to be read correctly, and **what** must be set to character() or a list with at least some character elements. The \f code, a form feed, is commented out–so is ignored.

The **fileEncoding** argument only applies to files and takes a single character string that contains an empty string or the name of the encoding in the file (run iconvlist() to see a list of encoding names). The argument, if not an empty string, tells R to recode the file. The default value of **fileEncoding** is "", that is, an empty string.

The **encoding** argument takes a single character string containing the encoding of the character strings in a file. The argument does not recode the strings. If the **file** argument is not the location of a computer file, the argument is ignored. The default value of **encoding** is "unknown".

The **text** argument takes a character vector (entered explicitly or as an object in the workspace) and allows the strings of text in the vector to be scanned. The argument is ignored if **file** is set to a value. There is no default value for **text**. A few of the examples in this section use **text** rather than **file**. See above.

The **skipNul** argument take a logical value. If set to TRUE, nul bytes are skipped. If FALSE, nul bytes cause an error. The default value of **skipNul** is FALSE.

To create a matrix or array, the call to scan() can be part of a call to matrix() or array(). For example:

```
> matrix( scan( text="1 2 3 4 5 6 7 8 9 10" ), 2, 5,
byrow=TRUE )
Read 10 items
     [,1] [,2] [,3] [,4] [,5]
[1,]   1    2    3    4    5
[2,]   6    7    8    9   10
```

More information about scan() can be found by using the Help tab in RStudio or by entering **?scan** at the R prompt.

The read.table() and Related Functions

The read.table() and related functions import data from a file or connection, where the file or connection is in the form of a matrix, or from value of the **text** argument. The functions create a data frame from the data. If the data is in a file, the location of the file is entered first in the call within quotation marks. The location of the file can be relative to the workspace or absolute, including URLs. To browse for a file, enter **file.choose()** for the quoted name (e.g., **read.table(file.choose())**). The read.table() function and the related read.csv(), read.csv2(), read.delim(), and read.delim2() functions are essentially the same function, differing only in the default values of the **sep, header, quote, dec, fill**, and **comment.char** arguments.

The functions can read all types of atomic data (except NULL): raw, logical, integer, double, complex, and character. From the R help page for the functions, R reads in the data as character data and then converts from character to one of the classes: raw, logical, integer, numeric, complex, factor, Date, or POSIXct.

The full set of arguments is **file**, **header**, **sep**, **quote**, **dec**, **numerals**, **row.names**, **col.names**, **as.is**, **na.strings**, **colClasses**, **nrows**, **skip**, **check. names**, **fill**, **strip.white**, **blank.lines.skip**, **comment.char**, **allowEscapes**, **flush**, **stringsAsFactors**, **fileEncoding**, **encoding**, **text**, and **skipNul**. The **file**, **sep**, **quote**, **dec**, **na.strings**, **skip**, **fill**, **strip.white**, **blank.lines.skip**, **comment.char**, **allowEscapes**, **flush**, **fileEncoding**, **encoding**, **text**, and **skipNul** arguments are as in scan(), except for some default values. The **file** argument has no default value in read.table() and the related functions. The **sep** argument equals "" in read.table(), "," in read.csv(), ";" in read. csv2(), and "\t" in read.delin() and read.delin2(). The **quote** argument equals "\"'" for read.table() and "\"" for the related functions. The **dec** argument has the default value of "." for read.table(), read.csv(), and read.delim() and the value of "," for read.csv2() and read.delim2(). The **fill** argument takes the default value of !blank.lines.skip in read.table() and TRUE in the related functions. The **comment.char** argument equals "#" in read.table() and "" in the related functions. The other arguments that are shared with scan() take the same default values as in scan().

The arguments that are not shared with scan() are **header**, **numeral**, **row.names**, **col.names**, **as.is**, **colClasses**, **nrow**, and **check.names**. The **header** argument tells the function whether to read a header from the first line; **numeral** tells how to handle numeric data points with more digits than double precision allows; **row.names** gives the names of the rows; **col.names** gives the names of the columns; **as.is** gives whether to convert character strings to factors; **colClasses** gives the class of each column; **nrow** gives the maximum number of rows to read; and **check.names** gives whether to check if the names of the columns are legal and unique.

The **header** argument takes a logical value. If **header** is set to TRUE, the first line read in the file is assumed to be a header. If set to FALSE, no header is read. The default value of **header** is FALSE in `read.table()` and TRUE in the related functions.

The **numeral** argument takes a single character string containing "allow.loss", "warn.loss", or "no.loss". If set to "allow.loss", the data is converted to double precision with no warning if the data object has too many digits; if set to "warn.loss", the data is converted to double precision with a warning; if set to "no.loss", the data is converted to a character string if **as.is** is TRUE or to a factor if **as.is** is FALSE. The default value of **numeral** is "allow.loss" for the five functions.

The **row.names** and **col.names** arguments are used to give names to the rows and columns of the data.frame. For **row.names**, the argument can be a character vector of length equal to the number of rows in the data. frame; the argument can be an integer specifying which column in the data.frame to use as row names; or the argument can be a character value containing the name of the column to be used as the row names. The row names do not cycle. The argument has no default value.

For **col.names**, the argument is a character vector of names for the columns. The vector must be of the same length as the number of columns. If **col.names** is not specified and **header** is **FALSE**, then the columns are named V1, V2,..., Vn, where **n** is the number of the last column. If **header** is **TRUE** and the first column does not have a name, while the rest of the columns do, then `read.table()` sets the first column as the row names.

The **as.is** argument takes a logical vector and affects data of the character type. If set to TRUE, character data is read as a character string (no change is made); if set to FALSE, character data are converted to factors. The **as.is** argument is by default a single value but can be a logical vector with a value for each column. A shorter vector can be entered also, with the values cycling across the columns. The default value of **as.is** is TRUE for all five of the functions.

The **colClasses** argument manually sets the class of each column and can be used in place of **as.is** to keep a column in character mode. The possible values for the column classes are NA, NULL, raw, logical, integer, numeric, complex, character, factor, Date, or POSIXct. The values are quoted, except for **NA** and **NULL**, and are entered as a vector. The values cycle if unnamed. The values can be assigned to just some of the names of the columns or to the full set of column names. If the value is **NA**, the normal conversion takes place. Otherwise, if possible, the column elements are coerced to the class listed for the column. If the value is NULL, the column is skipped when the file is read. The default value of **colClasses** is NA.

The **nrows** argument takes any object for a value but only affects the process of reading if the value is a positive integer. If a positive integer, the integer gives the maximum number of rows to be read. The default value of **nrows** is negative one, that is, all rows are read.

The **check.names** argument takes a single logical value. If set to TRUE, the column names are checked for legality and uniqueness. If there is a problem, R generates legal, unique values for the column names. If set to FALSE, the names are not checked. The default value of **check.names** is TRUE.

An example of reading the same file with read.table() and read.csv() is

```
> system( "cat ch9.tb2.txt" )
#junk,
one, two, three, four
1, 2, 3, 4
 2, 3, 4, 5

> read.table( file="ch9.tb2.txt", header=TRUE, sep="," )
  one two three four
1   1   2     3    4
2   2   3     4    5
```

```
> read.csv( file="ch9.tb2.txt", comment.char="#"  )
  one two three four
1   1   2     3    4
2   2   3     4    5
```

Note that the functions input and output across rows rather than down columns. The ch9.tb2.txt computer file contains a comment line and header. The column names and data points are separated by commas. Both functions give the same result, but the arguments that are set differ.

If the **text** argument is used to enter a table, the end of a row is indicated by \n. For example:

```
> read.table( text="1 2 3 4 \n 2 3 4 5" )
  V1 V2 V3 V4
1  1  2  3  4
2  2  3  4  5
```

Since the functions create a data frame out of the data, the types and classes of the elements need to only be consistent down the columns. An example of reading columns of different classes is

```
> cat(
+    '01 TRUE  1 1.1 1+0i "a"\n02 FALSE 2 2  2 "b"\n',
+    file="ch9.tb10.txt"
+ )
> system(
+    "cat ch9.tb10.txt"
+ )
01 TRUE  1 1.1 1+0i "a"
02 FALSE 2 2  2 "b"

> read.table(
+    file="ch9.tb10.txt"
+ )
```

```
   V1     V2 V3  V4    V5 V6
1  1    TRUE   1 1.1 1+0i   a
2  2 FALSE   2 2.0 2+0i   b
> read.table(
+    file="ch9.tb10.txt",
+    colClasses=c( V1="raw" )
+ )
   V1     V2 V3  V4    V5 V6
1 01    TRUE   1 1.1 1+0i   a
2 02 FALSE   2 2.0 2+0i   b
```

The computer file ch9.tb10.txt contains data that is of the raw, logical, integer, double, complex, and character classes. Note that the first column is read as an integer if the class is not specified in the call to read.table(). Note, also, that the columns are converted to the highest level of class contained in the column.

In the following example, column names are set, and the second column gives the row names. The ch9.tb10.txt computer file is read.

```
> read.table(
+    file="ch9.tb10.txt",
+    col.names=c( "col1", "col2", "col3", "col4", "col5", "col6" ),
+    row.names=2
+ )
        col1 col3 col4 col5 col6
TRUE     1    1  1.1 1+0i    a
FALSE    2    2  2.0 2+0i    b
```

Note that the six names are assigned to the six columns, and then column two is used for the names of the rows while the other columns retain the assigned names.

The other functions in the seven base packages that read spreadsheet style datasets are `read.dcf()`, for datasets in the Debian Control File format; `read.DIF()`, for datasets in the Data Interchange Format; `read.fortran()`, for files saved in a FORTRAN format; `read.ftable()`, for reading tables in the R flat table format; and `read.fwf()`, for files saved in a fixed width format.

A full description of the first five functions can be found by using the RStudio Help tab or by entering **?read.table** at the R prompt. For more information about the other functions in this section, use the RStudio Help tab or enter **?*name*** at the R prompt, where *name* is the name of the function (without the parentheses, e.g., ?read.dcf).

The readLines( ), read.socket( ), readClipboard( ), and readline( ) Functions

Some functions just read from connection functions. The `readLines()` function reads textual lines from a connection or file. The `read.socket()` function reads single character strings from a socket. The `readClipboard()` function reads the content of the clipboard (for Windows systems only). The `readline()` function reads single lines entered at the console.

The `readLines()` function has six arguments. The arguments are **con**, for the connection object to be read; **n**, for the number of lines to read; **ok**, for whether an error is given if **n** is larger than the number of lines in the connection; **warn**, for whether to give a warning if a file does not end in an EOL or embedded nuls are present; **encoding**, for the encoding of what is being read; and **skipNul**, for whether to skip embedded nuls.

The **con** argument takes either an object that is a connection or a character string containing the address of a file. From the help page for the `readLines()` function, if **con** is a character string, R opens a connection, if a connection is not already open, using `file()`–with the character string as the value of **description** and the **open** argument set to "rt". If the connection is already open, readLines() begins reading at the location R had reached before readLines() was called. The default value of **con** is stdin().

The **n** argument takes an integer value. If the integer is positive, the function reads n lines or to the end of the input if **n** is larger than the number of lines in the connection and the **ok** argument is set to TRUE. If **n** is greater than the number of lines and **ok** is set to FALSE, an error is returned. If **n** is negative, the full connection is read. The default value of **n** is minus one.

The **ok** argument takes a logical value. See the preceding paragraph for the effects of setting **ok** to TRUE and FALSE. The default value of **ok** is TRUE.

The **warn** argument takes a logical value. The argument is applicable to text files only. From the help page for readLines(), if **warn** is set to TRUE, R warns you if the end of the file does not have an EOL or if there are embedded nuls in the file. If set to FALSE, no warning is given. The default value of **warn** is TRUE.

The **encoding** and **skipNul** arguments are as in the section on scan(). For readLines(), the default values are "unknown" and FALSE, respectively. There are examples of running readLines() in the "Connections" section at the start of this chapter.

The read.socket() function reads single character strings from a socket connection and has three arguments. The arguments are **socket**, for the socket connection to be read; **maxlen**, for the maximum length in bytes of the character string to be read; and **loop**, for whether to wait until a value appears at the connection when there is nothing to read at the connection.

The **socket** argument takes an object that has been set equal to a socket connection. There is no default value for **socket**.

The **maxlen** argument takes a nonnegative integer giving the number of bytes to be read. The default value of **maxlen** is 256L.

The **loop** argument takes a logical value. If set to TRUE, `read.socket()` will continue to wait until a value appears at the connection. If set to FALSE, `read.socket()` does not wait. The default value of **loop** is FALSE.

The `readClipboard()` function reads a Windows system clipboard, where the contents can be in a variety of formats (see the help page for `readClipboard()` for a list of the standard formats) and takes two arguments. The arguments are **format**, for the format of the contents of the clipboard, and **raw**, for whether to read the clipboard as text or as raw data (which is used for binary data).

The **format** argument takes an integer specifying the format (the numbers associated with the formats are given at the help page for `readClipboard()`). The default value of **format** is 1, that is, read text.

The **raw** argument takes a logical value. If set to TRUE, the clipboard is read as raw data. If set to FALSE, the clipboard is read as text data. The default value of **raw** is FALSE.

The `readline()` function reads text interactively from the keyboard of the computer. The function takes one argument, **prompt**, for a string to be printed at the console that prompts you to enter data. The default value of **prompt** is `""`.

An example of calling `readline()` is

```
ch9.rlex = function() {
  ans = readline(
    "Are you tall? (y/n): "
  )
  if( ans=="y" | ans=="Y" ) {
    print( "YOU are tall." )
  }
  else {
    if( ans=="n" | ans=="N" ) {
      print( "YOU are not tall.")
    }
```

```
    else print( "Wrong answer." )
  }
}

ch9.rlex()
y
ch9.rlex()
N
ch9.rlex()
no
```

For more information about the readLines(), read.socket(), readClipboard(), and readline() functions, use the RStudio Help tab or enter **?*name*** at the R prompt, where *name* is the name of the function (without the parentheses, e.g., ?readLines).

The dget( ) and source( ) Functions

The dget() and source() functions read text and attempt to parse and evaluate the text. The dget() function reads text (including but not limited to functions saved with dput()). If the text is a function definition, the function is returned. (Note that, by default, any commenting in the function is removed.) Otherwise, R attempts to parse and evaluate the expressions in the text. For source(), the function parses and evaluates text that consists of expressions. For function definitions, by default, a list is returned. Both dget() and source() parse the text until the text that R cannot parse is encountered or until R reaches the end of the text.

The authors at the R project recommend against using dget() and dput() for transferring functions and datasets between workspaces, since they save and load in textual rather than binary format. For importing a text file containing a function that is stored or written externally, dget() works well. Scripts stored on the computer can be run with dget() but are more commonly run by source().

The dget() function has two arguments. The arguments are **file**, for the location of the text file, and **keep.source**, for whether to maintain the original formatting of a function.

The **file** argument can take for the value "", a character string containing the address of a file, or a connection object. There is no default value for **file**.

The **keep.source** argument takes a logical value. If set to TRUE, the function attempts to keep the formatting of a function. If set to FALSE, the formatting is the simplest formatting. The default value of **keep.source** is FALSE.

Scripts (files with an .R extension) are usually run with source(). The source() function takes 16 arguments and is a more sophisticated function than dget().

Some examples of running dget() and source() are

```
dget(
   ""
)
print( round( rnorm( 4 ), 2 ) )

ch9.dg1 = dget(
   ""
)
function() print( round( rnorm( 4 ), 2 ) )

ch9.dg1
ch9.dg1()

cat(
   "x=1:3\nprint( x )",
   file="ch9.dg2.txt"
)
```

```
system(
  "cat ch9.dg2.txt"
)

dget(
  "ch9.dg2.txt"
)
ch9.dg2=dget(
  "ch9.dg2.txt"
)
ch9.dg2

source(
  "ch9.dg2.txt"
)

cat(
  "function ( x = 1:3 )\n  print( x )",
  file="ch9.dg3.txt"
)
system(
  "cat ch9.dg3.txt"
)

ch9.dg3=dget(
  "ch9.dg3.txt"
)
ch9.dg3
ch9.dg3()

ch9.sc3 = source(
  "ch9.dg3.txt"
)
```

```
ch9.sc3
ch9.sc3$value()

cat(
  "function( x=4 )
print( round( rnorm( x ), 2 ) )",
  file="ch9.dg4.txt"
)
system(
  "cat ch9.dg4.txt"
+ )

dget(
  "ch9.dg4.txt",
  keep.source=TRUE
)
dget(
  "ch9.dg4.txt"
)
```

Note that in the first example, the text is entered at the console. In the first part of the example, the text is parsed and evaluated. In the second part, a function is entered and assigned to an object, so the text is parsed and evaluated, but the function is not run.

In the second example, dget() and source() read from the ch9.dg2.txt file on the computer, which is parsed and evaluated. Numbers are returned, since the text in the file is not a function definition.

In the third example, a function that is stored in the ch9.dg3.txt file on the computer is first read by dget() and saved to the ch9.dg3 object. Then ch9.dg3() is output and run. A vector of numbers is returned when the ch9.dg3() is run. Next, the file is read by source(). The result (which is a list) is saved to the ch9.sc3 object. The list is output, and the value element of the list (which contains the function) is run. The same vector of numbers is returned as with dget(). Note that dget() and source() give different results when the object that is read is a function definition.

In the fourth example, a function in a file on the computer is read with **keep.source** equal to TRUE, then with **keep.source** equal to FALSE (the default value). The first call returns the function as written. The second call simplifies the format of the code.

For more information about dget() and source(), use the RStudio Help tab or enter **?dget** and **?source**, respectively, at the R prompt.

The loadhistory( ) Function

The loadhistory() function loads a history file in text format into the workspace. The function takes one argument, **file**. The **file** argument takes a character string that contains the address of the file on the computer. The default value of **file** is ".Rhistory".

An example of saving and loading the workspace history is

```
> savehistory(
+   "ch9.Rhistory"
+ )
> loadhistory(
+   "ch9.Rhistory"
+ )
```

The history is saved in the ch9.Rhistory file and then loaded back into the workspace.

Some Other Functions That Read Textual Data

There are some other functions in the seven core packages of R that read specific kinds of R files that contain textual data. The functions are briefly covered in this section. The `citation()` function returns citation information for a package. The `readCitation()` function is run by the `citation()` function if a CITATION document exists for the package. The `readRegistry()` function (for Windows systems) returns registry keys and hives. The `readRenviron()` function reads environments contained in files on the computer named .Renviron or Renviron.site. (The information here is from the help pages for the functions.)

For more information about the functions in this section, use the RStudio Help tab or enter *?name* at the R prompt, where *name* is the name of the function (without parentheses, e.g., ?readCitation).

The load() and attach() Functions

The `load()` function is used to load objects saved externally by the `save()` function. When saved using `save()`, objects are saved in binary format by default. For this reason, the two functions are preferred to the use of `dput()` and `dget()` to save and load objects. The objects are loaded into the workspace under the name used when they were saved.

The `load()` function has three arguments. The arguments are **file**, for the name of the file or connection to be read; **envir**, for the environment into which to load the objects; and **verbose,** for whether to list the names of the objects that are loaded.

The **file** argument takes a character string or a one-element object of the `character` or `connection` class, where the string or object of the `character` class contains the address of a file and the object of the `connection` class contains a binary connection object (if default values are used in `load()` and `save()`). There is no default value for **file**.

The **envir** argument takes an object of the `environment` class. The default value of **envir** is parent.frame(), which returns the name of the environment from which `load()` was called.

The **verbose** argument takes a logical value. If set to TRUE, the names of the objects that are loaded are listed. If set to FALSE, nothing is printed during the loading. The default value of **verbose** is FALSE.

An example of calling `load()` is

```
save(
  atl.strm,
  atl.strm.plot.fun,
  file="ch9.ldex.bin"
)
load(
  "ch9.ldex.bin"
)
load(
  "ch9.ldex.bin",
  verbose=TRUE
)
```

Here, the atl.strm and atl.strm.plot.fun objects had been saved in the external file ch9.ldex.bin.

The `attach()` function, among other things, can be used to give access to R objects saved to a file on the computer by the `save()` function. The R objects are not actually loaded, but the computer file is put in the search stream. (To see the search stream, enter `search()` at the R prompt.)

The function takes four arguments. The arguments are **what**, for the address of the external file to be attached; **pos**, for the position at which to put the data file in the search stream; **name**, for the name to use for the attached data file; and **warn.conflicts**, for whether to warn you if there are objects of the same name elsewhere in the search stream.

The **what** argument takes a character string, or a one-element object of the character type, containing the address of the computer file. There is no default value for **what**.

The **pos** argument takes a positive integer value giving the position at which to put the computer file. The default value of **pos** is 2L (for the second position in the search stream.)

The **name** argument takes a character string, or a one-element object of the character type, containing an arbitrary name. The default value of **name** is deparse1(substitute(what), backtick=FALSE).

The **warn.conflicts** argument takes a logical value. If set to TRUE, you are warned if the assigned name is already in the search stream. If set to FALSE, you are not warned. The default value of **warn.conflicts** is TRUE.

An example of calling attach() for a file saved with save() is

```
rm(
  atl.strm
)
atl.strm

attach(
  "ch9.ldex.bin",
  name="one"
)
```

The following object is masked _by_ .GlobalEnv:

```
    atl.strm.plot.fun
```

```
nrow(
  atl.strm
)
ls(
  pat="atl.strm"
)
```

```
detach(
  one
)
atl.strm
Error: object 'atl.strm' not found
```

Here, atl.strm is removed from the workspace, but atl.strm.plot.fun is not. After ch9.ldex.bin is attached, atl.strm is accessible to the workspace. After ch9.ldex.bin is detached, atl.strm is no longer accessible. Note that the attach() function reports that the atl.strm.plot.fun object is already present in the search stream (in the workspace) since **warn.conflicts** is TRUE (the default value).

More information about load() and attach() can be found under the Help tab or by entering **?load** and **?attach**, respectively.

The readRDS() Function

The readRDS() function reads a single object if the object was saved with saveRDS() (which only saves single objects). Files saved with saveRDS() are saved in binary format. The readRDS() function has two arguments: **file**, for the name of the file or connection where the object was saved; and **refhook**, for a hook function.

The argument **file** takes a character string, a one-element object of the character class, or an object of a binary connection class. There is no default value for **file**.

To quote from the help page for readRDS(), the argument **refhook** is set to NULL or to "a hook function for handling reference objects." The default value is NULL.

Here is an example of calling readRDS():

```
saveRDS(
  atl.strm.plot.fun,
  "ASPF"
)
rm(
  atl.strm.plot.fun
)
ls(
  pat="atl.strm.plot.fun"
)

atl.strm.plot.fun = readRDS(
  "ASPF"
  )
ls(
  pat="atl.strm.plot.fun"
)
```

First, the atl.strm.plot.fun object is saved to the ASPE file using saveRDS(). Then, the object is removed from the workspace. Last, the file is loaded back into the workspace using readRDS(). (The atl.strm.plot.fun object is a function, not a dataset.)

More information about readRDS() can be found by using the Help tab in RStudio or by entering **?readRDS** at the R prompt.

The readBin( ), readChar( ), and unserialize( ) Functions

The `readBin()`, `readChar()`, and `unserialize()` functions read binary and raw data from connections. The `readBin()` function reads any kind of binary or raw file. The `readChar()` function reads both text and binary data but gives a warning if text is read. The `unserialize()` function reads files generated by the `serialize()` function.

The `readBin()` function has six arguments. The arguments are **con**, for the connection name; **what**, for the atomic type or class of the data to be read; **n**, for the number of records to be read; **size**, for the number of bytes in a record; **signed**, for whether to consider integers as having signs; and **endian**, for how the bytes are stored in the computer.

The **con** argument takes a character string with the address of a file (containing binary or raw data), an object of the `connection` type, or a character string containing raw data. There is no default value for **con**.

The **what** argument can take a value of a given type or class (i.e., a value of the `raw`, `logical`, `integer`, `double`, `numeric`, `complex`, or `character` type or class), an empty function call to one of the atomic types or classes (e.g., character()), or a character string containing the name of the type or class (e.g., "character"). The **what** argument has no default value.

The **n** argument takes an integer value and can be larger than the number of records in the connection (or file, or character string) being read. According to the help page for `readBin()`, R saves room for the amount of data specified by **n** (and **size**; see below). The default value of **n** is 1L.

The **size** argument takes an integer value giving the number of bytes in a record. The default value of size is NA_integer_. According to the help page for `readBin()`, R uses the "natural" number of bytes by default, and **size** cannot be changed from the default for `raw` and `complex` types of data.

The **signed** argument takes a logical value. If these three conditions are true: (1) **signed** is set to TRUE, (2) **what** equals an integer, integer(), or the character string, "integer", and (3) **size** equals one or two, then the integers are signed (can be negative). If **signed** is set to FALSE and the second two conditions are true, the integers are unsigned (are nonnegative). If **what** is not an integer, integer(), or "integer", **signed** is ignored (all according to the help page for readBin()).

The **endian** argument takes one of two character strings, "little" or "big", or a function that returns one of the two character string. The value is platform specific. The default value of **endian** is .Platform$endian, which returns "little" on my macOS system, my Windows 10 system, and my Linux Mint system.

The readChar() function has three arguments. The arguments are **con**, for the connection; **nchars**, for the number of characters to read; and **useBytes**, for whether to count characters or bytes in locales in which characters have more than one byte.

The **con** argument takes a character string containing the address of a binary or text file, an object that has been set equal to a connection function, or vector of the raw type. There is no default value for **con**.

The **nchars** argument takes a vector of nonnegative integers. The function consecutively reads the number of characters given by the elements of the vector and creates a character string for each integer. The function returns a vector of the character strings that are read. (The readChar() argument starts reading a new string wherever the function left off, so the connection is read and put into strings in order.) According to the help page for readChar(), while zero is an acceptable value in the integer vector, NA is not. There is no default value for **nchars**.

The **useBytes** argument takes a logical value. If set to TRUE, **nchars** counts bytes instead of characters for locales that have multibyte characters. If set to FALSE, characters are read. The default value of **useBytes** is FALSE.

An example of running `readBin()` and `readChar()` is

```
writeBin(
  "one, two, three",
  "ch9.rbex.bin"
)

readBin(
  "ch9.rbex.bin",
  character()
)
readBin(
  "ch9.rbex.bin",
  raw(),
  n=100
)

readChar(
  "ch9.rbex.bin",
  nchars=15
)
readChar(
  "ch9.rbex.bin",
  nchars=c( 3, 2, 3, 2, 5 )
)
```

Note that `writeBin()` writes the data while both `readBin()` and `readChar()` can read the data. The **what** argument in `readBin()` and the **nchar** argument in `readChar()` affect how the file is read.

The `unserialize()` function has two arguments. The arguments are **connection**, for the connection containing the serialized data, and **refhook**, for the hook function, if there is one.

The **connection** argument takes a raw vector, a one-element object of the raw class, or an object of the connection class that has been opened to read a binary connection. The raw vector or object would contain the data or the location of the serialized file to be read. The connection object would be connected to a serialized file. There is no default value for **connection**.

The **refhook** argument takes the value NULL or a hook function. The default value of **refhook** is NULL.

Three examples of calling unserialize are

```
serialize(
  "one, two, three",
  NULL
)
unserialize(
  serialize(
    "one, two, three",
    NULL
  )
)

ch9.serex = serialize(
  "one, two, three",
  connection=NULL
)
unserialize(
  ch9.serex
)

ch9.sercon = gzfile(
  "ch9.serex.bin",
  "wb"
)
```

```
serialize(
  "one, two, three",
  connection=ch9.sercon
)

close(
  ch9.sercon
)
ch9.sercon = gzfile(
  "ch9.serex.bin",
  "rb"
)
unserialize(
  connection=ch9.sercon
)
close(
  ch9.sercon
)
```

In the first example, the **connection** argument is set to NULL, so serialize() returns a raw vector. The call to unserialize() returns the value serialized by serialize(). Nothing is saved.

In the second example, **connection** equals NULL, again, but the result of serialize() is saved to an object in the workspace. The unserialize() function, with the object name as the value of **connection**, returns the value that was serialized.

In the third example, an external binary connection is opened for writing, and a character string is serialized to the file set in the connection. Then the connection is closed, and a binary connect is opened for reading. The unserialize() function, with **connection** set to the connection name, reads the file and returns the original character string. The read connection is then closed.

If the connections are not handled carefully, then errors can occur. You can run `closeAllConnectins()` and start over if you run into errors.

More information about `readBin()`, `readChar()`, or `unserialize()` can be found under the Help tab in RStudio or by entering **?readBin, ?readChar()**, or **?serialize** at the R prompt, respectively.

R Datasets and the library( ), attach( ), and data( ) Functions

Many of the packages in R come with datasets. A dataset can be an atomic object, a data frame, or another kind of list. Some datasets are found in the **datasets** package, which is one of the packages installed by default in R. We use the datasets package to illustrate the three functions covered in this section.

To access the datasets in the **datasets** package, check the box to the left of **datasets** under the Packages tab in RStudio or enter **library(datasets)** at the R prompt. To see the datasets in the **datasets** package, select **datasets** under the Packages tab in RStudio or enter **library(help=datasets)** at the R prompt. Once the library is loaded, the datasets in **datasets** are accessible. (For any library, once the library is loaded, the datasets in the library are accessible like any object in the workspace.)

You can use the `attach()` function to attach a specific dataset and get easy access to variables in a dataset (which can be in a package or in the workspace). If accessing a dataset in a package, the package must be installed but need not be loaded. Only datasets that are data frames or some other kinds of lists can be attached. (Environments can also be attached.) See the "The load() and attach() Functions" section for the arguments to `attach()`.

The `attach()` function attaches the dataset into a position in the search stream. The first position (position 1) of the search stream is the workspace. By default, the `attach()` call attaches the dataset in the second position and pushes the other items in the search stream up one position. The position at which to attach the dataset may also be specified in the call to attach() by setting the **pos** argument.

When searching for an object, R uses the first object with the given name that R finds in the search stream, starting the search with the first position. When attaching the dataset, unless a dataset is part of a loaded package, both the package and the dataset name are required, separated by two colons and unquoted (e.g., **attach(loo::milk)**). Attached datasets should be detached after you are done with them (e.g., **detach(loo::milk)**.

Once a dataset has been attached, the variables in the dataset are accessible by name, if there are not already variables existing in the search stream with the name. If variables in the search stream exist with the name, the variable must be referenced with the package and dataset names (e.g., colorspace::USSouthPolygon$x). The USSouthPolygon dataset in the colorspace package has the x, y, and z variables.

Two examples of attaching a dataset and referencing a variable in the dataset are

Example 1.

```
search()
names(
  loo::milk
)
attach(
  loo::milk
)

search()
loo::milk$mass[ 1:5 ]
mass[ 1:5 ]
```

Example 2.

```
names(
  colorspace::USSouthPolygon
)
attach(
  colorspace::USSouthPolygon
)

search()
colorspace::USSouthPolygon$x[ 1:5 ]
x

detach(
  colorspace::USSouthPolygon
)
detach(
  loo::milk
)
search()
```

In the first example, the names() function returns the names of the variables in the milk dataset. The names of the variables in the dataset are not masked (are not present elsewhere in the search stream.) The mass variable in the milk dataset, which is in the loo package, can be referenced by mass or loo::milk$mass.

In the second example, the names of the variables in the USSouthPolygon dataset are masked by variables in the workspace. So the x variable in the USSouthPolygon dataset, which is in the colorspace package, must be referenced by colorspace::USSouthPolygon$x. Both datasets that were attached are detached at the end of the second example.

The data() function can load objects that are in packages that have been installed and can list datasets that are available in the search stream. However, the function is "under construction." Not everything works.

(According to the help page for `data()`, files that have been saved on the computer with the extensions .R, .r, .RData, .rda, .tab, .txt, .TXT, .csv, or .CSV can be loaded with `data()`, but I have not been able to figure out how to do so given the instructions on the help page.)

The arguments to `data()` are ..., for objects to be loaded; **list**, for a list of objects to be loaded; **package**, for the packages in which to look for the objects; **lib.loc**, for the locations on the computer of the packages or external files containing the objects; **verbose**, for outputting extra information about the loading of the objects; and **envir**, for the environment into which to put the objects when loaded.

The **...** argument takes character strings, or objects of the `character` type, containing the names of objects to be loaded. The values are separated by commas in the call. The objects can be in any installed package. There is no default value for **...**.

The **list** argument contains the same type of information as the **...** argument, but in the form of a list of character vectors. The default value for **list** is character().

The **package** argument takes a vector of the `character` type and lets you specify in which package(s) to look for the objects. The default value of **package** is NULL, that is, all packages and files in the search stream are searched.

The **lib.loc** argument takes a vector of the `character` type and gives the location(s) of the R library(ies) in which to look. The default value of **lib. loc** is NULL, that is, libraries known by R are searched.

The **verbose** argument takes a logical value. If set to TRUE, R returns information about the call that is not normally given. If set to FALSE, the extra information is not returned.

The **envir** argument takes a value of the `environment` class and gives the environment into which the objects are to be put. By default, **envir** is set to .GlobalEnv.

An example of loading a specific dataset into the workspace is

```
library(
  datasets
)
airmiles
ls(
  pattern="air"
)
data(
  "airmiles",
  package="datasets"
)
ls(
  pattern="air"
)
```

The airmiles dataset is available when dataset is loaded but is not in the workspace. The call to data() puts airmiles in the workspace.

If data() is called with neither of the first two arguments set to a value(s), R searches the search list for datasets. The object that is returned is of the packageIQR class, which class, according to the help page for data(), is under development. Currently, if there are no datasets in the given search stream, data() returns "no data sets found." If there are datasets present, data() returns a four-element list quietly (without outputting the list). The names of the four elements of the list that is returned quietly are "title", "header", "results", and "footer". To see the names of the datasets that were found, append **$results** to the data() call.

This second example looks for datasets in the graphics and colorspace packages:

```
data(
  package="graphics"
)
data(
  package="graphics"
)$results

data(
  package="colorspace"
)
data(
  package="colorspace"
)$results
```

Note that the calls to data() with **$results** appended returned a list with the elements "Package", "LibPath", "Item", and "Title". For the graphics package, the list is empty, since there are no datasets in the graphics package. For the colorspace package, there are two datasets: USSouthPolygon and max_chroma_table.

More information about the three functions can be found by using the Help tab in RStudio or by entering **?load** for load(), **?attach** for attach(), or **?data** for data() at the R prompt.

Probability Distributions and the Function sample( )

R has a wealth of random number generators. For most of the random number generators in the stats package, the random number generator is one of four functions associated with a probability distribution. All four functions are covered here and have the same basic form for most of the probability distributions.

(Note that the random number generator seed can be set using the set.seed() function. See the help page for Random for information about the functions related to random number generation, including set.seed().)

Probability Distributions

For most of the probability distributions in the **stats** package, there are four functions associated with a distribution: *ddist()*, *pdist()*, *qdist()*, and *rdist()*, where *dist* describes the distribution. For example, for the normal distribution, *dist* equals **norm**, so the functions are dnorm(), pnorm(), qnorm(), and rnorm(). Not all distributions have all four.

The first function is the function for the density of the probability distribution. The function, *ddist()*, gives the heights of the probability density function at specified values of a vector of numbers. Here, *dist* is the name of the distribution.

The second function, *pdist()*, returns values of the cumulative probability distribution. The function, by default, gives the areas under the probability density function to the left of and including the specified values of a vector of numbers. Here, *dist* is the name of the distribution.

The third function returns quantiles. The function, *qdist()*, takes a vector of probabilities as the first argument. If the distribution is continuous, by default, *qdist()* gives the values on the real line for which the areas to the left of the values equal the probabilities in the vector. If the distribution is discrete, the function returns the values for which the cumulative probabilities including the outcomes of lesser value than the values are less than the probabilities in the vector and, when the values are included, the cumulative probabilities are greater than or equal to the probabilities in the vector. Here, *dist* is the name of the distribution.

The fourth function is the random number generator. The function, *rdist()*, generates a given number of pseudorandom variables from the distribution.

For the first three functions, the vectors can be vectors of length one. For the fourth function, the first argument should be a numeric vector of length one.

The four functions have arguments to specify the standard parameters of the given distribution. For many of which there are defaults, for example, for the normal distribution, the arguments are **mean** and **sd** and are set equal to **0** and **1** by default. (Both the variables **mean** and **sd** can be entered as vectors and will cycle. The vectors must be numeric or logical. Logical vectors are coerced to numeric.) The distribution names used in the **stats** package are given in Table 9-1 along with the parameter arguments for the distributions.

Table 9-1. *Probability Distributions in the Stats Package*

Distribution name in R	Parameters of the distribution
beta	shape1, shape2, npc=0
binom	size, prob
birthday	classes=365, coincident=2 (for qbirthday(), instead of setting p, prob, with a default value of 0.5, is set)
cauchy	location=0, scale=1
chisq	df, npc=0
exp	rate=1
f	df1, df2, npc
gamma	shape, rate=1, scale=1/rate
geom	Prob
hyper	m, n, k
lnorm	meanlog=0, sdlog=1
multinom	size, prob (prob=NULL for dmultinom())
nbinom	size, prob, mu
norm	mean=0, sd=1
pois	lambda
signrank	n
t	df, ncp
tukey	nmeans, df, nranges=1
unif	min=0, max=1
weibull	shape, scale=1
wilcox	m, n

The prefixes are d, p, q, and r. The multinom function only has d and r. The tukey function only has p and q. The birthday function only has p and q and does not have a log.p argument. (From the CRAN help page for distributions.)

For the four functions, the first argument is required and does not have a default. For the density functions, the first argument **x** is a vector of real numbers or values that can be coerced to real numbers. For the cumulative probability functions, the first argument **q** is also a vector of real numbers or values that can be coerced to real numbers. For the quantile functions, the first argument **p** is a vector of probabilities or values that can be coerced to a value between zero and one inclusive. For the random number generators, the first argument **n** (**nn** for the hypergeometric, sign rank, and Wilcox distributions) is a positive integer, or a value that can be coerced to an integer, that tells R how many numbers to generate.

In general, for the density functions, if the values of the first argument are to be considered as logs of the values of interest, the logical argument **log** is set to **TRUE**. For the probability and quantile functions, the logical argument **log.p** is set to TRUE if the values that are for the probabilities are entered or output as logs of the probabilities. The default values of **log** and **log.p** are FALSE for the distributions that use the arguments.

In general, for the cumulative probability and quantile functions, whether to use the upper tail or the lower tail of the distribution can be set using the logical argument **lower.tail**. If set to TRUE, the probability of the lower tail is found. If set to FALSE, the probability of the upper tail is found. (Lower tails are the area under the distribution function for values less than or equal to the values of the first argument, and upper tails are the area under the distribution function for values greater than the values of the first argument.) The default value of **lower.tail** is TRUE.

Also, in general, parameters can be entered as vectors and will cycle. If an illegal value for a parameter is entered, the functions give an error. An example of calling the four functions for the binomial distribution is

```
round(
    dbinom(
        0:5,
        5,
        0.4
    ),
    3
)
round(
    pbinom(
        0:5,
        5,
        0.4
    ),
    3
)
qbinom(
    0:5/5,
    5,
    0.4
)
rbinom(
    6,
    5,
    0.4
+ )
```

Here, the sample size equals five, and the probability of a success equals 0.4. The possible outcomes are zero, one, two, three, four, or five successes. The dbinom() function returns the probability of each outcome. The pbinom() function returns the cumulative probability distribution of the possible outcomes (e.g., the probability of zero or one success is 0.337). The qbinom() function returns the outcomes associated with the probabilities 0.0, 0.2, 0.4, 0.6, 0.8, and 1.0 (using the cumulative probabilities associated with the six outcomes). The rbinom() function returns six pseudorandom values from the binomial distribution.

Use the Help tab in RStudio or enter **?distribution** at the R prompt for the help page on the distributions and generators in the **stats** package. The other six base packages do not contain probability distribution functions. Some other packages do. Many of the distributions in other packages can be found at the website https://cran.r-project.org/web/views/Distributions.html. For more information about a specific probability distribution, use the Help tab in RStudio or enter **?d*dist*** at the R prompt, where *dist* is the name of the distribution from Table 9-1 (except for the tukey and birthday distributions, for which **?p*dist*** works).

The sample() Function

Sometimes, a random sample is needed rather than random numbers. The sample() function takes a random sample of atomic objects, list objects, or any other mode object for which length is defined.

The sample() function takes four arguments. The first argument, **x**, is the object to be sampled. If **x** is a single positive real number greater than one, sample() samples from the sequence from 1 to the real number rounded down to an integer. If **x** is an object that can be coerced to a vector or a single positive number and no other arguments are given, sample() returns a permutation of the object or of the sequence from one to **x** rounded down to an integer, respectively. There is no default value for **x**.

The second argument, **size**, is the number of items to be sampled. The **size** argument can be a nonnegative integer or a real number that can be rounded down to a nonnegative integer. There is no default value for **size**. If **size** is not set, **size** is set to the length of **x**, if the length of **x** is greater than one, or to **x,** if **x** is set to one nonnegative number.

The third argument is the logical argument **replace**, which tells `sample()` whether to sample with replacement. If set to TRUE, the sampling is with replacement. If set to FALSE, the sampling is without replacement. (If **size** is larger than the length of **x, or x if x is an integer**, and **replace** is **FALSE**, then `sample()` gives an error.) The default value of **replace** is **FALSE**, which is to sample without replacement.

The fourth argument is **prob** and gives a list of weights for the sampling. The **prob** argument must be one of the following: (1) NULL; (2) a vector that can be coerced to numeric of the same length as **x** (if the length of **x** is greater than one); or (3) a vector that can be coerced to numeric of length given by the value of **x** rounded down to an integer (if **x** is a single number). The value of **prob** must have elements that can be coerced to nonnegative numeric elements and for which at least half of the coerced elements are nonzero. The coerced elements of **prob** need not sum to one.

For example:

```
sample(
  10
)
sample(
  10,
  5
)
```

```
sample(
  c( "a1", "a2", "a3" ),
  6,
  replace=TRUE
)
sample(
  11:21,
  prob=1:11
)
```

More information about sample() can be found by using the Help tab in RStudio or by entering **?sample** at the R prompt.

Manually Entering Data and Generating Data with Patterns

Data can be entered manually using the c() function (where the **c** stands for *collect*). Sometimes, data with a certain pattern is needed, for example, in setting up indices for matrix or array manipulation or as input to functions. There are a few of the functions in R that give patterned results, which results can be useful. Sometimes, indexed names are needed for dimensions in a vector, matrix, or array. The paste() function can be used to create indexed names.

The c( ) Function

The c() function collects objects together into a single object. The objects to be collected are separated by commas within the call to c(). The objects can be expressions of the NULL, raw, logical, integer, numeric, character, list, and expression classes and/or objects of the above-listed classes. Objects can also be functional calls that return any of the aforementioned classes.

If all of the objects in the call are atomic objects, the c() function collects the objects into a vector of the elements making up the objects. The class of the resulting vector is the highest level class within the elements of the vector, where the levels of the classes increase in the order NULL, raw, logical, integer, double, complex, and character.

An example of the hierarchy follows:

```
rw = as.raw(
   c( 36, 37, 38, 39 )
)
rw
c(
    rw,
    rw
)
c(
    rw,
    TRUE
)
c(
    rw,
    40L
)
c(
    rw,
    40.5
)
c(
    rw,
    1+1i
)
```

```
c(
  rw,
  "six"
)
```

The conversion from `raw` is automatic except for the conversion to `character`, which maintains the `raw` values.

The `c()` function has two possible named arguments. The arguments are **recursive**, for whether to treat lists recursively, and **use.names**, for whether to keep names for named values.

The **recursive** argument takes a logical value. If **recursive** is set to **TRUE** and the collection contains a list but not an expression, then the list is taken apart to the lowest level of the individual elements in the list and a vector of atomic elements is returned. The object takes on the class of the highest level of class in the object. If **recursive** is **FALSE**, the resulting object becomes a list. The default value of **recursive** is **FALSE**.

The **use.names** argument also takes a logical value. If set to TRUE, the elements of the vector that is returned by `c()` retain the names that they are assigned in the call. If set to FALSE, the names are dropped. The default value of **use.names** is TRUE.

Names can be assigned to the elements of the object created by `c()` by setting the elements equal to a name in the listing, for example:

```
c(
  a=1,
  b=2,
  3
)
```

Here, the first two elements are assigned the names a and b, while the third element is not assigned a name.

In the hierarchy of classes, `list` is above the atomic classes but below `expression`. If an expression is included in the call to `c()`, then the result has the `expression` class.

An example for objects of class list and expression follows:

```
ch9.lst2 = list(
  matrix(
    1:4,
    2,
    2,
    dimnames=list(
      NULL,
      c( "cl1", "cl2" )
    )
  ),
  c(
    "abc",
    "cde"
  )
)
c(
  ch9.lst2,
  1:2
)
c(
  ch9.lst2,
  1:2,
  recursive=TRUE
)
```

```
ch9.expr = expression(

  y ~ x,
  `1`
)
c(
  ch9.lst2,
  ch9.expr
)
```

In the first call to c(), an object of the list class is returned. In the second call, an object of the character class is returned. In the third call, an object of the expression class is returned.

More information about c() can be found by using the Help tab in RStudio or by entering **?c** at the R prompt.

The seq() and rep() Functions

The seq() and rep() functions are used for sequences and repeated patterns. In the simplest form, using seq() is the same as using the colon operator to create a sequence. However, seq() can create a more sophisticated sequence than the colon operator. The rep() function repeats the first argument to the function a specified number of times, where there are two possible ways to do the repetition.

The seq() Function

The seq() function has six arguments. The first two arguments are the starting and ending values of the sequence and are named **from** and **to**. The **from** and **to** arguments can take logical and numeric values. For logical values, **TRUE** is coerced to one, and **FALSE** is coerced to zero. Both **from** and **to** are set to 1 by default.

The third argument is **by**. The **by** argument gives the value by which to increment the sequence. The argument can take logical and numeric values; however, it cannot equal **FALSE** since **FALSE** coerces to zero and **by** cannot equal zero. The argument does not have to divide into the difference between **to** and **from** evenly. The sequence will stop at the largest value less than or equal to **to** if **to** is greater than **from** (except when the largest value is just a tad larger than **to** and rounding brings the number down to **to**). If **to** is less than **from**, then **by** must be negative, and the sequence stops at the smallest value greater than or equal to **to** (with the exception that a value just a tad smaller will round up). The default value of **by** is ((to-from)/(length.out-1)), if **by** is not set.

The fourth argument is **length.out**. The **length.out** argument can be used in place of **by**. The argument takes a single value that can be NULL, TRUE, or a positive number and gives the length of the sequence to be output. If **length.out** is a number but not an integer, the number is rounded up to an integer. By default, **length.out** is set to **NULL** (i.e., **length.out** is 1+(to-from)/by if **by** is set or length(along.with) if **along.with** is set).

The fifth argument is **along.with**. The **along.with** argument is also used in place of **by**. The argument takes any object that is a vector. The length of the sequence to be output is given by the length of **along.with**. The default value of **along.with** is NULL.

Only one of **by**, **length.out**, and **along.with** is set. The sixth argument is the **...** argument, for arguments to other methods called within the call to seq().

Some examples follow:

```
seq(
  -3.3
)
```

Entering just one value without a name gives a sequence from one to the largest integer less than or equal to the value for positive values or the smallest integer greater than or equal to the value if the value is negative.

```
seq(
    3,
    10
)
```

When two values are entered without names, the first is interpreted as the **from** value, the second is interpreted as the **to** value, and **by** is set equal to one.

```
seq(
    3,
    10,
    2
)
```

When three values are entered without names, the first is interpreted as the **from** value, the second is interpreted as the **to** value, and the third is interpreted as the **by** value.

```
seq(
    3,
    10,
    len=5
)
```

Here, **length.out** is shortened to **len**. Five equally spaced values are returned.

```
seq(
  3,
  10,
  along=c( 1, 2, 1, 2 , 1 )
)
```

Here, **along.with** is shortened to **along**. Again, five equally spaced values are returned.

```
seq(
  c( 1, 2, 1, 2 )
)
```

If a vector with more than one element is entered as the only argument, a sequence starting with one is created. The **by** argument equals one, and the length of the result equals the length of the vector.

```
seq(
  len=4
)
seq(
  7,
  along=c( 1, 2, 1, 2 )
)
seq(
  7,
  len=4
)
```

Entering **length.out** or **along.with** alone or with a value for **from** returns a vector starting with the value of **from** and with **by** equal to 1. The length of the result will be correct.

For long sequences, there are lower-level functions that are faster than seq() (see the help page for seq()). For information about seq(), use the Help tab in RStudio or enter **?seq** at the R prompt.

The rep() Function

The rep() function repeats the first argument in a pattern determined by the other arguments. The first argument can be any type of object that can be coerced to a vector. The other three arguments are **times**, **each**, and **length.out**. The default values for **times**, **each**, and **length.out** are **1**, **1**, and **NA**, respectively.

The **times** argument is a vector of values that can be coerced to integer. The argument must be either a single value or of the same length as the first argument. If the argument takes a single value, the first argument is repeated the number of times of the single value.

If the **times** argument is of length equal to the length of the first argument, then each element of the first argument is repeated the number of times indicated by the corresponding element of the **times** argument. The **times** argument is the second argument to rep(), for example:

```
rep(
  0,
  5
)
rep(
  1:3,
  3
)
```

```
rep(
  1:3,
  2:4
)
```

Here, the second argument is not explicitly called **times**, but **times** implicitly takes on the value.

The **each** argument can be any object that can be coerced to a vector of integers, where the first element is nonnegative. Only the first element of the object is used. The argument tells rep() to repeat each element of the first argument the value of **each** times, for example:

```
rep(
  1:3,
  each=3
)
```
```
rep(
  1:3,
  each=3,
  times=2
)
rep(
  rep(
    1:3,
    times=2:4
  ),
  each=2
)rep(
```

```
rep(
  1:3,
  times=2:4
),
times=2
)
```

The last argument is **length.out**. The argument can take any value that can be coerced to an integer vector and for which the first element is nonnegative. Only the first element is used. If **length.out** is set to a value, only the number of elements given by the value of the argument is returned. For example:

```
rep(
  rep(
    1:3,
    times=2:4
  ),
  times=2,
  len=10
)
```

Here, **length.out** is shortened to **len**.

More information about rep() can be found under the Help tab in RStudio or by entering **?rep** at the R prompt.

Combinatorics and Grid Expansion

Combinatorics is a subject about the combinations that can be made from a set of discrete values. Combinations are all of the combinations that are possible from a discrete set of values for a given number of elements in each combination, where no element is repeated. Permutations are the set of all possible permutations of a given size from a discrete set of elements. Grid expansion is about the expansion of different sets of elements so that each element of each set is linked with every element of the other sets.

Probably the easiest way to see what the combinations, permutations, and grid expansion involve is by showing some examples. Three functions that are relevant are combn(), permsn() (which is in the prob library), and expand.grid().

The combn() function takes five arguments. The arguments are **x**, for the discrete set from which the combinations are formed; **m**, for the number of elements to include in each combination; **FUN**, for an optional function to operate on the elements of the combinations; **simplify**, for whether to return a vector or matrix or to return a list; and **...**, for any arguments to the value of FUN.

The **x** argument can take either a single positive integer or any object that can be coerced to a vector. If **x** is a single positive integer, the sequence from one to **x** becomes the discrete set. The **x** argument has no default value.

The **m** argument takes a nonnegative number that is less than or equal to the length of **x** if **x** is a vector and less than or equal to **x** if **x** is a single positive integer. If **m** is not an integer, the number is rounded down to an integer. If **m** equals zero, a single zero is returned by combn(). The **m** argument has no default value.

The **FUN** argument takes either NULL or the name of a function (unquoted and without parentheses). The default value of FUN is NULL.

The **simplify** argument takes a logical value. If set to **TRUE**, a vector or matrix is returned. If **FALSE**, a list is returned. The default value is **TRUE**.

The **...** argument contains any arguments necessary for the value of **FUN**.

Two examples of calling `combn()` are

```
combn(
  1:3,
  2
)
combn(
  3,
  2,
  FUN=sum,
  simplify=FALSE
)
```

Note that the combinations are down in the columns of the matrix in first call to `combn()`. With **simplify** equal to the default value TRUE, a matrix is returned. In the second call, the combinations are the same as in the first call (since **x** equal to 3 is equivalent to **x** equal to 1:3), but **FUN** is set to sum, so each combination is summed, and **simplify** is set to FALSE, so a list is returned.

The `permsn()` function is in the **prob** package. Since the package is not one of the packages installed by default, the package may need to be installed. (See Chapter 1.) If the package is installed, the package must be loaded in RStudio or with

```
library( prob )
```

at the R prompt.

The `permsn()` function has just two arguments, **x** and **m**, which are as described for `combn()`. An example for `permsn()` is

```
library(
  prob
)
```

```
permsn(
  3,
  2
)
```

Note that the permutations are in the columns of the matrix. Also note that while combn() just has the combination (1,2), permsn() includes both (1,2) and (2,1) (and so forth). The permsn() function returns a matrix.

The expand.grid() function has three arguments. The arguments are ..., for the objects out of which to make a grid; **KEEP.OUT.ATTRS**, for whether to keep dimension and dimension name attributes; and **stringsAsFactors**, for whether to convert character vectors to factors.

The ... argument takes objects, separated by commas, that must be able to be coerced to a vector. The function returns the vectors crossed with each other in a data frame. There is no default value for ....

The **KEEP.OUT.ATTRS** argument takes a logical value. If set to TRUE, the attributes are kept. If set to FALSE, the attributes are not kept. The default value of **KEEP.OUT.ATTRS** is TRUE.

The **stringsAsFactors** argument takes a logical value. If set to TRUE, character vectors are converted to factors. If set to FALSE, the character vectors remain as vectors of the character class. The default value of **stringsAsFactors** is TRUE.

An example of calling expand.grid() is

```
expand.grid(
  a=1:2,
  b=3:4,
  c=5:6
)
```

Here, the combinations are across the rows.

More information about combn(), permsn(), and expand.grid() can be found under the Help tab in RStudio or by entering **?combn**, **?prob::permsn**, and **?expand.grid** at the R prompt. Note that if the **prob package** is not installed, the second command will not work.

The paste( ) and paste0( ) Functions

This chapter ends with the paste() and paste0() functions. The functions are used to create character strings out of many types of objects. One of the useful applications of paste() is the creation of dimension names.

Other than the objects to be strung together, which are separated by commas, paste takes three arguments. The arguments are **sep**, for the character(s) to put between the values that are pasted together; **collapse**, for what to put between values if the pasted values are collapsed together; and **recycle0**, for how to process character(0)'s.

The **sep** argument takes a character string or a one-element character object. To set the value to nothing, set **sep** equal to "" or use paste0() rather than paste() (paste0() is the same as paste() except that the separator is always ""). The default value of **sep** is a white space (" ").

The **collapse** argument takes NULL, a character string, or a one-element character vector for a value. The default value of **collapse** is NULL.

The **recycle0** argument takes a logical value. If set to TRUE, character vectors with zero length are processed as is. If set to FALSE, zero length character vectors are set to "". The default value of **recycle0** is FALSE.

Here is an example of three simple applications of paste(). The third example would be appropriate for creating dimension names.

```
paste(
  1:3
)
```

```
paste(
  "a",
  1:3
)
paste0(
  "a",
  1:3
)
```

The next three examples show how **collapse** behaves and how to use **recycle0**.

```
paste0(
  "a",
  1:3,
  collapse=".."
)
paste0(
  character(0),
  1:3,
  recycle0=TRUE
)
> paste0(
  character(0),
  1:3,
  recycle0=FALSE
)
```

You can find more information about paste() under the Help tab in RStudio or by entering **?paste** at the R prompt.

CHAPTER 10

Exporting from R

Being able to export from R makes R more useful. Objects or expressions may be exported to files, connections, or the console and objects. Since RStudio does not have specialized methods for exporting objects (except for documents in the Source subwindow–covered in the last section of Chapter 2), only command line R methods are covered here. In this chapter, we discuss exporting from the command line to external files on the computer, to connections (note that the first section of Chapter 9 gives most of the connection functions and the setting for the connections), and to the console and objects.

There are several functions that export to external files, to connections, and/or to the console and objects, 18 of which we will go over in this chapter. The first function is `sink()`, which sinks output that would normally be displayed at the console to an external file. The output is in text format. Next are the `cat()` and `write()` functions. The `cat()` and `write()` functions write atomic vectors and objects of the `symbol` type to a connection, an external file, or the console, in text format.

For objects that can be coerced to a data frame, the `write.table()`, `write.csv()`, and `write.csv2()` functions write the object to a connection, an external file, or the console (or an object at the console) while maintaining the data frame structure. (The `write.dcf()` and `write.ftable()` functions, listed in Table 10-1, also write tabular data but are not discussed here.) The `writeLines()`, `write.socket()`, and `writeClipboard()` functions write text to, respectively, any kind of connection, a socket connection, and the clipboard (for Windows only).

© Margot Tollefson 2022
M. Tollefson, *R 4 Quick Syntax Reference*, https://doi.org/10.1007/978-1-4842-7924-3_10

The dput() function writes text or a single object, and the dump() function writes one or more named objects. Both write to a connection, a file, or the console (or object) in text format. The savehistory() function saves a copy of the session history to a file on the computer in text format.

The next three functions we discuss are save(), save.image(), and saveRDS(). These functions save objects to a connection or file in binary format, by default, and are the functions of choice to transfer data sets and functions between workspaces. Last, the writeBin(), writeChar(), and serialize() functions write in binary or raw (a text format) format to a connection (which can be to a file on the computer or the console). Note that output at the console can, also, be cut and pasted to an external file.

There are functions that convert data frames to Excel, SPSS, SAS, and Stata formats and a function that writes tabular atomic data more efficiently than write.table() in packages other than the seven core packages. We cover the functions briefly at the end of this chapter.

A table of the importing and exporting functions mentioned in Chapters 9 and 10 is given in Table 10-1. Note that many of the input and output functions are paired.

Connection Functions That Write

Most of the connection functions are covered in the first section of Chapter 9, along with the various ways a connection can be opened. From the help page for connections, only file() and the socket connection functions can be opened for both reading and writing in the same call to the function. (But the help page also says that fifo() can be opened for both.) And that url(), URLs in general, and unz() cannot be opened for writing.

The other connection functions at the help page that can be opened for writing are gzfile(), bzfile(), xzfile(), and pipe(). Also from the help page, to open a connection to the clipboard for writing in the macOS operating system, assign **pipe("pbcopy", "w")** to an object. And in

Linux, **pipe("xclip -i", "w")** opens the clipboard for writing. The function `writeClipboard()` can be used for Windows (see "The writeLines(), write. socket(), and writeClipboard() Functions" section of this chapter).

The `stdout()` and `stderr()` functions connect to the console and are used to write to the console (and can sink output or error messages to a file when used with the `sink()` function; see below). The `stdout()` function writes output, and the `stderr()` function writes error messages. Neither has any arguments, and neither can be opened or closed. Both are always open.

The sink( ) Function

The **sink()** function sends output from command line entries to a file or connection. The **sink()** function continues writing as commands are entered and return output until **sink()** or **sink(NULL)** is entered at the R prompt. The function takes four arguments: **file**, **append**, **type**, and **split**.

The **file** argument tells `sink()` where to write the output. If writing to an external file on the computer, the write location is a character argument containing a computer address within quotes. The address can be relative to the workspace folder or absolute. Otherwise, file is set to a connection (which can be opened for writing). (Note that the option **file=""** is not acceptable for `sink()`.)

The second argument, **append**, tells `sink()` whether to append or overwrite the file or connection. The argument takes a logical value. For **append** equal to **TRUE**, the file or connection is appended. For **FALSE**, the file or connection is overwritten. The default value of **append** is **FALSE**.

The third argument, **type**, tells `sink()` which of two possible streams to sink. The argument takes a character string, which can be **"output"** or **"message"**. For **"output"**, the output stream is sent to the file. For **"message"**, any messages generated by the command are sent to the file. The default value of **type** is **"output"**.

The fourth argument, **split**, takes a logical value that tells sink() how to split the stream. If set to **TRUE**, the output stream is sent to both the file and the console. If **FALSE**, the output stream is not sent to the console. The default value of **split** is **FALSE**.

An example of the use of sink() follows:

```
> sink(
+    "ch10.f1.txt"
+ )
> round(
+    rnorm( 5 ),
+    3
+ )
> sink()
> system(
+    "cat ch10.f1.txt"
+ )
[1]  0.795  0.568 -0.704  1.291  0.817
```

In the example, five standard normal pseudorandom variates, rounded to three decimal places, are sunk to the "ch10.f1.txt" file. The contents of the file are returned by the system() function and the operating system cat command. Note that the entries at the R prompts are not output to the file.

For more information about sink(), use the Help tab in RStudio or enter **?sink** at the R prompt.

The cat() and write() Functions

The cat() and write() functions write atomic vectors and objects of the symbol type to a file, connection, or the console (or object). The cat() function writes in a line until the line break characters, "\n", occur or until conditions given by the **fill** argument are met (see below). The write() function writes in tabular format. Both functions write text.

The cat() function has six arguments. The arguments are **...**, **file**, **sep**, **fill**, **labels**, and **append**. (Note that since **...** is the first argument, the other arguments, if set, must be referenced by their full names in a call to the function.) The value(s) of the first argument is output to the console, by default. (The cat() function actually returns NULL and the function does so invisibly, i.e., you can set the call to an object name and the object will contain NULL, but NULL is not visibly returned by the call).

The **...** argument takes values of the atomic types and the symbol type, whether objects or expressions. The values are separated by commas in the argument and are printed out by cat(), without quotes, in a line or lines. There is no default value for **...**.

The **file** argument takes one of the following: a connection either open for writing or able to be opened for writing; a character string giving the address of an existing file on the computer or a file to be written to the computer; a character string containing the pipe symbol and an operating system command (i.e., "|cat ch10.f1.txt"); or a character string containing nothing (i.e., "").

If **file** is an open connection, the function starts writing to the file where R had previously stopped. Otherwise, the connection is opened–with the **open** argument set to "wt" (i.e., open for writing text). According to the help page for cat(), the file is closed after the call.

If **file** is a character string containing a file address, cat() writes to the file. If the character string is a pipe with a command, cat() runs the command in the operating system terminal and returns the result. If set to "", cat() writes to stdout(). The default value of **file** is "".

The **sep** argument takes a character vector of arbitrary length giving the character(s) to separate the values being written. The vector cycles. The default value of **sep** is " " (i.e., a whitespace).

The **fill** argument takes either a single numeric value or a single logical value. If equal to a number greater or equal to one, the number is rounded down to an integer, and the integer gives the maximum width of a line, in character spaces. The value of **sep** is placed to the right of each element

315

and is counted in the count of character spaces, even if a whitespace. So if **fill** is 3, each element is one character, and **sep** is one whitespace, only one element fits on a line. But if **fill** is 4, two elements fit. However, if an element is wider than the value of **fill**, the entire element is printed and does wrap–at least on my MacBook Air computer.

If **fill** equals TRUE, the value of width is what the options() function gives for the value of width (i.e., the line width is the value that entering options("width") at the R prompt returns). On my MacBook Air computer, the value of width depends on the sizing of the console window in RStudio and changes when the window is resized.

If **fill** equals FALSE, there is no limit to the line width and lines wrap if the width of the console (or external file) is exceeded, at least on my MacBook Air computer. A line break occurs when an "\n" occurs, either as part of a larger character string or as an individual element. The default value of **fill** is FALSE.

The **labels** argument takes a character vector of arbitrary length. (The values cycle and extra values do not return an error.) The values are row names for the lines of the output if **fill** does not equal FALSE. Otherwise, **labels** is ignored. The default value of **labels** is NULL.

The **append** argument takes a single logical value and only has an effect if cat() writes to a file on the computer. If set to TRUE, cat() appends the file. If set to FALSE, cat() overwrites the file. The default value of **append** is FALSE.

The values of **…** are entered as single vectors (e.g., as a collection of vectors and expressions collected using c()).

Some examples of setting arguments in cat() are

```
> cat(
+     "zzzzzzz",
+     2:3,
+     "\n"
+ )
```

```
zzzzzzz 2 3

> cat(
+     "zzzzzzz",
+     2:3,
+     fill=3
+ )
zzzzzzz
2
3

> cat(
+   "zzzzzzz",
+   2:3,
+   sep=c( "", "-", "+" ),
+   fill=10,
+   labels=paste0( "row:", 1:3 )
+ )
row:1 zzzzzzz
row:2 2-3

> cat(
+   "zzzzzzz",
+   2:3,
+   file="ch10.f2.txt",
+   fill=TRUE
+ )
> cat(
+   file="|cat ch10.f2.txt"
+ )
zzzzzzz 2 3

> cat(
```

```
+    "zzzzzzz",
+    2:3,
+    file="ch10.f2.txt",
+    fill=TRUE,
+    append=TRUE
+ )
> cat(
+    file="|cat ch10.f2.txt"
+ )
zzzzzzz 2 3
zzzzzzz 2 3
```

In the first call, all the arguments with defaults are set to their default values, so the values in **...** are printed in a line. Since an "\n" is the last value of **...**, cat() returns an end of line. As a result, the second call starts on the next line. Otherwise, the call starts to the right of the values that are printed from the first call.

In the second call, **fill** is set to 3, so each value has a line. In the third call, **sep** is set to a three-element character vector containing an empty string, a string with a minus sign, and a string with a plus sign; **fill** is set to 10; and **labels** is set to three five-character values. So zzzzzzz is on one line, and 2 and 3 share a line. The values 2 and 3 are separated by a minus sign. The two lines are labeled. The third values of **sep** and **labels** are ignored.

In the fourth call, **file** is set to the ch10.f2.txt file name and **fill** is set to TRUE, so one line is written to ch10.f2.txt. The fifth call returns the contents of ch10.f2.txt. In the sixth call, **file** is set to the same file name, **fill** is set to TRUE, and **append** is set to TRUE, so the ch10.f2.txt file is appended with the same line. The seventh call returns the contents of the appended file (i.e., two lines of the same data).

According to the help page for write(), the function is a wrapper for cat(). The function writes an atomic vector, or a vector of the symbol type, in tabular form. The arguments of write() are **x**, **file**, **ncolumns**, **append**, and **sep**. The **file**, **append**, and **sep** arguments are as in cat(), except that the default value of file is "data" rather than the "" in write().

The first argument, **x,** is the vector to be written. The argument is usually an atomic vector but can also be a vector of the symbol type. Atomic vectors are coerced to the type of the highest-level element in the vector, where the type levels, from lowest to highest, are NULL, raw, logical, integer, double, complex, and character.

The second argument is **ncolumns**. The **ncolumns** argument can be logical, numeric, or complex, and if it is not an integer, it is coerced to an integer (see Chapter 4). The argument gives the number of columns for the exported table. By default, the argument takes the value **if(is. character(x)) 1 else 5** (i.e., if the data is of the character type, the output matrix has one column; otherwise, the output matrix has five columns).

The input vector need not be of a length divisible by **ncolumns**. In other words, the last row need not be complete.

An example follows:

```
> x=1:4
> y=5:8
> b = rep(
+    " ",
+    4
+ )
> z=rbind(
+    x,
+    y
+ )
```

```
> w=paste0(
+    "a",
+    1:3
+ )
> write(
+    c(
+      x,
+      y,
+      b,
+      z,
+      b,
+      w
+    ),
+    file="",
+    ncol=4,
+    sep=" + "
+ )
1 + 2 + 3 + 4
5 + 6 + 7 + 8
  +   +   +
1 + 5 + 2 + 6
3 + 7 + 4 + 8
  +   +   +
a1 + a2 + a3
```

Note that when entered separately, **x** and **y** each output as a row. When **x** and **y** are bound together into a two-row matrix using `rbind()`, `write()` goes down the columns to read and writes the result across the rows. Also note that there are four columns as specified by **ncol** and that there are only three elements in the last row.

You can find more information about write() by using the Help tab in RStudio or by entering **?write** at the R prompt.

The write.table() and Related Functions

The write.table(), write.csv(), and write.csv2() functions also export matrices and data frames in tabular text format. The three functions are essentially the same function, but with different defaults. All of the defaults for write.table() can be changed. For write.csv() and write.csv2(), the default values for **append**, **col.names**, **sep**, **dec**, and **qmethod** cannot be changed.

The functions have 12 arguments. The arguments are **x**, **file**, **append**, **quote**, **sep**, **eol**, **na**, **dec**, **row.names**, **col.names**, **qmethod**, and **fileEncoding**.

The **x** argument is the object to be exported and must be an object that can be coerced to a data frame. There is no default value for **x**.

The **file** argument gives the location to which to write the data frame. The argument takes a character string containing the address of the file, relative to the workspace or absolute; the empty character string ""; or a connection that is open for writing. If **file** equals "", then the functions export to the console (or to stdout() if stdout() is not the console). The value of **file** is "" by default.

The **append** argument is a logical argument. If **append** is **TRUE**, then the file is appended with the new data frame. If **FALSE**, the file is overwritten. The default value of **append** is **FALSE**.

The **quote** argument is either logical or a numeric vector of column numbers and gives rules for placing quotes around elements. If set to TRUE, in the columns of the data frame that contain character type values, the values are quoted, as are the row names, and the column names. If set to an integer vector of column numbers, only the row names, the column names, and those columns containing `character` type data and corresponding to a number in the vector are quoted. If set to **FALSE**, nothing is quoted. The default value of **quote** is **TRUE**.

The **sep** argument is a character argument and gives the separator to be used between the elements of the exported data. The separator is entered within quotes. For `write.table()`, `write.csv()`, and `write.csv2()`, the default values of **sep** are a whitespace, a comma, and a semicolon, respectively (i.e., " ", ",", and ";").

The **eol** argument is an argument of the `character` type and gives the end of line delineator. The correct value for **eol** varies with the operating system. By default, **eol** is equal to "\n".

The **na** argument is also a character argument and gives the string to be output where data is missing. The default value is "NA".

The **dec** argument is another character argument and gives the character to be used as the decimal point. By default, **dec** equals "." for `write.table()` and `write.csv()` and equals "," for `write.csv2()`.

The **row.names** argument is either a logical value or a character vector of row names of length equal to the number of rows. Note that if **row.names** is set to **TRUE** or to a character vector of names, `write.table()` treats the row names differently than `write.csv()` and `write.csv2()`. If a column of row names is in the data frame to be exported, the `write.table()` function does not create a blank character string for the name of the row name column, while `write.csv()` and `write.csv2()` do. If **row.names** is equal to **FALSE**, there is no difference between the two with regard to row names since no row names are exported.

If no row names are given, row names are not present in the data frame (e.g., if a matrix without row names is entered for **x**), and **row.names** is **TRUE**, then the rows are given names, starting with "1" and incrementing by one with each row. By default, **row.names** equals **TRUE**.

The **col.names** argument is either logical or a character vector of column names of length equal to the number of columns. For `write.table()`, if **col.names** is set equal to **TRUE**, either the column names are taken from the data frame or, if no names are present in the data frame, column names are created starting with "V1" and incrementing the integer by one for each new column. If column names are supplied, the column names are set equal to the supplied names.

As noted previously, for `write.table()`, by default, no column name value is given for the column of row names if the row name column exists in the exported file. However, if **col.names** is set equal to **NA**, then columns are treated the same as for **col.names** set equal to **TRUE** except that a blank character string is added for the row name column. If **row.names** equals **FALSE**, then setting **col.names** equal to **NA** gives an error. If **col.names** is set equal to **FALSE**, no column names are assigned in the exported file. The default value of **col.names** for `write.table()` is TRUE.

For `write.csv()` and `write.csv2()`, the default value for **col.names** depends on the value of **row.names**. The default cannot be changed. If **row.names** equals **TRUE**, **col.names** is set to **NA**. Otherwise, **col.names** is set equal to **TRUE**. In either case, column names are given by either the names in the data frame or, if there are no column names in the data frame, names starting with "V1" and with the integer incrementing by one for each new column.

The next argument is **qmethod,** which can take the value "escape" or "double". The argument gives instructions for double quoted values. (See the help page for `write.table()` for more information.) The default value of **qmethod** is "escape".

The last argument is **fileEncoding**, which need not be assigned but if assigned tell R how to encode the output (e.g., in UTF-8 format). The default value of **fileEncoding** is "".

Here are some examples (the object `ch10.mat` is a matrix with row and column names):

```
> ch10.mat = matrix(
+    1:4+0.0,
+    2,
```

```
+     2,
+     dimnames=list(
+         c( "r1", "r2" ),
+         c( "c1", "c2" )
+     )
+ )
> ch10.mat
   c1 c2
r1  1  3
r2  2  4

> write.table(
+   ch10.mat
+ )
"c1" "c2"
"r1" 1 3
"r2" 2 4

> write.table(
+   ch10.mat,
+   col.names=NA
+ )
"" "c1" "c2"
"r1" 1 3
"r2" 2 4

> write.table(
+   ch10.mat,
+   col.names=FALSE
+ )
"r1" 1 3
"r2" 2 4
```

```
> write.csv(
+    ch10.mat
+ )
"","c1","c2"
"r1",1,3
"r2",2,4

> write.csv2(
+    ch10.mat,
+    quote=FALSE
+ )
;c1;c2
r1;1;3
r2;2;4
```

First, the ch10.mat matrix is generated, and the contents of the matrix are printed. Then write.table() is called three times; first using default values, second with **col.names** set to NA, and third with **col.names** to FALSE. Last, write.csv() is called using default values, and write.csv2() is called with **quote** set to FALSE.

There are no corresponding write functions for read.delim() and read.delim2(). Tab delineated, tabulated data can be written using the write.table() function and setting **sep** to "\t". The write.dcf() and write.ftable() functions exist, but there are no write functions corresponding to the read.DIF(), read.fortran(), and read.fwf() functions.

To access the help page for write.table(), write.csv(), and write. csv2(), use the Help tab in RStudio or enter **?write.table** at the R prompt.

The writeLines( ), write.socket( ), and writeClipboard( ) Functions

The writeLines(), write.socket(), and writeClipboard() functions write text to a connection. For writeLines(), the connection can be to a file on the computer or to stdout(); for write.socket(), the connection is a socket connection; and for writeClipboard(), the connection is to the computer clipboard (and is used only with Windows operating systems).

The writeLines() function has four arguments. The arguments are **text**, **con**, **sep**, and **useBytes**.

The **text** argument takes a vector of the character type or an object or expression that can be coerced to an atomic vector and that is made up of character elements (e.g., a matrix or array of the character type). There is no default value for **text**.

The **con** argument takes either a writable connection or a character string containing an address on the computer. According to the help page for writeLines(), if set to an address, the function calls the file() function with **description** set equal to the value of **text** and **open** set equal to "wt".

If set to a connection and the connection is already open, writeLines() begins writing to the connection where the previous writing had stopped. Otherwise, the connection is just opened. When the call is done, whether **con** is set to a character string or a connection, the connection is closed (all according to the help page for writeLines()). The default value of **con** is stdout().

The **sep** argument gives the value of the separator to be written between the elements of **text** and can take any character vector. (If longer than one element, writeLines() only uses the first element of the vector and no warning is given.) The default value of **sep** is "\n", which (according to the help page for writeLines()) generates the line feed character used by the operating system. So each element of the character vector is on a different line.

The **useBytes** argument tells writeLines() how to handle bytes when writing characters and takes a logical value. See the help page for writeLines() for the effect of setting the value to TRUE. The help page says that the value of FALSE is appropriate for most tasks that do not require expertise. The default value of **useBytes** is FALSE.

Some examples of calling writeLines() are

```
> ch10.vec.chr = c(
+    "one",
+    "two"
+ )
> ch10.vec.chr
[1] "one" "two"

> writeLines(
+      ch10.vec.chr
+ )
one
two

> writeLines(
+      ch10.vec.chr,
+      sep="\t"
+ )
one    two

> writeLines(
+      ch10.vec.chr,
+      sep="-+-"
+ )
one-+-two-+-

> writeLines(
+      ch10.vec.chr,
```

```
+      con="ch10.wl.txt",
+      sep="-+-\n"
+    )
> cat(
+      file="| cat ch10.wl.txt"
+ )
one-+-
two-+-

> wlcon = file(
+      "ch10.wl.txt",
+      open="at"
+ )

> writeLines(
+      ch10.vec.chr,
+      con=wlcon,
+      sep="-+-"
+ )

> close( wlcon )
> cat(
+    file="| cat ch10.wl.txt"
+ )
one-+-
two-+-
one-+-two-+-
```

First, the character vector ch10.vec.chr is generated and printed. Then writeLines() is called with **text** set equal to ch10.vec.chr and with default values for the other arguments. The elements of ch10.vec.chr are written on separate lines and are unquoted.

In the second call, **sep** is set to "\t", so the elements are on one line and each is appended with a tab. In the third call, sep is set to "-+-", so the elements are on one line and -+- is appended to each element.

In the fourth call, **con** is set to "ch10.wl.txt" and **sep** to "-+-\n". The elements are written to the "ch10.wl.txt" file in two lines with -+- appended to each element.

In the fifth call, **con** is set equal to a connection generated by the file() function with **description** equal to "ch10.wl.txt" and **open** equal to "at" (for appending the file). The **sep** argument is set to "-+-". Note that the connection must be closed before the vector is written to the file. The writeLines() function appends one line to the file. The line contains one-+-two-+-.

The write.socket() function writes a single character string to a socket and returns the number of bytes that are written. The function has two arguments: **socket** and **string**.

The **socket** argument gives the name of the socket (the socket can be generated with the make.socket() function). There is no default value for **socket**.

The **string** argument gives the string to be written and takes a single character string or a one-element character object. There is no default value for **string**.

The writeClipboard() function writes to the Windows clipboard. The function takes two arguments: **str** and **format**.

The **srt** argument give the text to be written to the clipboard and takes a vector of the character or raw type. There is no default value for **str**.

The **format** argument gives the format of what is being written to the clipboard and takes a single integer value. The formats are listed at the help page for readClipboard(), along with the integer associated with each format. The default value of format is 1.

To access the help page for writeLines(), write.socket(), and writeClipboard(), use the Help tab in RStudio or enter **?writeLines**, **?read.socket**, and **?clipboard** at the R prompt, respectively.

The dput( ) and dump( ) Functions

The dput() and dump() functions write objects that are in the workspace (and, for dput(), expressions) in text format to a file, connection, or the console. The dput() function writes a single object (or expression), and the name of the object is not kept, while the dump() function can write multiple objects, along with the names of the objects.

The dput() function has three arguments. The arguments are **x**, **file**, and **control**.

The **x** argument gives the text to be written and takes an (unquoted) expression or an (unquoted) object name. There is no default value for **x**.

The **file** argument gives the location at which to write and takes a character string, a one-element character object, or a connection name for a value. The character string or object should contain the address of the file to be written to (or written) or be set to "" for writing to the console. A connection should be writable. The default value for **file** is "".

The **control** argument gives deparsing options for deparsing the objects to be written. The argument takes the value NULL or a character vector. The possible values, and descriptions of the effects of the values, are found at the help page for **deparseOpts**. According to the help page for dput(), for complex objects, the deparsing may not give the original object. Also, for the simplest deparsing, set control equal to NULL, and for the clearest deparsing, set control equal to "all". The default value of **control** is c("keepNA", "keepInteger", "niceNames", "showAttributes").

Some examples of calling dput() are

```
> ch10.dp.fun = function(){
+    # example for dput()
+    b = rnorm( 5 ) # normal random number generator
+    b
+ }

> dput(
```

```
+   ch10.dp.fun
+ )
function ()
{
    b = rnorm(5)
    b
}

> dput(
+   ch10.dp.fun,
+   control=NULL
+ )
function ()
{
    b = rnorm(5)
    b
}

> dput(
+   ch10.dp.fun,
+   control="all"
+ )
function(){
  # example for dput()
  b = rnorm( 5 ) # normal random number generator
  b
}

> dput(
+   1L:3L
+ )
1:3
> dput(
```

```
+    1L:3L,
+    control=NULL
+ )
1:3
> dput(
+    1L:3L,
+    control="all"
+ )
1:3
```

First, the ch10.dp.fun object is set equal to a function with comments. Then ch10.dp.fun is written to the console using the default value of **control**, the NULL value for **control**, and the "all" value for **control**. The first two calls give the same result (no comments and no space around the five in rnorm()), but the third call returns the function as entered. Last, the 1L:3L expression is entered for **x** in the three calls. There is no difference between the results from the three calls.

The dump() function takes a vector of object names and exports the contents of the objects to a file in text format. (The source() function reads the dumped file into a two-element list containing the value read and a logical value indicating if the result is visible. If more than one object is dumped, only the last object is sourced.)

The first argument to dump() is **list** and is a collection of the objects to be dumped. To enter the objects into the function, the object names are collected into a character vector with the object names in quotes.

For example:

```
> a = function(){
+    print( 1:4 )
+ }
> b = expression( x~y )
> c = list( 1:4, "a" )
```

```
> d = c( 1, 2, 3, 4 )

> dump(
+        c(
+            "a",
+            "b",
+            "c",
+            "d"
+        ),
+        file=""
+ )
a <-
function(){
  print( 1:4 )
}
b <-
expression(x ~ y)
c <-
list(1:4, "a")
d <-
c(1, 2, 3, 4)
```

Other than the vector of named objects, the function takes the **file**,
append, **control**, **envir**, and **evaluate** arguments.

The **file** argument contains the location to which the function writes
and takes either a character string or a connection object. For a computer
address, the address is quoted, so the value of **file** is either a character
string or a character object. (A computer address can be either relative to
the working directory or an absolute address.) If the argument is set to "",
the dump goes to the console or `stdout()` if `stdout()` is not the console. If
file is set to a connection object, the connection must writable. The default
value of **file** is **"dumpdata.R"**.

The **append** argument takes a logical variable. If **append** is **TRUE** and dump() **writes to a file**, dump() appends the objects to the file. If **FALSE**, the file is overwritten. The default value of **append** is **FALSE**.

The **control** argument behaves the same as in dput(). The default value of **control** in dump() is "all".

The **envir** argument tells dump() in which environment to look for the objects to be dumped. The argument takes a value of the environment type. The default value of **envir** is **parent.frame()**.

The **evaluate** argument (and the **control** argument) has to do with saving and reloading objects (where dump() is used to save and source() is used to load the objects). **The** argument tells R whether to evaluate promises and takes a logical variable. If set to TRUE, promises are evaluated. If set to FALSE, promises are not evaluated. The default value **evaluate** is **TRUE**.

You can access the help pages for dput() and dump() under the Help tab in RStudio or by entering **?dget** and **?dump** at the R prompt, respectively.

The savehistory() Function

The savehistory() function saves the current history to a file on the computer in text format. The function takes one argument, **file**. The **file** argument takes a character string that contains the address for the file on the computer. The default value of **file** is ".Rhistory".

An example of calling savehistory() is

```
> savehistory(
+    "ch10.Rhistory"
+ )
> rh = readLines(
+    "ch10.Rhistory"
+ )
```

```
> rh[ 511:512 ]
[1] "\"ch10.Rhistory\"" ")"
```

First, the history is saved. Then `readLines()` reads the history into the rh object. Last, the last two lines of rh are displayed (the history has 512 lines for my system).

More information about `savehistory()` can be found under the Help tab in RStudio or by entering **?savehistory** at the R prompt.

The save( ) and save.image( ) Functions

The `save()` function saves R objects, by default in binary form, to a file or connection. The saved objects can be loaded into a workspace using `load()`, or sometimes `data()`, or can be attached to a workspace using `attach()`. (See Chapter 9 for information about `load()`, `data()`, and `attach()`.) The `save.image()` function saves the workspace (i.e., all the files present in the workspace) to a file on the computer.

Any type of object can be saved using `save()`. When reloaded, the objects are loaded into the workspace under their original names and are not displayed at the console. The function has the ten arguments **...**, **list**, **file**, **ascii**, **version**, **envir**, **compress, compression_level, eval.promises**, and **precheck**.

The names of the objects to be saved can be entered in two ways: symbols or character strings containing the object names, separated by commas (**...**), or a character vector containing the quoted names of the objects (**list**). (Both **...** and **list** can be set in a call to `save()`.)

The **file** argument gives the location where the objects are to be saved and takes an object or expression of the `character` or `connection` type. If of the `character` type, the value must contain the address where the file is to be saved. If a connection, the connection must be writable in binary format. There is no default value for **file**.

The **ascii** argument tells save() whether to write in the ASCII format. The argument takes a logical value. If set to TRUE, the ASCII format is applied. If set to FALSE, a binary file is created. For **ascii** set to NA, see the help page for save(). The default value of **ascii** is FALSE.

From the help page for save(), the **version** argument tells save() which version of the workspace format to use. The choices are NULL (for the current default format) and 1, 2, or 3 (for the default formats in R 0.99.0 to R 1.3.1; R 1.4.0 to 3.5.0; and after R 3.5.0, respectively).

The **envir** argument gives the environment in which to find the object(s). The argument takes a value of the environment type. The default value of **envir** is parent.frame().

The **compress** argument indicates whether to do compression or what kind of compression to do. The argument takes a logical or character value. If set to TRUE, "gzip" compression is done. If set to FALSE, no compression is done. Setting the value equal to "gzip," "bzip2," or "xz" tells save() to use the given method of compression. (According to the help page for save(), this argument is ignored if the **file** argument is a connection or if the workspace format is version 1.) The default value of **compress** is isTRUE(!ascii) (i.e., if **ascii** is FALSE, compression is done).

The **compression_level** argument gives the level of compression if **compress** is not equal to FALSE. If the compression method is "gzip", the default level is "6". For "bzip2" or "xz", the default level is "9".

The **precheck** argument takes a logical argument that, when set equal to TRUE, tells save() to check to see if an object exists before opening a file or connection. If set equal to FALSE, the file or connection is opened even if nothing is saved. According to the help page for save(), for version 1, **precheck** does not apply.

An example of calling save() (and load()) is

```
> save(
+   "ClintonCorpus",
+   "mat",
```

```
+   list=c(
+     "junk",
+     "trst"
+   ),
+   file="ch10.bin"
+ )

> load(
+   "ch10.bin",
+   ver=TRUE
+   )
Loading objects:
  junk
  trst
  ClintonCorpus
  mat

> class(
+   junk
+ )
[1] "list"
> class(
+   trst
+ )
[1] "asS4"
attr(,"package")
[1] ".GlobalEnv"
> class(
+   ClintonCorpus
+ )
[1] "SimpleCorpus" "Corpus"
> class(
```

```
+    mat
+ )
[1] "matrix" "array"
```

Here, four objects are saved to the file "save.bin" and are then reloaded. The four objects belong to different classes.

The save.image() function writes the entire workspace to a file on the computer. The workspace can be saved to any file (e.g., save.image("ch10.RData")).

The function has five arguments: **file, version, ascii, compress,** and **safe**. The arguments, except **safe**, have the same descriptions and take the same types of values, as the same arguments in save(), except that the value of **file** must be an address on the computer for save.image(). The default values in save.image() are ".RData" for **file**, NULL for **version**, FALSE for **ascii**, and !ascii for **compress**.

The **safe** argument takes a logical argument that, when set equal to TRUE, tells save() to open a temporary file when saving a workspace in case the save fails. But setting **safe** to TRUE causes the save to use more disk space during the saving. If set equal to FALSE, the workspace can be lost if the save fails. The default value of **safe** is TRUE.

For more information about save() and save.image(), use the Help tab in RStudio or enter **?save** at the R prompt.

The saveRDS() Function

The saveRDS() function saves a single object to a file. Objects saved with saveRDS() can be loaded with readRDS() (see Chapter 9 for a description of readRDS()). The arguments of saveRDS() are **object, file, ascii, compress**, and **refhook**.

The **object** argument is set equal to the name of the object, which is not quoted. There is no default value for **object**.

The **file** argument gives where to save the object. The argument takes a character string containing an address on the computer, "", or a connection object. The default value of **file** is "".

The **ascii** argument behaves the same as for save(). The default value of **ascii** is FALSE in saveRDS().

The next argument is **version**, giving the version of R to apply when saving the object. The argument takes the value NULL or the integer values 2 and 3. From the help page for saveRDS(), setting **version** equal to NULL tells the function to use the default value (currently 3–for R 3.5.0 and later). The legal options for **version** are 2 (for R 1.4.0 to 3.5.0) and 3. The default value of **version** is NULL.

The **compress** argument behaves like in save(). The default value of compress in saveRDS() is TRUE.

See the help page for information about the **refhook** argument. The default value of **refhook** is NULL in saveRDS().

For more information about saveRDS(), use the Help tab in RStudio or enter **?saveRDS** at the R prompt.

The writeBin( ), writeChar( ), and serialize( ) Functions

The writeBin(), writeChar(), and serialize() functions write binary or raw formatted data to a connection, computer file, or the console (for raw data). The writeBin() function writes any atomic vector in the binary or raw format. The writeChar() function writes a vector of the character type in the binary or raw format. The serialize() function serializes an R object or expression in the binary or raw format. (Serializing transforms an object to a form than can be easily sent digitally between systems.)

The writeBin() function has five arguments. The arguments are **object**, **con**, **size**, **endian**, and **useBytes**.

The **object** argument takes a vector of an `atomic` type for a value. There is no default value for **object**.

The **con** argument gives the location at which to save the object. The argument takes one of the following: a character string containing an address on the computer; the `raw()` function (with any or no value for the argument); or an object of the `connection` class that is open, or can be opened, for writing in the binary format. Raw data can be output to the console or an object by setting **con** equal to a `raw()` function call. If the connection is open, `writeBin()` starts writing where R stopped before the call to `writeBin()`. There is no default value for **con**.

According to the help page for `readBin()`, the **size** argument gives the number of bytes for an element of the byte stream. Also, the argument takes an integer value, including the NA_integer_ value. And if set to NA_integer_, the "natural" size is applied. And **size** cannot be changed if the vector is of the `raw` or `complex` type. The default value of **size** is NA_integer_.

The **endian** argument gives the order in which bytes are processed. The argument takes either the character string "big" or "little". The default value of endian is .Platform$endian, which returns "little" on the operating system of my MacBook Air computer and my computers running the Windows 10 operating system and the Linux Mint operating system.

For **useBytes**, see the description of `writeLines()` in the "The writeLines(), write.socket(), and writeClipboard() Funtions" section of this chapter. The default value of **useBytes** is FALSE in `writeBin()`.

An example of calling `writeBin()` is

```
> writeBin(
+    object=1:3,
+    con=raw()
+ )
 [1] 01 00 00 00 02 00 00 00 03 00 00 00
> readBin(
```

```
+       writeBin(
+          1:3,
+          raw()
+        ),
+        what=integer(),
+        n=3
+ )
[1] 1 2 3
```

First, `writeBin()` converts a vector containing the integers one through three to raw format and returns the raw vector to the console. Then, the raw vector is converted back to an integer vector using `readBin()`. Note that the connection is set to `raw()` in `writeBin()` and to a vector of the `raw` type in `readBin()`.

The `writeChar()` function writes a character vector, (in binary or raw format) to a connection, an address on the computer, or to the console (or object). The function has five arguments, **object**, **con**, **nchars**, **eos**, and **useBytes**.

The **object** argument gives the vector to be written. The argument takes an object of the `character` class or an expression giving a vector of the `character` type. There is no default value for **object**.

The **con** argument gives the location at which to write the vector. The argument takes a connection object, a character string containing an address on the computer, or a call to `raw()` (with any or no value for the argument). There is no default value for **con**.

The **nchars** argument gives the number of characters to write from each element of **object**. The argument takes a nonnegative vector of the `integer` type, the length of which must be less than or equal to the number of elements in **object**. Also, if the value of an element of **nchars** is greater than the number of characters in the corresponding element of **object**, extra zero bytes are added to fill out the element. If the length of **nchars** is less than the length of **object**, only the elements included in **nchars** are written. A value of zero for an element of **nchars** suppresses the writing of the element. The default value of **nchars** is nchar(object, type = "chars") (e.g., nchar(c("a", "ab", "abc"), type="chars") equals c(1,2,3)).

The **eos** argument gives the character string to write at the end of what is written for a given element of **object** (for the elements of **object** that corresponds to an element in **nchars**). The **eos** argument takes NULL or a single character string for a value. The NULL value tells R to not include an end of string value or an ASCII nul (an embedded nul). If the value is not NULL, according to the help page for readChar(), the value is followed by an ASCII nul. If **con** is a call to raw(), **eos** must be NULL if readChar() is to read the output. The default value of **eos** is "".

For **useBytes**, see the description of writeLines() in the "The writeLines(), write.socket(), and writeClipboard() Functions" section of this chapter. The default value of **useBytes** is FALSE in writeChar().

Some examples of calling writeChar() are

```
> ch10.rc.1 = writeChar(
+       object=c( "a", "ab", "abc" ),
+       con=raw(),
+       nchars=c( 1, 2, 3 ),
+       eos=NULL
+ )

> readChar(
+       con=ch10.rc.1,
+       nchars=c( 1, 2, 3 )
+ )
[1] "a"    "ab"   "abc"

> ch10.rc.2= writeChar(
+       c( "a", "ab", "abc" ),
+       raw(),
+       c( 1, 0, 3 ),
```

```
+     eos=NULL
+ )

> readChar(
+     ch10.rc.2,
+     c( 1, 3 )
+ )
[1] "a"    "abc"

> writeChar(
+   object=c( "a", "ab", "abc" ),
+   con="ch10.rc.1.bin",
+   nchars=c( 1, 2, 3 ),
+   eos=""
+ )

> readChar(
+   con="ch10.rc.1.bin",
+   nchars=c( 1, 2, 3 )
+ )
[1] "a" "" "b"
Warning message:
In readChar(con = "ch10.rc.1.bin", nchars = c(1, 2, 3)) :
  truncating string with embedded nuls

> readChar(
+   "ch10.rc.1.bin",
+   c( 2, 3, 4 )
+ )
[1] "a"    "ab"  "abc"
Warning message:
In readChar("ch10.rc.1.bin", c(2, 3, 4)) :
  truncating string with embedded nuls
```

```
> readChar(
+   "ch10.rc.1.bin",
+   c( 3, 4, 5 )
+ )
[1] "a" "b" "c"
Warning message:
In readChar("ch10.rc.1.bin", c(3, 4, 5)) :
  truncating string with embedded nuls
```

The first call to writeChar() writes a raw vector to the ch10.rc.1 object. The readChar() function reads the object and returns the original character vector. The **eos** argument is set to NULL in writeChar(), so setting **nchars** to the same value in both the write and the read functions gives the correct result.

In the second call to writeChar(), the second element of the integer vector is set to zero, so the second element is ignored. Setting **nchars** to a two-element vector returns the two elements that were written. Note that **con** was set to raw() in both calls to writeChar().

In the third call to writeChar(), **con** is set to the file name "ch10. rc.1.bin", and **eos** is set to "". The **object** argument is the same character vector as in the first two calls. Three attempts to read "ch10.rc.1.bin" are shown. Since **eos** is not NULL, but "", there is one more character to count in each element.

The first call to readChar() has **nchars** set to the same value as set in the writeChar() call. The function reads one character for the first element ("a"), two characters for the second element ("", an embedded nul, and the "a" part of "ab"), and three characters for the third element (the "b" part of "ab", "", an embedded nul, and the "a" part of "abc"). Note that, with **eos** set to "", an embedded nul (an ASCII nul) terminates each string and readChar() does not read past an embedded nul in a string. Also, the function does not count the embedded nul as a character. And a warning is given that embedded nuls were encountered.

The second call to readChar() reads the elements correctly. The **nchars** argument has the function read two characters for the first element ("a" and ""), three characters in the second element ("ab" and ""), and four characters in the third element ("abc" and ""). An embedded nul warning is given.

The third call to readChar() reads three characters for the first element ("a", "", an embedded nul, and the "a" part of "ab"), four characters for the second element (the "b" part of "ab", "", an embedded nul, and the "ab" part of "abc"), and two characters for the third element (the "c" part of "abc", "", and an embedded nul–the last three characters are not there, so nothing is read).

The serialize() function attempts to serialize an R object and write the result in binary or raw format to an open connection or to the console or an object (for output of the raw type only). The function takes six arguments. The arguments are **object**, **connection**, **ascii**, **xdr**, **version**, and **refhook**.

The **object** argument can be any R object. There is no default value for **object**.

The **connection** argument gives the location at which to write the output. The argument takes the NULL value or a connection object that is open for writing. There is no default value for **connection**.

The **ascii** argument tells R whether to output ASCII (raw) or binary data. The argument takes a logical value. If set to TRUE or NA, ASCII data is output. If set to FALSE, binary data is output. The default value of **ascii** is FALSE.

The **xdr** argument can speed up writing between systems (see the help page for serialize() for more information). The argument takes a logical value. The default value of **xdr** is TRUE.

For the **version** and **refhook** arguments, see the section on writeRDS(). The default value of both is NULL in serialize().

Some examples of calling serialize() are

```
> ch10.sr.fun = function( x=1:3 ) {
+   print( x ) # example
+ }
> ch10.sr.fun
function( x=1:3 ) {
  print( x ) # example
}

> ch10.sr.txt = serialize(
+   object=ch10.sr.fun,
+   connection=NULL,
+   ascii=TRUE
+ )
> ch10.sr.txt[ 1:12 ]
 [1] 41 0a 33 0a 32 36 32 34 30 31 0a 31
> unserialize(
+   ch10.sr.txt
+ )
function( x=1:3 ) {
  print( x ) # example
}

> srcon = gzfile(
+   "ch10.sr.bin",
+   "w+b"
+ )
> serialize(
+   object=ch10.sr.fun,
+   connection=srcon
+ )
NULL
> close( srcon )
```

```
> srcon = gzfile(
+    "ch10.sr.bin",
+    "r+b"
+ )
> unserialize(
+    srcon
+ )
function( x=1:3 ) {
  print( x ) # example
}
> close( srcon )
```

First, the ch10.sr.fun object is generated and printed. Second, serialize() is called with ch10.sr.fun assigned to **object**, **con** set to NULL, and **ascii** set to TRUE, so a raw vector is returned. The raw vector is assigned to the ch10.sr.txt object. The first 12 raw numbers in ch10.sr.txt are printed, and the object is unserialized with unserialize(). The function is returned as originally written.

In the second call to serialize(), first, a connection is opened using gzfile() with set **description** equal to "ch10.sr.bin" and **open** equal to "w+b". The connection is assigned to the srcon object. Next, serialize is called with **object** equal to ch10.sr.fun and **con** equal to srcon. (By default, **ascii** equals FALSE.) Then the srcon connection is closed and reopened with **open** set equal to "r+b" (if **open** were set to "w+b" after srcon was closed, the contents of the file would be truncated, i.e., erased). Last, srcon is unserialized using unserialize() and then closed. The function is returned as originally written.

Matching Importing and Exporting Functions

Many of the importing and exporting functions are paired with each other. For example: source() with dump(); save() with load(), data(), or attach(); dput() with dget(); or write.table() with read.table(). Table 10-1 gives importing and exporting functions based on pairing.

Table 10-1. *Paired Import and Export Functions*

Importing	Exporting	Use
	sink( )	Writes output from the console in text format to a file or connection; stops the writing by entering sink(NULL)
scan( )	cat( )	Reads and writes vector data in text format to a file, a connection, or the console
	write( )	Writes vector data in tabular form and text format to a file, connection, or the console
read.table( ) read.csv( ) read.csv2( ) read.delim( ) read.delim2( )	write.table( ) write.csv( ) write.csv2( )	Read and write a matrix or data frame in text format to a file, connection, or the console; maintain the original structure
read.dcf( ) read.ftable( ) read.DIF( ) read.fortran() read.fwf( )	write.dcf( ) write.ftable( )	Read and write files in Debian Control File format and in R flat file format (both text formats); read files in Data Interchange Format, Fortran format, and fixed width format (all text formats); read from or write to a file, connection, or the console

(continued)

Table 10-1. (*continued*)

Importing	Exporting	Use
readLines( )	writeLines( )	Reads and writes lines of text from and to a connection (including a file or the console) in text format
read.socket( )	write.socket( )	Reads and writes character strings from and to a socket in text format
readClipboard( )	writeClipboard( )	Reads and writes from and to the clipboard (Windows systems only)
readline( )		Reads from the console using the keyboard in text format
dget( )	dput( )	Reads and writes an object to a file, connection, or the console in text format; does not include the object name
source( )	dump( )	Sources and writes objects from or to a file, connection, or the console in text format; includes the object names
readCitationFile( )		Used with citation(), reads a package citation, if the citation exists, in a package description
readRegistry( )		Reads registry keys and hives (Windows systems only)
readRenviron( )		Reads an .Renviron or Renviron.site file on the computer (for R environments)
loadhistory( )	savehistory( )	Loads and saves an .Rhistory file from or to the computer

(*continued*)

Table 10-1. (*continued*)

Importing	Exporting	Use
load( ) data( ) attach( )	save( ) save.image( )	Read and write objects, by default in binary format, from and to a connection or file; save. image() saves all the objects in a workspace to a file with the .RData extension
readRDS( )	saveRDS( )	Reads and writes an object, by default in binary format, from and to a connection or file
readBin( )	writeBin( )	Reads and writes binary data in binary or raw format from or to a connection, file, or the console (for the raw format)
readChar( )	writeChar( )	Reads and writes text data in binary or raw format from or to a connection, file, or the console (for the raw format)
unserialize( )	serialize( )	Unserializes and serializes data in binary or raw format to a connection or the console (for the raw format)

Other Exporting Functions

Like the functions that read in data, there are a variety of other functions that write data. The CRAN page on the **rio** package (for importing and exporting data) lists many of the packages and what they do. The CRAN vignette can be found at https://cran.r-project.org/web/packages/rio/vignettes/rio.html.

For SPSS, SAS, and Stata, the write.foreign() function that can be found in the **foreign** package can import and export in the correct format. The write.foreign() function also exports in some other formats. Other exporting functions can be found in the **foreign** package.

The **foreign** package is one of the packages installed by default. To see the contents of **foreign**, click on foreign in the list of packages under the Packages tab in RStudio or enter **help(package=foreign)** at the R prompt. To load **foreign**, check the box to the left of foreign under the Packages tab in RStudio or enter **library(foreign)** at the R prompt.

A newer package to read and write SPSS, SAS, and Stata files is the **haven** package. The package is not installed by default, unlike the **foreign** package, so **haven** must be installed before you can inspect or load it.

For Excel, there is the **xlsx** package specifically for working with Excel. The **xlsx** package is not a default package in R, so it must be installed. For older Excel files, the **readxl** package has functions to write and read the Excel files. Like the **xlsx** package**, readxl** is not installed by default, so it must be installed before it is inspected or loaded.

The function write.matrix() is in the **MASS** package, which is a package that is installed by default, but not loaded by default. The package can easily be inspected or loaded. According to the writers at the R project, write.matrix() is much faster than write.table() for large data sets, so the function may be preferable if a matrix or data.frame is large and the data frame contains columns of just one type. The function only exports in one atomic type (which is why write.matrix() is faster than write.table()).

CHAPTER 11

Descriptive Functions and Manipulating Objects

For arrays, matrices, vectors, lists, and expressions, in command line R, there are a number of functions that describe various attributes of an object. In RStudio, many attributes, such as the number of columns in a matrix or the length of a list, are given to the right of the object name under the Environment tab in the upper right window. Also, there are functions that manipulate objects to create new objects.

The functions covered in this chapter are `dim()`, `nrow()`, `NROW()`, `ncol()`, `NCOL()`, `length()`, `nchar()`, and `nzchar()` (descriptive functions) and `cbind()`, `cbind2()`, `rbind()`, and `rbind2()` (functions that manipulate objects.) Also, some apply functions and the `sweep()`, `scale()`, and `aggregate()` functions (functions that apply a function to the elements of an object or expression); `table()`, `tabulate`, and `ftable()` (table functions); and `grep()`, `grepl()`, `agrep()`, `grepRaw()`, `sub()`, `gsub()`, `regexpr()`, `gregexp()`, `regexec()`, `gregexec()`, `substr()`, `substring()`, and `strsplit()` (string functions.)

© Margot Tollefson 2022
M. Tollefson, *R 4 Quick Syntax Reference*, https://doi.org/10.1007/978-1-4842-7924-3_11

Descriptive Functions

The descriptive functions describe qualities of objects. This section discusses some descriptive functions that are useful when writing functions or creating objects. The functions are dim(), nrow(), ncol(), NROW(), NCOL(), length(), and nchar().

The dim() Function

If multiple dimensions make sense for an object or expression (e.g., matrices, data frames, tables, and arrays), the dim() function returns the number of levels in each of the dimensions of the object. For objects or expressions that do not have multiple dimensions, dim() returns **NULL**. The dimensions of the object can be changed if the product of the original dimensions equals the product of the dimensions of the result. You assign the vector of new dimensions to the call to dim().

The function has one argument, **x**, which gives the object or expression to be examined. The argument takes any R object or legal expression. The **x** argument has no default value.

Examples of calling dim() are

```
> ch11.v.1 = 1:2
> ch11.v.2 = 3:5
> ch11.v.1 %o% ch11.v.2 %o% ch11.v.1
dim(
  ch11.v.1
)
dim(
  ch11.v.1 %o% ch11.v.2 %o% ch11.v.1
)
```

```
ch11.v.3 = ch11.v.1 %o% ch11.v.2
ch11.v.3
dim(
  ch11.v.3
)
dim(
  ch11.v.3
  ) = c( 3, 2 )
ch11.v.3
```

First, the ch11.v.1 and ch11.v.2 vectors are assigned values, and the outer product of ch11.v.1 with ch11.v.2, with ch11.v.1 is output. Then the dim() function is called with **x** set to ch11.v.1 and **x** set to ch11.v.1%o%ch11.v.2%o% ch11.v.1. The first call returns NULL, since ch11.v.1 has one dimension. The second call returns 2 3 2, for two levels, three levels, and two levels, respectively, in the first, second, and third dimensions.

Then the two-by-three ch11.v.3 matrix is generated from ch11.v.1%o%ch11.v.2, and dim() is applied to ch11.v.3, returning 2 3. In the last call to dim(), ch11.v.3 is changed from a two-by-three matrix to a three-by-two matrix by assigning c(3,2) to dim(ch11.v.3).

You can find more information about dim() by using the Help tab in RStudio or by entering **?dim** at the R prompt.

The nrow(), ncol(), NROW(), and NCOL() Functions

For matrices, data frames, and arrays, nrow() and ncol() give the number of levels in the first and second dimensions of the matrix, data frame, or array, respectively. Other classes of objects return **NULL**.

The `nrow()` and `ncol()` functions have one argument, **x**. The argument takes any R object or legal expression. There is no default value for **x**. Sometimes, vectors must be treated as matrices or arrays. The `NROW()` and `NCOL()` functions treat vectors as one-column matrices but otherwise are the same as `nrow()` and `ncol()`.

Some examples follow:

```
> ch11.v.1 %o% ch11.v.2
nrow(
  ch11.v.1 %o% ch11.v.2
)
ncol(
  ch11.v.1 %o% ch11.v.2
)
nrow(
  ch11.v.1
)
NROW(
  ch11.v.2
)
NCOL(
  ch11.v.2
)

# length()

ch11.mat = matrix(
  1:4,
  2,
  2
)
```

```
ch11.mat
length(
  ch11.mat
)

ch11.list = list(
  ch11.mat,
  c(
    "abc",
    "cde"
  )
)
ch11.list
length(
  ch11.list
)

ch11.fun = log
length(
  ch11.fun
)
```

You can find more information about nrow(), ncol(), NROW(), and NCOL() by using the Help tab in RStudio or by entering **?nrow** at the R prompt.

The length() Function

The next descriptive function we describe is length(). The function has one argument, **x**. The argument can be any type of object or expression. For values of the atomic types (e.g., NULL, vectors, matrices, arrays), length() returns the number of elements in the value. For values of the list type (e.g., data frames), length() returns the number of the lowest-level elements (e.g., the number of columns in a data frame). For the three types of functions (closure, builtin, and special), length() returns one. For values of the environment type, length() returns the number of objects in the environment. For values of the S4 type, length() returns one.

For values of the symbol type, length() returns one. For values of the language type, length() returns the number of arguments entered in the creation of the call. For values of the expression type, length() returns the number of elements in the expression.

The length of an object (or expression) of one of the atomic types or of the list type can be assigned using length(). For objects of other types, an attempted length() assignment returns an error. For the atomic types, setting the length to a value larger than **the length of x** generates **NAs** for the extra elements. Setting the length shorter than **the length of x** removes elements. In either case, a vector is returned—unless the length is not changed, in which case the original object is returned. For objects of list type, lengthening the list adds **NULL** elements at the lowest level while shortening the list removes elements at the lowest level.

Some examples follow:

```
ch11.mat = matrix(
   1:4,
   2,
   2
)
ch11.mat
length(
   ch11.mat
)
```

```
ch11.list = list(
  ch11.mat,
  c(
    "abc",
    "cde"
  )
)
ch11.list
length(
  ch11.list
)

ch11.fun = log
length(
  ch11.fun
)

ch11.env = .GlobalEnv
length(
  ch11.env
)

ch11.S4 = RCE.p1
ch11.S4
length(
  ch11.S4
)

ch11.sym = as.symbol(
  1:4
)
ch11.sym
```

```
length(
  ch11.sym
)

ch11.lang = call(
  "lm",
  y~x
)
ch11.lang
length(
  ch11.lang
)

ch11.exp = expression(
  ch11.call,
  sin( 1:5/180 * pi )
)
ch11.exp
length(
  ch11.exp
)

ch11.mat.2 = ch11.mat
length(
  ch11.mat.2
) = 6
ch11.mat.2

ch11.mat.2 = ch11.mat
length(
  ch11.mat.2
) = 3
ch11.mat.2
```

```
ch11.mat.2 = ch11.mat
length(
  ch11.mat.2
) = 4
ch11.mat.2

ch11.list
length(
  ch11.list
) = 3
ch11.list

length(
  ch11.list
+ ) = 3
) = 1
ch11.list
```

In the first part of the example, the length is found for each kind of object. First, the ch11.mat matrix is defined and output. The length of the two-by-two matrix is found to be four, for the four elements of the matrix. Then, the ch11.list list is defined and output. The length of the list is found to be two since the list has two elements. Next, ch11.fun is set equal to the log function. The length of ch11.fun is found to be one.

Then, ch11.env is set equal to the global environment, and the value of ch11.env is returned. The environment is found to have a length of 441, for the 441 objects in the environment. Then, ch11.S4 is set equal to RCE. p1 (an object of the S4 class generated in Chapter 7), and ch11.S4 is output. The length of ch11.S4 is found to be one.

Then, the ch11.sym object is set equal to as.symbol(1:4) and output. The length of ch11.sym is found to be one. Then, the ch11.lang object is set equal to a call, and the value is output. The length of ch11.lang is found to be two since there are two arguments in the call() function. Then, the

ch11.exp object is set equal to an expression and output. The length of c11.
exp is found to be two since there are two arguments in the expression()
function.

In the second part of the example, different lengths are set for ch11.
mat and ch11.list. For ch11.mat, ch11.mat.2 is set equal to ch11.mat. Then,
the length of ch11.mat.2 is set to six. The 1:4 vector is returned, appended
with two NAs. Then, the ch11.mat.2 is set equal to ch11.mat again, and the
length of ch11.mat.2 is set to three. The 1:3 vector is returned. Then, ch11.
mat.2 is set to ch11.mat for the third time. The length of ch11.mat.2 is set to
four, and ch11.mat.2 is returned and is the original two-by-two matrix.

Next, the length of ch11.list is set to three, and ch11.list is output. A
third element has been added and has the value NULL. Last, the length of
ch11.list is set to one, and ch11.list is output. The ch11.list object has just
one element, containing the original two-by-two matrix in ch11.mat.

You can find more information about length() by using the Help tab
in RStudio or by entering **?length** at the R prompt.

The nchar() and nzchar() Functions

The nchar() function counts characters in objects that can be coerced
to the character type. The nzchar() function returns a logical vector
indicating which elements contain nonempty strings.

The nchar() function has four arguments: **x**, **type**, **allowNA**, and
keepNA. The **x** argument is the object to be counted and takes any value
that can be coerced to the character type. The nchar() function coerces
x to character, and the characters to be counted are the characters in each
element of the coerced object. Quotes are not counted.

The **type** argument is a character argument and can take on the values
of "**bytes,**" "**chars,**" or "**width.**" If "**bytes**" is chosen, the bytes of the strings
are counted. If "**chars**" is chosen, the standard text number of characters
is counted. If "**width**" is chosen, the number of characters that the cat()

function would assign the strings is counted. The default value is "**chars.**" Usually, there is no difference between the three.

The **allowNA** argument is a logical argument. If set equal to **TRUE**, strings that are not valid are set equal to **NA**. If set equal to **FALSE**, strings that are not valid give an error and cause the function to stop. The default value is **FALSE**.

The **keepNA** argument is a logical argument that tells nchar() whether to convert NAs to character strings or to keep them as **NA**s. The default value is **NA**, which tells nchar() to set the argument to TRUE if **type** is "bytes" or "char" and to FALSE if **type** is "width." If the argument is a data frame, since a data frame is a list, each column is converted to a character string, and the NAs are also made into character strings before the counting done by nchar() (whether keepNA is set to TRUE or FALSE). For vectors, matrices, and arrays, NAs are not converted to strings.

Some examples of calling nchar() are

```
ch11.list = list(
  matrix(
    1:4,
    2,
    2
  ),
  c(
    "abc",
    "cde"
  ),,
  NULL
)
ch11.list
as.character(
  ch11.list
)
```

```
nchar(
  ch11.list
)

ch11.df=data.frame(
  1,
  NA,
  12
)
as.character(
  ch11.df
)
nchar(
  ch11.df,
  keepNA=FALSE
)
nchar(
  ch11.df,
  keepNA=TRUE
)

ch11.mat.2 = as.matrix(
  ch11.d
)
as.character(
  ch11.mat.2
)
nchar(
  ch11.mat.2,
  keepNA=FALSE
)
```

```
nchar(
  ch11.mat.2,
  keepNA=TRUE
)

# nzchar()

nzchar(
  c( "1", NA, "12", "" ),
  keepNA=FALSE
)
nzchar(
  c( "1", NA, "12", "" ),
  keepNA=NA
)
nzchar(
  c( "1", NA, "12", "" ),
  keepNA=TRUE
)
```

First, the ch11.list object is redefined (from the last section), output, converted to character, and counted. Next, the ch11.df data frame is created (and contains NA for the second element), coerced to character, and counted with **keepNA** set to FALSE and with **keepNA** set to TRUE. There is no difference in the counts for the two values of **keepNA** since coercing data frames to character converts NAs to strings. Last, the ch11.mat.2 matrix is generated out of ch11.df (by calling as.matrix()), converted to character, and counted with **keepNA** set to FALSE and **keepNA** set to TRUE. With **keepNA** set to FALSE, the NA is converted to a string. With **keepNA** set to TRUE, the NA remains a missing value and is returned as such.

The nzchar() function returns a vector of TRUEs, FALSEs, and NAs that depend on whether an element of a character vector is a nonempty string, an empty string, or is missing. The function returns a logical vector of the same length as the object being tested.

The function has two arguments: **x** and **keepNA**. The **x** argument is set to the object or expression to be tested and can take any value that can be coerced to a character vector. The **keepNA** argument takes a logical value, which can be TRUE, FALSE, or NA. If **keepNA** is TRUE, NAs return NAs; if FALSE or NA, NAs return TRUE. The default value of **keepNA** is FALSE.

Three examples of calling nzchar() are

```
[1]   TRUE    NA  TRUE FALSE
```

In the first two calls to nzchar(), **keepNA** is set to FALSE and NA, respectively. Both calls return TRUE for the NA value in the character vector and FALSE for the "" value. In the third call, **keepNA** is set to TRUE. The NA value returns NA, and the "" value returns FALSE. For all three calls, the "1" and "12" values return TRUE.

You can find more information about nchar() and nzchar() by using the Help tab in RStudio or by entering **?nchar** at the R prompt.

Manipulating Objects

There are functions that manipulate R objects, which can make programming easier. This subsection covers some of the functions, including cbind(), rbind(), cbind2(), rbind2(), apply(), lapply(), rapply(), sapply(), vapply(), tapply(), mapply(), eapply(), sweep(), scale(), aggregate(), table(), tabulate(), and ftable().

The cbind(), rbind(), cbind2(), and rbind2() Functions

The cbind() and rbind() functions are self-explanatory for vectors, matrices, and data frames. The cbind() function binds columns. The rbind() function binds rows. (The cbind2() and rbind2() functions are used internally by cbind() and rbind() if S4 objects are present in the call to cbind() or rbind(). They are S4 generic functions. The second two functions give the same result as the first two functions if a call just contains S3 objects.)

There are two arguments for cbind() and rbind(), except when the first argument contains data frames. The arguments are **…** and **deparse. level**. For data frames, there are three more arguments: **make.row.names**, **stringsAsFactors**, and **factor.exclude**.

The **…** argument takes vectors, matrices, data frames, lists, and some S4 objects as values, where the objects or expressions are separated by commas in the call.

The **deparse.level** argument is used to create column labels for objects that are not matrixlike. The argument takes a single value that must be coercible to the integer type. The legal values, after coercion, are the values **0**, **1**, and **2**, although any value that can be coerced to an integer works. Values that do not give 1 or 2 when coerced to an integer give the same result as 0. The default value of **deparse.level** is 1.

The **make.row.names** argument takes a logical value. If set to TRUE, R generates unique names for the rows. If set to FALSE, no names are generated. The default value of **make.row.names** is TRUE.

The **stringsAsFactors** argument tells R whether to change character columns to factor columns. The argument takes a logical value. If set to TRUE, factors are generated from columns of the character type. If set to FALSE, character columns remain of the character type. The default value of **stringsAsFactors** is FALSE (which is different from earlier versions of R).

The **factor.exclude** argument tells R whether to keep an NA level for factor columns. If set to TRUE, an NA level is kept. If set to FALSE, an NA level is not kept. The default level of **factor.exclude** is TRUE.

For atomic vectors, vectors being bound do not have to be of the same length. The vectors cycle with themselves and with higher dimensional objects.

For higher dimensional atomic objects, the objects will not cycle. If, for rbind(), the numbers of columns do not match or, for cbind(), the numbers of rows do not match, an error is given. The resulting object takes on the type of the highest level object entered, where the hierarchy, from lowest to highest, is raw, logical, integer, double, complex, character, and list.

If a data frame is included in the objects to be bound and a list that is not a data frame is not included, then the result is a data frame. In that case, any character columns are changed to factors only if **stringsAsFactors** is set to TRUE.

For data frames, unlike for matrices, two objects for which the number of rows is multiples of each other can be combined with cbind(). Similarly, objects that have the number of columns multiples of each other can be combined with rbind(). The rows or columns cycle.

For lists that are not matrixlike, when combined, cbind() and rbind() return the type and number of elements in each of the lowest-level elements of the list, creating a matrix of the types. Lists can also be bound with nonlist objects. The result will be a list, but the nonlist arguments will not be converted like the list part of the result.

For time series, cbind() gives a multivariate time series, whereas for rbind(), the time series reverts to a plain matrix.

Some examples follow:

```
rbind(
  1:2,
  3:5
)
```

```
cbind(
  1:3,
  ch11.mat
)
cbind(
  1:3,
  data.frame( ch11.mat )
)
cbind(
  1:4,
  data.frame( ch11.mat )
)

ch11.list.2 = list(
  one=1:3,
  two=1:5
  )
ch11.list.2
rbind(
  ch11.list,
  ch11.list.2
)
cbind( ch11.list.2,
       1:2,
       1:3
     )
cbind( ch11.list.2,
       1:2,
       1:3,
       deparse.level=0
     )
```

```
cbind(
  ch11.list.2,
  1:2,
  1:3,
  deparse.level=2
)
```

First, the vectors 1:2 and 3:5 are row bound. A warning is given because the length of 1:2 is not a multiple of the length of 3:5. That is, three is not a multiple of two. The vector 1:2 cycles. Next, the vector 1:3 is column bound with the ch11.mat matrix (a two-row matrix). Since the length of 1:3 is larger than the number of rows in ch11.mat and not a multiple of the number of rows in ch11.mat, only the first two elements of 1:3 are included and a warning is given.

Next, we attempt to column bind 1:3 to a data frame generated out of c11.mat. The attempt fails. Then we column bind 1:4 to the same data frame, which succeeds because four is a multiple of two. The data frame repeats in the rows.

Next, the ch11.list.2 list is generated and output. The ch11.list is row bound to ch11.list.2. A matrix of list descriptions is returned. Then ch11.list.2 is column bound with the vectors 1:2 and 1:3. Note that even though the length of 1:3 is not the same as the number of rows of the list, the binding is done–but a warning is given. Then, the cbind() function is called three times, with the value of **deparse.level** being 1 (the default), 0, and 2, respectively. The **deparse.level** argument affects the names given to the columns.

You can find more information about cbind() and rbind() by using the Help tab in RStudio or by entering **?cbind** at the R prompt. (For cbind2() and rbind2(), enter **?cbind2**.)

The Apply Functions

There are several functions in R for applying a function over a subset of an object, eight of which are covered here. The eight functions are `apply()`, `lapply()`, `rapply()`, `sapply()`, `vapply()`, `tapply()`, `mapply()`, and `eapply()`. The functions to be applied can be user defined, which can be quite useful.

The apply() Function

The `apply()` function applies a function over a dimension(s) in an array (including matrices). The function has four arguments: **X**, **MARGIN**, **FUN,** **...** (where **...** is for any arguments to the function assigned to **FUN**), and **simplify**.

The first argument **X** takes any multiple dimension object that can be coerced to an array with `as.matrix()` or `as.array()`. There is no default value for **X**.

The second argument **MARGIN** gives the margin(s) over which the function is to operate. For matrices, setting **MARGIN** to one applies the function over the rows (across the columns). For **MARGIN** set to **two**, the function is applied over the columns (down the rows). For higher dimension arrays, the value of **MARGIN** gives the dimension(s) over which to apply the function. There is no default value for **MARGIN**.

The **FUN** argument takes an unquoted function name (without parentheses) giving the function to be applied to the margin(s). You can also enter arithmetic operators by enclosing the operators within quotes. (Any arguments to the function are entered next, separated by commas.) There is no default value for **FUN**.

The **simplify** argument takes a logical value. If set to TRUE, the result is simplified as much as possible. If set to FALSE, no simplification is done. The default value of **simplify** is TRUE.

The result is an array, matrix, or vector (atomic or list).
Some examples follow:

```
ch11.mat.3 = matrix(
  1:4,
  2,
  2,
  dimnames=list(
    c( "r1", "r2" ),
    c( "c1", "c2" )
  )
)
ch11.mat.3

apply(
  X=ch11.mat.3,
  MARGIN=1,
  FUN=sum
)

apply(
  X=ch11.mat.3
  MARGIN=1,
  FUN=sum,
  simplify=FALSE
)

round(
  apply(
    ch11.mat.3,
    1,
    pnorm,
```

```
    3,
    2
  ),
  3
)

round(
  apply(
    ch11.mat.3,
    1,
    pnorm,
    3,
    2
  ),
  3
)

ch11.array = array(
  1:8,
  c( 2, 2, 2 ),
  dimnames=list(
    c( "x1", "x2" ),
    c( "y1", "y2" ),
    c( "z1", "z2" )
  )
)

ch11.array

apply( ch11.array,
       c( 1, 3 ),
       mean
)
```

First the ch11.mat.3 matrix is generated and output (with row and column labels). Then, the first call to apply() finds the sums of the rows in ch11.mat.3, with **simplify** taking the default value of TRUE. An atomic vector is returned containing the sums of the rows and labeled with the row labels. The second call sets **simplify** to FALSE, and a list is returned containing the same information.

In the third call to apply(), **MARGIN** is set to one, and the arguments to pnorm() are the rows in ch11.mat.3 for **q**, **three** for the value of **mean**, and **two** for the value of **sd** (pnorm() returns cumulative probabilities for the normal distribution). A matrix is returned, with the cumulative probabilities for the first row of ch11.mat.3 in the first column and the cumulative probabilities for the second row of ch11.mat.3 in the second column. The cumulative probabilities are rounded to three decimal places.

Next, the ch11.array array is generated and output. Then, apply() finds the mean of the y values for each combination of the x and z values (the mean of each row in the array, as output). The **MARGIN** argument was set to c(1,3). A matrix with the x labels on the rows and the z labels on the columns is returned.

You can find more information about apply() by using the Help tab in RStudio or by entering **?apply** at the R prompt.

The lapply(), sapply(), vapply(), and rapply() Functions

The lapply(), sapply(), and vapply() functions apply a function to the elements of a list and work with vectors (including atomic vectors, lists, and expressions). The three functions take the **X**, **FUN**, and **...** arguments. The functions sapply() and vapply() also take other arguments.

If **X** is not a list, then **X** is coerced to a list. The elements of **X** must be of the correct type for the function being applied.

The `lapply()` function is the simplest with just two arguments plus any arguments to the function to be applied. The `sapply()` function takes four arguments plus any extra arguments for the function to be applied. The `vapply()` function also takes four arguments plus any extra for the function to be applied.

The lapply() Function

The `lapply()` function takes the **X**, **FUN**, and **...** (for any extra arguments for **FUN**) arguments. The function that is the value of **FUN** is applied to every element of the vector or to every second level element of the list. The result is a list.

Two examples follow:

```
ch11.list.3 = list(
  1:7,
  3:4
)
ch11.list.3

lapply(
  ch11.list.3,
  sum
)

lapply(
  1:2,
  "^",
  2
)
```

First the ch11.list.3 list is generated and output. Then the `lapply()` function finds the sums of the two elements of ch11.list.3. A list containing the sums is returned. Last, `lapply()` is applied to the vector containing the integers one through two. The function that is applied is ^ (for raising to a power), and the argument to ^ is two (for squaring the values in **X**). A list containing two elements is returned with the square of one in the first element and the square of two in the second element.

The sapply() Function

The `sapply()` function also operates on vectors, including lists and expressions. The function takes the **X**, **FUN**, **...**, **simplify,** and **USE.NAMES** arguments.

The **simplify** argument can be logical or the character string "array". The **simplify** argument tells `sapply()` to simplify the list to a vector or matrix if **TRUE** and to an array if set to "array". No simplification is done if set equal to **FALSE**. For **FALSE**, a list is returned. The value **TRUE** is the default of **simplify** in `sapply()`.

The **USE.NAMES** argument takes a logical value. For an object of the `character` type, the **USE.NAMES** argument tells `sapply()` whether to use the elements of the object as names for the result. If set to TRUE, the elements are used. If set to FALSE, names are not assigned. The default value of **USE.NAMES** is **TRUE**.

An example follows:

```
sapply(
  ch11.list.3,
  sum
)
```

```
ch11.char = paste0(
  "a",
  7:9
  )
ch11.char

sapply(
  ch11.char,
  paste0,
  "b"
)
sapply(
  ch11.char,
  paste0,
  "b",
  USE.NAMES=FALSE
)
```

First, the sums of the two elements of the ch11.list.3 list are returned as a vector, since **simplify** is TRUE by default. Next, the ch11.char vector is generated and output. Using sapply(), the paste0() function is applied to the elements of the vector, first with **USE.NAMES** equal to TRUE (the default value), then with **USE.NAMES** equal to FALSE. Both calls return a vector, the first with named elements and the second with elements that are not named.

The vapply() Function

The vapply() function assigns a structure to the output of the function. The function returns an array, matrix, or vector of objects of the kind given by the **FUN.VALUE** argument. The function has the **X**, **FUN**, **FUN.VALUE**, **…**, (for any arguments to **FUN**), and **USE.NAMES** arguments.

The **X**, **FUN**, and **...** arguments are as in `lapply()`. The **FUN.VALUE** argument is the structure for the output from the function. The structure is the structure of the result of applying **FUN** to a single element of **X**. Dummy values of the correct type are used in the structure. The number and type of the dummy elements must be correct. Any extra arguments for **FUN** are placed after **FUN.VALUE**. The USE.NAMES argument is as in `sapply()`. The default value of **USE.NAMES** in `vapply()` is **TRUE**.

An example follows:

```
set.seed( 49676 )
ch11.val=1:2
round(
  vapply(
    X=ch11.val,
    FUN=rnorm,
    FUN.VALUE=matrix( 0.1, 2, 2 ),
    n=4,
    sd=1
    ),
  3
)
```

In the example, ch11.val is a vector of means entered into the `rnorm()` function (`rnorm()` returns normal random variates). The other arguments to `rnorm()` are **n**, set to four, and **sd**, set to one. The call returns an array, with the matrices in the first two dimensions. The result is rounded to three decimal places with the `round()` function.

The rapply() Function

The `rapply()` function operates on an object or expression of the `list` type, recursively. The function takes six arguments: **object, f, classes, deflt, how**, and **...** (for the arguments to **f**).

The **object** argument takes a list or list-like value. There is no default value for **object**.

The **f** argument gives the function to be applied to the elements and takes the name of a function (unquoted and without parentheses). The name can also be an operator within quotes (e.g., "+"). There is no default value for **f**.

The **classes** argument takes a character vector containing the name(s) of the class(es) on which to operate. If the class of an element of the list is not included in the vector, the function to which **f** is set is not applied to the element. The default value of **classes** is "ANY" (i.e., any class is acceptable).

The **deflt** argument is set to the value to be given to an element if the function assigned to **f** cannot be applied to the element because the class is wrong. The default value of **deflt** is NULL (i.e., the element is not included in the output).

The **how** argument gives the structure of what is output. The argument takes one of the character strings: "unlist", "replace", and "list." If set to "unlist", a vector of the results from applying the function (or setting the value of the element to the value of **deflt**) to the unlisted list is returned.

If set to "replace", a list with the same structure as the original list is returned. The list has the result of applying **f** to the elements in the elements–except for the elements for which **f** could not be applied. For those elements, the original element is returned.

If set to "list", `rapply()` behaves like the function behaves with **how** set to "replace", except that, for elements for which **f** could not be applied, the value of **deflt** is returned. (If the default value of **deflt** is used, NULL is returned for the element.)

The **...** argument is last, so if arguments are to be set in the function given by **f**, the arguments must be last in the call and the other arguments must be set. Or if the arguments to the function given by **f** are named, the arguments can be placed anywhere in the call, but the other arguments must also be named.

Some examples of calling `rapply()` are

```
ch11.list.4 = list(
  list(
    1:3,
    4:5
  ),
  paste0(
    "p",
    1:3
  )
)
ch11.list.4
  rapply(
    ch11.list.4,
    sum,
    classes="integer"
  )
  rapply(
    ch11.list.4, sum,
    classes="integer",
    deflt=NA
  )
  rapply(
    ch11.list.4, sum,
    classes="integer",
    deflt=NA,
    how="replace"
  )
```

```
rapply(
  ch11.list.4, sum,
  classes="integer",
  deflt=NA,
  how="list"
)
rapply(
  ch11.list.4,
  paste0,
  classes="character",
  deflt=NULL,
  how="unlist",
  ":"
)
```

First, the ch11.list.4 list is defined and output. The list contains two elements. The first element is a list with two integer vectors for elements, and the second element is a three-element character vector.

Then, rapply() is called with **f** set to sum and **classes** set to "integer". A two-element vector is returned containing the sums of the elements in the first element of ch11.list.5 (six and nine).

The second call to rapply() has **sum** and **classes** set like in the first call, but with **deflt** set to NA. The call returns a three-element vector containing six, nine, and NA.

The third call is like the second call except that **how** is set to "replace". A two-element list is returned with the first element a list with the first element being six and the second element being nine. The second element is the character vector in the original list.

The fourth call is like the third call except that **how** is set to "list". The result is the same as the result in the third call, except that the second element is NA.

The fifth call has **f** set to paste0, **classes** set to "character", **deflt** set to NULL, **how** set to "unlist", and **...** set to ":". The call returns a three-element character vector with : appended to the elements in the original vector.

To find more information about lapply(), sapply(), and vapply(), use the Help tab in RStudio or enter **?lapply** at the R prompt. For rapply(), search under **rapply**.

The tapply() Function

The tapply() function applies functions to tabulated data. The arguments to the function are **X**, **INDEX**, **FUN**, **...**, **default**, and **simplify**.

The **X** argument must be an atomic object or expression and is coerced to a vector. The argument can be a contingency table created by table(). (The length of **X** is then the product of the dimensions of the contingency table.) There is no default value for **X**.

The **INDEX** argument gives the groups over which to apply the function given by **FUN** (see below). The argument must be a vector that can be coerced to a factor or a list of vectors that can be coerced to factors. The length of **X** and the length(s) of the factor vectors must all be the same. There is no default value for **INDEX**.

The **FUN** argument gives the function to be applied to the grouped values. The argument takes the same values as in apply()–except that the value can equal NULL. (For NULL, the returned values give the group into which each element of **X** falls.) The default value of **FUN** is NULL.

The **...** argument is for any arguments to the value of **FUN**. (Since **default** and **simplify** come after **...**, the two arguments must be referenced with their full names in calls to the function.)

According the help page for tapply(), the **default** argument is only used if **simplify** is TRUE and the function given by **FUN** returns one atomic value for each group. The argument gives the value to which the elements of the array to be returned are set before the array is filled with the result from the function set in **FUN**. The default value for **default** is NA.

The **simplify** argument tells rapply() whether to return an atomic array if the value of **FUN** returns a single atomic value for each group. If set to TRUE, an atomic array is returned. If set to FALSE, a list array is returned. The default value of **simplify** is **TRUE**.

Some examples follow:

```
ch11.ta.1 = sample(
  1:4,
  100,
  re=TRUE
)
ch11.ta.2 = sample(
  5:6,
  100,
  re=TRUE
)
ch11.ta.1[ 1:8 ]
ch11.ta.2[ 1:8 ]

ch11.ta.f = paste0(
  "a",
  c( 1, 1, 2, 2 )
)
ch11.ta.f.1 = paste0(
  "a",
  c( 1, 1, 2, 2, 1, 1, 2, 2 )
)

ch11.ta.f.2 = paste0(
  "b",
  c( 3, 4, 3, 4, 3, 4, 3, 4 )
)
```

```
table(
  ch11.ta.1
)

tapply(
  table( ch11.ta.1 ),
  ch11.ta.f,
  NULL
)

table( ch11.ta.1 )
tapply(
  table( ch11.ta.1 ),
  ch11.ta.f,
  mean
)

tapply(
  table( ch11.ta.1 ),
  ch11.ta.f,
  "^",
  2
)

table(
  ch11.ta.1,
    ch11.ta.2
)

tapply(
  table(
    ch11.ta.1,
    ch11.ta.2
  ),
```

```
list(
    ch11.ta.f.1,
    ch11.ta.f.2
  ),
  NULL
)

tapply(
  table(
      ch11.ta.1,
      ch11.ta.2
  ),
  list(
    ch11.ta.f.1,
    ch11.ta.f.2
  ),
  mean
)
```

First, two samples of 100 values are taken–from the 1:4 vector and the 5:6 vector, respectively. The first eight elements of both samples are output. Then, three factor vectors are generated, one with four elements to be used with the first sample and two with eight elements to be used for the contingency table resulting from crossing the two samples. The second and third factor vectors are associated with the first and second samples, respectively.

Next, the one-dimensional table based on the first factor vector is output and used in the first call to tapply(). In the call, **X** is set to the table, **INDEX** is set to the first factor vector, and **FUN** is set to NULL. The function returns a vector containing one, one, two, and two, so a function assigned to **FUN** is applied to the first and second elements of the table and to the third and fourth elements.

Then, the same call is run with **FUN** set to mean. A vector containing the means of the first two elements of the table and the second two elements of the table is returned by `tapply()`.

Next, the same call is run with **FUN** equal to "^" and the argument of ^ set to 2 (the individual values are squared). A two-element list array is returned containing two values in each element. The values are the values in the table raised to the power of two. The first element contains the values for which the factor vector equals one. The second element contains the values for which the factor vector equals two.

Next, `table()` is run on the two samples using the two factor vectors. The four-by-two table is output. Then, `rapply()` is called with **X** set to the table, **INDEX** set to a list containing the second and third factor vectors, and **FUN** set to NULL. The result is a vector with one, three, two, and four repeated twice. The length of the vector is eight, which is the product of four (for the four unique values in the first sample) and two (for the two unique values in the second sample). The vector indicates that the function in **FUN** operates on the rows of the table.

Next, `tapply()` is run as in the last paragraph except that **FUN** is set to mean. A four-element matrix (a matrix is an array) is returned with the means associated with factors of the first sample in the rows and the means associated with factors of the second sample in the columns.

You can find more information about `tapply()` by using the Help tab in RStudio or by entering **?tapply** at the R prompt.

The mapply() Function

The `mapply()` function applies a function over a group of vectors (which can be atomic or list or both) elementwise. The values, over all the vectors and for a given element (first, second, etc.), are acted on together by the function. If the vectors in the group of vectors are not the same length, the vectors cycle out to the length of the longest vector(s). The result is an atomic vector, matrix, or array, or a list.

The `mapply()` function takes five arguments. The arguments are **FUN**, **...**, **MoreArgs**, **SIMPLIFY**, and **USE.NAMES**.

The **FUN** argument is the function to be applied. The argument takes the same kinds of values as in `apply()`. There is no default value for **FUN** in `mapply()`.

The **...** argument refers to the vectors on which the **FUN** argument operates and may be atomic and/or list vectors. Or the values can be objects or expressions that can be coerced to vectors.

If the function given by **FUN** only takes named arguments, the values for the arguments are entered in the order of the vectors (unless, for a given argument, the elements in the vector are all given the name of the argument). Or if an argument takes the same value for all elements in a vector, the value can be entered using the **MoreArgs** argument (see below). If more vectors are entered than there are arguments in the function, an error is given.

If the function to be applied contains the **... argument**, there is no limit on the number of vectors in the group. The arguments after the **... argument** must be named if entered. (Note that arguments, in an element and over the group of vectors, follow the standard rules for the arguments to a function.)

The vectors are separated by commas in the call. If the vector is a list, the elements of the list can be any type of object or expression. The elements of the vectors (list or atomic) must be legal for the function to be applied. If an object that is not a vector is entered, `mapply()` attempts to coerce the object to a vector. There are no default values for **...**.

The **MoreArgs** argument also gives arguments to the function assigned to **FUN**. The values of the arguments must be together in an object or expression of the `list` type and must be named. (Note that, unlike arguments in the vectors in **...**, only one value can be assigned to the name of an argument in the list.) By default, **MoreArgs** equals **NULL**.

The **SIMPLIFY** argument tells `mapply()` to attempt to simplify the result to a vector or matrix. The effect of the argument is as in `sapply()`. The default value of **SIMPLIFY** is **TRUE**.

The **USE.NAMES** argument tells `mapply()` to use the names of the elements or, if the vector is of the `character` type, the characters themselves, as names for the output. By default, the value of **USE.NAMES** is **TRUE**.

Some examples follow:

```
set.seed( 43529 )

ch11.ma.1 = matrix(
  1,
  4,
  4
)
ch11.ma.2 = round(
  matrix(
    runif( 9 ),
    3,
    3
  ),
  2
)
ch11.ma.2
ch11.ma.3 = 1:2

round(
  mapply(
    det,
    list(
      ch11.ma.1,
      ch11.ma.2
```

```
    )
  ),
  4
)

round(
  mapply(
    mean,
    list(
      ch11.ma.1,
      ch11.ma.2,
      ch11.ma.3
    )
  ),
  3
)

mapply(
  sum,
  list(
    ch11.ma.1,
    ch11.ma.2
    ),
  ch11.ma.3,
  MoreArgs=NULL,
  SIMPLIFY=TRUE,
  USE.NAMES=TRUE
)
```

```
round(
  mapply(
    cor,
    list(
      1:16 + runif( 16 )*4,
      1:9 + runif( 9 )*4
    ),
    list(
      1:16,
      1:9
    ),
    MoreArgs=list(
        method="kendall"
    )
  ),
  3
)
```

First, the random seed is set, the ch11.ma.1 and ch11.ma.2 matrices and the ch11.ma.3 vector are generated, and the ch11.ma.2 matrix is output. Then mapply() is called with **FUN** set to det (for the determinant of a matrix) and ... set to the list(ch11.ma.1, ch11.ma.2) vector. The call returns the determinants of ch11.ma.1 and ch11.ma.2, rounded to four decimal places.

Then mapply() is called with **FUN** set to mean (for the mean value of the contents of an object) and ... set to the list(ch11.ma.1, ch11.ma.2, ch11.ma.3) vector. A three-element numeric vector, containing the means of the values in ch11.ma.1, ch11.ma.2, and ch11.ma.3, respectively, is returned, rounded to three decimal places.

Next, mapply() is called with **FUN** set to sum (for the sum of each element in the objects that are entered through the ... argument, summed across the objects) and ... set to the list(ch11.ma.1, ch11.ma.2) and ch11.ma.2 vectors. The sums over ch11.ma.1 and ch11.ma.3[1] and over ch11.ma.2 and ch11.ma.3[2] are returned in a two-element vector.

Last, mapply() is called with **FUN** set to cor (for the correlation between two vectors), **...** set to two lists (the first containing 1:16 plus a random vector and 1:9 plus a random vector and the second containing 1:16 and 1:9), and **MoreArgs** set to list(method="kendall"). A two-element vector is returned containing the correlations between the elements of the two vectors. The Kendall Rank Correlation method is used to find the correlations, rounded to three decimal places.

You can find more information about mapply() by using the Help tab in RStudio or by entering **?mapply** at the R prompt.

The eapply() Function

The eapply() function applies a function to most or all of the objects in an environment and returns a list to the console. The function has five arguments: **env, FUN, ..., all.names,** and **USE.NAMES**.

The **env** argument gives the name of the environment. The argument takes an object or expression of the environment class. There is no default value for **env**.

The **FUN** argument is the function to be applied. The argument takes the same kind of values as in apply(). There is no default value for **FUN**.

The **...** argument gives any arguments to the function to be applied. The arguments are separated by commas in the call to eapply(). There are no default values for **...**.

The **all.names** argument takes a logical value, indicating whether to include objects whose names begin with a period or not. If set to TRUE, objects that begin with a period are operated on by the function to be applied. If set to FALSE, the objects are not included. The default value of **all.names** is FALSE.

The **USE.NAMES** argument takes a logical value, indicating whether the resultant list has names assigned to the elements or not. If set to TRUE, names are assigned. If set to FALSE, names are not assigned. The default value of **USE.NAMES** is TRUE.

An example of applying eapply() follows:

```
set.seed( 38994 )
ch11.en = new.env()
ch11.en

ch11.en$a = 1:10
ch11.en$b = 11:20
ch11.en$c = rnorm( 100 )

ls(
    ch11.en
)

lapply(
  eapply(
    ch11.en,
    sd
  ),
  round,
  3
)
```

Here, an environment is created and populated with three numeric objects. The sd() function (which finds the standard deviation of the values in a numeric object) was applied to the three objects, and the resultant standard deviations were returned to the console as a three-element list. Finally, lapply() is applied to the list to round the output to three decimal places.

More information about eapply() can be found by using the Help tab in RStudio or by entering **?eapply** at the R prompt.

The sweep() and scale() Functions

The sweep() function operates on arrays (including matrices and vectors), and the scale() function operates on numeric matrixlike objects. The sweep() function sweeps out a margin(s) of an array (e.g., the columns of a matrix) with values (e.g., the column means) using a function (e.g., the subtraction operator). The scale() function by default centers and normalizes the columns of matrices by subtracting the mean and dividing by the standard deviation for each column.

The sweep() Function

The sweep() function has six arguments. The arguments are **x**, **MARGIN**, **STATS**, **FUN**, **check.margin**, and **....**

The **x** argument gives the array to be swept and takes an object or expression of the array class. The array can be of any atomic mode.

The **MARGIN** argument gives the margins over which the sweep is to take place and takes an integer vector. For a matrix, **MARGIN** can equal **1**, **2**, or **1:2** (or **c(1,2)**). If **MARGIN** equals **1:2**, the entire matrix is swept, rather than the sweeping being done by column or row. For an array of more than two dimensions, **MARGIN** can be any subset of the margins, including all of the margins.

The **STATS** argument gives the value(s) to sweep with. For example, to use column means, the apply() function can be applied (e.g., **apply(mat,2,mean)** would work as a value for **STATS**, where **mat** is the matrix being swept). The value(s) for **STATS** cycles.

The **FUN** argument is the function to use. The argument takes the same kinds of values as in the apply() function. The value for **FUN** can be any function legal for the values of the array (e.g., **paste** can be used with arrays of mode character). By default, **FUN** equals "-", the subtraction operator.

The **check.margin** argument tells sweep() whether to check to see if the dimensions or length of **STATS** agrees with the dimensions given by **MARGIN**. If set to TRUE and the dimensions do not match, just a warning is given. The function does not stop but cycles the values in **STATS**. If set to FALSE, no checking is done. The default value of **check.margin** is **TRUE**.

The **...** argument gives any extra arguments to the function set to **FUN**. There are no default values for **....**

An example follows (note that different platforms can generate different numbers from the same seed):

```
set.seed( 36694 )

ch11.mat.4 = matrix(
  sample(
    1:8
  ),
  2,
  4
)
ch11.mat.4
ch11.cent = sweep(
  ch11.mat.4,
  1,
  apply(
    ch11.mat.4,
    1,
    mean
  )
)
ch11.cent
round(
  sweep(
    ch11.cent,
    1,
```

```
    apply(
      ch11.mat.4,
      1,
      sd
    ),
    "/"
  ),
  3
)
```

First, the random seed is set, and the ch11.mat.4 matrix is generated and output. Then, the ch11.cent matrix is generated with the sweep() function. Since **MARGIN** is set equal to one, the mean() function finds the mean of each row (and the sd() function finds the standard deviation of each row). In ch11.cent, the mean of each row has been subtracted from the elements in each row of ch11.mat.4. The subtraction function is the default, so it need not be entered. In the second call to sweep(), the centered elements in ch11.mat.4 are divided by the standard deviations of the rows. The resulting matrix (which now has standardized values in the rows) is returned. The results are rounded to three decimal places.

You can find more information about sweep() by using the Help tab in RStudio or by entering **?sweep** at the R prompt.

The scale() Function

The scale() function is used to scale the columns of a matrix (i.e., to center the column to a specified center and to scale the column to a specified standard deviation). The scale() function has three arguments: **x**, **center**, and **scale**.

The **x** argument takes a matrix or matrixlike numeric object (e.g., a data frame or time series matrix). There is no default value for **x**.

The **center** argument can take either a logical value or a numeric vector of length equal to the number of columns in **x**. If set to **TRUE**, the column mean is subtracted from each element in a column. If set to a vector of numbers, then each number is subtracted from the elements in the corresponding column of the number. If set to **FALSE**, nothing is subtracted. The default value of **center** is **TRUE**.

The **scale** argument also takes a logical value or a vector of numbers. If **scale** is set equal to **TRUE**, each centered (if centering has been done) element is divided by the standard deviation of the elements in the column (where **NA**s are ignored and the division is by n-1). If **scale** is set equal to a vector of numbers, each element of a column (centered, if centering has been done) is divided by the corresponding number in **scale**. (Dividing by zero will give a **NaN** but will not stop the execution.) If **scale** is set equal to **FALSE,** no division is done. The default value of **scale** is **TRUE**.

An example follows:

```
ch11.mat.5 = t(
  ch11.mat.4
)
round(
  t(
    scale(
      ch11.mat.5
    )
  ),
  3
)
ch11.mat.6 = matrix(
  c(
    1:8,
    NA,
```

```
    2
  ),
  2,
  5
)
ch11.mat.6
round(
  scale(
    ch11.mat.6,
    center=rep(
      3,
      5
    ),
    scale=rep(
      4,
      5
    )
  ),
  3
)
+   3
+ )
      [,1] [,2] [,3] [,4]   [,5]
[1,] -0.50 0.00 0.50 1.00     NA
[2,] -0.25 0.25 0.75 1.25 -0.25
attr(,"scaled:center")
[1] 3 3 3 3 3
attr(,"scaled:scale")
[1] 4 4 4 4 4
```

First, the ch11.mat.5 matrix is set equal to the transpose of the ch11.
mat.4 matrix (i.e., columns become rows and rows become columns).
Then, the `scale()` function is run on the ch11.mat.5 matrix. The result is
rounded to three decimal places and transposed back to a two-by-three
matrix. Note that the resulting matrix is the same as the matrix result in
the section on `sweep()`. Also, `scale()` returns the scaled matrix, the values
used to center the elements, and the values used to scale the elements.

Next, the ch11.mat.6 matrix is generated and output. The matrix
contains an NA. Then, `scale()` is run on the matrix, with **center** equal to
a vector of five threes and **scale** equal to a vector of five fours. The result is
rounded to three decimal places and output. The NA remains an NA.

For more information about `scale()`, use the Help tab in RStudio or
enter **?scale** at the R prompt.

The aggregate(), table(), tabulate(), and ftable() Functions

Like the apply functions, the `aggregate()` function finds statistics for
groups within an object or expression. The `table()`, `tabulate()`, and
`ftable()` functions create contingency tables out of data.

The aggregate() Function

The `aggregate()` function applies a function to the elements of an object
based on the values of another object. The object to be operated on is
either a time series, a data frame, or an object that can be coerced to a
data frame. The values of the other object must be a list with elements that
can be interpretable as factors and, at the second level, must be of length
equal to the rows of the data frame or time series. The aggregating can also
depend on a formula containing objects in a data frame and/or the global
environment. The function treats data frames, formulas, and time series
differently.

Data Frames

For data frames, the arguments are **x**, **by**, **FUN**, **...**, **simplify**, and **drop**.

The **x** argument takes a data frame. The **by** argument takes an object of the list type consisting of elements that can be interpreted as factors. The elements of **by** are used to group the rows of **x**.

The **FUN** argument is the function to be applied, and **...** are any extra arguments for that function. The **simplify** argument tells aggregate() whether to try to simplify the result to a vector or matrix. The default value of **simplify** is **TRUE**. The **drop** argument is a logical variable. If TRUE, unused combinations for the **by** factors are dropped. Starting with R 3.5.0, the default value of **by** is TRUE.

The result of aggregate() for a data frame is a data frame. An example follows:

```
ch11.df=data.frame(
  y1=1:3,
  y2=7:9,
  x=c(
    1,
    2,
    1
  )
)
ch11.df

aggregate(
  ch11.df[ , 1:2 ],
  by=list(
    ch11.df$x
  ),
  FUN=sum
)
```

The function finds the sums in each column of ch11.df[,1:2] for the two grouping values in **x**.

Formulas

For data frames, a formula may be used to classify **x** rather than using the **by** argument. Also, objects in the global environment can make up the formula. For the formula option, the arguments are **formula**, **data**, **FUN**, **...**, **subset**, and **na.action**. The **formula** argument takes the form **y~x**, where **y** is a numeric vector or matrix and **x** is a formula such as **x1** or **x1+x2**, where both **x1** and **x2** can be interpreted as factors. (See the help page for formula for the ways of setting up formulas.)

The **data** argument gives the name of the data frame and need not be included if the objects in the formula are strictly from the global environment. The **FUN** argument is the function to be applied, and **...** contains any extra arguments for **FUN**. There is no default value for **FUN** if a formula is used. The **subset** argument gives the rows of the data frame on which to operate. The **na.action** argument gives the choice for how to handle missing values and is a character string. The default value is **na. omit**, which tells aggregate() to omit missing values. There are no other options for **na.action** at the help page.

An example, using the data frame ch11.df (see above), follows:

```
aggregate(
  cbind( y1, y2 )~x,
  data=ch11.df,
  FUN=sum
)
```

The formula gives the same result as in the last example. Note that the **by** variable covered in the last section must be a list while the right side of a formula covered in this section cannot be a list.

Time Series

Time series have both a frequency and a period. In R, the inverse of the frequency gives the length of the subperiods in a period. For example, a year can be the period of interest. Then, the months have a frequency of 12 while having subperiods of 1/12.

For time series, the arguments are **x**, **nfrequency**, **FUN**, **ndeltat**, **ts. eps**, and **....** The **x** argument must be a time series (an object or expression of the ts class). The **nfrequency** argument is the number of subperiods for each period after **FUN** has operated on the time series. The value must divide evenly into the original time series frequency. For a monthly time series, aggregating to a quarter can be done by setting **nfrequency** to four. The argument equals **one** by default. (The original time series frequency divided by **nfrequency** gives the number of elements that are grouped together—on which **FUN** operates.)

The **FUN** argument is the function to be applied, and **...** gives any extra arguments to **FUN**. (The **...** argument is at the end of the argument list.) The **FUN** function must be legal for the values of the time series and is **sum** by default.

The **ndeltat** argument tells aggregate() the length of the subperiods for the output (in terms of the period) and equals **one** by default. The argument is the value of one divided by **nfequency**. The product of the frequency of the original time series and **ndeltat** must be an integer.

Either **nfrequency** or **ndeltat** can be set but not both. The product of **nfrequency** and the inverse of **ndeltat** should be an integer.

The **ts.eps** argument gives the tolerance for accepting that **nfrequency** divides evenly into the frequency of the time series. By default, **ts.eps** equals **getOption("ts.eps")**, which value can be found by entering **options("ts.eps")** at the R prompt. The value is numeric and can be set manually.

401

Some examples of calling `aggregate()` with a time series follow:

```
ch11.ts=ts(
  cbind(
    1:8,
    9:16
  ),
  start=c(
    1,
    1
  ),
  freq=4
)
ch11.ts
aggregate(
  ch11.ts,
  nfreq=2
)
```

First, the ch11.ts time series object is generated and output. Each period has four observations, and two periods are generated. Then `aggregate()` is run twice, first with **nfrequency** set to two and then with **ndeltat** set to two. With **nfrequency** set to two (i.e., ndeltat=1/2), two rows are summed, since the new subperiod is one half of the original frequency. With **ndeltat** set to two (i.e., **nfreq=1/2**), all eight rows are summed, since the new subperiod is twice the original frequency (of four). Note that **nfrequency** can be less than one but must give an integer if multiplied by the **frequency**.

You can find more information about `aggregate()` by using the Help tab in RStudio or by entering **?aggregate** at the R prompt.

The table(), as.table(), and is.table() Functions

There are three functions associated with creating tables using table(). The table() function creates a contingency table from atomic data or some lists. The data must be able to be interpreted as factors. The result has the table class. The as.table() function attempts to coerce an object to table class. The is.table() function tests if an object is of table class.

The arguments to table() are **...**, **exclude**, **useNA**, **dnn**, and **deparse.level**.

The **...** argument refers to the objects that are to be cross classified. The objects are separated by commas and, for atomic objects, must all have the same length. For list objects, the second level elements must all have the same length and be atomic. Atomic and list objects cannot be combined in a call to table().

The **exclude** argument gives values to be excluded from the contingency table. By default, **exclude** equals **if(useNA=="no") c(NA, NaA)**, which tells table() not to set a level for missing values or illegal values (such as one divided by zero) if the **useNA** argument equals "**no**" (see below).

The **useNA** argument is a character argument and can take on the value "**no**", "**ifany**", or "**always**". For "**no**", no level is set for missing values. For "**ifany**", a level is set if missing values are present. For "**always**", a level for missing values is always set. The default level is "**no**".

The **dnn** argument gives dimension names for the contingency table and takes an object or expression of the list type. The default value is list. names(...). (The list.names() function is defined in table() and gives the names of the dimensions being tabulated; see below.)

The **deparse.level** argument takes an integer value that can be **0**, **1**, or **2**. The argument controls list.names() if **dnn** is not given. For **zero**, no names are given. For **one**, the column names are used. For **two**, column names are deparsed. The default value of **deparse.level** is **one**.

Some examples of calling `table()` follow:

```
set.seed( 36694 )
ch11.smp.1=sample(
  2,
  100,
  replace=TRUE
)
ch11.smp.2=sample(
  4:6,
  100,
  replace=TRUE
)
ch11.smp.2[10]=NA
table(
  ch11.smp.1,
  ch11.smp.2
)
table(
  ch11.smp.1,
  ch11.smp.2,
  useNA="ifany"
)
```

First, two samples of 100 pseudorandom variates are generated, and an NA is put into the second sample. Then, `table()` is run twice on the two samples to generate two contingency tables: once with default values for the arguments and once with **useNA** set to "ifany". Note that the first table does not include the missing value, but the second does. Otherwise, the tables are the same.

The as.table() function has the **x** and **...** arguments. The **x** argument is the object to be coerced to the table class. The argument must be of the numeric mode. The **...** argument provides any arguments for lower-level functions.

The is.table() function takes the **x** argument and returns **TRUE** if **x** is of table class and **FALSE** if not.

You can find more information about table(), as.table(), and is.table() by using the Help tab in RStudio or by entering **?table** at the R prompt.

The tabulate() Function

The tabulate() function coerces numeric or factor objects to vectors and bins the result. The arguments of tabulate() are **bin** and **nbins**. The **bin** argument is the object to be binned. If the object is of the double class, then the elements are rounded down to integers. The resulting integers must be positive. If an illegal element is present in the value of **bin**, the element is ignored.

The **nbins** argument gives the largest integer to be binned and by default equals **max(1, bin, na.rm=T)** (i.e., one or the largest value in **bin**, assuming the largest value in **bin** is larger than or equal to one). Any NAs are removed.

If **nbins** is smaller than the largest value in **bin**, then only those values with a value less than or equal to **nbins** are binned. All of the integers between one and **nbins** are binned even if there are zero elements in a given bin. The function creates a vector without labels. The bins always start with one.

Two examples of calling `tabulate()` follow:

```
tabulate(
  c(
    -3.5,
    0.9,
    1,
    4,
    5.6,
    5.4,
    4,
    1,
    3
  )
)
tabulate(
  c(
    -3.5,
    0.9,
    1,
    4,
    5.6,
    5.4,
    4,
    1,
    3
  ),
  nbins=3
)
```

In the examples, after the value of **bin** is coerced to the integer class, there are two ones, zero twos, one three, two fours, and two fives for both calls to tabulate(). In the second call, **nbins** is set to three.

The tabulate() function is good when all of the bins, including those with zero elements, are needed. You can find more information about tabulate() by using the Help tab in RStudio or by entering **?tabulate** at the R prompt.

The ftable() Function

The ftable() function creates a matrix out of a contingency table (i.e., makes a flat table). The arguments to ftable() are **...**, **exclude**, **row.vars**, and **col.vars**.

The **...** argument can be any objects or expressions that can be coerced to vectors and that can be interpreted as factors. The values are entered into the call to ftable() first and are separated by commas. The argument can also be a list whose elements can be interpreted as factors. The resultant vectors or list elements must all be the same length. Or the argument can be an object or expression of the table or ftable class.

The **exclude** argument gives the values to be excluded when building the flat table. By default, **exclude** equals **c(NA, NaN)**.

The **row.vars** and **col.vars** arguments give the dimensions to put in the rows and columns. The values can go from one to the number of dimensions in the table (e.g., a table with three dimensions can have **row. vars** and **col.vars** equal to **1:2** and **3**; or **2:1** and **3**; or **1** and **3**; or **c(3,1)** and **2**; etc.). If some dimensions are not included, the cells for the included dimensions contain the sums over the respective cells of the dimensions that are not included.

Some examples follow:

```
set.seed( 38794 )
ch11.smp.3 = sample(
  7:8,
  100,
  replace=TRUE
)

ftable(
  ch11.smp.1,
  ch11.smp.2,
  ch11.smp.3
)

ftable(
  list(
    ch11.smp.1,
    ch11.smp.2,
    ch11.smp.3
  ),
  row.vars=3,
  col.vars=2:1
)

ftable(
   table(
    ch11.smp.1,
    ch11.smp.2,
    ch11.smp.3
   ),
  row.vars=2,
  col.vars=3
)
```

First, ch11.smp.3 is generated (and contains a sample of 100 pseudorandom variates from the vector 7:8). Then, the three samples (ch11.smp.1, ch11.smp.2, and ch11.smp.3) are entered directly into ftable(). The default values are used in the call to ftable(). The first two dimensions are in the rows; the third is in the columns.

In the second call, the three samples are entered into ftable() as a list. The third dimension is in the rows, and the second and then first dimensions are in the columns (since **row.vars** is set to three and **col.vars** is set to two through one).

In the third call, the three samples are entered into the call as a table. The second dimension is in the rows, and the third dimension is in the columns (since **row.vars** is set to two and **col.vars** is set to three). The cells contain the sum over the first dimension for each second and third crossed level.

You can find more information about ftable() by using the Help tab in RStudio or by entering **?ftable** at the R prompt.

Some Character String Functions

There are a number of functions for searching for patterns in character strings and for replacing parts of strings with other strings based on matching. This section covers the grep functions, the sub functions, the regexpr and regexec functions, the str functions, and the character case transformation functions.

The grep Functions

The grep() and grepl() functions search for matches to a pattern in a vector of character strings. The grep() function returns either the index or the value of those strings that contain the pattern. The grepl() function returns a logical vector of the same length as the character vector, with elements equal to TRUE if there is a match, and FALSE if there is not a match, for each element of the character vector.

The arguments of grep() are **pattern, x, ignore.case, perl, value, fixed**, and **useBytes**. The **pattern** argument is the value to be matched and takes an object or expression that is of, or can be coerced to (by using as. character()), the character type. If the argument contains more than one element, only the first one is used. The **x** argument is the character vector in which to look for the matches. There are no default values for **pattern** or **x**.

The **ignore.case** argument tells grep() to ignore case in doing the matching if set equal to TRUE. The default value of **ignore.case** is FALSE. The **perl** and **fixed** arguments tell grep() what type of matching to do (see the help page for regex for more information). Both arguments are FALSE by default. The **value** argument tells grep() to return the value of the element if set to TRUE and the index of the element if set to FALSE. The default value of **value** is FALSE. The **useBytes** argument, if set to TRUE, tells grep() to match byte-wise rather than character-wise. The default value of **useBytes** is FALSE. The **inverse** argument, if set equal to TRUE, tells grep() to return the elements that do not contain matches rather than those that do. The default value of **inverse** is FALSE.

The grepl() function takes the same arguments as grep() except that there are no argument **value** or **invert**. The function returns a logical vector of the same length of **x**, indicating whether there is a match or not.

The agrep() and agrepl() functions are similar to grep() and grepl(), except that agrep() and agrepl() do "fuzzy" matching. See the help page for agrep() for more information on how the matching can be done.

Some examples of calling grep(), grepl(), agrep(), and agrepl() are

```
ch11.char.1=c(
  "achar1",
  "achar2",
  "achar3"
)
ch11.char.1
```

```
grep(
  "achar",
  ch11.char.1
)

grep(
  "1",
  ch11.char.1,
  value=TRUE
)

grep(
  "Achar",
  ch11.char.1
)

grep(
  "Achar",
  ch11.char.1,
  ignore.case=TRUE
)

grep( "Achar",
      ch11.char.1,
      ignore.case=TRUE,
      invert=T
)

grepl(
  "1",
  ch11.char.1
)
```

```
grepl(
  "Achar",
  ch11.char.1
)

agrep(
  "Achar",
  ch11.char.1
)

agrepl(
  "Achar",
  ch11.char.1
)
```

First, the ch11.char.1 character vector is generated. Then five calls to grep() are made. The first call returns one, two, and three (for the indices of the ch11.char.1 vector, since the "achar" character string appears in all of the elements of ch11.char.1).

The second call returns "achar1" since **pattern** equals one and **value** is set to TRUE. The "achar1" character string is the value of the only element of ch11.char.1 that contains one. The third call returns integer(0) since no element of ch11.char.1 contains "Achar". The fourth call repeats the third call with **ignore.case** set to TRUE. The three indices are returned since "Achar" matches "achar" if case is ignored. The fifth call repeats the fourth call with **invert** set equal to TRUE. The call returns integer(0).

Next, two calls to grepl() are made. The first call takes the same arguments as the second call to grep() and returns TRUE, FALSE, and FALSE. The second call uses the same arguments as the third call to grep() and returns FALSE, FALSE, and FALSE.

Last, fuzzy matching is done with agrep() and agrepl(). The call to agrep() takes the same arguments as the third call to grep(). Unlike the call to grep(), agrep() returns the indices one, two, and three (since "Achar" and "achar" match under fuzzy matching). Similarly, agrepl() returns TRUE, TRUE, and TRUE, for the same argument values.

The grepRaw() function does pattern matching for raw vectors. The function takes the **pattern**, **x**, **offset**, **ignore.case**, **value**, **fixed**, **all**, and **invert** arguments.

The **pattern** argument is the pattern to be matched and can be a raw vector or a single character string. The **x** argument is also a raw vector or a single character string and is the object in which to search for the pattern. In grepRaw(), before the search, the character strings are converted to raw vectors using the charToRaw() function.

The **offset** argument gives the index of the raw vector at which to start searching. The value must be able to be coerced to a positive integer. If the value is an object of length greater than one, only the first element is used. The default value for **offset** is 1L.

The **ignore.case** argument, if set equal to TRUE, tells grepRaw() to match both capital letters and lowercase letters given a letter of either case. The default value is FALSE.

The **value** argument, if set equal to TRUE, returns the first raw vector containing the match or a list of the raw vectors containing the matches, depending on whether the **all** argument (see below) is FALSE or TRUE. If **value** is FALSE, either the index of the first element of the first match, or the indices of the first elements of all the matches, is returned, depending on the value of the **all** argument (FALSE or TRUE, respectively). The default value of **value** is FALSE.

The **all** argument tells grepRaw() to just return the first match if set equal to FALSE and all matches if set equal to TRUE. The default value is FALSE. The **fixed** and **invert** arguments are as defined for grep() and by default are FALSE.

Some examples of calling grepRaw() are

```
charToRaw(
  "abc123"
)

grepRaw(
  "b",
  "abc123"
)

grepRaw(
  "b",
  "abc123",
  value=TRUE
)

grepRaw(
  "B",
  "abc123",
  value=TRUE,
  ignore.case=T
)

charToRaw(
  "abab"
)

grepRaw(
  "ab",
  "abab"
)
```

```
grepRaw(
  "ab",
  "abab",
  all=TRUE
)

grepRaw(
  "ab",
  "abab",
  value=TRUE,
  all=TRUE
)

grepRaw(
  "ab",
  "Abab",
  value=TRUE,
  all=TRUE
)

grepRaw(
  "ab",
  "Abab",
  value=TRUE,
  all=TRUE,
  ignore.case=TRUE
)
```

First, the "abc123" character string is displayed in raw format. Then, grepRaw( ) is called three times, with **pattern** equal to "b", "b", and "B", respectively, in the calls, and with **x** equal to "abc123" for all three calls. The function returns two, for the second character in "abc123", 62 for the raw value of "b" (**value** is set to TRUE), and 62 for the raw value of "b" (**value** is set to TRUE and **ignore.case** is set to TRUE), respectively.

Then, the "abab" character string is displayed in the raw format, and three calls to grepRaw() are made with **pattern** set to "ab" and **x** set to "abab". In the three calls, default values are used; **all** is set to TRUE; and both **value** and **all** are set to TRUE, respectively. The values one and one and three and a list with two elements, each containing 61 62, are returned (since the first match starts with the first character of **x**; the first second match starts with the third character of **x**; and because there are two instances of "ab" in "abab" and the raw version of "ab" is 61 62).

In the last two calls to grepRaw(), **pattern** is set to "ab" and **x** is set to "Abab". The two calls have **value** and **all** set to TRUE. The second call also has **ignore.case** set to TRUE. The calls return a one-element list containing 61 62 and a two-element list containing 41 62 and 61 62, respectively. The raw format of "A" is 41.

The sub() and gsub() functions can replace a substring, in the element(s) of any object or expression that can be coerced to a character vector, with a new string. The arguments to both functions are **pattern**, **replacement**, **x**, **ignore.case**, **perl**, **fixed**, and **useBytes**. The only new argument is **replacement**, the replacement value. The replacement value must be an object or expression that can be coerced to a character string. If the replacement object has more than one element, only the first element is used, and a warning is given. The sub() function replaces the first occurrence of the pattern in each element of **x**. The gsub() function replaces all occurrences of the pattern.

For example:

```
> sub( "b1", "c", c( "b1b2b1", "cb1" ) )
[1] "cb2b1" "cc"
> gsub( "b1", "c", c( "b1b2b1", "cb1" ) )
[1] "cb2c" "cc"
```

In the call to sub(), the first occurrence of "b1" is replaced with "c" in each of the elements of **x**. In the call to gsub(), all occurrences of "b1" are replaced with "c" in the elements of **x**.

The `regexpr()`, `gregexpr()`, `regexec()`, and `gregexec()` functions return the location and length of a string within an element of a character vector (plus some attributes). For `regexpr()`, a vector with attributes is returned. For the other functions, an object of the `list` type is returned with one element for each element of the character vector. For all the functions, minus one is returned if no match is found in an element.

The arguments to the four functions are **pattern**, **text**, **ignore.case**, **perl**, **fixed**, and **useBytes**. Here, **text** is the object in which to search for the pattern. The other arguments are as described previously.

The `regexpr()` function finds the first occurrence of the pattern for each element of **text** and returns a vector with attributes. The vector is a vector of integers, where for each element in **text**, the integer is the position of the first occurrence of the pattern in the element. If the pattern is not in the element, a minus one is returned.

The first attribute of the result is "match.length" (a vector of integers that contains the number of characters or bytes, depending on whether **useBytes** is FALSE or TRUE, in the first match of the pattern). Again, if there is no match, minus one is returned. Two other possible attributes are "index.type" and "useBytes".

To separate out the vector from the attributes, you can use the `as.vector()` function on the result. To access the attributes, you can use the `attr()` function.

The `gregexpr()` function finds all matches to the **pattern** argument in each element of **text**. The function takes the same arguments as `regexpr()` and returns a list of the same length as **text**. The first element of the list contains the information for the first element of **text**; the second element, information about the second element of **text**; and so forth. The structure of each element of the list is structured like the output from `regexpr()` except the reference is to all matches in the element rather than for the first match in each element.

The regexec() function is regexpr() with output in the form of gregexpr(). The gregexec() function returns matrices instead of vectors. Otherwise, gregexec() is like gregexpr().

Some examples of regexpr(), gregexpr(), regexec(), and gregexec() are:

```
regexpr(
  "ab",
  c(
    "abab",
    "ba"
  )
)

ch11.rg=gregexpr(
  "ab",
  c(
    "abab",
    "ba"
  )
)

ch11.rg
as.vector(
  ch11.rg[[1]]
)

attr(
  ch11.rg[[1]],
  "match.length"
)
```

```
regexec(
  "ab",
  c(
    "abab",
    "ba"
  )
)

ch11.rg.2=gregexec(
  "ab",
  c(
    "abab",
    "ba"
  )
)

ch11.rg.2
as.vector(
  ch11.rg.2[[1]][ 1, ]
)

attr(
  ch11.rg.2[[1]],
  "match.length"
)
```

In the four examples, **pattern** is set to "ab", and **text** is set to c("abab", "ba"). For regexp(), a vector of one and minus one is returned (since **pattern** is matched by the first two characters in the first element of **text** and is not matched in the second element). The match.length attribute is a vector consisting of two and minus one (since the pattern consists of two characters and there is a match in the first element of **text** and no match in the second).

For gregexpr(), the ch11.rg object is set equal to the call to gregexpr(). The object is a list. The first element of ch11.rg is a vector with attributes and consists of one and three (since the second, and last, match to **pattern** starts with the third character of the first element of **text**). The second element of ch11.rg consists of a vector with attributes that takes the value of minus one (since the pattern makes no match in the second element of text).

For regexec(), the function returns the same structure as gregexpr(), but only the first match is returned for each element of **text**. For gregexec(), if there is more than one match, the function returns a matrix with attributes rather than a vector with attributes. Otherwise, the function returns a vector with attributes.

Some other functions and a help page of interest are regmatchs(), for use with regexp(), gregexp(), regexec(), and gregexec(), to remove or replace text in a character vector; regex, for a help page giving the structure of regular expressions and the use of wildcards in expressions; and glob2rx(), for converting expressions with wildcards to regular expressions.

For more information on grep(), grepl(), sub(), gsub(), regexpr(), gregexpr(), regexec(), and gregexec(), use the Help tab in RStudio or enter **?grep** at the R prompt. For more information about agrep() or grepRaw(), use the Help tab in RStudio or enter **?agrep** or **?grepRaw** at the R prompt.

Functions to Manipulate Case in Character Strings

Four functions that can be used to change the case of a character string are tolower(), toupper(), casefold(), and chartr(). The tolower() and toupper() functions take one argument, **x**, which can be any object that can be coerced to the character type by using as.character(). The functions change the case of the entire vector, either to lower- or uppercase. Characters that are not letters are not changed.

The casefold() function has two arguments: **x** and **upper**. The **x** argument is as in tolower() and toupper(). The **upper** argument takes a logical value. If set to TRUE, casefold() behaves like toupper(). If set to FALSE, casefold() behaves like tolower(). The default value of **upper** is FALSE.

The chartr() function changes characters in a vector to other characters. The function takes three arguments: **old**, **new**, and **x**. The **old** and **new** arguments must be character strings and of the same length. The characters to be replaced make up **old**, while the replacement characters are in **new**, where there is a one-to-one transformation between the two. The **x** argument gives the vector on which to operate and takes a character vector. Each character in **old** and the elements of **x** is evaluated separately. Characters can be referred to by a range.

Some examples of tolower(), toupper(), casefold(), and chartr() follow:

```
tolower(
  c(
    "Jane Doe",
    "John Doe"
  )
)

casefold(
  c(
    "Jane Doe",
    "John Doe"
  )
)
```

```r
toupper(
  c(
    "Jane Doe",
    "John Doe"
  )
)
casefold(
  c(
    "Jane Doe",
    "John Doe"
  ),
  upper=TRUE
)
chartr(
  "ao",
  "oa",
  c(
    "Jane Doe",
    "John Doe"
  )
)
chartr(
  "a-e",
  "ABCDE",
  c(
    "Jane Doe",
    "John Doe"
  )
)
```

Clearly, `tolower()` and `casefold()` with the default value for **upper** give the same result (of changing the case to lowercase in a character vector). The same goes for `toupper()` and `casefold()` with **upper** set to TRUE (and the case being uppercase).

In the first call to `chartr()`, a's are changed to o's and o's to a's in the elements of the character vector. In the second call, the lowercase letters a through e are changed to the uppercase letters A through E in the elements of the character vector.

More information about `tolower()`, `toupper()`, `casefold()`, and `chartr()` can be found by using the Help tab in RStudio or by entering **?tolower** at the R prompt.

The substr(), substring(), and strsplit() Functions

The `substr()` and `substring()` functions work with character strings by specifying where on the string to operate on the string. The functions either return a portion of the character string or replace a portion of the string with a value that is assigned to the function call. The `strsplit()` function splits a character string into smaller strings based on the value of another character string.

The `substr()` function, which either returns or replaces a substring of a string, has three arguments: **x**, **start**, and **stop**. The **x** argument takes a character vector (the vector on which `substr()` operates). The **start** argument tells `substr()` how far into each character string in **x** to go before selecting or changing the substring. The **stop** argument tells `substr()` where to stop selecting or replacing the character string. Both **start** and **stop** take nonnegative integer vectors, which cycle through the elements of **x**. Both vectors can be shorter or longer than the length of **x**. Any of the integers in the vectors can be larger than the number of characters in an element of **x**. Neither **start** nor **stop** has a default value.

The `substring()` function performs much like `substr()`, except that the three arguments are **text**, **first**, and **last**. Also, the **last** argument has the default value of 1000000L, so it need not be specified.

For both `substr()` and `substring()`, assigning a value to the function call replaces the selected characters by the assigned value. For assignments, **x** must be an object rather than an expression. Also, the assigned value must be a character vector. The character vector need not be the same length as **x** and will cycle. Both functions return a vector with the same length as **x**.

If the assigned value is shorter than the selected portion of a string, only the characters out to the length of the assigned value are changed. If the value is longer than the selected characters, only the portion of the assigned value that fits in the selected portion is changed.

The `strsplit()` function splits the elements of a character vector into a list of smaller vectors based on a character vector or an object that can be coerced to a character vector. The function has five arguments: **x**, **split**, **fixed**, **perl**, and **useBytes**.

The arguments **fixed**, **perl**, and **useBytes** are as described previously and on the help page. The **x** argument is the object to be split and must be a character vector. The **split** argument is set to the character vector used for the splitting. The elements of **split** are not included in the split and cycle through the elements of **x**. For splitting on periods, use the string "[.]" rather than ".". To split the string into individual characters, set **string** to "", NULL, or character(0).

Some examples of calling `substr()`, `substring()`, and `strsplit()` are

```
substr(
  c(
    "Jane Doe",
    "John Doe",
    "Ms. X"
  ),
```

```
  2,
  7
)
substr(
  c(
    "Jane Doe",
    "John Doe",
    "Ms. X"
  ),
  c(
    6,
    6,
    0
  ),
  c(
    8,
    8,
     0
  )
)
ch11.char.2 = c(
  "Jane Doe",
  "John Doe",
  "Ms. X"
)
substr(
  ch11.char.2,
  6,
  7
) = "SoA"
ch11.char.2
```

```
substring(
  ch11.char.2,
  c(
    2,
    2,
    4
  )
) = "osa"
ch11.char.2

strsplit(
  "a.b.b",
  "b."
)

strsplit(
  "a.b.b",
  "."
)

strsplit(
  "a.b.b",
  "[.]"
)

strsplit(
  c(
    "a.b.b",
    "d.f.d"
  ),
  ""
)
```

In the first example, `substr()` operates on the second through seventh characters in each element of the vector. In the second example, `substr()` operates on the sixth through eighth characters in the first two elements and does not operate on the third element. Note that for the third element, "" is returned. In the third example, only two characters are replaced, characters six and seven even though the assigned value has three characters.

For the `substring()` example, only **first** is set, so `substring()` replaces as many characters after the first as are in the assigned value "osa" (up to the lengths of the character strings in the **x** vector). For the `strsplit()` examples, the splitting values are "b.", ".", "[.]", and "".

More information about `substr()` and `substring()` can be found by entering **?substr** at the R prompt or by using the Help tab in RStudio. For `strsplit()`, use the Help tab in RStudio or enter **?strsplit** at the R prompt.

PART V

Flow Control

CHAPTER 12

Flow Control

Flow control statements are used to repeat a series of tasks a number of times or to direct flow based on a logical object. For persons who came into programming in the age of FORTRAN and BASIC, using loops is very comfortable. (In looping, either an index is used to apply a group of expressions to each element of an object or a group of expressions is repeated until a condition is met.) In R, the better choice, if possible, is to select multiple indices of an object(s) (for an object(s) with dimensions) and to operate of the selection, instead of looping through each individual index. For many of the tasks that can be done by flow control statements, using indices is faster than looping.

That said, the control statements are **if**, **if/else**, **while**, **for**, and **repeat**. They are sometimes necessary and often useful. In this chapter, we give syntax for the flow control statements. We give examples of the use of flow control in Chapter 13.

Brackets "{}" and the Semicolon ";"

Curly brackets are used to enclose sections of code. Brackets can be used with **if**, **else**, **while**, **for**, and **repeat** flow control statements to delineate the section of code on which the control statement is to operate, both within functions and at the R console.

Brackets can also be used without an accompanying flow control statement, directly at the R console. Starting with an opening bracket, code statements can be entered one line at a time. The statements do not execute until the closing bracket is entered.

The semicolon is used to include more than one statement on one line. A statement is not evaluated until the statement before it has finished executing. If the first statement is a flow control statement followed by a single statement of code, the control flow must finish before the second statement executes. However, if the two (or more) statements are enclosed in an opening and a closing bracket after a flow control statement, all the statements within the brackets are executed together, based on the flow control statement.

The "if" and "if/else" Control Statements

The **if** control statement takes a logical object and executes code if the object is true. If the object is not true, then (optionally) different code given by an **else** statement executes.

The logical object must be an object that can be coerced to the logical type. If the logical object is of length greater than one, only the first element of the object is used.

The **if** statement can take the following forms:

```
if ( 'logical object' ) 'single code statement'
if ( 'logical object' ) 'single code statement'; 'single code
statement'
if ( 'logical object' ) { 'more than one code statement
separated by semicolons' }
if ( 'logical object' ) {
    'lines of code statements'
}
```

These four forms are not exhaustive of the possible forms. In the second form, the second statement will execute even if the logical object is false since the two statements are not enclosed in brackets.

If the **logical object** is false, then the option exists to have R execute different code by using an **else** statement. Usually, **if** and **else** statements are within the brackets of another statement (e.g., a function definition or a **for** statement). If the **if** and **else** statements are not within brackets, the **else** statement must be on the same line as the closing bracket of the **if** statement (or if there are no brackets in the **if** statement, on the same line as the last command of the **if** statement). No semicolon is placed between the **if** statement(s) and **else**.

For the control statements **if** and **else**, two examples of form follow:

```
if ( 'logical object' ) 'single code statement' else 'single
code statement'

{ if ( 'logical object' ) {
   'lines of the code statements'
}
else {
   'lines of the code statements'
} }
```

Again, the two forms are not exhaustive. If no **else** control statement is present and **logical object** is false, then the code statements associated with the **if** statement are skipped.

The "while" Control Statement

The **while** control statement executes a block of code while a logical condition is true. Again, the logical object must be an object that can be coerced to the logical type. If the logical object is of length greater than one, only the first element of the object is used. Care should be taken that the logical condition will eventually be met as the code runs. Otherwise, an "infinite" loop will occur, and the code will have to be stopped manually.

Some of the forms the control statement can take are

```
while ( 'logical object' ) 'single code statement'
while ( 'logical object' ) 'single code statement'; 'single
code statement'
while ( 'logical object' ) { 'multiple code statements
separated by semicolons' }
while ( 'logical object' ) {
    'lines of code statements'
}
```

Again, the forms shown are not exhaustive of the possible forms. Note that for the second form, the second statement does not execute until the while loop is ended since the two statements are not in brackets.

The "for" Control Statement

The **for** control statement instructs R to loop through a section of code for a set number of times. There are various ways that the looping can be done based on the looping criteria.

The looping criteria can be quite flexible. The simplest form is

```
for ( i in 1:n )
```

where **i** is an object that indexes from **1** to **n** and where **n** is an integer.

In general, the syntax of the flow control statement for **for** loops is

```
for ( 'indexing variable' in 'vector object' )
```

where **indexing variable** is a variable whose value changes at each iteration of the loop and **vector object** contains the values that **indexing value** takes. The vector object can be any object that can be coerced to a vector, including objects of the list and expression types.

The **indexing variable** object takes the values of **vector object** sequentially. Usually, the indexing variable is used in the code statements executed by the **for** loop.

Note that if the vector object is created using the function seq() within the **for** statement and the seq() argument **along.with** (which can be abbreviated **along**) is used, seq() gives the indices of the elements of **along.with** rather than the values of the object.

Some forms of a **for** loop are the following:

```
for ( 'looping criteria' ) 'single code statement'
for ( 'looping criteria' ) 'single code statement'; 'single
code statement'
for ( 'looping criteria' ) { 'multiple code statements
separated by semicolons' }
for ( 'looping criteria' ) {
    'lines of code statements'
}
```

Again, the four forms are not exhaustive of the possible forms. In the second form, the code after the semicolon does not execute until after the **for** loop is finished since the two statements are not in brackets.

According to the CRAN help page for flow control, the value of the indexing variable can be changed in the code statements referenced by **for** but, at the start of the next loop, reverts to the next indexed value of the variable. At the end of the looping, the value of **indexing variable** in the global environment is the final value of the indexing variable in the loop.

The "repeat" Control Statement

The **repeat** flow control statement repeats a section of code until a stopping point is reached. The stopping point must be programmed into the section of code. Unlike **while**, **repeat** does not have a logical object as part of the control statement, and unlike **for**, no looping index is part of the control statement. The following are two forms for repeat:

```
repeat { 'some code statements separated by semicolons' }
repeat {
    'lines of code statements'
}
```

Again, the two are not exhaustive. Infinite loops are possible with **repeat**, so use caution.

The Statements "break" and "next"

The **break** and **next** statements are used for flow control within those sections of code controlled by one of the flow controllers.

The **break** statement tells R to leave a **for**, **while**, or **repeat** loop or an **if** section and go to the first statement after the loop or section.

The **next** statement tells R to stop executing the code statements in a **for** or **while** loop and start again at the beginning of the loop with the indexing variable taking on the next value of the indexing variable.

Nesting

Any of the flow control statements can be nested within other flow control sections of code. For the sake of clarity and to prevent subtle bugs, you can use brackets at all levels when nesting flow control sections within other flow control sections.

Most of the information presented here on flow control is from the CRAN help page on controlling flow, which can be found by using the Help tab in RStudio or by entering **?Control** at the R prompt.

CHAPTER 13

Examples of Flow Control

This chapter gives some examples of flow control as well as ways to do the examples using indexing. The first example uses nested **for** loops and **if/else** statements. The second example uses the **while** statement. The third example is of nested **for** loops. The fourth example uses a **for** loop, an **if** statement, and a **next** statement. The fifth example is of a **for** loop, a **repeat** loop, an **if** statement, and a **break** statement.

Nested "for" Loops with an "if/else" Statement

In this example, we do an element-by-element substitution into a matrix based on an **if/else** test.

First, a two-by-five matrix **ch13.mat** is generated, and the matrix is displayed. Next, two **for** loops cycle through the row and column indices of **ch13.mat**. At each cycle, a set of **if/else** statements test whether the element in the matrix is greater than five.

If the value of the element is greater than five, the value of the element is replaced with one. If not, control goes to the **else** statement. Within the **else** statement, the value of the element is replaced by zero.

Last, the resultant matrix is displayed. The example follows:

© Margot Tollefson 2022
M. Tollefson, *R 4 Quick Syntax Reference*, https://doi.org/10.1007/978-1-4842-7924-3_13

```
> ch13.mat = matrix(
+    1:10,
+    2,
+    5
+ )
> ch13.mat
      [,1] [,2] [,3] [,4] [,5]
[1,]    1    3    5    7    9
[2,]    2    4    6    8   10

> for ( i in 1:2 ) {
+    for ( j in 1:5 ) {
+       if ( ch13.mat[ i, j ] > 5 ) ch13.mat[ i, j ] = 1
+       else ch13.mat[ i, j ] = 0
+    }
+ }
> ch13.mat
      [,1] [,2] [,3] [,4] [,5]
[1,]    0    0    0    1    1
[2,]    0    0    1    1    1
```

Using Indices

Doing the same substitution without loops is easier. First, the **ch13.mat**
matrix is generated and displayed. Next, the elements in **ch13.mat** are set
equal to the new values based on the original values. Note that the order in
which the substitution is done matters, since one is less than six. Last, the
resultant matrix is displayed.

The example follows:

```
> ch13.mat = matrix(
+    1:10,
```

```
+    2,
+    5
+ )
> ch13.mat
      [,1] [,2] [,3] [,4] [,5]
[1,]    1    3    5    7    9
[2,]    2    4    6    8   10

> ch13.mat[ ch13.mat <= 5 ] = 0
> ch13.mat[ ch13.mat > 5 ] = 1
> ch13.mat
      [,1] [,2] [,3] [,4] [,5]
[1,]    0    0    0    1    1
[2,]    0    0    1    1    1
```

On my MacBook Air computer, using a matrix with 10,000 rows and 50 columns, both methods took less than a second.

Sometimes, the clarity of the code justifies code that takes slightly longer to run. Also, the difference in time varies with the size of the data set on which the code operates.

A "while" Loop

In this example, a **while** loop is used to find how many iterations it takes for a sum of variables distributed randomly and uniformly between zero and one to be greater than five.

After initially setting the seed for the random number generator and setting the objects **n** and **ch13.sum** to zero, a **while** loop is started to increment **n** and to add values to **ch13.sum**. A number, generated using the random number generator for the uniform distribution (i.e., the runif() function), is added to **ch13.sum** at each iteration. When **ch13.**

sum is greater than five, the looping stops and the values for **n** and **ch13. sum** are printed out.

The example follows:

```
> set.seed( 129435 )
> n = 0
> ch13.sum = 0
> while ( ch13.sum <= 5 ) {
+    ch13.sum = ch13.sum + runif( 1 )
+    n = n + 1
+ }
> n
[1] 7
> ch13.sum
[1] 5.179325
```

Using Indices

To do the same task using indices, a vector of uniform random variables is generated of length much greater than what would be expected for the result of the sum.

Then, the function cumsum(), which creates a cumulative sum along a vector, is used to find when the sum is greater than five. The **ch13.sum** object results from applying the cumsum() function to the uniform random variates. Since the elements of **ch13.sum** are always greater than zero, the accumulated sum always increases along the vector.

Next, the function length() is used to find the number of elements for which the sum is less than or equal to five. Note that one is added to the number to give the value of **n**. Then, the values for **n** and **ch13.sum** are printed out, where **ch13.sum** equals ch13.sum[n].

The example follows:

```
> set.seed( 129435 )
```

```
> ch13.sum = runif( 25 )
> ch13.sum = cumsum( ch13.sum )
> n = length( ch13.sum[ ch13.sum <= 5  ] ) + 1
> ch13.sum = ch13.sum[ n ]
> n
[1] 7
> ch13.sum
[1] 5.179325
```

The random number generator is set to the same seed value for both parts of the example, so the results for the two are the same since the same first seven numbers are generated.

On my computer, if I substitute 1000000 for 5 in the preceding examples, and 3000000 for 25, the method using looping takes 3 to 4 seconds, while the method using indices takes less than a second. Here, the difference is speed justifies the more confusing code.

Nested "for" Loops

Sometimes, the differences between the columns of a matrix are needed. In this example, nested **for** loops are used to find the differences.

First, the **ch13.mat.2** matrix is generated with two rows and four columns and is assigned column names. Next, the matrix is displayed. Then, the **ch13.mat.2p** matrix of zeroes with two rows and six columns is generated to hold the result of the differences, and the matrix is assigned blank column names. (Note that the number of columns in **ch13.mat.2p** equals p(p-1)/2, where **p** is the number of columns in **ch13.mat.2**.)

Next, a counter **k** for the columns in the **ch13.mat.2p** matrix is set to zero. As the two **for** loops increment, **k** increases by one at each step.

Then, the two **for** loops are run. In the loops, the elements of **ch13. mat.2p** are filled with differences between the different columns in **ch13.**

441

mat.2. The two loops loop through the columns in the **ch13.mat.2** matrix in such a way that no column combinations are repeated, and the two columns are never the same. At each step, the columns of **ch13.mat.2p** are assigned names based on the names in **ch13.mat.2**.

Last, the resulting **ch13.mat.2p** matrix is displayed.

The example follows:

```
> ch13.mat.2 = matrix(
+    1:8,
+    2,
+    4
+ )
> colnames( ch13.mat.2 ) = paste0(
+    "c",
+    1:4
+ )
> ch13.mat.2
     c1 c2 c3 c4
[1,]  1  3  5  7
[2,]  2  4  6  8

> ch13.mat.2p = matrix(
+    0,
+    2,
+    6
+ )
> colnames( ch13.mat.2p ) = rep(
+    "",
+    6
+ )
> ch13.mat.2p

[1,] 0 0 0 0 0 0
```

```
[2,] 0 0 0 0 0 0

> k=0
> for ( i in 1:3 ) {
+    for ( j in ( i+1 ):4 ) {
+        k = k+1
+        ch13.mat.2p[ , k ] = ch13.mat.2[ , i ] - ch13.
         mat.2[ , j ]
+        colnames( ch13.mat.2p )[ k ] = paste0(
+          colnames( ch13.mat.2 )[ i ],
+          "-",
+          colnames( ch13.mat.2 )[ j ]
+        )
+    }
+ }
> ch13.mat.2p
     c1-c2 c1-c3 c1-c4 c2-c3 c2-c4 c3-c4
[1,]   -2    -4    -6    -2    -4    -2
[2,]   -2    -4    -6    -2    -4    -2
```

Using Indices

To do this problem using indices, two vectors of indices are created.

First, the initial **ch13.mat.2** matrix is displayed. Then, two vectors of indices of the same length, **ind.1** and **ind.2**, are created. The respective indices in the two sets are never the same, and all possible combinations of the indices are present and present only once. Some column indices appear more than once in both sets of indices.

Next, the resultant **ch13.mat.3p** matrix is created by subtracting the columns of **ch13.mat.2** in the second index set from the columns of **ch13. mat.2** in the first index set. Then, the column names for **ch13.mat.3p** are created and assigned using paste0() and the two index vectors.

443

Last, the **ch13.mat.3p** matrix is displayed. The example follows:

```
> ch13.mat.2
     c1 c2 c3 c4
[1,]  1  3  5  7
[2,]  2  4  6  8

> ind.1 = rep(
+    1:3,
+    3:1
+ )
> ind.1
[1] 1 1 1 2 2 3

> ind.2 = numeric( 0 )
> for( i in 2:4 ) ind.2 = c(
+    ind.2,
+    i:4
+ )
> ind.2
[1] 2 3 4 3 4 4

> ch13.mat.3p = ch13.mat.2[ , ind.1 ] - ch13.mat.2[ , ind.2 ]
> colnames( ch13.mat.3p ) = paste0(
+    "c",
+    ind.1,
+    "-c",
+    ind.2
+ )
> ch13.mat.3p
     c1-c2 c1-c3 c1-c4 c2-c3 c2-c4 c3-c4
[1,]    -2    -4    -6    -2    -4    -2
[2,]    -2    -4    -6    -2    -4    -2
```

Note that a **for** loop is used to create the second set of indices. Also, the matrices **ch13.mat.2p** and **ch13.mat.3p** are the same.

For large matrices, the second method is a little faster than the first. On my computer, column differences for two matrices each with 40,000 rows and 40 columns were found by the two methods. The two methods both gave the same 40,000-by-780 matrix. The looping method took about 1 second, and the indexing method took less than 1 second. The second method is a bit clearer.

A "for" Loop, "if" Statement, and "next" Statement

In this example, standard normal random numbers are generated and compared to 2.1158. Only those values that are less than or equal to 2.1158 are kept. The numbers are plotted in a histogram.

First, the seed for the random number generator is set to an arbitrary value. Then, the **ch13.vec** object is set equal to the empty numeric value. In the **for** loop that comes next, for 10,000 iterations, a standard normal random number is generated at each iteration. If the number is larger than 2.1158, the next loop starts. Otherwise, the number is added to a vector of numbers. A histogram is plotted on the final vector. See Figure 13-1 for the result.

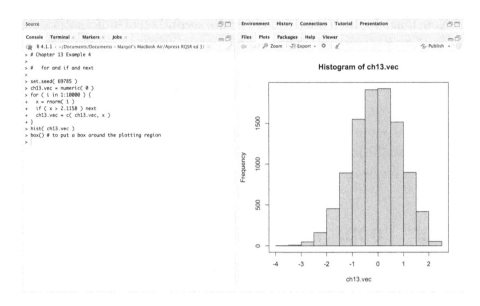

Figure 13-1. *Using a loop to generate a histogram of random standard normal variates that are less than 2.1158*

The example follows:

```
> set.seed( 69785 )
> ch13.vec = numeric( 0 )
> for ( i in 1:10000 ) {
+    x = rnorm( 1 )
+    if ( x > 2.1158 ) next
+    ch13.vec = c( ch13.vec, x )
+ }
> hist( ch13.vec )
> box() # to put a box around the plotting region
```

Using Indices

Using indices is much simpler. First, the random number generator seed is set to the same value as for the first part of this example. Next, a vector of standard normal random variables of length 10,000 is generated. Next, only those values in the vector that are less than or equal to 2.1158 are kept. Last, a histogram on the vector is generated. The histogram is shown in Figure 13-2.

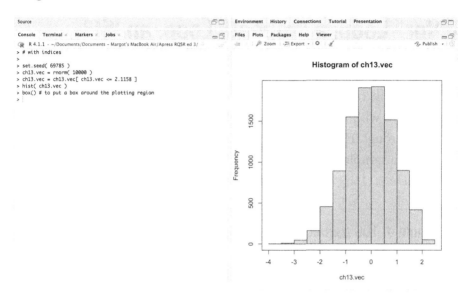

Figure 13-2. *Using indices to generate a histogram of random standard normal variates that are less than 2.1158*

The example follows:

```
> set.seed( 69785 )
> ch13.vec = rnorm( 10000 )
> ch13.vec = ch13.vec[ ch13.vec <= 2.1158 ]
> hist( ch13.vec )
> box() # to put a box around the plotting region
```

Note that the two histograms are the same since the seeds are the same and the same 10,000 numbers are used.

If 10,000 is increased to 100,000 above, on my computer, the method using loops takes about 17 seconds while the method using indices takes less than 1 second. The second method is also clear.

A "for" Loop, a "repeat" Loop, an "if" Statement, and a "break" Statement

In this example, random samples of size 100 of standard normal numbers are generated within a **repeat loop**. The **repeat loop** is within a **for** loop that goes through 10,000 iterations.

For each sample, the sum of the sample is divided by ten and then compared to 2.1158.

A sample of 100 pseudorandom standard normal variates is generated using rnorm(). The expected values of the generated numbers are zero, the standard deviations are one, and the numbers are generated independently, so the mean of the numbers has a standard error of one divided by ten. Consequently, the sample mean divided by the standard error of the mean is a standard normal variate and is equal to the sample sum divided by ten.

If the value is less than 2.1158, then the **repeat** loop continues. Otherwise, the **repeat** loop stops; the number of times through the loop (which is the number of trials until a false positive occurs) is recorded; and the next **for** loop starts. At the end, the vector of the numbers of times through the loop is plotted in a histogram, and the mean and median of the numbers of times are found.

First, the seed for the random number generator is set. Then, the **ch13. vec.2** vector is created to hold the results. The vector has an element for each iteration of the **for** loop. Next, the **for** loop opens, and the counter **n** is set to zero. Then, the **repeat** loop opens.

At the beginning of the **repeat** loop, the counter **n** is incremented by one. Then, the sample is taken, summed, and divided by ten. The result is set equal to **x**. Next, the value of **x** is compared to 2.1158 in an **if** statement. If the value is greater than 2.1158, then the value of **ch13.vec.2** for index **i** is set equal to the counter **n**, and a **break** statement breaks the function out of the **repeat** loop. Otherwise, the **repeat** loop continues looping.

At the end, hist() is run to create a histogram of **ch13.vec.2**; mean() is run to find the mean of **ch13.vec.2**; and median() is run to find the median of **ch13.vec.2**. See Figure 13-3 for the histogram.

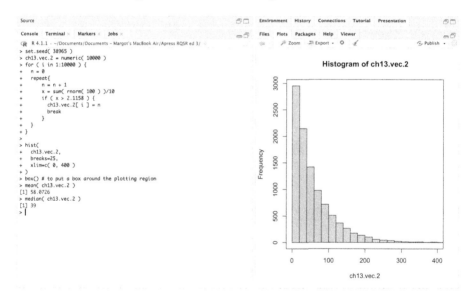

Figure 13-3. *The numbers of times needed until the result exceeds 2.1158 for sums of 100 standard normal variates divided by 10 (by using a **for** loop)*

The example follows:

```
> set.seed( 38965 )
```

```
> ch13.vec.2 = numeric( 10000 )
> for ( i in 1:10000 ) {
+    n = 0
+    repeat{
+        n = n + 1
+        x = sum( rnorm( 100 ) )/10
+        if ( x > 2.1158 ) {
+           ch13.vec.2[ i ] = n
+           break
+        }
+    }
+ }

> hist(
+    ch13.vec.2,
+    breaks=25,
+    xlim=c( 0, 400 )
+ )
> box() # to put a box around the plotting region
> mean( ch13.vec.2 )
[1] 58.0726
> median( ch13.vec.2 )
[1] 39
```

Note that the mean of **ch13.vec.2** is 58.0726, which is close to the expected number of trials before seeing an event with a probability of 0.017181 of occurring (i.e., one divided by 0.017181 or 58.204). However, the sample median (at 39) is much smaller than the sample mean (at 58.0726) since the distribution of the number of trials until a false positive occurs is highly skewed. (There is a large difference between the mean and the median of a distribution if a distribution is highly skewed, so a large difference would be expected in the mean and median from a random sample from the distribution.)

The median of this kind of distribution (the geometric distribution) is the log of 0.5 divided by the log of the quantity one minus the probability of a false positive (i.e. for this example, $\log(0.5)/(1 - \log(0.017181))$ or 39.996). Note that, over repeated sampling, about 50% of the time the number of trials until the first false positive will be less than or equal to the median.

Using Indices

To do this example using indices, we found the **repeat** loop necessary, but that the **for** loop could be dispensed with.

The random number generator seed is set to the same number as in the first part of this example. The **ch13.vec.3** and **xr** objects are set to the empty **numeric** value.

Next, the **repeat** loop opens. The **x** matrix is defined as a matrix with 100 rows and 1000 columns. The elements of **x** are 100,000 pseudorandomly generated standard normal variates generated with rnorm().

Next, the function colSums() is used to sum each column of the matrix, the result is assigned to **x**, and **x** is divided by ten. Then, the **xr** object is collected with the **x** object (using the c() function) and assigned to **x** (the **xr** object is initially an empty object); the **w** object is set equal to a vector of the indices of the elements of **x** that are greater than 2.1158; and the object **lw** is set equal to the length of **w**.

Next, the **ch13.vec.3** object is set equal to itself collected with the **w** vector minus the vector containing zero collected with the **w** vector with the last element removed (which gives the vector of the number of trials until the false positives occur.) Then R tests to see if **ch13.vec.3** is longer than 10,000 elements. If **ch13.vec.3** is long enough, the **repeat** loop stops.

If **ch13.vec.3** is not longer than 10,000, then **lr** is set to the length of **xr** (the initial value of **xr** is an empty numeric value), and **xr** is set equal to the values of **x** that occur after the last occurring false positive. (If the last false positive occurs at the last element of **x**, **xr** is set to an empty numeric object.) The repeat loop continues until **ch13.vec.3** is longer than or of length 10,000; then R breaks out of the loop.

Next, only the first 10,000 elements of **ch13.vec.3** are kept; the histogram of **ch13.vec.3** is generated using hist(); the mean of **ch13. vec.3** using mean(); and the median of **ch13.vec.3** using median(). See Figure 13-4 for the histogram.

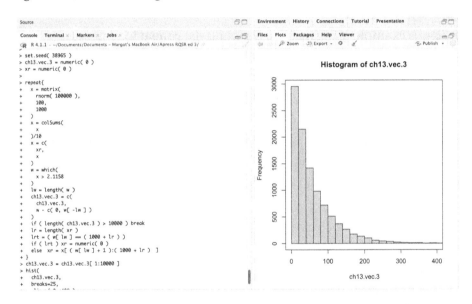

Figure 13-4. *The numbers of times needed to exceed 2.1158 for sums of 100 standard normal variables divided by 10 (using indices)*

The example follows:

```
> set.seed( 38965 )
> ch13.vec.3 = numeric( 0 )
> xr = numeric( 0 )
```

```
> repeat{
+   x = matrix(
+     rnorm( 100000 ),
+     100,
+     1000
+   )
+   x = colSums(
+     x
+   )/10
+   x = c(
+     xr,
+     x
+   )
+   w = which(
+     x > 2.1158
+   )
+   lw = length( w )
+   ch13.vec.3 = c(
+     ch13.vec.3,
+     w - c( 0, w[ -lw ] )
+   )
+   if ( length( ch13.vec.3 ) > 10000 ) break
+   lr = length( xr )
+   lrt = ( w[ lw ] == ( 1000 + lr ) )
+   if ( lrt ) xr = numeric( 0 )
+   else  xr = x[ ( w[ lw ] + 1 ):( 1000 + lr )  ]
+ }
> ch13.vec.3 = ch13.vec.3[ 1:10000 ]
> hist(
+   ch13.vec.3,
+   breaks=25,
```

```
+    xlim=c( 0, 400 )
+ )
> box() # to put a box around the plotting region
> mean( ch13.vec.3 )
[1] 58.0726
> median( ch13.vec.3 )
[1] 39
```

Once again, the result is the same as in the last example since the same pseudorandom variates are generated.

The first method takes quite a bit longer than the second method when fit with a large number of trials. If the length of **ch13.vec.2** and **ch13.vec.3** is increased to 100,000 from 10,000, the looping method takes about 28 seconds on my MacBook Air computer, and the indexing method takes about 19 seconds. Note that in running the second part of this example, I found that setting the initial matrix to too few or too many columns slowed the running time. One thousand columns worked the best of the numbers I tried.

CHAPTER 14

The ifelse( ) and switch( ) Functions

The functions `ifelse()` and `switch()` execute flow control at the console or within a function or script. The `ifelse()` function evaluates a logical expression and chooses one of two values based on the result. The `switch()` function takes a value as an argument and returns another value based on the value of the first argument.

The ifelse( ) Function

The `ifelse()` function chooses what value to return based on whether the first argument has the value TRUE or FALSE. The function has three arguments: **test**, **yes**, and **no**. The **test** argument takes an object or expression of the `logical` type, or any object or expression that can be coerced to the `logical` type (e.g., objects of the atomic types, other than the `raw` or `NULL` types, or objects of `list` type where there is only one level of depth to the list and where each element has only one value.) The **yes** argument takes an object or expression containing the value(s) to be returned when **test** is TRUE. The **no** argument is set to the object or expression to be returned when **test** is FALSE.

© Margot Tollefson 2022
M. Tollefson, *R 4 Quick Syntax Reference*, https://doi.org/10.1007/978-1-4842-7924-3_14

Each element of **test** is tested separately. Elements of the character type and missing elements return **NA**. Otherwise, the value that is returned for a given element is the value in the same position in the value of **yes** or **no**. For example, if **test** is the vector c(TRUE,TRUE,FALSE,TRUE), **yes** is the vector c(1,2,1,2), and **no** is c(4,5,6,4), then ifelse() returns c(1,2,6,2).

That is:

```
> ifelse(
+    c( TRUE, TRUE, FALSE, TRUE ),
+    c( 1, 2, 1, 2 ),
+    c( 4, 5, 6, 4 )
+ )
[1] 1 2 6 2
```

If possible, the result has the same dimensions as the **test** argument. Otherwise, a vector of the list type and of length equal to the length of **test** is returned.

For example:

```
> ch14.mat = matrix(
+    0:3,
+    2,
+    2
+ )
> ch14.mat
     [,1] [,2]
[1,]    0    2
[2,]    1    3
> ch14.list = list(
+    ch14.mat,
+    c( "a", "b", "c" )
+ )
> ch14.list
```

```
[[1]]
     [,1] [,2]
[1,]    0    2
[2,]    1    3

[[2]]
[1] "a" "b" "c"

> ifelse(
+    ch14.mat,
+    1:4,
+    30:33
+ )
     [,1] [,2]
[1,]   30    3
[2,]    2    4

> ifelse(
+    ch14.mat,
+    1:4,
+    ch14.list
+ )
[[1]]
     [,1] [,2]
[1,]    0    2
[2,]    1    3

[[2]]
[1] 2

[[3]]
[1] 3
[[4]]
[1] 4
```

First, the four-element, two-by-two ch14.mat matrix and the two-element ch14.list list are created and output.

In the first call to ifelse(), **test** is set to ch14.mat. The first element of ch14.mat is zero, so the element has the coerced value of FALSE. The other elements coerce to TRUE. (See the section on the integer type in Chapter 4 for integer coercion rules.) The **yes** and **no** arguments are also set to two-by-two matrices. A two-by-two matrix is returned by ifelse() with the first element from the respective value of **no** and the other elements from the respective values of **yes**.

In the second call to ifelse(), the **no** argument is replaced with ch14.list, while **test** and **yes** remain the same. The first element of ch14.list is the ch14.mat matrix. The second element of ch14.list is a character vector with three elements. The call to ifelse() returns a four-element list instead of a matrix, with ch14.mat as the first element and the other elements from the second, third, and fourth elements of **yes**. (Note that since the first element of **ch14.mat** results in a **FALSE** and the first element of **ch14.list** is a matrix, in the second call to ifelse(), a list is generated by the call.)

If the length of **test** is less than the length of **yes** and/or **no**, only those elements in **yes** and/or **no** up to the length of **test** are returned.

For example:

```
> ifelse(
+    c( TRUE, FALSE ),
+    1:5,
+    10:15
+ )
[1]  1 11
```

In the example, **test** has two elements, so two elements are returned by the call. The first element of **yes** is **one** and the second element of **no** is **eleven**, so a vector containing one and 11 is returned.

If **test** is longer than **yes** and/or **no**, the **yes** and/or **no** argument(s) cycles.

For example:

```
> ifelse(
+    c( TRUE, FALSE, FALSE, FALSE, TRUE ),
+    1:3,
+    10:12
+ )
[1]   1 11 12 10   2
```

The **test** argument has five elements. The **yes** and **no** arguments have three elements each and cycle out to c(1,2,3,1,2) and c(10,11,12,10,11), respectively. It follows that c(1,11,12,10,2) is returned when **test** is set to c(TRUE, FALSE, FALSE, FALSE, TRUE).

If the types of the resulting elements are not the same, then the result will have the type of the element with the highest level in the hierarchy of types, where the levels for atomic and list objects and expressions are (from lowest to highest) logical, integer, double, complex, character, and list. Objects of the **NULL** and raw types give an error.

Two examples are

```
> ifelse(
+    c( TRUE, FALSE, FALSE, FALSE, TRUE ),
+    1:5+1i,
+    1:5
+ )
[1] 1+1i 2+0i 3+0i 4+0i 5+1i
> ifelse(
+    c( TRUE, FALSE, FALSE, FALSE, TRUE ),
+    as.raw( 2:6 ),
+    as.raw( 12:16 )
+ )
Error in ans[ypos] <- rep(yes, length.out = len)[ypos] :
```

incompatible types (from raw to logical) in subassignment
type fix

A function can be used as the value for any of the three arguments.
Functions are evaluated when accessed or returned.

For example:

```
> ch14.fun = function(
+    mu,
+    se=1,
+    alpha=.05
+    ){
+    q_value = qnorm(
+       1-alpha/2,
+       mu,
+       se
+    )
+    q_value
+ }

> ifelse(
+    0:3,
+    round(
+       ch14.fun( 1:2 ),
+       3
+    ),
+    round(
+       ch14.fun( 3 ),
+       3
+    )
+ )
[1] 4.96 3.96 2.96 3.96
```

First, the `ch14.fun()` function is defined. Then `ifelse()` is called with
test set to zero through three (i.e., coercing to FALSE, TRUE, TRUE, TRUE).
So the value of **no** is returned for the first element of the result, and the
values of the second, first, and second elements of **yes** are returned for the
second, third, and fourth elements of the result, respectively.

The `ifelse()` function can be nested. For example, a first-order
Markov chain of length six with two states, where the transition matrix is

$$\begin{bmatrix} 0.7 & 0.3 \\ 0.8 & 0.2 \end{bmatrix},$$

can be generated using nested `ifelse()` functions. That is, letting "A" be
the first state and "B" be the second state:

```
> set.seed( 6978 )
> mc="A"
> for ( i in 2:6 ) {
+     rn = runif( 1 )
+     mc = c(
+       mc,
+       ifelse(
+         mc[ i-1 ] == "A",
+         ifelse(
+           rn <= 0.7,
+           "A",
+           "B"
+         ),
+         ifelse(
+           rn <= 0.8,
+           "B",
+           "A"
+         )
```

```
+       )
+     )
+ }
> mc
[1] "A" "A" "B" "B" "B" "B"
```

First, the mc object is set to "A". Within the for loop, a random number from the uniform distribution with end points at zero and one (i.e., the default values for `runif()`) is generated. Then a letter is added to mc based on the value of the randomly generated number and the value of the previous letter. If the previous letter is "A" and the random number is less than or equal to 0.7, "A" is added, and if greater than 0.7, "B" is added. If the previous letter is "B" and the random letter is less than or equal to 0.8, "B" is added, and if greater than 0.8, "A" is added.

You can find more information about `ifelse()` by using the Help tab in R Studio or by entering **?ifelse** at the R prompt.

The switch() Function

The `switch()` function chooses a value to be returned based on the value of the first argument to the function. The function has two arguments: **EXPR** and **...** (where **...** can take any number of arguments). The **EXPR** argument tells `switch()` which of the arguments of **...** to return. (According to the writers at CRAN, the **EXPR** argument should always be placed first in the argument list, even if explicitly named.) Like the `ifelse()` function, the `switch()` function can be nested.

The **EXPR** argument must be numeric, logical, complex, character, or **NA**, and it must consist of a single element. The values of the **...** argument can be of any type and dimension. Commas separate the values.

If **EXPR** is numeric, the number is rounded down to an integer; if logical, **TRUE** is coerced to **1** and **FALSE** to **0**; and if complex, the imaginary part is discarded, the real part is treated like numeric, and a warning is given. The function returns the argument indicated by **EXPR**. For example, if **EXPR** is 3, then the fourth argument is returned.

That is:

```
> switch(
+    3,
+    5, "a", "b", 6
+ )
[1] "b"
```

If the first argument is larger than the number of arguments in ..., is less than one, or is **NA**, then a NULL object is returned, quietly (a result returned quietly is not displayed at the console but can be assigned to an object.)

For example:

```
> switch(
+    0,
+    1, 2, 3
+ )
> ch14.sw = switch(
+    0,
+    1, 2, 3
+ )
> ch14.sw
NULL
```

In the example, calling switch() does not return anything to the console, since **EXPR** equals zero. But setting the call to an object outputs NULL to the object.

A character string for **EXPR** causes switch() to behave differently. The function looks at the names of the arguments following the character string to try to find a match. All the following arguments must be named except (possibly) one argument without a name.

If there is an argument without a name, then that argument becomes the default value if there is no match to the character string. If there is no argument without a name, then the default value is NULL.

Some examples are

```
> switch(
+     "e",
+     a=1, b=2, c=3, d=4,
+     e=round( ch14.fun( 0 ), 3 )
+ )
[1] 1.96
> switch(
+     "e",
+     a=1, b=2, c=3, d=4,
+     25
+ )
[1] 25

> switch(
+     "e",
+     a=1, b=2, c=3, d=4
+ )
> typeof(
+     switch(
+         "e",
+         a=1, b=2, c=3, d=4
+     )
+ )
[1] "NULL"
```

In the first call to switch(), the argument named **e** is set to a call to ch14.fun() rounded to three decimal places. In the second call, there is no argument named **e**, but there is an unnamed argument with the value 25, which is returned. (The unnamed argument can appear anywhere in the listing except as the first argument. Also, if more than one unnamed argument is entered, then switch() returns an error.) In the third call, there is no argument named **e** and no unnamed argument, so the call returns NULL, quietly.

With a character string for the first argument, the subsequent arguments need not be assigned a value, only a name. If the character string matches a name without a value, then switch() continues along the listing of the arguments and returns the value of the next argument with a value. If none of the subsequent arguments are set to a value, switch() returns NULL, invisibly.

Two examples are

```
> switch(
+   "b",
+   a=1, b=, c=3, d=
+ )
[1] 3

> switch(
+   "b",
+   a=1, b=, c=, d=
+ )
> typeof(
+   switch(
+     "b",
+     a=1, b=, c=, d=
+   )
+ )
[1] "NULL"
```

In the first call to switch(), **b** is not set to a value, but the next argument **c** is. The value of **c** is returned. In the second call, **b** and no arguments to the right of **b** are set to a value, so NULL is returned, quietly. The type of the result is returned as NULL by the typeof() function.

Note that the value of **EXPR** is enclosed in quotes if the value is of the character type, while the names of the arguments entered through the **...** argument are usually not (sometimes names are backquoted).

You can find more information about switch() by using the Help tab in RStudio or by entering **?switch** at the R prompt.

PART VI

Some Common Functions, Packages, and Techniques

CHAPTER 15

Some Common Functions

This chapter covers some common functions in R. The first section discusses the `options()` function, which sets the default options for R. The second section describes the `round()`, `signif()`, and `noquote()` functions, which are used in formatting objects. The third section discusses the `format()`, `print()`, and `plot()` functions for displaying objects. The functions in the third section operate differently on different classes of objects, so they are generic functions. The fourth section goes over the `eval()`, `attributes()`, `attr()`, and `summary()` functions. The functions return evaluated expressions, the attributes of an object, a specific attribute of an object, and a summary of the contents of an object, respectively. The `eval()` and `summary()` functions are generic functions, but `eval()` has just one method. The fifth section introduces the `deriv()`, `numericDeriv()`, and `integrate()` functions. The functions take derivatives of or integrate numeric vectors. The `parse()` and `deparse()` functions are covered in the sixth section. The functions read and return text and attempt to interpret the text as R language. In the seventh section, we cover the `anova()`, `coef()`, `effects()`, `residuals()`, `fitted()`, `vcov()`, `confint()`, and `predict()` functions. The functions operate specifically on models and are generic functions.

© Margot Tollefson 2022
M. Tollefson, *R 4 Quick Syntax Reference*, https://doi.org/10.1007/978-1-4842-7924-3_15

The options() Function

Currently on my macOS system, there are 67 options in base R and 103 options in base RStudio (here, base refers to the packages loaded by default). Options are loaded when the packages that use the options are loaded. To see a list of the options on your computer and their set values, enter **options()** at the R prompt. The options for all loaded packages are in the list.

To see the value(s) of specific options, enter options(*"opt1"*, *"opt2"*, ... , *"opt_n"*) at the R prompt, where **opt1** through **opt_n** are the names of the options (e.g., options("stringsAsFactors")). To access the value(s) of an option, use getOption(*"opt"*), where **opt** is the name of the option (e.g., get Option("stringsAsFactors")).

To set option values, enter options(*opt1=value1, opt2=value2, ... , opt_n=value_n*) at the R prompt, where **opt1** through **opt_n** are the options and **value1** through **value_n** are the values to be assigned to the options (e.g., options(stringsAsFactors=TRUE).) Note that for getting and accessing an option, the option is entered as a character string (in quotes), whereas for setting a value, the option is entered as an argument (no quotes).

When options are changed during an R session, the change is only good for the session. If the .Rprofile exists in the folder that contains the .RData and .Rhistory files, the .Rprofile file tells R what functions to run at startup. Putting lines in the .Rprofile file to run options() in order to assign values to specific options tells R to set those options when the R session opens.

To change the values of the option defaults, do one of the following. If the .Rprofile file does not already exist in the folder that contains .RData and .Rhistory, you can create the file. The .Rprofile file must be a plain text file with no extension. If the file already exists, you can edit the file. Note that if .Rprofile is changed for a given workspace and the change affects a function defined in the workspace, the function will not run in a different workspace without making the same change in the .Rprofile of that workspace.

As an example, the contents of .Rprofile might be the following:

```
options(
  defaultPackages=c(
    getOption( "defaultPackages" ),
    "MASS"
  ),
  contrasts=c(
    "contr.sum",
    "contr.poly"
  )
)
```

Here, the package **MASS** is added to the packages that are loaded at startup, and the contrast method for unordered factors is changed from the default "contr.treatment" to "contr.sum".

A small subset of the options in the full set of options is the following:

> **continue**: A character string—gives what R prints at the console when more than one line is used for R code; the default value is "+ ".
>
> **contrasts**: Character strings—the types of contrasts to use for factor data in linear models; the default values are "contr.treatment" for unordered contrasts and "contr.poly" for ordered contrasts; other possible values are "contr.sum" and "contr. helmert";information about the contrasts can be found by using the Help tab in RStudio or by entering **?contrasts** at the R prompt.

defaultPackages: Character strings—the packages to be loaded by default when R is run; the default values are "datasets", "utils", "grDevices", "graphics", "stats", and "methods" (base is always loaded).

digits: An integer—the recommendation for the number of digits to be returned for numbers; R does not necessarily use the recommended number; the default value is seven.

editor: A character string—gives the editor that the edit() function calls; the default value varies with operating system; see the help page for edit() for more information.

expressions: An integer—how deep nesting can go; the value can be between 25 and 500,000; the default value is 5000.

na.action: A character string giving a function name—gives the option for missing values; the default value is "na.omit"; other values are "na.fail", "na.pass", and "na.exclude"; see the help page for na.fail() for more information.

scipen: An integer—an option that gives R a tendency toward either scientific notation (negative integers) or fixed notation (positive integers); see the options() help page for more information; the default value is zero.

show.coef.Pvalues: A logical value—an option that tells R whether to show p values in the summary() output from linear models; the default value is TRUE.

show.signif.stars: A logical value—an option that tells R whether to show stars to give significance levels in the `summary()` output from linear models; the default value is TRUE.

stringsAsFactors: A logical value—tells `data.frame()` and `read.table()` whether to convert character strings to factors; the default value is FALSE; do not convert strings.

OutDec: Single character string—gives the value to use for a decimal point; the default value is ".".

prompt: A character string—the value to use as the R prompt; the default value is ">".

ts.eps: A numeric value—the tolerance level for comparing time periods in more than one time series; the default value is 1.0e-5.

For more about the startup process or for descriptions of the options and the packages to which they belong, use the Help tab in RStudio or enter **?Startup** (for the startup process) or **?options** (for information on the options) at the R prompt.

The round(), signif(), and noquote() Functions

The `round()`, `signif()`, and `noquote()` functions make output easier to read.

The round( ) Function

The round( ) function rounds the elements in an object or expression of the integer, double or complex type to a given number of digits. The function returns an object of the same dimensions as the original object.

The function takes two arguments: the object to be rounded (**x**) and the number of digits to which to round (**digits**). For positive numbers, **digits** gives the number of places to the right of the decimal point at which to round. For negative number, **digits** gives the number of places to the left of the decimal point at which to round.

The **x** argument takes values as described in the first paragraph of this section. The **digits** argument takes an object or expression of the logical, integer, or numeric type. Logical values are coerced to the integer type, and values of the double type are rounded to the nearest integer.

If **digits** is not a single value, then the elements of **digits** are applied down the dimensions of **x**, and for a dimension, while the rounding is done correctly, the number of places output is given by the largest value of **digits** in the dimension. (Note that vectors have only one dimension.) If **digits** is shorter than the length of **x**, the elements of **digits** cycle out to the last element of **x**.

Some examples are

```
> set.seed( 69239 )

> round(
+    c(
+       1.2344,
+       5.67,
+       1234.567
+       ),
+    3
+ )
[1]     1.234    5.670 1234.567
```

```
> round(
+    rnorm( 3, 2 ) + 62,
+    -1
+ )
[1] 70 60 60

> round(
+    1.34+3.0i,
+    1
+ )
[1] 1.3+3i

> round(
+      x=array(
+          1:8 + 0.2345,
+          c( 2, 2, 2 )
+      ),
+      digits=1:3
+ )
, , 1

      [,1]  [,2]
[1,] 1.20 3.235
[2,] 2.23 4.200

, , 2

      [,1] [,2]
[1,] 5.230 7.20
[2,] 6.234 8.23
```

Note that in the first three examples, within a vector, all the values returned have the same number of places after the decimal point, if there is one, except the real and imaginary parts of the complex number, which are treated separately.

For the fourth example, **x** is set to a two-by-two-by-two array, and **digits** is set to the one through three integer vector. The function outputs an array of the same dimensions as **x**. The two elements in the first column of the first matrix (associated with first element of the third dimension) round to one and two digits, respectively, and output with two decimal places. The elements in the second column round to three and one digit(s), respectively, and output with three decimal places.

For the matrix associated with the second element of the third dimension, the elements of the first column round to two and three digits, respectively, and output with three decimal places. For the second column, the elements of the column round to one and two digits, respectively, and output with two decimal places.

See the help page of round() for rounding rules if the last digit in **x** equals five. The default value for **digits** is zero.

The help page for round() can be found by using the Help tab in R or by entering **?round** at the R prompt.

The signif() Function

The signif() function rounds the elements of an object or expression of the logical, integer, or numeric type to a given number of significant digits. The function takes two arguments: the object or expression to be rounded (**x**) and the number of significant digits (**digits**) for the result. The arguments take the same types of values as in round() (see the last section.) And, like round(), the function outputs an object with the same dimensions as the value of **x**. If **digits** is longer than one, the argument acts in the same way as in round().

Some examples are

```
> set.seed( 69239 )
> signif(
+    c(
```

```
+      1.2344,
+      5.67,
+      1234.567
+    ),
+    3
+ )
[1]    1.23    5.67 1230.00

> signif(
+    rnorm( 3, 2 ) + 62,
+    -1
+ )
[1] 70 60 60

> signif(
+    1.34+3.0i,
+    1
+ )
[1] 1+3i

> signif(
+    array(
+        1:8 + 0.2345,
+        c( 2, 2, 2 )
+    ),
+    1:3
+ )
, , 1

     [,1] [,2]
[1,]  1.0 3.23
[2,]  2.2 4.00

, , 2
```

```
       [,1] [,2]
[1,] 5.20  7.0
[2,] 6.23  8.2
```

Note that, as in the round() function, in signif(), all the returned numbers go out to the same number of decimal places within the vectors. But for signif(), the significant digits are limited to the integer given by **digits**. If a value less than one is given for **digits**, then the number of significant digits is set to one. The default value for **digits** is six.

For more information about signif(), use the Help tab in RStudio or enter **?signif** at the R prompt.

The noquote() Function

The noquote() function returns output where the quotes have been removed from any character strings in the object. The function takes one argument **obj**, which can be any type of object.

An example is

```
> c(
+      " a",
+      "bc",
+      "d"
+ )
[1] " a" "bc" "d"
> noquote(
+      c(
+           " a",
+           "bc",
+           "d"
+      )
+ )
[1]  a bc d
```

478

More information about noquote() can be found by using the Help tab in RStudio or by entering **?noquote** at the R prompt.

The format(), print(), and plot() Functions

The format(), print(), and plot() functions behave differently depending on the class of the object on which the functions operate (i.e., they are generic functions). Methods (the way the function behaves given the class of the first argument) are defined for them. In S3, the methods are already created. In S4 and Reference Class, methods are created by the user depending on a user-defined class(es). This section covers S3 methods for the preceding three functions.

For a given generic function, to see the classes that have special methods for the function, enter **methods(*function*)** at the R prompt, where *function* is the name of the function (e.g., enter methods(format) for the methods of the format() function). Or for operators, enter methods("*operator_symbol*") where *operator_symbol* is the operator symbol (e.g., enter methods("+") for the methods of the plus operator).

In RStudio, entering the name of a generic function in the search box under the Help tab will open a drop-down menu with the function name followed by a period. Usually the name of a class comes after the period (e.g., plot.acf gives the help page for the method of plot() if the first argument to plot() is of the acf class). The menu is in alphabetical order. If the menu is longer than the space available, entering one letter after the period will list the classes starting with that letter. Sometimes, the extension after the period do not refer to a method, but a separate function (e.g., the plot.design() function is a separate function). If the function as displayed in the Usage section of the help page for the function contains the extension, then the function is a separate function.

R automatically uses the method for a class if the first argument of the function is of the class. The class extension is usually not included and sometimes gives an error if added. For example, plot(a.ts) and plot.ts(a. ts) give the same result if a.ts is an object of the ts class, while if a.lm is an object of the lm class, plot(a.lm) runs but plot.lm(a.lm) gives an error.

If there is no special function for the class of the object, then the default method is used (if there is a default method). For information about the default method of a generic function, use the Help tab in RStudio or enter **?*function*.default** at the R prompt, where *function* is the name of the function (e.g., **?plot.default**).

The format( ) Function

The format() function has 103 methods on my macOS system, including the default method. The function returns a character version of atomic objects and, for many list objects, reduced character versions of the list. The function takes several arguments that can structure the output to make a visually nice result. The arguments vary from method to method.

Two examples are

```
> ch15.date = as.Date(
+    x=1:3,
+    origin="2014-3-9"
+ )
> ch15.date
[1] "2014-03-10" "2014-03-11" "2014-03-12"
> format(
+    ch15.date,
+    "%m/%d/%Y"
+ )
[1] "03/10/2014" "03/11/2014" "03/12/2014"
```

```
> ch15.list = list(
+    c( "a", "b", "c" ),
+    matrix(
+       1:4, 2, 2,
+       dimnames = list(
+          c( "r1", "r2" ),
+          c( "c1", "c2" )
+       )
+    )
+ )
> ch15.list
[[1]]
[1] "a" "b" "c"

[[2]]
   c1 c2
r1  1  3
r2  2  4

> format(
+    ch15.list
+ )
[1] "a, b, c"    "1, 2, 3, 4"
```

In the first example, the ch15.date object is set equal to three dates (which are in the default format for dates in R). Then, format() outputs ch15.date in the traditional American format. In the second example, ch15.list is set equal to a list containing a character vector and a numeric matrix. Acting on ch15.list, the format() function returns two character strings containing the contents of the character vector and the matrix, respectively. Note that for lists, the default method of format() is applied.

For more information about `format()`, use the Help tab in RStudio or enter **?format** or **?format.ext** at the R prompt, where **ext** is the extension for the class. The possible extensions can be found in RStudio as described previously or by entering methods(format) at the R prompt.

The print() Function

The `print()` function prints objects. The function has 276 methods on my macOS system, including default. The methods can take a variety of arguments depending on the class of the object to be printed. Some useful ones that are available for many classes are **quote**, which is a logical argument that tells print whether to print quotes or not; **print.gap**, which is an integer argument that tells `print()` how many spaces to put between columns for matrices, arrays, and data frames; and **right**, which is a logical argument that tells print whether to right or left justify strings. For example:

```
> ch15.mat = matrix(
+    pasteO( "m", 1:8 ),
+    2,
+    4,
+    dimnames=list(
+       rep( "", 2 ),
+       rep( "", 4 )
+    )
+ )

> print(
+    ch15.mat
+ )

 "m1" "m3" "m5" "m7"
 "m2" "m4" "m6" "m8"
```

```
> print(
+    ch15.mat,
+    quote=FALSE,
+    right=TRUE,
+    print.gap=3
+ )
     m1     m3     m5     m7
     m2     m4     m6     m8
```

First, the ch15.mat matrix is generated and printed using the default values for the arguments in the default method of `print()`. Then, the ch15. mat is printed with quote set to FALSE, right set to TRUE, and print.gap set to three in the default method of `print()`.

To find more information about `print()` and the various print methods, use the Help tab in RStudio or enter **?print** or **?print.ext**, where **ext** is the extension for the class of the object, at the R prompt.

The plot() Function

The `plot()` function is one of the functions that makes plots. The function has 41 methods on my macOS system, including default. Plotting in R can go from simple descriptive plots to very sophisticated plots. The subject deserves and has a book of its own (*Visualizing Data in R 4: Graphics Using the base, graphics, stats, and ggplot2 Packages*, Tollefson, M. (2021), Apress); consequently, it will not be covered here. Information about `plot()` can be found by using the Help tab in RStudio or by entering **?plot** or **?plot.ext**, where **ext** is the extension for the class of the object to be plotted.

The eval(), attributes(), attr(), and summary() Functions

The eval(), attributes(), attr(), and summary() functions evaluate or give information about an object or expression. Some objects or expressions are unevaluated, some have attributes as well as a value, and some return information of interest when summarized. We go over the four functions given previously in this section.

The eval() Function

The eval() function evaluates objects or expressions. For some objects or expressions, the object or expression is not evaluated when returned. The eval() function evaluates such objects or expressions. If the object or expression is evaluated when returned, the eval() function passes the result through. (The function has one method, eval.parent().)

The eval() function has three arguments: **expr**, **envir**, and **enclos**. The **expr** argument gives the expression to be evaluated. The **envir** gives the environment in which to evaluate the expression. The **enclos** argument gives the enclosing environment(s) in which to look if the environment of **envir** does not contain an object in the expression.

The **expr** argument can take an object or expression of the language type; of the promise type; of the atomic or list type; of the special, builtin, or closure type; or of the environment type (as given on the help page for eval()). There is no default value for **expr**.

According to the help page for eval(), the **envir** argument takes an object of the environment type, a data frame or other list, a pair list, NULL, or an integer that refers to a stack number (see the help page for sys. call() for more information about the stack). Also, if **envir** is set to NULL, eval() looks for objects in the environment given by **enclos**. The default value of **envir** is parent.frame().

The **enclos** argument takes the NULL value or an object or expression of the `environment` class. The default value of **enclos** is if(is.list(envir) || is.pairlist(envir)) parent.frame() else baseenv() (i.e., if the value of **envir** is a list or pairlist, **enclos** is set to parent.frame(); otherwise, the argument is set to baseenv()).

An example of calling `eval()` is

```
> call(
+    "cospi",
+    x=0:4
+ )
cospi(x = 0:4)

> eval(
+    call(
+       "cospi",
+       x=0:4
+    )
+ )
[1]   1 -1   1 -1   1

> x
[1] 1 2 3 4 5
```

The `call()` function returns an unevaluated object of the `language` type. Note that setting the value of x in the call to `call()` does not change the value of x in the workspace. (See the section on the `language` type in Chapter 4 for more on the `call()` function.)

You can also see the section on taking derivatives and integrating (below) for an example of calling `eval()`. For more information about the function, use the Help tab in RStudio or enter **?eval** at the R prompt.

The attributes() and attr() Functions

Some objects and expressions have attributes associated with the object or expression. The `attributes()` function returns the attributes. The `attr()` function accesses a specific attribute. (The `attributes()` and `attr()` functions are not generic functions.)

The `attributes()` function has one argument **x**. The **x** argument takes any object or expression. If the object or expression has attributes, a list of the attributes is returned. If **x** has no attributes, NULL is returned. Attributes can be assigned to an object by setting a call to `attributes()` equal to a list that contains the attributes or to NULL—which removes the attributes. There is no default value for **x**.

The `attr()` function has three arguments: **x**, **which**, and **exact**. The **x** argument is as in `attributes()`. The **which** argument gives the name of the attribute to be accessed. The **exact** argument tells whether to use exact matching when matching the value of **which**.

The **which** argument takes a character string containing the name of the attribute to be accessed. There is no default value for **which**.

The **exact** argument takes a logical value. If the argument is set to TRUE, the match to the attribute name must be exact. If **exact** is set to FALSE, the name can be shortened to a unique version. The default value of **exact** is FALSE.

The value of an attribute can be set or changed with `attr()`. The assignment is as described for `attribute()`. For assignments, the value of **which** must be TRUE.

Some examples of `attributes()` and `attr()` are

```
> attributes(
+    1:10
+ )
NULL
```

```
> attributes(
+   cbind(
+     1:10,
+     1:10
+   )
+ )
$dim
[1] 10   2

> attributes(
+   cbind(
+     a=1:10,
+     b=1:10
+   )
+ )
$dim
[1] 10   2

$dimnames
$dimnames[[1]]
NULL

$dimnames[[2]]
[1] "a" "b"

> attr(
+   cbind(
+     a=1:10,
+     b=1:10
+   ),
+   "dimnames"
+ )[[ 2 ]]
[1] "a" "b"
```

```
> ch15.mat.2 = ch11.mat.3
> ch15.mat.2
   c1 c2
r1  1  3
r2  2  4

> attr(
+      ch15.mat.2,
+      "dimn"
+ )
[[1]]
[1] "r1" "r2"

[[2]]
[1] "c1" "c2"

> attr(
+      ch15.mat.2,
+      "dimnames"
+ ) = NULL

> ch15.mat.2
      [,1] [,2]
[1,]    1    3
[2,]    2    4
```

In the three calls to attributes(), the value of **x** goes from a vector to a matrix to a matrix with dimension names. The value NULL, the dim attribute, and the dim and dimnames attributes are returned, respectively, for the calls.

In the first call to attr(), the dimnames attribute is returned. Only the second value of the list is requested and output. In the second call to attr(), **x** is set to ch15.mat.2 and **which** to "dimnames". The call sets the dimnames attribute to NULL. The ch15.mat.2 matrix that is used in the call is output before and after the call and is missing dimension names after the call.

More information about `attributes()` and `attr()` can be found by using the Help tab in RStudio or by entering **?attributes** or **?attr**, respectively, at the R prompt.

The summary() Function

The `summary()` function has 49 methods on my macOS system, including default. For some classes of objects or expressions (e.g., the output from `lm()`), `summary()` is subscriptable and returns variables that are not returned by the objects or expressions of the class.

Some examples follow:

```
> set.seed( 69235 )
> x = sample(
+    3,
+    1000,
+    replace=TRUE
+ )
> y = sample(
+    4:5,
+    1000,
+    replace=TRUE
+ )
> ch15.tab = table( x, y )

> ch15.tab
   y
x     4   5
  1 175 136
  2 176 166
  3 176 171
```

```
> summary( ch15.tab )
Number of cases in table: 1000
Number of factors: 2
Test for independence of all factors:
    Chisq = 2.346, df = 2, p-value = 0.3094
> ch15.ar = array(
+    1:8,
+    c( 2, 2, 2 )
+ )
> ch15.ar
, , 1

     [,1] [,2]
[1,]    1    3
[2,]    2    4

, , 2

     [,1] [,2]
[1,]    5    7
[2,]    6    8

> summary( ch15.ar )
   Min. 1st Qu.  Median    Mean 3rd Qu.    Max.
   1.00    2.75    4.50    4.50    6.25    8.00

> set.seed( 69235 )
> ch15.lm = lm(
+    I( 1:10 + rnorm( 10, 1:10 ) ) ~ I( 1:10 )
+ )
> ch15.lm
```

```
Call:
lm(formula = I(1:10 + rnorm(10, 1:10)) ~ I(1:10))

Coefficients:
(Intercept)        I(1:10)
    -1.130          2.199

> summary( ch15.lm )

Call:
lm(formula = I(1:10 + rnorm(10, 1:10)) ~ I(1:10))

Residuals:
    Min       1Q    Median      3Q      Max
-1.12127 -0.29107   0.03822  0.41509  0.87602

Coefficients:
             Estimate Std. Error t value Pr(>|t|)
(Intercept) -1.13027    0.46886  -2.411   0.0425 *
I(1:10)      2.19884    0.07556  29.099 2.11e-09 ***
---
Signif. codes:  0 '***' 0.001 '**' 0.01 '*' 0.05 '.' 0.1 ' ' 1

Residual standard error: 0.6863 on 8 degrees of freedom
Multiple R-squared:  0.9906,    Adjusted R-squared:  0.9895
F-statistic: 846.8 on 1 and 8 DF,  p-value: 2.106e-09
```

More information about summary() can be found by using the Help tab in RStudio or by entering **?summary** or **?summary.ext** (where *ext* is the extension for the class of the object, at the R prompt.)

491

The deriv(), numericDeriv(), and integrate() Functions

The deriv() function (and the related deriv3() and D() functions) finds the first or first and second derivatives (or the partial derivatives) of a function with respect to the variable(s) in the function. (For D(), the function must be a one-variable function and only the first derivative can be found.) Part of what the deriv() function returns is the formula for the derivative(s) (or partial derivatives). Also by using the result from the call to deriv(), for a set of points, the values of the function and the gradient (and possibly the hessian) of the function can be calculated at points.

The numericDeriv() function takes the derivative of a one-variable function numerically and returns a vector of gradients at given points. The integrate() function uses a numerical method to find the integral between two points (on the x axis) of a one-variable function.

The deriv() and Related Functions

The deriv() function takes a function and returns an expression definition or a function definition. The formula(s) for the derivative(s) (or partial derivatives) of the function is part of the returned expression() or function() statement. When evaluated or run, respectively, the expression() or function() statement returns the values of the function that was entered into deriv(), calculated at a set of points. Also returned is the value(s) of the derivative(s) (and possibly the partial derivatives) at the points, which values are returned as an attribute(s).

The values of the points are the values of object(s) in the workspace with the same name(s) as the variable(s) in the function. Or the values are entered as arguments(s) (with the correctly assigned names) in a call to a function generated by deriv(). The objects or arguments need not be the same length and will cycle out to the length of the longest object or argument.

The gradient (values of the first derivative or partial derivatives at the points) and, possibly, the hessian (values of the second derivative or partial second derivatives at the points) are returned as the gradient and hessian attributes.

The deriv() function has six arguments. The arguments are **expr**, **namevec**, **function.arg**, **tag**, **hessian**, and **....**

The **expr** argument gives the function for which the derivative(s) is to be found. The argument takes a call to call(), a call to expression(), and a call to quote() that contains the formula defining the function, or a formal formula (with a tilde, where the left side of the formula is ignored and should not be included and the right side contains the formula of the entered function). There is no default value for **expr**.

The **namevec** argument takes a character vector containing the name(s) of the argument(s) for which to find the derivative(s). The name(s) of the variable(s) need not be part of the formula or exist in the global environment, but at least one name must be given. The NA and NULL values give an error. There is no default value for **namevec**.

The **function.arg** argument tells R what to return from a call to deriv(). The argument takes the NULL value, the NA value, or a logical value. Or the argument takes a character vector containing the names of the variables that must be entered into a call to the function generated by deriv(). Or the argument takes a function definition (where the body of the function is {} and the names of the variables that must be entered into the call to the function are included within the parentheses of the function definition).

If set to NULL or FALSE, an expression definition is returned. If not set to NULL or FALSE, the argument tells deriv() to return a function definition. If set to TRUE or NA, all the variables named in **namevec** must be manually entered in a call to the function returned by deriv(). If not set to NULL, FALSE, TRUE, or NA, the value of **function.arg** gives the argument(s) that must be manually entered when the function returned by deriv() is run. The default value of **function.arg** is NULL.

The **tag** argument gives the prefix for the names of any arguments created when finding the derivative(s) (e.g., for tag set to ".var", the first two names would be .var1 and .var2). The argument takes a character string. The default value of **tag** is ".expr".

The **hessian** argument tells deriv() whether to return the second derivative (or the partial second derivatives) of the function set by **expr**. If TRUE, the first and second derivatives are returned. If FALSE, only the first derivative(s) is returned. In deriv(), the default value of **hessian** is FALSE.

The **...** argument gives any arguments to the value of **expr** that are not the variable(s) for which the derivatives are to be found. The argument is optional.

The deriv3() function is the same as the deriv() function except that the default value of **hessian** is TRUE in deriv3().

The D() function finds the derivative of a one-variable function. The function takes two argument: **expr** and **name**. The **expr** argument is the same as in deriv() and deriv3(), except that the formal formula method cannot be used. The **name** argument is the same as **namevec** in deriv() and deriv3(), with the restriction that name must contain only one element.

Some examples of calling deriv(), deriv3(), and D() are

```
> x=1:2
> y=3

> deriv(
+    ~x^2*y,
+    c("x", "y" ),
+    function.arg=FALSE
+ )
expression({
    .expr1 <- x^2
    .value <- .expr1 * y
    .grad <- array(0, c(length(.value), 2L), list(NULL, c("x",
        "y")))
```

```
    .grad[, "x"] <- 2 * x * y
    .grad[, "y"] <- .expr1
    attr(.value, "gradient") <- .grad
    .value
})
> eval(
+   deriv( ~x^2*y,
+          c( "x", "y" ),
+           function.arg=FALSE
+        )
+ )
[1]  3 12
attr(,"gradient")
      x y
[1,]  6 1
[2,] 12 4

> deriv(
+   ~x^2*y,
+   c( "x", "y" ),
+   function.arg="x"
+ )
function (x)
{
    .expr1 <- x^2
    .value <- .expr1 * y
    .grad <- array(0, c(length(.value), 2L), list(NULL, c("x",
        "y")))
    .grad[, "x"] <- 2 * x * y
    .grad[, "y"] <- .expr1
    attr(.value, "gradient") <- .grad
    .value
}
```

```
> deriv(
+    ~x^2*y,
+    c( "x", "y" ),
+    function.arg=function( x ) {}
+ )( x=2:3 )
[1] 12 27
attr(,"gradient")
      x y
[1,] 12 4
[2,] 18 9

> deriv3(
+    ~x^2*y,
+    c( "x", "y" ),
+    function.arg=function( x ) {}
+    )( x=2:3 )
[1] 12 27
attr(,"gradient")
      x y
[1,] 12 4
[2,] 18 9
attr(,"hessian")
, , x

      x y
[1,] 6 4
[2,] 6 6

, , y

      x y
[1,] 4 0
[2,] 6 0
```

```
> attributes(
+    deriv3(
+       ~x^2*y,
+       c( "x", "y" ),
+       function.arg=function( x ) {}
+    )( x=2:3 )
+ )
$gradient
      x y
[1,] 12 4
[2,] 18 9

$hessian
, , x

      x y
[1,] 6 4
[2,] 6 6

, , y

      x y
[1,] 4 0
[2,] 6 0

> summary(
+    attributes(
+      deriv3(
+        ~x^2*y,
+        c( "x", "y" ),
+        function.arg=function( x ) {}
+      )( x=2:3 )
+    )
+ )
```

```
          Length Class   Mode
gradient 4         -none- numeric
hessian  8         -none- numeric

> D(
+    quote( sinpi( x ) ),
+    "x"
+ )
cospi(x) * pi
> eval(
+    D(
+       quote( sinpi( x ) ),
+       "x"
+    )
+ )
[1] -3.141593  3.141593
```

For the examples, in the workspace, **x** equals the integer vector one through two and **y** equals three. For the examples involving `deriv()` and `deriv3()`, the function to be analyzed is x squared times y, and the value of **expr** is set to a formula. The variables in the formula are **x** and **y**.

In the first call to `deriv()`, **function.arg** is set to FALSE, so an expression definition is returned. The partial derivative with respect to **x** is 2 times **x** times **y**, and the partial derivative with respect to **y** is **x** squared. In the next call (to `eval()`), the same call is evaluated with the values of **x** and **y** in the workspace. The call to `eval()` returns the vector three and 12 (which are the values returned by the **expr** function given the values of **x** and **y** in the workspace) and the gradient attribute. The gradient attribute has two values for **x** and two values for **y**. The values for x are six and 12 (2*x*y), and for y, the values are one and four (x^2).

In the second call to `deriv()`, **function.arg** is set to "x", so a function definition is returned. In the third call, **function.arg** is set to function(x){} (which has the same effect as the value set in the second call.)

The third call runs the function that is returned. The function is run (with **x** set to the vector two through three) by appending the call with (x=2:3). Note that in the third call, **x** must be entered manually into the call to the function resulting from running `deriv()` (because **function.arg** is set to a function definition that has **x** as an argument) and that **y** need not be entered (since **y** is not part of the function definition). The value of **y** in the workspace is accessed when the function is run. The function returns 12 and 27 and the gradient attribute. The gradient attribute equals 12 and 18 for **x** and four and nine for **y**.

For the first call to `deriv3()`, the values of the partial second derivatives are returned in the hessian attribute. Otherwise, the call is the same as the third call to `deriv()`. The second derivative with respect to x is two times y; with respect to x and y is two times x; and with respect to y is zero. The values of the hessian attribute for x are six and six; for x and y are four and six; and for y are zero and zero.

The second call to `deriv3()` is enclosed in an `attributes()` call. The gradient and hessian attributes are returned. The third call is the second call enclosed within a call to `summary()`. The summary function returns the name, number of values, class, and type of the two attributes. Note that the values that are returned by `deriv3()` for the attributes have no class.

The last two calls are to the `D()` function. The entered function is the sine of the quantity pi times x. The entered function is enclosed in a `quote()` function. The `D()` function returns the formula for the first derivative of the entered function: pi times the cos of the quantity pi times x.

The last call in the example is the first call to `D()` placed within a call to `eval()`. The calls return the value of the derivative at **x** for **x** equal to one and two (**x** equal to one and two is the value of **x** in the workspace and is equivalent to 180 and 360 degrees of arc).

More information about deriv(), deriv3(), and D() can be found under the Help tab in RStudio or by entering **?deriv** at the R prompt.

The numericDeriv() Function

Unlike deriv(), which uses the formula of the function to find the derivative or partial derivatives of a function, the numericDeriv() function uses a numeric method. The function returns the values of the entered function for objects in the enclosing environment. The derivative or partial derivatives are estimated for each row of values generated by the objects and are returned as the gradient attribute. If the objects are not of the same length, the values in the shorter objects cycle out to the longest length. For numericDeriv(), the variables of the function must be of the double type.

The numericDeriv() function has six arguments. The arguments are **expr**, **theta**, **rho**, **dir**, **eps**, and **central**.

The **expr** argument gives the formula of the function for which the derivatives are to be evaluated. The argument takes the same kinds of values as in deriv(), except that objects or expressions of the formula type are not allowed. The formula to which **expr** is set must return a vector of the double type. There is no default value for **expr**.

The **theta** argument gives the variables of the entered function for which derivatives or partial derivatives are to be found. The object that is returned by numericDeriv() as the gradient attribute is a matrix. The matrix has a row for each data point and a column for each value of the variables entered in the **theta** argument. The argument takes a character vector of the names of variable(s). There is no default value for **theta**.

The **rho** argument gives the environment in which to find the variables of the entered function. The argument takes an object or expression of the environment type. The default value of **rho** is parent.frame().

According to the help page for numericDeriv(), the **dir** argument gives the direction for finite differences and usually takes a value of the double type that is between minus one and one. The default value of **dir** is one.

The **eps** argument gives the step size for the numeric integration. The argument takes a positive number of the double type. The default value of **eps** is .Machine$double.eps ^ (1/if(central) 3 else 2).

The **central** argument tells numericDeriv() whether to take steps centered on a value or steps starting at a value. If set to TRUE, steps are centered, with **eps** subtracted from and added to the value. The divisor is then two times **eps**. If set to FALSE, the value is the starting point, **eps** is added to the value to get the end point, and the divisor is **eps**. According to the help page for numericDeriv(), the first option is slower, but more accurate. The default value of **central** is FALSE.

Some examples of calling numericDeriv() are

```
> x = 1:2 + 0.0
> y = 3 + 0.0
> numericDeriv(
+    quote( x^2*y ),
+    "y"
+ )
[1]  3 12
attr(,"gradient")
     [,1]
[1,]    1
[2,]    4

> numericDeriv(
+    quote( x^2*y ),
+    c( "y", "x" )
+ )
[1]  3 12
```

```
attr(,"gradient")
      [,1] [,2] [,3]
[1,]    1   6    0
[2,]    4   0   12
```

Note that adding 0.0 to 1:2 and 3 converts 1:2 and 3 from the integer type to the double type. Also, the value of **expr** in the two calls to numericDeriv() is the same as the value in the calls to deriv(). And the variables in the function have the same values. The first call to numericDeriv() has "y" as the value of **theta**, so the partial derivatives with respect to y are evaluated numerically at each of the two data points and are returned in a one-column matrix. The values agree with the values from deriv(). In the second call, **theta** is set to c("y","x"). The resulting gradient matrix has three columns, one for the single value of y and two for the two values of x. The values for both y and x agree with the result from deriv().

More information about numericDeriv() can be found under the Help tab in RStudio or by entering **?numericDeriv** at the R prompt.

The integrate() Function

The integrate() function finds the definite integral over a function with just one argument that varies. The function performs numerical integration. The lower and upper limits for the integral are set in the call to integrate(). The function returns the value and tolerance of the integral visibly and a list with the elements: value, abs.error, subdivisions, message, and call, invisibly.

The integrate() function has ten arguments (the last two are not used.) The eight arguments that are used are **f, lower, upper, ..., rel.tol, abs.tol, subdivisions**, and **stop.on.error**.

The **f** argument gives the function to be integrated and takes a value of the closure, special, or builtin type (i.e., an object of the function mode).

If the value is a function name, rather than a function definition, the name can be quoted. The function must have one, and just one, argument that is not set in the **... argument** (see below). The function must do a one-to-one mapping of numeric values to numeric values and must return a vector. There is no default value for **f**.

The **lower** and **upper** arguments give the end points (on the x axis) for the integral. The arguments can take values of the `logical`, `integer`, `double`, and `complex` types. For values of the types other than `double`, the values are coerced to the `double` type (see the `as.double()` function in Chapter 4). The value of **lower** can be larger than the value of **upper**, but then the sign of the integral is reversed (minus becomes plus and vice versa). The limits can equal -Inf and/or Inf (minus and plus infinity.) There are no default values for **lower** and **upper**.

The **...** argument allows for other arguments to the function to be entered. The arguments must be named and should take only one value. The argument(s) must be in the argument list of the function definition if **f** is set to a function definition. Otherwise, the argument(s) must be arguments to the function to which **f** is set. There are no default values for **...**.

According to the help page for `integrate()`, the **subdivisions** argument gives the maximum number of subdivisions for the integration. The default value of **subdivisions** is 100L.

Also according to the help page for `integrate()`, the **rel.tol** and **abs.tol** arguments give the acceptable relative and absolute tolerances. The default values of **rel.tol** and **abs.tol** are .Machine$double.eps^0.25 and rel.tol, respectively.

The **stop.on.error** argument tells `integrate()` whether to always stop if there is an error or to let some errors occur without stopping the call. If set to TRUE, the function always stops when an error occurs. If set to FALSE, the function continues to run for some errors. The default value of **stop.on.errors** is TRUE.

Some examples of calling integrate() are

```
> integrate(
+    sinpi,
+    0,
+    1
+ )
0.6366198 with absolute error < 7.1e-15

> integrate(
+    dnorm,
+    5,
+    Inf,
+    mean=5
+ )
0.5 with absolute error < 4.7e-05

> ch15.int = integrate(
+    function( a, x ) a*x^2,
+    0,
+    1,
+    a=3
+ )

> ch15.int
1 with absolute error < 1.1e-14

> ch15.int[1:5]
$value
[1] 1

$abs.error
[1] 1.110223e-14
```

```
$subdivisions
[1] 1

$message
[1] "OK"

$call
integrate(f = function(a, x) a * x^2, lower = 0, upper = 1, a = 3)
```

The first call to integrate() gives the integral from zero radians to one times pi radians (from zero degrees to 180 degrees) of the sine function. The returned value is two divided by pi.

The second call finds the integral from five to plus infinity for the normal probability density function that has its mean equal to five and its standard deviation equal to one (the probability that the normally distributed variate is larger than the mean of the distribution). The returned value is 0.5, as expected.

The third call is set equal to ch15.int. The call finds three times the integral of x squared, with the integration limits set to zero and one. As expected, one is returned as the value of the integral (since the indefinite integral of x squared is one-third x cubed). Entering ch15.int at the R prompt gives what is returned visibly by integrate(). Entering ch15.int[1:5] gives the five elements of the list that is returned invisibly by integrate().

More information about integrate() can be found under the Help tab in RStudio or by entering **?integrate** at the R prompt.

The parse() and deparse() Functions

The parse() function takes text that is R code and generates an object of the expression type from the text. The deparse() function takes R code and returns a character string of the code.

The parse() Function

The parse() function has seven arguments. The arguments are **file, n, text, prompt, keep.source, srcfile,** and **encoding**.

If a file or connection is the source of the code, the **file** argument gives the file location or the connection object from which the code is to be read. If **file** is set to "" and **text** (see below) is missing or NULL, parse() reads from the console. If the source of the code is an object or expression of the character type, then the object or expression is assigned to **text** rather than **file**. The **text** argument takes precedence over the **file** argument.

The **file** argument takes either a character string containing the address of a file on the computer, a connection object (see Chapter 9 for the kinds of connection objects), or the value "". The default value of **file** is "".

The **n** argument gives the maximum number of separate code segments to include in the object that is to be output (which will be of the expression type). The argument takes any logical, integer, double, or complex value. If not of the integer type, the value is coerced to the integer type (see as.integer() in Chapter 4). If longer than one element, only the first element is used. If between minus one and one (not inclusive), expression() is returned. If **n** is less than or equal to minus one, NULL, or NA, all segments are returned. The default value of **n** is NULL.

The **text** argument can take an object or expression of the character type, where the character string(s) in the object or expression contains R code. The code is entered into an expression definition, with a separate element for each character string if the length of the character object or character expression is greater than one.

The **text** argument can also take code that is not quoted. If the code is unquoted, parse() evaluates the code and puts the result into an expression definition.

If code that is not legal for R in entered through **file** or **text**, an error occurs and R exits parse() with a comment. The default value of **text** is NULL.

The **prompt** argument gives the command line prompt to use when parsing from the console. The argument takes a single character string. The default value of prompt is "?".

When parsing from the console, parse() looks for you to enter the number of lines of code given by **n**. If **n** is not set, just one line can be entered. If **n** is between minus one and one, an empty call to expression() is output. If **n** is greater than or equal to one and you do not enter all **n** lines or if **n** is less than or equal to minus one, parse() keeps prompting you for lines. Pressing the Ctrl and D keys together outputs what has been entered in an expression() definition. Pressing the Esc key exits parse() without outputting the result. (The keys work on my macOS, Windows 10, and Linux Mint systems.)

The **keep.source** argument tells parse() whether to keep the information about the source of the text that is read. If neither **file** nor **text** is set; **keep.source** is set to either TRUE or FALSE; and **srcfile** is one of not set, set to NULL, or set to a character string (see below), then no attributes are added to the value returned by parse(). If **file** and **text** are not set, **keep.source** is set to either TRUE or FALSE, and **srcfile** is set to a call to srcfile() (see below), attributes are added, but the text is not read correctly.

If **file** is set, **text** is not set, and **keep.source** is set to TRUE, attributes are added; if **keep.source** is set to FALSE and **srcfile** is set to a call to srcfile() (see below), attributes are added; otherwise, if **keep.source** is set to FALSE, no attributes are added.

If **file** is not set, **text** is set, and **keep.source** is set to TRUE, then when **srcfile** (see below) is either not set or set to a call to `srcfile()`, attributes are added, and when **srcfile** is set to NULL or a character string, no attributes are added. If **file** is not set, **text** is set, and **keep.source** is set to FALSE, when **srcfile** (see below) is not set, set to NULL, or set to a character vector, no attributes are added, and when **srcfile** is set to a call to `srcfile()`, attributes are set.

The default value of **keep.source** is getOption("keep.source"), which on my macOS system is TRUE.

The **srcfile** argument, in some cases, provides the text to be parsed into the expression definition output by `parse()`. The argument takes four kinds of values: no value, a NULL value, a character string, and a call to the `srcfile()` function. If **srcfile** is set to a call to `srcfile()` and either **file** or **text** is set, then `parse()` reads from the source file, except when **file** is set and **keep.source** is set to TRUE. Otherwise, `parse()` reads from the console, the value of **file**, or the value of **text**. The default value of **srcfile** is not set in the call to `parse()`.

The **encoding** argument gives the encoding of the text that is read. The default value of **encoding** is "unknown".

Some examples of calling `parse()` are

```
> cat(
+    "c( 2, 9 )\nc( 9, 8 )\n",
+    file="ch15.src.txt"
+ )
> system(
+    "cat ch15.src.txt"
+ )
c( 2, 9 )
c( 9, 8 )

> cat(
+    "c( 2, 3 )\nc( 9, 2 )\n",
```

```
+    file="ch15.src.2.txt"
+ )
> system(
+    "cat ch15.src.2.txt"
+ )
c( 2, 3 )
c( 9, 2 )
> ch15.par.1T = parse(
+    ,
+    2,
+    ,
+    "P>",
+    TRUE,
+    srcfile( "ch15.src.txt" )
+ )
P>1:10
P>3:7

> ch15.par.1T
expression(c( 2, c( )
> attributes( ch15.par.1T )
$srcref
$srcref[[1]]
c( 2

$srcref[[2]]
c(

$srcfile
ch15.src.txt

$wholeSrcref
c( 2, 9 )
c( 9, 8 )
```

```
> ch15.par.1F = parse(
+    ,
+    2,
+    ,
+    "P> ",
+    FALSE,
+    srcfile( "ch15.src.txt" )
+ )
P> 1:10
P> 3:7

> ch15.par.1F
expression(c( 2, c( )
> attributes( ch15.par.1F )
$srcref
$srcref[[1]]
c( 2

$srcref[[2]]
c(

$srcfile
ch15.src.txt

$wholeSrcref
c( 2, 9 )
c( 9, 8 )

> ch15.par.2T = parse(
+    "ch15.src.txt",
+    2,
+    ,
+    "P> ",
+    TRUE,
```

```
+    srcfile( "ch15.src.2.txt" )
+ )
> ch15.par.2T
expression(c( 2, 9 ), c( 9, 8 ))
> attributes( ch15.par.2T )
$srcref
$srcref[[1]]
c( 2, 9 )

$srcref[[2]]
c( 9, 8 )

$srcfile
ch15.src.txt

$wholeSrcref
c( 2, 9 )
c( 9, 8 )

> ch15.par.2F = parse(
+    "ch15.src.txt",
+    2,
+    ,
+    "P> ",
+    FALSE,
+    srcfile( "ch15.src.2.txt" )
+ )

> ch15.par.2F
expression(c( 2, 3 ), c( 9, 2 ))
> attributes( ch15.par.2F )
$srcref
$srcref[[1]]
```

```
c( 2, 3 )

$srcref[[2]]
c( 9, 2 )

$srcfile
ch15.src.2.txt

$wholeSrcref
c( 2, 3 )
c( 9, 2 )

> ch15.par.3T = parse(
+    ,
+    2,
+    "c( 2, 6 )",
+    "P> ",
+    TRUE
+ )

> ch15.par.3T
expression(c( 2, 6 ))
> attributes( ch15.par.3T )
$srcref
$srcref[[1]]
c( 2, 6 )

$srcfile
<text>

$wholeSrcref
c( 2, 6 )

> ch15.par.3F = parse(
+    ,
+    2,
```

```
+    "c( 2, 6 )",
+    "P> ",
+    FALSE
+ )

> ch15.par.3F
expression(c(2, 6))
> attributes( ch15.par.3F )
NULL

> ch15.par.4T = parse(
+    ,
+    2,
+    "c( 2, 6 )",
+    "P> ",
+    TRUE,
+    NULL
+ )

> ch15.par.4T
expression(c(2, 6))
> attributes( ch15.par.4T )
NULL

> ch15.par.4F = parse(
+    ,
+    2,
+    "c( 2, 6 )",
+    "P> ",
+    FALSE,
+    NULL
+ )
```

```
> ch15.par.4F
expression(c(2, 6))
> attributes( ch15.par.4F )
NULL
```

First, the ch15.src.txt and ch15.src.2.txt computer files are generated and printed. Then, `parse()` is run with both **file** and **text** not set, **keep. source** set to TRUE and then FALSE, and **srcfile** set to srcfile("ch15.src. txt"). With **keep.source** set to either TRUE or FALSE, text is entered from the console and attributes are printed, but what is read is not read correctly (either for the text from the console or the text in the source file) except for the wholeSrcref attribute, which returns the contents of the file given by the **srcfile** argument.

In the second set of calls, **file** is set to "ch15.src.txt", and **srcfile** is set to srcfile("ch15.src.2.txt"). For **keep.source** set to TRUE, the text is read correctly from "ch15.src.txt" and attributes are added. For **keep.source** set to FALSE, the text is read correctly from "ch15.src.2.txt" and attributes are added.

Next, **text** is set to "c(2,6)" and **srcfile** is not set. With **keep.source** set to either TRUE or FALSE, the text is read correctly, but attributes are only added when **keep.source** is set to TRUE.

In the fourth set of calls, the same values as in the third set of calls are used, except that **srcfile** is set to NULL. Once again, the text is read correctly, but attributes are not added for either value of **keep.source**.

For more information about `parse()`, use the Help tab in RStudio or enter **?parse** at the R prompt.

The deparse() Function

The `deparse()` function converts R code to a character string. The function runs the code, returns the result to the console, and generates a character string containing some form of the code. According to the help page for the function, `deparse()` is often called when creating labels for the axes of a plot.

The deparse() function has five arguments. The arguments are **expr**, **width.cutoff**, **backtick**, **control**, and **nlines**.

The **expr** argument gives the object or expression to be converted and takes any value that is legal for R code. The object or expression should not be in quotes. There is no default value for **expr**.

The **width.cutoff** argument gives the number of bytes into the value of **expr** at which to try breaking the line on which the expression is being entered. According to the help page for deparse(), R does not break a line within an expression. The argument takes a value of the integer type between 20 and 500, inclusive. The default value of **width.cutoff** is 60L.

The **backtick** argument tells deparse() whether to put backticks around object names that require a backtick if used outside the function. The default value of **backtick** is mode(expr)%in%c("call", "expression", "(", "function") (i.e., if **expr** is of the call, expression, (, or function mode, then set **backtick** to TRUE; otherwise, set **backtick** to FALSE).

The **control** argument gives the options to use when converting **expr**. The argument takes a character vector. The possible values for the elements can be found at the help page for deparseOpts. The default value of **control** is c("keepNA", "keepInteger", "niceNames", "showAttributes").

The **nlines** argument gives the maximum number of lines to convert and should take a value of the integer type. However, NA and values of the NULL, logical, double, complex, character, and list types do not give an error. A value of the NULL, character, and list types is converted to NA (sometimes with a warning and sometimes without) unless, for the character type, the value is a character string containing one integer, for which **nlines** is set to the value of the integer. A value of the logical type is coerced to one if TRUE and zero if FALSE. A value of the double type is rounded down to an integer. For a value of the complex type, the complex part is discarded with a warning, and the real part is rounded down to an integer.

If the coerced value of **nlines** is NA or less than one, all lines are read. If greater than or equal to one, the argument gives the number of lines (number of elements for a vector) that are converted. The default value of **nlines** is -1L.

Some examples of calling deparse() are

```
> ch15.dep = c(
+    list( 1:3 ),
+    list( 7:8 ),
+    list( c( 9, 8, 10 ) )
+ )
> deparse(
+    ch15.dep
+ )
[1] "list(1:3, 7:8, c(9, 8, 10))"

> deparse(
+    ch15.dep,
+    width.cutoff=20L
+ )
[1] "list(1:3, 7:8, c(9, 8, " "10))"

> deparse(
+    ch15.dep,
+    width.cutoff=20L,
+    nlines=1
+ )
[1] "list(1:3, 7:8, c(9, 8, "

> deparse(
+    ch15.dep,
+    width.cutoff=20L,
+    nlines=NA
```

```
+ )
[1] "list(1:3, 7:8, c(9, 8, " "10))"
```

First, the ch15.dep list is assigned a value with three elements. Then, deparse() is called with **expr** set to ch15.dep and the other arguments taking the default values. One character string is returned. The second call is like the first, except that **width.cutoff** is set to 20L (the smallest possible value). The call returns a two-element character vector. The first element containing 23 characters (using nchar()) with three blanks. The second element contains four characters, with no blanks.

The third call is like the second call, except that **nlines** is set to one. Only the first element of the vector returned in the second call is returned. The fourth call is like the third call, except that **nlines** is set to NA. Both elements of the vector from the second call are returned.

More information about deparse() can be found under the Help tab in RStudio or by entering **?deparse** at the R prompt.

Some Functions for Models: anova(), coef(), effects(), residuals(), fitted(), vcov(), confint(), and predict()

While print(), plot(), and summary() have methods for model classes such as **lm** and **glm**, the functions also cover many other classes. The anova(), coef(), effects(), residuals(), fitted(), vcov(), confint(), and predict() functions are generic functions and are written for model classes.

For the examples in this section, we use the following liner model (an ordinary least squares regression on y on x):

```
> set.seed( 69235 )
> x=1:5
```

```
> y = rnorm( 5 )
> ch15.lm.2 = lm(
+    y~x
+ )
```

The anova() function has seven methods on my macOS system and returns an ANOVA table for a model.

For example:

```
> methods( anova )
[1] anova.glm*      anova.glmlist* anova.lm*       anova.lmlist*
[5] anova.loess*    anova.mlm*     anova.nls*
see '?methods' for accessing help and source code

> round(
+    anova( ch15.lm.2 ),
+    4
+ )
Analysis of Variance Table

Response: y
          Df Sum Sq Mean Sq F value Pr(>F)
x          1 0.0020  0.0020  0.0052 0.9469
Residuals  3 1.1348  0.3783
```

The coef() function has six methods on my macOS system, including default, and returns the coefficients of a model.

For example:

```
> methods( coef )
[1] coef.aov*      coef.Arima*    coef.default* coef.listof*
[5] coef.maov*     coef.nls*
see '?methods' for accessing help and source code
```

```
> round(
+   coef( ch15.lm.2 ),
+   3
+ )
(Intercept)              X
    -0.716         0.014
```

The effects() function has two methods (**lm** and **glm**) on my macOS system and returns the treatment effects of a model.

For example:

```
> round(
+   effects( ch15.lm.2 ),
+   3
+ )
(Intercept)              X
     1.508         0.044         0.817         0.554

    -0.401
attr(,"assign")
[1] 0 1
attr(,"class")
[1] "coef"
```

The residuals() function has eight methods on my macOS system, including default. The function returns the residuals of a model.

For example:

```
> methods( residuals )
[1] residuals.default*         residuals.glm
residuals.HoltWinters*
[4] residuals.isoreg*          residuals.lm
residuals.nls*
[7] residuals.smooth.spline* residuals.tukeyline*
see '?methods' for accessing help and source code
```

```
round(
+   residuals( ch15.lm.2 ),
+   3
+ )
     1      2      3      4      5
-0.416 -0.017  0.669  0.374 -0.611
```

The fitted() function has five methods on my macOS system, including default, and returns the fitted values for a model.

For example:

```
> methods( fitted )
[1] fitted.default*        fitted.isoreg*        fitted.kmeans*
[4] fitted.nls*            fitted.smooth.spline*
see '?methods' for accessing help and source code

> round(
+   fitted( ch15.lm.2 ),
+   3
+ )
     1      2      3      4      5
-0.702 -0.688 -0.674 -0.660 -0.646
```

The vcov() function has eight methods on my macOS system and returns the estimated variance-covariance matrix of the coefficients of the model. There is no default method.

For an example:

```
> methods( vcov )
[1] vcov.aov*          vcov.Arima*        vcov.glm*
vcov.lm*
[5] vcov.mlm*          vcov.nls*          vcov.summary.glm* vcov.
summary.lm*
see '?methods' for accessing help and source code
```

```
> round(
+    vcov( ch15.lm.2 ),
+    3
+ )
           (Intercept)       X
(Intercept)      0.416 -0.113
X                -0.113  0.038
```

The confint() function has four methods on my macOS system, including default. The function returns confidence intervals for the coefficients of a model.

For example:

```
> methods( confint )
[1] confint.default confint.glm*    confint.lm      confint.nls*
see '?methods' for accessing help and source code
> round(
+    confint( ch15.lm.2 ),
+    3
+ )
              2.5 % 97.5 %
(Intercept) -2.769  1.336
X           -0.605  0.633
```

The predict() function has 16 methods on my macOS system and returns predictions from the model. For some classes of objects, predict() can return confidence or prediction intervals for the predicted values. If a model fit by lm() is used for the first argument in predict(), then the intervals are an option. For our **ch15.lm.2** model and for finding 95% confidence intervals for the predicted values, an example follows:

```
> methods( predict )
 [1] predict.ar*                   predict.Arima*
predict.arima0*
 [4] predict.glm                   predict.HoltWinters*
predict.lm
 [7] predict.loess*                predict.mlm*
predict.nls*
[10] predict.poly*                 predict.ppr*
predict.prcomp*
[13] predict.princomp*             predict.smooth.spline*
predict.smooth.spline.fit*
[16] predict.StructTS*
see '?methods' for accessing help and source code

> round(
+    predict(
+    ch15.lm.2,
+    interval="confidence"
+    ),
+    3
+ )
    fit    lwr    upr
1 -0.702 -2.218 0.814
2 -0.688 -1.760 0.384
3 -0.674 -1.550 0.201
4 -0.660 -1.732 0.412
5 -0.646 -2.162 0.870
```

More information for the functions in this section can be found by using the Help tab in RStudio or by **entering ?*function*** or **?*function.ext*** at the R prompt, where *function* is the function name and *ext* is the extension for the class.

CHAPTER 16

The base, stats, and graphics Packages

In this chapter, we take a quick look at the base, stats, and graphics packages (three of the packages loaded by default in R). The base package contains things such as the trigonometric function and other mathematical functions, many of the **as.** and **is.** functions, the arithmetic operators, the flow control statements, some apply functions, and many other basic functions in R.

The stats package contains many basic statistical functions, such as functions to find the median, the standard deviation, and the variance. It also includes the functions associated with common probability distributions as well as many more statistical functions. The graphics package contains the basic plotting functions (except `plot()`) and ancillary functions used by `plot()` and other plotting functions.

The other packages loaded by default are datasets, which contains data sets; utils, which contains utility functions; grDevices, which contains information used in plotting, such as fonts and colors; and methods, which contains functions and information for working with S4 (formal) methods and classes.

For a list of the functions in a package with clickable links to the function help pages, you can use the Packages tab in RStudio and select the package name or enter **help(package=*package.name*)** or **library(help=*package. name*)** at the R prompt, where *package.name* is the name of the package.

The source of the information in this chapter is the R help pages.

© Margot Tollefson 2022
M. Tollefson, *R 4 Quick Syntax Reference*, https://doi.org/10.1007/978-1-4842-7924-3_16

The base Package

The base package contains many functions basic to R. The list of links to the help pages for base is 30 pages long. This section covers the reserved words, the built-in constants, the trigonometric and hyperbolic functions, the exponential and log functions, the functions related to the beta and gamma functions, some other mathematical functions, and functions for complex numbers, matrix functions, and a few other functions. It also discusses some other functions in the base package.

Reserved Words

The reserved words in R are if, else, repeat, while, for, function, next, break, in, TRUE, FALSE, Inf, NULL, NA, NaN, NA_integer_, NA_real_, NA_complex_, NA_character_, ..., ..1, ..2, and so forth. See Table 16-1.

For more information, enter **?Reserved** at the R prompt or use the Help tab in RStudio.

Table 16-1. *The Reserved Words in R*

if	else	repeat	While	for
in	next	break	function	TRUE
FALSE	Inf	NULL	NA	NAN
NA_integer_	NA_real_	NA_complex_	NA_character_	
'...'	'.._1'	'.._2'	. . . .	'.. _n'

Built-in Constants

The built-in constants in R are **LETTERS**, which are the 26 letters in the English alphabet and which are capitalized; **letters**, which are the 26 letters in the English alphabet and which are lowercase; **month.abb**, which are three-letter abbreviations of the names of the months in English; month.name, which are the names of the months in English; and **pi**, the mathematical constant π. See Table 16-2 for a listing of the constants.

You can find more information about the constants by using the Help tab in RStudio or by entering **?Constants** at the R prompt.

Table 16-2. *The Built-in Constants in R*

Constants	Description
LETTERS	The 26 capital letters
letters	The 26 lowercase letters
month.abb	The 12 names of the months abbreviated to three letters
month.name	The 12 names of the months
pi	π; 1/2 the circumference of a unit circle

Trigonometric and Hyperbolic Functions

The trigonometric and hyperbolic functions available in R are the cosine (cos()), the cosine for which the argument is multiplied by pi before the cosine is taken (cospi()), the sine (sin()), the sine for which the argument is multiplied by pi before the sine is taken (sinpi()), the tangent (tan()), the tangent for which the argument has been multiplied by pi before the tangent is taken (tanpi()), the inverse cosine (acos()), the inverse sine (asin()), two versions of the inverse tangent (atan() and atan2()), the hyperbolic cosine (cosh()), the hyperbolic sine (sinh()), the hyperbolic tangent (tanh()), the inverse hyperbolic cosine (acosh()), the inverse hyperbolic sine (asinh()), and the inverse hyperbolic tangent (atanh()).

Angles are entered into the functions as radians (an angle in radians equals pi divided by 180 times the angle measured in degrees), except for `cospi()`, `sinpi()`, and `tanpi()`. For `cospi()`, `sinpi()`, and `tanpi()`, angles are entered as fractions of a circle times two (e.g., one is equivalent to 180 degrees, since 180 degrees is one-half of a circle). For the inverse functions, the angles are returned in radians. (Note that the result in degrees equals 180 divided by pi times the result that is returned in radians.) The argument(s) to the functions must be of the `logical`, `integer`, `double`, or `complex` type, except for `cospi()`, `sinpi()`, and `tanpi()`, which cannot be of the `complex` type. Values of the `logical` type are coerced to the `integer` type (see `as.integer()` in Chapter 4).

For the inverse cosine and sine, the values must be between minus one and one, inclusive. For other values, the result is **NaN**. For the inverse tangent, `atan()` takes one argument (which can be any object or expression of the `logical`, `integer`, `double`, or `complex` type), and the result falls between minus pi divided by two ($-\pi/2$, which is equivalently $-90°$) and pi divided by two ($\pi/2$, which is equivalently $90°$).

The `atan2()` function takes two arguments. The function returns the inverse tangent of the ratio of the two arguments, with the first argument being the numerator and the second the denominator. Both arguments of the function take any object or expression of the `logical`, `integer`, `double`, or `complex` type (logical values are coerced to the `integer` type). The arguments can be of different lengths and will cycle.

The tangent of x, for any number x, is the sine of x divided by the cosine of x. Since the function `atan2()` finds the angles associated with numbers in both a numerator and a denominator, the angles can fall in any quadrant, rather than just between minus pi divided by two and pi divided by two (between $-90°$ and $90°$). It follows that the function returns angular results between minus pi ($-\pi$, or equivalently $-180°$) and pi (π, or equivalently $180°$).

The quadrant of the angle depends on the signs on the arguments for the numerator and the denominator. (The quadrants start at the positive x axis and take up 90 degrees of arc. The quadrant number increases in the counterclockwise direction.) For the sign combinations, +/+ puts the angle in the first quadrant (0 to π/2), +/– puts the angle in the second quadrant (π/2 to π), –/– puts the angle in the third quadrant (-π to -π/2), and –/+ puts the angle in the fourth quadrant (-π/2 to 0). Also, zero in the denominator returns pi divided by two (π/2, or equivalently 90°) or minus pi divided by two (–π/2, or equivalently -90°), depending on the sign of the numerator.

The hyperbolic functions can also take any object or expression of the `logical`, `integer`, `double`, or `complex` type (logical values are coerced to the `integer` type). For the inverse of the hyperbolic functions, any values in the argument for `acosh()` must be between one and plus infinity, inclusive; the argument of `asinh()` can be any object or expression of the `logical`, `integer`, `double`, or `complex` type; and the values in the argument of `atanh()` must be between minus one and one, inclusive. For `acosh()` and `atanh()`, illegal values return NaN and a warning.

Arguments to the trigonometric and hyperbolic functions can be vectors, matrices, data frames, or arrays. For arguments with more than one element, the operation is carried out elementwise. For `atan2()`, which takes two arguments, the arguments cycle. The functions return an object of the same dimension(s) as the argument(s) to the function.

See Table 16-3 for a listing of the functions, with restrictions.

You can find more information about the trigonometric and hyperbolic functions by using the Help tab in RStudio or by entering **?Trig** and **?cosh**, respectively, at the R prompt.

Table 16-3. *The Trigonometric and Hyperbolic Functions*

Function	R Function	Restrictions
cosine	cos(x)	x; logical, integer, numeric, or complex; logical coerced to numeric
sine	sin(x)	see cosine
tangent	tan(x)	see cosine
cosine with pi	cospi(x)	x; logical , integer, or double; logical coerced to integer
sine with pi	sinpi(x)	See cosine with pi
tangent with pi	tanpi(x)	See cosine with pi
inverse cosine	acos(x)	x; $-1 \leq x \leq 1$
inverse sine	asin(x)	See inverse cosine
inverse tangent	atan(x)	See cosine
""	atan2(y,x)	y, x; see cosine for legal values for both y and x; inverse of tangent of **y** divided by **x**; maintains quadrant information
hyperbolic cosine	cosh(x)	See cosine
hyperbolic sine	sine(x)	See cosine
hyperbolic tangent	tanh(x)	see cosine
inverse hyperbolic cosine	acosh(x)	x; $1 \leq x \leq \infty$
inverse hyperbolic sine	asinh(x)	See cosine
inverse hyperbolic tangent	atanh(x)	x; $-1 \leq x \leq 1$

Exponential and Log Functions

There are two exponential functions in the base package: exp() and expm1(). There are five logarithmic functions: log(), logb(), log10(), log2(), and log1p().

The exp() function returns the value of Euler's number (i.e., *e*) raised to the power of the argument of the function (i.e., e^x). The expm1() function returns Euler's number raised to the value of the argument, from which quantity one is subtracted (i.e., $e^x - 1$). The expm1() function is useful for data where the smallest value is zero (e.g., count data). The exponential functions can find the result for any value of the logical, integer, double, or complex type (logical values are coerced to the integer type).

The log() and logb() functions return the logarithms of the values in the first argument of the function. The base for the logarithm is set by the second argument. For both functions, the default base is Euler's number (i.e., the functions return natural logarithms by default). The log() function is an S4 generic function as well as an S3 function. The logb() function is just an S3 function.

For the log10() and log2() functions, the base of the logarithm is ten and two, respectively (i.e., $log10(x)$ is the value for which $10^{log10(x)}$ is *x* and $log2(x)$ is the value for which $2^{log2(x)}$ is *x*). The preceding four functions find logarithms for nonnegative values of the integer or double type and for any values of the complex or logical type (logical values are coerced to the integer type). The legal types for the second argument are the same as the legal types for the first argument. The first and second arguments need not be the same length and will cycle.

The log1p() function returns the logarithm of values to which one has been added (i.e., $log(x + 1)$). Like the expm1() function, log1p() is useful for data where the smallest value is zero. The first argument of the function takes values of the logical, integer, or double type (logical values are coerced to the integer type). The integer and double values must be greater than or equal to minus one (i.e., ≥ -1). The second argument takes the same types of values as in the log() function.

The value returned for the log of zero, one, or Inf varies with the value of the base. For the two functions for which the base can be assigned, the log of zero returns -Inf for all bases except zero and Inf. For zero or Inf, taking the log of zero returns NaN.

Taking the log of one returns zero for all bases except when the base is set to one. For one, taking the log of one returns NaN.

The log of Inf returns -Inf when the base is set to legal values less than one (i.e., $0 \leq base < 1$) and Inf for values of base greater than or equal to one, except when the value of base is Inf (i.e., when $1 \leq base < Inf$). When the base is set equal to Inf, the function returns NaN. All other legal values for the two arguments give results other than NaN.

See Table 16-4 for a listing of the exponential and logarithmic functions.

For more information about the functions, use the Help tab in RStudio or enter **?log** at the R prompt.

Table 16-4. *The Exponential and Logarithmic Functions*

Function	Function in R	Arguments
Exponential	exp(x)	x; -Inf≤x≤Inf
Exponential minus one	expm1(x)	See exp()
Logarithm (S3 and S4 generic)	log(x, base)	x, base=exp(1); 0≤x≤Inf, 0≤base≤Inf (0,0), (0,Inf), (1,1), and (Inf,Inf) return NAN
Logarithm (S3 only)	logb(x, base)	See log()
Logarithm, base is 10	log10(x)	x; 0≤x≤Inf
Logarithm, base is 2	log2(x)	See log10()
Logarithm of x plus 1, base is e	log1p(x)	x; -1≤x≤Inf

Beta- and Gamma-Related Functions

The functions related to the beta and gamma functions are `beta()`, `lbeta()`, `gamma()`, `lgamma()`, `psigamma()`, `bigamma()`, `trigamma()`, `choose()`, `lchoose()`, `factorial()`, and `lfactorial()`. In R, these functions are called the *Special* functions. The arguments to these functions must be of the `logical`, `integer`, or `double` type (logical values are coerced to the `integer` type). The function returns a result with the same dimensions as the argument. The elements of the arguments cycle.

The `beta()` and `lbeta()` functions take the **a** and **b** arguments and return the value of the beta function or the natural logarithm of the value of the beta function, respectively. Both **a** and **b** must be nonnegative. Negative numbers return **NaN,** with a warning.

The `gamma()`, `lgamma()`, `psigamma()`, `digamma()`, and `trigamma()` functions take the **x** argument and, for `psigamma()`, the **deriv** argument. The **x** argument can be any number except zero or the negative integers (for which **NaN**s are returned with a warning). The `gamma()` and `lgamma()` functions return the value of the gamma function and the natural logarithm of the absolute value of the gamma function, respectively. The `psigamma()` function returns the derivative of the natural logarithm of the gamma function to the order given by **deriv**. The **deriv** argument must be set to an integer greater than or equal to zero. Otherwise, **NaN**s are returned, with a warning. By default, **deriv** equals zero. The `digamma()` function returns the value of the first derivative of the natural logarithm of the gamma function, while `trigamma()` returns the second derivative.

The `choose()` and `lchoose()` functions return binomial coefficients and the natural logarithms of the absolute values of binomial coefficients, respectively. The `choose()` function is the familiar "**n** choose **k**" if **n** is a positive integer and **k** is a nonnegative integer less than or equal to **n**.

Both functions take the **n** and **k** arguments. The **n** argument can be any object or expression of the `logical`, `integer`, or `double` type (logical values are coerced to the `integer` type). The **k** argument can be any object or expression of the `logical`, `integer`, or `double` type (logical values are coerced to the `integer` type and double-precision values are rounded to integers). The arguments need not be the same length and cycle out to the longer argument. If **k** contains numbers that are negative when rounded, the function returns **0** for the numbers.

The `factorial()` and `lfactorial()` functions return the factorial value and the natural logarithm of the absolute value of the factorial value, respectively. The factorial of a number is defined as gamma(x+1) for any value of **x** that is a real number. For x a positive integer, the factorial equals x factorial (i.e., (x)(x-1)(x-2)...(2)(1), denoted by x!).

The functions take one argument, **x**. The value of **x** can be any object or expression of the `logical`, `integer`, or `double` type (logical values are coerced to the `integer` type). For **x** equal to zero, factorial(x) equals one. Negative integers return NaNs with a warning.

See Table 16-5 for a listing of the functions.

You can find more information about the functions by using the Help tab in RStudio or by entering **?Special** at the R prompt.

Table 16-5. *The Beta, Gamma, and Related Functions*

Function	Function in R	Arguments
Beta	beta(a, b)	a, b; both integers ≥ 0
Natural log of beta	lbeta(a, b)	See beta
Gamma	gamma(x)	x, any real number; zero and negative integers return NaN
Natural log of the absolute value of gamma	lgamma(x)	x, any real number; zero and negative integers return Inf
nth derivative of natural log of the gamma function where **deriv** equals **n**	psigamma(x, deriv=0)	x, any real number; deriv, an integer ≥ 0; returns NaNs where not defined
First derivative of the natural log of the gamma function	digamma(x)	x, any real number; returns NaNs where not defined
Second derivative of the natural log of the gamma function	trigamma(x)	See digamma
Binomial coefficients	choose(n, k)	n, any real number k, any real number; rounds to the nearest integer, negative integers return 0
Natural log of the absolute value of the binomial coefficients	lchoose(n, k)	See binomial coefficients
Factorial	factorial(x)	x, any real number; factorial(x) equals gamma(x+1); negative integers return NaN
Natural log of the absolute value of the factorial	lfactorial(x)	x, any real number; lfactorial(x) equals lgamma(x+1); negative integers return Inf

Miscellaneous Mathematical Functions

Some other mathematical functions include the following:

sum() for the sum of the elements of an object

prod() for the product of the elements of an object

cumprod() for the cumulative product over an atomic object

cumsum() for the cumulative sum over an atomic object

mean() for the mean of the elements of an object

range() for the range of the elements of an object

rank() for the ranks of the elements of an object

order() for indices giving the order of the elements of an object; with more than one object, the order of the first object, using the second object for ties, and so forth; used to reorder vectors, matrices, data frames, and arrays; x[order(x)] equals sort(x)

sort() for sorting the elements of objects

max() for the maximum of the elements in an object, can be character

min() for the minimum of the elements in an object, can be character

cummax() for the cumulative maximum over an atomic object

cummin() for the cumulative minimum over an atomic object

pmax() for multiple vectors or matrices (will cycle)—returns the maximum across rows between objects

pmin() for multiple vectors or matrices (will cycle)—returns the minimum across rows between objects

abs() for the absolute values of the elements of an object

sign() for the signs of the elements of an object—returns 1 for positive numbers, –1 for negative numbers, and 0 for zeroes

sqrt() for the square roots of the elements of an object

ceiling() for rounding the elements of an object up to an integer

floor() for rounding the elements of an object down to an integer

trunc() for truncating the elements of an object to the decimal point

zapsmall() for setting very small numbers to zero

Atomic vectors, matrices, arrays, and data frames of the legal types can be used for these functions. The results of these functions are various kinds of objects, depending on the function. For some of the functions, the result returns a property of the data. For the other functions, the function is applied elementwise, and the result has the same dimensions as the argument.

See Table 16-6 for a listing of the functions with restrictions.

You can find more information about any of these functions by using the Help tab in RStudio or by entering **?*function.name*** at the R prompt, where *function.name* is the name of the function.

Table 16-6. *Some Other Mathematical Functions*

Function in R	Restrictions
sum(..., na.rm=FALSE)	..., logical, numeric, and complex objects separated by commas; can mix modes; returns a single value na.rm, logical; if an NA is present and na.rm is set to FALSE, returns NA; if TRUE, ignores the NA; NaN similar but are treated differently for complex numbers
prod(..., na.rm=FALSE)	See sum()
cumsum(x)	Raw, logical, numeric, or character object; will be coerced to numeric; character objects that are not a number in quotes return NAs; returns vector
cumprod(x)	See cumsum()
mean(x, trim=0, na.rm=FALSE, ...)	x, logical, numeric, or complex object; returns a single value; for complex trim must equal zero trim, $0 \leq \text{trim} \leq .5$; is proportion of elements to trim before taking the mean na.rm, logical; if an NA is present and na.rm is FALSE, returns NA; if TRUE, ignores NA; NaN the same ... any arguments to be passed to lower-level functions called by mean()

(*continued*)

Table 16-6. (*continued*)

Function in R	Restrictions
`range(..., na.rm=FALSE)`	..., logical, numeric, and character objects separated by commas; can mix modes; returns two values na.rm, logical; if an NA is present and na.rm is set to FALSE, returns NA; if TRUE, ignores the NA; NaN the same

`rank(x, na.last=TRUE,`
`ties.method=c(`
`"average", "first",`
`"random", "max",`
`"min"))`
	x, logical, numeric, complex, or character object
	na.last, logical or character; if TRUE, NAs and NaNs are ranked last; if FALSE, they are first; if NA, they are discarded; if "keep," they keep their place in the order; NaNs return NAs; returns a vector
	ties.method, character; method for setting a value for ties; the default is "average"

`order(...,`
`na.last=TRUE,`
`decreasing=FALSE)`
	..., logical, numeric, complex, or character vectors of the same length—can use just one vector—can mix modes; returns a permutation of indices of length equal to the length of the vector(s)
	na.last, logical; for TRUE, NAs are placed last; for FALSE, NAs first; for NA, NAs are removed
	Decreasing, logical; must be TRUE or FALSE; if TRUE, order is decreasing; if FALSE, increasing

(*continued*)

Table 16-6. (*continued*)

Function in R	Restrictions
sort(x, decreasing=FALSE, na.last=NA, ...)	x, logical, numeric, complex, or character object; sorts real and imaginary parts of complex separately; returns a vector
	Decreasing, logical; if TRUE, sorts in decreasing order, if FALSE, increasing; must be TRUE or FALSE
	na.last, logical; if TRUE, NAs are put last; if FALSE, they are put first; if NA, they are discarded; NaNs are put last
	..., any arguments to be passed on to lower-level functions called by sort()
max(..., na.rm=FALSE)	..., logical, numeric, complex, and character objects separated by commas; do not need to be of the same length; can mix modes; returns a single value
	na.rm, logical; if an NA is present and na.rm is set to FALSE, returns NA, if TRUE, ignores the NA
min(..., na.rm=FALSE)	See max()
cummax(x)	See cumsum()
cummin(x)	See cumsum()
pmax(..., na.rm=FALSE)	..., logical, numeric, and character objects separated by commas; do not need to be of the same length— cycle; can mix modes; returns a vector or matrix
	na.rm, logical; if an NA is present and na.rm is set to FALSE, returns NA; if TRUE, ignores the NA

(*continued*)

Table 16-6. (*continued*)

Function in R	Restrictions
pmin(..., na.rm=FALSE)	see pmax()
abs(x)	Logical, numeric, or complex objects; logical coerced to numeric; returns object of same dimensions
sign(x)	Logical or numeric object; returns object of same dimensions
sqrt(x)	See abs(); negative real numbers return NaN
ceiling(x)	Logical or numeric object; logical coerced to numeric; returns object of same dimensions
floor(x)	See ceiling()
trunc(x, ...)	x, logical or numeric object; logical coerced to numeric; returns object of same dimensions ..., any arguments to be passed on to lower-level functions called by trunc()
zapsmall(x, digits= getOptions("digits"))	x, logical, numeric, or complex object; returns object of same dimensions Digits, numeric; will round to an integer

Complex Numbers

The following functions are for complex numbers:

Re(): The real part of a complex number

Img(): The imaginary part of a complex number

Arg(): The angle from the x axis in radians of the line between the origin and the complex number

Mod(): The modulus of a complex number; equals the length of the line between the origin and the complex number

Conj(): The complex conjugate of a complex number

The functions take objects or expressions of the logical, integer, double, or complex type for arguments. Values of the logical type are coerced to the integer type. The result has the same dimensions as the argument.

You can find more information about the complex functions in the section on complex(), as.complex(), and is.complex() in Chapter 4 by using the Help tab in RStudio or by entering **?complex** at the R prompt.

Matrices, Arrays, and Data Frames

There are functions for matrices, arrays, and data frames in the base package that we have not yet covered.

Some of the functions include the following:

aperm(), which permutes an array.

kronecker(), which returns the matrix or array that is the Kronecker **product** of two objects and where **product** is a specified function. The two objects can be vectors, matrices, and/or arrays. The dimensions of the result are the products of the dimensions of the two objects.

append(), which appends elements to a vector (including lists and data frames) at a specified location on the vector. Lists and data frames return a list.

col(), which returns a matrix of the same dimensions as the argument and which contains the column indices in the columns or a matrix of factors with each column one factor.

row(), which returns a matrix of the same dimensions as the argument and which contains the row indices in the rows or a matrix of factors with each row one factor.

slice.index(), which generalizes row() and col() to arrays, more than one dimension can be selected.

colMeans(), which returns the means of the columns of a data frame or matrix or the means for given dimensions for an array—going from the first dimension to the specified dimension.

rowMeans(), which returns the means of the rows of a data frame or matrix or the means over dimensions of an array—going from the specified dimension plus one to the last dimension.

colSums(), which returns the sums of the columns of a data frame or matrix or the sums for an array—going from the first dimension to the specified dimension.

rowSums(), which returns the sums of the rows or a data frame or matrix—going from the specified dimension plus one to the last dimension.

rowsum(), which sums over rows of a matrix or data frame in groups set by the **group** variable.

determinant(), which returns the modulus, or the logarithm of the modulus of the determinant, and the sign of the modulus.

eigen(), which returns the eigenvalues and eigenvectors of a matrix.

kappa(), which calculates the condition of a square matrix.

norm(), which returns the norm of a matrix calculated by the **one, infinity, Frobenius, maximum modulus**, or **spectral** (or **2**) method

Some functions used in model fitting are the following:

backsolve(), which solves a matrix equation where the matrix on the left of the equation is upper triangular

forwardsolve(), which solves a matrix equation where the matrix on the left of the equation is lower triangular

chol(), the Cholesky decomposition of a square positive definite matrix

chol2inv(), the inverse of a positive definite matrix using the Cholesky decomposition of the matrix

qr(), the QR decomposition of a matrix

svd(), a singular value decomposition of a matrix

The **LINPACK** argument is defunct or deprecated in chol.default(), chol2inv(), and svd().

See Table 16-7 for a listing of the functions with arguments.

Table 16-7. *Some Functions for Matrices, Arrays, and Data Frames*

Function in R	Restrictions
`aperm(a, perm=NULL, resize=TRUE, ...)`	a, matrix or array perm, NULL, integer or character vector; gives order of the dimensions by index or character string; if not NULL, must be of length equal to the dimensions of **a** and a permutation of the dimensions of **a**; NULL returns the dimensions reversed Resize, logical; must be TRUE or FALSE ..., any arguments to be passed to lower-level functions
`kronecker(X, Y, FUN="*", make.names=FALSE, ...)`	X, Y, vectors, matrices, and arrays; do not have to be of the same mode; must be legal for the function **FUN** FUN, a function; can be a character string make.names, logical; must be TRUE or FALSE; does not work with all functions ..., any arguments for the function **FUN**
`append(x, values, after=length(x))`	x, a vector values, an object or expression to be appended after, an integer giving where on x to append values
`col(x, as.factor=FALSE)`	x, any matrix as.factor, logical; must be TRUE or FALSE
`row(x, as.factor=FALSE)`	See col()

(continued)

Table 16-7. (*continued*)

Function in R	Restrictions
slice.index(x, MARGIN)	x, an array MARGIN, an integer vector giving the dimension(s) to index
colMeans(x, na.rm=FALSE, dims=1)	x, logical, numeric, or complex matrix, data frame, or array na.rm, logical; must be TRUE or FALSE dims, numeric; $1 \leq dims \leq n-1$, where n is the number of dimensions
rowMeans(x, na.rm=FALSE, dims=1)	See colMeans()
colSums(x, na.rm=FALSE, dims=1)	See colMeans()
rowSums(x, na.rm=FALSE, dims=1)	See colMeans()
rowsum(x, group, reorder=TRUE, na.rm=FALSE, ...)	x, any numeric matrix group, a vector or factor of length equal to the number of rows in x—used for grouping reorder, logical; must be TRUE or FALSE na.rm, logical; must be TRUE or FALSE ..., any arguments to be passed to or from lower-level functions
determinant(x, logarithm=TRUE, ...)	x, a logical or numeric square matrix; logical coerced to numeric logarithm, logical; must be TRUE or FALSE ..., ignored

(*continued*)

Table 16-7. (*continued*)

Function in R	Restrictions
eigen(x, symmetric, only.values=FALSE, EISPACK=FALSE)	x, a logical, numeric, or complex square matrix; logical coerced to numeric symmetric, logical; if TRUE, matrix is assumed symmetric; if FALSE, not only.values, logical; if TRUE, only eigenvalues are returned; if FALSE, both eigenvalues and eigenvectors are returned EISPACK, logical; defunct and ignored
kappa(z, exact=FALSE, norm=NULL, method= c("qr", "direct"), ..)	z, logical or numeric square matrix; logical coerced to numeric exact, logical; must be TRUE or FALSE norm, character; must be NULL, "O", or "I"—for norm one and norm infinite method, character; must be "qr" or "direct"; default is "qr" ..., any arguments to lower-level functions
norm(x, type= c("O","I","F","M","2")	x, logical, numeric, or complex matrix; logical and complex are coerced to numeric type, character; default value is "O"

(*continued*)

Table 16-7. (*continued*)

Function in R	Restrictions
backsolve(r, x, k=ncol(r), upper.tri=TRUE, transpose=FALSE)	r, upper triangular matrix of mode logical, numeric, or complex—logical and complex values are coerced to numeric x, vector or matrix of mode logical, numeric, or complex—logical and complex values are coerced to numeric k, numeric—rounds down to an integer; $1 \leq k \leq ncol(r)$; is the number of columns in "r" to use upper.tri, logical; for TRUE, the upper triangle is used; for FALSE, the lower is used transpose, logical; for TRUE, **r** is transposed in the formula
forwardsolve(l, x, k=ncol(l), upper.tri=FALSE, transpose=FALSE)	l, lower triangular matrix of mode logical, numeric, or complex—logical and complex values are coerced to numeric x, a vector or matrix of mode logical, numeric, or complex—logical and complex values are coerced to numeric k, numeric—rounds down to an integer; $1 \leq k \leq ncol(l)$; the number of columns in "l" to use upper.tri, logical; for TRUE, the upper triangle is used; for FALSE, the lower is used transpose, logical; for TRUE, **l** is transposed in the formula

(*continued*)

Table 16-7. (*continued*)

Function in R	Restrictions
chol(x, pivot=FALSE, LINPACK=FALSE, tol=-1, ...)	x, raw, logical, or numeric matrix—where raw and logical matrices are coerced to numeric; must be square and positive definite
	pivot, logical; for TRUE, pivot; for FALSE, do not pivot
	LINPACK (deprecated), logical; for TRUE, use LINPACK; for FALSE, do not use LINPACK
	tol, numeric; tolerance when pivot=TRUE and LINPACK=FALSE
	..., any arguments to be passed to lower-level functions
chol2inv(x, size=NCOL(x), LINPACK=FALSE)	x, matrix for which the first **size** columns are a Cholesky decomposition
	size, numeric, logical, or complex—logical and complex coerced to numeric; $1 \leq$ size $\leq$ ncol(x)
	LINPACK, logical; defunct—no longer used
qr(x, tol=1e-7, LAPACK=FALSE, ...)	x, logical, numeric, or complex matrix; logical matrices are coerced to numeric
	tol, numeric; tolerance for singularity
	LAPACK, logical; if FALSE, qr() uses LINPACK
	..., any arguments to be passed to lower-level functions
svd(x, nu=min(n,p), nv=min(n,p), LINPACK=FALSE)	x, logical, numeric, or complex matrix; logical matrices are coerced to numeric
	nu, integer; $0 \leq$ nu $\leq$ n; n = nrow(x)
	nv, integer; $0 \leq$ nv $\leq$ p; p = ncol(x)
	LINPACK, logical; defunct and ignored

More about matrices can be found in section "Matrix Operators and Functions" in Chapter 3. You can find more information about the functions here by using the Help tab in RStudio or by entering ?*function.name* at the R prompt, where *function.name* is the name of the function.

A Few Other Functions and Some Comments

A few other functions that are often useful are

> R.home(), R.Version(), dir(), getwd(), setwd(), system(), all.equal(), Identical(), unique(), duplicated(), (and anyDuplicated()), rle(), (and inverse.rle()), jitter(), pretty(), cut(), rev(), hexamode(), margin.table(), prop.table(), try(), warning(), suppressWarnings(), warnings(), stop() and gc().

> For the functions, we will just describe what they do. You can find more information about the functions by using the Help tab in RStudio or by entering ?*function.name* at the R prompt, where *function.name* is the name of the function.

The following are the function descriptions:

> R.home() gives the full path to the directory containing the R program.

> R.Version() gives the R version and other information about the version.

> dir() returns the contents of a directory on the hard drive.

> getwd() returns the computer directory (folder) in which R is operating.

548

setwd() sets the default computer directory (folder) in which R reads and saves files.

system() runs a system command from inside R (the command is entered in quotes).

all.equal() tests if two objects are nearly equal.

Identical() tests if two objects are identically equal.

unique() returns a vector with any duplicated elements in the original vector removed. The function only works on vectors, including vectors of the list type.

duplicated() and anyDuplicated() look for duplicates. For vectors, including lists, duplicated() returns a vector of the same length containing **FALSE** for elements that are not duplicated and for the first instance of elements that are duplicated. The function returns **TRUE** for the rest of the duplicates. For matrices and data frames, rows are compared. The function anyDuplicated() counts how many differing elements have duplicates, or duplicated rows for matrices and data frames.

rle() (and inverse.rle()) returns the value and number of times the value is repeated (consecutively) in a vector, or reverses the process.

jitter() adds a little jitter (noise) to the elements of numeric objects. The arguments to jitter() control how much jitter is added.

pretty() takes any object that can be coerced to numeric and returns a vector of evenly spaced values close to a given length and similar to the values in the original object.

cut() cuts a numeric vector into factors and returns a factor vector with the factor names in the place of the original elements. The object to be cut can be any object that can be coerced to vector but must be numeric. The break points and factor names can be assigned, but cut() creates break points and factor names from the break points by default.

rev() reverses the order of the elements of an object and returns a vector. The object can be atomic or any type where reversing the order makes sense, like the list, expression, and call types.

hexmode() returns the hexadecimal value of a number.

margin.table() takes a logical, numeric, or complex object and returns margin sums for a margin in a table.

prop.table() takes a logical, numeric, or complex object and returns the object divided by the sum of the elements in the object. Logical objects are coerced to numeric, and the real and imaginary parts of complex objects are treated separately.

try() attempts to execute an expression or function and returns an error message or the result of the execution. Errors do not stop the program.

warning() generates warning messages from within an expression or function.

warnings() returns the warning messages if a program has run with warnings.

suppressWarnings() suppresses warnings generated by an expression.

stop() tells R to stop the execution of a function. If stop() has a character string for an argument, the character string prints when stop() executes. The function is very useful for the process of debugging a function as well as for checking if conditions are met for objects entered into a function.

gc() garbage collection—cleans up the session.

There are many other functions in the base package, many of which have to do with the running of R. The **as.** and **is.** functions are prevalent. On the help page for the base package, there are 53 links for **as.** functions and 43 links for **is.** functions. The Bessel functions and bitwise logical functions are also part of the base package.

If you are interested in what is in the listings, select the link to the base package under the Packages tab in RStudio or enter **help(package=base)** at the R prompt.

The stats Package

The stats package contains items such as basic descriptive statistics, probability distributions, tests, functions to fit models, clustering functions, some plotting functions, and other functions used for outputting results. The list of links to the help pages for the stats package is 18 pages long (enter **help(package=stats)** at the R prompt to see the list). In this chapter, we cover the basic descriptive statistics, the tests, clustering and other functions for multivariate data, and modeling functions, but in little detail. The probability distributions can be found in Chapter 9.

Basic Descriptive Statistics

Some of the basic statistical functions in the stats package include the following (note that the mean() function is in the base package):

> weighted.mean(), which finds the weighted mean of an object

> sd(), which finds the standard deviation of an object

> var(), which finds the variance of a vector or the covariance matrix of a matrix or data frame

> cov(), which finds the covariance matrix of a matrix or data frame—more flexible than var()

> cov.wt(), which finds the weighted covariance or correlation matrix of a matrix or data frame

> cor(), which finds the correlation between vectors or within matrices and data frames

> cov2cor(), which converts a covariance matrix (or other symmetric positive definite matrix) to a correlation matrix

> median(), which finds the median of the elements of an object

> mad(), which finds the median absolute deviation of the elements of an object

> IQR(), which finds the interquartile range of the elements of an object

> quantile(), which finds specific quantiles of the elements in an object

fivenum(), which finds Tukey's five-number
summary for the elements in an object (the
summary() function also returns the five-number
summary, along with the mean of the elements)

boxplot.stats(), returns a four-element list, with
the statistics used in boxplots as the first element

ave(), which uses a function to operate on groups of
rows, for an object with rows, based on factor values

xtabs(), which creates a contingency table based
on a formula

cancor(), which finds the canonical correlation
between two matrices

dist(), which finds a type of average difference
between the rows of a matrix, based on the type of
distance and the power used to find the average

mahalanobis(), which finds the Mahalanobis
distance between rows of a matrix

r2dtable(), which creates a random two-way
table based on marginal values—using Patefield's
algorithm

simulate(), which simulates observations from a
model that has been fitted

See Table 16-8 for a listing of the functions, with arguments.

You can find more information about the functions by using the Help
tab in RStudio or by entering **?***function.name* at the R prompt where
function.name is the name of the function.

Table 16-8. *Basic Statistical Functions in the stats Package*

Function in R	Description
weighted.mean(x, w, ..., na.rm=FALSE)	Finds the weighted mean of x, where x is coerced to a vector
sd(x, na.rm=FALSE)	Finds the standard deviation x, where x is coerced to a vector; divides by the square root of (n-1)
var(x, y=NULL, na.rm=FALSE, use)	Finds the variance of x if x is a vector or the covariance of x and y or the covariance matrix of x if x is a matrix or data frame; divides by (n-1)
cov(x, y=NULL, use="everything", method=c("pearson", "kendall", "spearman"))	Finds the covariance between x and y if y is given or the covariance matrix of x if x is a matrix or data frame; more options are available than with var( )
cov.wt(x, wt=rep(1/ nrow(x), nrow(x)), cor=FALSE, center=TRUE, method=c("unbiased", "ML"))	Finds the weighted covariance matrix or weighted correlation matrix of x, where x is a matrix or data frame
cor(x, y=NULL, use="everything", method=c("pearson", "kendall", "spearman"))	Finds the correlation between x and y if y is supplied or within x if just x is supplied, where x is a vector, matrix, or data frame
cov2cor(V)	Converts a symmetric matrix of the integer or double type to a correlation matrix if V is a positive definite matrix (i.e., could be a covariance matrix), otherwise just passes the matrix through

(continued)

Table 16-8. (*continued*)

Function in R	Description
median(x, na.rm=FALSE)	Finds the median of the elements of x
mad(x, center=median(x), constant=1.4826, na.rm= FALSE, low=FALSE, high=FALSE)	Finds the median absolute deviation of x
IQR(x, na.rm=FALSE, type=7)	Finds the interquartile range of x
quantile(x, probs=seq(0,1,.25), na.rm=FALSE, names=TRUE, type=7, ...)	Finds the quantiles of x for the values of probs
fivenum(x, na.rm=FALSE)	Finds Tukey's five-number summary for x (the summary() function also returns the five-number summary, along with the mean of x)
boxplot.stats(x, coef = 1.5, do.conf = TRUE, do.out = TRUE)	Returns a list of information about the data: the five-number summary, the sample size, the upper and lower limits of the notch if do.conf is TRUE, and the outliers if do.out is TRUE
ave(x, ..., FUN=mean)	The function in FUN operates on groups of the elements of x, where the grouping variables are in the argument ...

(*continued*)

Table 16-8. (*continued*)

Function in R	Description
xtabs(formula=~., data=parent.frame(), subset, sparse=FALSE, na.action, exclude= c(NA,NaN), drop.unused. levels=FALSE)	Creates a contingency table based on the formula, where the variables on the right side of the formula are used to group the object on the left
cancor(x, y, xcenter=TRUE, ycenter=TRUE)	Finds canonical correlation between the matrices x and y
dist(x, method="euclidean", diag=FALSE, upper=FALSE, p=2)	Finds distance between rows of a matrix, where the type of distance is specified by method
mahalanobis(x, center, cov, inverted=FALSE)	Finds the Mahalanobis distance between rows of a matrix
r2dtable(n, r, c)	Creates a random table based on marginal totals for the rows and columns
simulate(x, nsim=1, seed=NULL, ...)	Simulates observations from the model given in x; x is a model

Some Functions That Do Tests

There are functions in the stats package that do hypothesis tests. Some of the functions include the following:

> ansari.test() for the Ansari-Bradley test for testing for a difference between the scale parameters of two samples.
>
> bartlett.test() for the homogeneity of variances.

`binomial.test()` for exact tests using the binomial distribution.

`Box.test()` for the Box-Pierce and Ljung-Box tests—used in time series to test for independence.

`chisq.test()` for testing count data using Pearson's test.

`cor.test()` for correlations in paired samples.

`fisher.test()` for contingency tables using Fisher's exact test.

`fligner.test()` for the Fligner-Killeen test for homogeneity of variances.

`friedman.test()` for the Friedman rank sum test.

`kruskal.test()` for the Kruskal-Wallis rank sum test.

`ks.test()` for the Kolmogorov-Smirnov tests on one or two samples.

`mantelhaen.test()` for the Cochran-Mantel-Haenszel chi-squared test for count data.

`mauchly.test()` for the test of sphericity developed by Mauchly.

`mcnemar.test()` for the chi-squared test for count data developed by McNemar.

`mood.test()` for the two sample tests of scale developed by Mood.

`oneway.test()` for testing for equal means if the layout is one way.

`pairwise.prop.test()` for comparing proportions pairwise.

`pairwise.t.test()` for comparing t tests pairwise.

`pairwise.wilcox.test()` for comparing Wilcox on rank sum tests pairwise.

`poisson.test()` for an exact test using the Poisson distribution.

`power.anova.test()` to find powers for a balanced one-way analysis of variance.

`power.prop.test()` to find the powers for comparing two proportions.

`power.t.test()` for the powers in one and two sample t tests.

`PP.test()` for the Phillips-Perron test to test for unit roots in time series data.

`prop.test()` for testing proportions.

`prop.trend.test()` for testing trend in proportions.

`quade.test()` for the Quade test.

`shapiro.test()` for the Shapiro-Wilk test for normality.

`t.test()` for doing a t test.

`TukeyHSD()` finds confidence intervals for the coefficients of a model that take into account that more than one hypothesis is being tested—for analysis of variance models.

var.test() for an F test to compare two variances.

wilcox.test() for Wilcoxon rank sum and
sign tests.

The tests are listed with arguments in Table 16-9.

For more information about any of the tests, use the Help tab in
RStudio or enter **?***function.name* at the R prompt, where *function.name* is
the name of the function.

Table 16-9. *Some Tests in stats*

Test
ansari.test(x, y, alternative=c("two-sided", "less", "greater"), exact=NULL, conf. int=FALSE, conf.level=0.95, . . .)
bartlett.test(x, g, ...)
biniom.test(x, n, p=0.5, alternative=c("two-sided", "less", "greater"), conf. level=0.95)
Box.test(x, lag=1, type=c("Box-Pierce", "Ljung-Box"), fitdf=0)
chisq.test(x, y=NULL, correct=TRUE, p=rep(1/length(x), length(x)), rescale.p=FALSE, B=2000)
cor.test(x, y, alternative=c("two.sided", "less", "greater"), method=c("pearson", "kendall", "spearman"), exact=NULL, conf.level=0.95, continuity=FALSE, . . .)
fisher.test(x, y=NULL, workspace=200000, hybrid=FALSE, control=list(), or=1, alternative="two.sided", conf.int=TRUE, conf.level=0.95, simulate.p.value=FALSE, B=2000)
fligner.test(x, g, . . .)

(continued)

Table 16-9. (*continued*)

Test

friedman.test(y, groups, blocks, ...)

kruskal(x, g, ...)

ks.test(x, y, ..., alternative=c("two-sided", "less", "greater"), exact=NULL)

mantelhaen.test(x, y=NULL, z=NULL, alternative=c("two.sided", "less", "greater"), correct=T, exact=F, conf.level=0.95)

mauchly.test(object, ...)

mcnemar.test(x, y=NULL, correct=TRUE)

mood.test(x, y, alternative=c("two.sided", "less", "greater"), ...)

oneway.test(formula, data, subset, na.action, var.equal=FALSE)

pairwise.prop.test(x, n, p.adjust.method=p.adjust.methods, ...)

pairwise.t.test(x, g, p.adjust.method=p.adjust.methods, pool.sd=!paired, paired=FALSE, alternative=c("two.sided", "less", "greater"), ...)

pairwise.wilcox.test(x, g, p.adjust.method=p.adjust.methods, paired=FALSE, ...)

poisson.test(x, T=1, r=1, alternative=c("two-sided", "less", "greater"), conf. level=0.95)

power.anova.test(groups=NULL, n=NULL, between.var=NULL, within.var=NULL, sig. level=0.05, power=NULL)

power.prop.test(n=NULL, p1=NULL, p2=NULL, sig.level=0.05, power=NULL, alternative=c("two-sided", "one.sided"), strict=FALSE)

power.t.test(n=NULL, delta=NULL, sd=1, sig.level=0.05, type=c("two.sample", "one.sample", "paired"), alternative=c("two.sided", "one.sided"), strict=FALSE)

(continued)

Table 16-9. (*continued*)

Test
PP.test(x, lshort=TRUE)
prop.test(x, n, p=NULL, alternative=c("two-sided", "less", "greater"), conf. level=0.95, correct=TRUE)
prop.tend.test(x, n, score=seq_along(x))
quade.test(y, …)
shapiro.test(x)
t.test(x, y=NULL, alternative=c("two-sided", "less", "greater"), mu=0, paired=FALSE, var.equal=FALSE, conf.level=0.95, …)
TukeyHSD(x, which, order=FALSE, conf.level=0.95, …)
var.test(x, y, ratio=1, alternative=c("two-sided", "less", "greater"), conf.level=0.95, …)
wilcox.test(x, y=NULL, alternative=c("two-sided", "less", "greater"), mu=0, paired=FALSE, exact=NULL, correct=TRUE, conf.int=FALSE, conf.level=0.95, …)

Some Modeling Functions in stats

There are functions in the stats package that do modeling, including the following:

>   Time Series:

>   acf() to estimate autocorrelation and autocovariance in time series

>   pacf() to estimate partial autocovariances and autocorrelations for a time series

ccf() to estimate cross correlation and cross covariance for two time series

acf2AR() to exactly fit an autoregressive model to an autocorrelation function

ar() to fit a time series autoregressive model

arima() to fit an autoregressive integrated moving average to time series data

arima.sim() to do simulations from an ARIMA model

cpgram() to plot a cumulative periodogram for time series data

spec() to find the spectral density for time series data

fft() for fast discrete Fourier transforms for time series data

mvfft() for fast discrete Fourier transforms for matrices

filter() for linear filtering of time series

KalmanForcast(), KalmanLike(), KalmanRun(), KalmanSmooth(), and makeARIMA() for Kalman filtering

decompose() to decompose seasonal patterns using moving average

stl() to use the loess method to seasonally decompose a time series

StrucTS() to fit a structural time series model

Models:

`aov()` to fit an analysis of variance model

`approx()` and `approxfun()` to do linear interpolation

`density()` for kernel density estimation

`ecdf()` for the empirical cumulative distribution function

`glm()` to fit a generalized linear model

`isoreg()` isotonic or monotone regression

`line()` to fit a line robustly—based on Tukey's Exploratory Data Analysis

`lm()` to fit a linear model

`loess()` to fit a local polynomial model

`loglin()` to fit a loglinear model

`lsfit()` to fit a least squared linear model with one explanatory variable

`manova()` to fit multiple analysis of variance models

`medpolish()` for a median polish of a matrix

`nls()` to fit a nonlinear least squares model

`ppr()` to fit a projection pursuit regression model

`smooth.spline()` to fit a smooth spline model

Smoothers:

`ksmooth()` to smooth using a kernel smoother

`smooth()` which creates a smoother version of a noisy set of data using Tukey's running median smoothers—usually used for time series

`supsmu()` for Friedman's super smoother

Tools:

`add1()` to find those single terms that can be added or dropped from a model, fit the models, and tabulate the results of the fitting

`AIC()` and `BIC()` to find Akaike's "Information Criterion" or the "Schwarz-Bayesian criterion" for an appropriate model

`complete.cases()` to find complete cases for a sequence of vectors, matrices, or data.frames

`step()` to use the AIC to choose a model using a stepwise algorithm

`update()` for updating a model

`contrasts()` to set or get contrasts for a factor object

`poly()` and `polym()` to create orthogonal polynomials of the desired degree

`nlm()` to find a minimum of a nonlinear model

`optim()`, `optimHess()`, `optimise()`, and `optimize()` to optimize a function

`profile()` to profile models (generic function)

There are many functions in the stats package that support the modeling functions, which we do not cover. You can find more information at the help pages for the individual functions: either use the Help tab in RStudio or enter *?function.name* at the R prompt where *function.name* is the name of the function.

Clustering Algorithms and Other Multivariate Techniques

Some of the functions used in multivariate analysis for clustering and working with multivariate data are the following:

cut.dendrogram() for a general tree structure.

dendrapply() to apply a function to all nodes of a dendrogram.

as.dendrogram() to give an appropriate object to the class dendrogram.

labels.dendrogram() gives the ordering of or the labels of the leaves on a dendrogram.

merge.dendrogram() merges two dendrograms.

order.dendrogram() gives the ordering or the labels of the leaves of a dendrogram.

reorder.dendrogram() for reordering a dendrogram maintaining the initial constraints.

rev.dendrogram() reverses the order of the nodes in a dendrogram.

str.dendrogram() displays the internal structure of a dendrogram.

cutree() for cutting a tree into groups.

hclust() for hierarchical clustering.

identify.hclust() to identify clusters.

kmeans() for k-means clustering.

prcomp() does principal component analysis.

princomp() also does principal component analysis.

cmdscale() for classical multidimensional scaling.

cophenetic() for cophenetic distances in hierarchical clustering.

factanal() for factor analysis.

loadings() printing loadings from a factor analysis.

promax() used for rotation of axes in factor analysis.

varimax() used for rotation of axes in factor analysis.

The stats package also contains several probability distributions (see Chapter 9); eight **as.** functions; six **is.** functions; a number of plotting functions (like heatmap()) and 19 **plot.** functions (which are specific for many of the classes associated with modeling functions); functions used in kernel estimation; ancillary functions for models (like the seven **model.** functions); seven **na.** functions (to handle missing data); 13 **predict.** functions (for model output), 28 **print.** functions (for printing output); and nine **summary.** functions (for summarizing output).

For more information about any of the functions, use the Help tab in RStudio or enter ?*function.name* at the R prompt where *function.name* is the name of the function.

The graphics Package

The graphics package does not contain the plot() function anymore (the function was recently moved to the base package). The graphics package does contain several methods for plot(). The ancillary functions for plot() are also in the graphics package. There are several plotting functions for specific types of plots (like histograms and bar charts).

The list of links to the help pages for graphics is three pages long (from entering **help(package=graphics)** at the R prompt). In this section, we cover the specific types of plots and a few other functions related to plotting.

The following are the functions in the graphics package that do specific types of plots:

assocplot() for a Cohen-Friendly association plot; used for contingency tables; will work with any matrix that is logical or numeric.

barplot() for a bar plot; takes vector or matrix objects, which are of mode logical or numeric, for the heights of the bars.

boxplot() for box plots; logical or numeric vectors, matrices, arrays, data frames, and some lists can be used as input to the function.

bxp() for box plots of summaries.

cdplot() for a conditional density plot.

coplot() for scatter plots using a conditioning variable.

contour() and filled.contour() for a contour plot and a contour plot where the regions between the contours are filled with different colors.

curve() for plotting a one-variable function that is a one-to-one mapping.

dotchart() for a Cleveland dot plot; numeric vectors and matrices can be used for the plot.

fourfoldplot() for a fourfold plot of 2 x 2 x k contingency tables.

hist() for histograms; gives histograms for numeric vectors, matrices, and arrays.

matplot() for plotting a vector or the columns of a matrix on a single plot.

mosaicplot() for mosaic plots; takes numeric or logical arguments that are vectors, matrices, data frames, or arrays; is meant for contingency tables.

pairs() for scatter plots of paired variables; takes numeric vectors, matrices, and data frames as input; creates a matrix of plots.

persp() for a perspective plot; does three-dimensional plotting.

pie() for pie charts; uses numeric vectors, matrices, and arrays as input.

smoothScatter() for a smoothed version of scatter plots—which are colored; is copyrighted by M. P. Wand.

spineplot() for spine plots; uses a logical, numeric, or complex matrix as input to the plot; logical and complex matrices are coerced to numeric; was developed for two-way contingency tables.

stars() for star or segment plots; uses a numeric matrix or data frame for the input to the plot.

stem() for a stem and leaf plot; uses a numeric vector, matrix, or array as the input to the plot

stripchart() for a one-dimensional scatter plot.

sunflowerplot() for a sunflower plot, which is a scatter plot in which points with duplicates have sunflower leaves for the duplicated points; uses a logical, numeric, or complex vector, matrix, or data frame for the input to the plot.

There are also some functions in the graphics package that control the screen for plotting functions. The splitscreen() function and its ancillary functions, close.screen(), erase.screen(), and screen(), are used to split the plotting screen into regions and to plot to the regions. The frame() and plot.new() functions open a new frame for plotting.

The par() function in the graphics package is like options(), except the function is for plotting options and contains the options used by many plotting functions. When a session starts, the options in par() are the default options. To see the list of options, call par() with no arguments. The options can be changed at any time (in the same way that options are changed in options()). Calling par() opens a new plotting frame.

The function plot() (in the base package) is the basic plotting function in R and has a number of ancillary functions in the graphics package (like lines(), points(), and box()). Twelve methods for plot() are found in the graphics package. We do not cover plot() in this book.

You can find more information about the functions in the graphics package by using the Help tab in RStudio or by entering ?*function.name* at the R prompt where *function.name* is the name of the function.

CHAPTER 17

Tricks of the Trade

This book would not be complete without advice on some tricky parts of R. When it seems that everything is set up right, but things still do not do what you expect and you do not know why, this chapter can help. This chapter also describes some not-so-obvious parts of R. Also, we give some new parts of R.

Value Substitution: NA, NaN, Inf, and –Inf

This section has to do with missing data (i.e., **NAs**) or illegal elements (i.e., **NaNs**, **Infs**, or **–Infs**). Say you want to substitute a value, for example, **0**, for missing values. The intuitive approach would be to enter something like the following:

```
mat[ mat==NA ] = 0
```

This does not work. What does work is to enter the following:

```
mat [ is.na( mat ) ] = 0
```

For example:

```
> ch17.mat = matrix(
+    c(
+      1,
+      NA,
+      3,
```

© Margot Tollefson 2022

M. Tollefson, *R 4 Quick Syntax Reference*, https://doi.org/10.1007/978-1-4842-7924-3_17

```
+     4
+   ),
+   2,
+   2
+ )
> ch17.mat
     [,1] [,2]
[1,]   1    3
[2,]   NA   4

> ch17.mat[ ch17.mat==NA ] = 0
> ch17.mat
     [,1] [,2]
[1,]   1    3
[2,]   NA   4

> ch17.mat[ is.na( ch17.mat ) ] = 0
> ch17.mat
     [,1] [,2]
[1,]   1    3
[2,]   0    4
```

The same method works for illegal values. The values **NaN, Inf**, and **–Inf** are defined in R for illegal operations.

For example:

```
> 1/0
[1] Inf
> -1/0
[1] -Inf
> 0/0
[1] NaN
> log( -1 )
```

```
[1] NaN
Warning message:
In log(-1) : NaNs produced
```

In this example, dividing a positive number by zero results in plus infinity; dividing a negative number by zero gives negative infinity; dividing zero by zero is not defined, so **NaN** is returned. Trying to find the logarithm of minus one returns **NaN** with a warning since the logarithm of minus one is not defined.

The functions is.finite(), is.infinite(), and is.nan() take the place of is.na() in tests for finite, **Inf** and **–Inf**, and **NaN** elements.

For example:

```
> ch17.mat.2 = matrix(
+    c(
+      1,
+      NaN,
+      Inf,
+      -Inf
+    ),
+    2,
+    2
+ )
> ch17.mat.2
     [,1] [,2]
[1,]    1  Inf
[2,]  NaN -Inf

> ch17.mat.2[ is.finite( ch17.mat.2 ) ] = 2
> ch17.mat.2
     [,1] [,2]
[1,]    2  Inf
[2,]  NaN -Inf
```

```
> ch17.mat.2[ is.infinite( ch17.mat.2 ) ] = 3
> ch17.mat.2
      [,1] [,2]
[1,]    2    3
[2,]  NaN    3
> ch17.mat.2[ is.nan( ch17.mat.2 ) ] = 4
> ch17.mat.2
      [,1] [,2]
[1,]    2    3
[2,]    4    3
```

Note that is.infinite() treats **Inf** and **–Inf** the same.

The function sign() returns **–1** for an argument equal to **–Inf**. As a result, a simple way to handle the sign problem is to take the sign of the object first and then multiply the absolute value of the object resulting from the substitution by the sign object after assigning a number to **–Inf**. For example:

```
> ch17.mat.3=matrix(
+    c(
+       1,
+       2,
+       Inf,
+       -Inf
+    ),
+    2,
+    2
+ )
> ch17.mat.3
      [,1] [,2]
[1,]     1  Inf
[2,]     2 -Inf
```

```
> ch17.sg.mat.3 = sign( ch17.mat.3 )
> ch17.sg.mat.3
      [,1] [,2]
[1,]    1    1
[2,]    1   -1
> ch17.mat.3[ is.infinite( ch17.mat.3 ) ] = 4
> ch17.mat.3
      [,1] [,2]
[1,]    1    4
[2,]    2    4
> ch17.mat.3 = ch17.sg.mat.3*abs( ch17.mat.3 )
> ch17.mat.3
      [,1] [,2]
[1,]    1    4
[2,]    2   -4
```

For more information, you can use the Help page in RStudio. Or for more information about **NA** and is.na(), enter **?is.na** at the R prompt. For **NaN**, **Inf**, **–Inf**, is.nan(), is.finite(), and is.infinite(), enter **?is.finite** at the R prompt.

If Statements and Logical Vectors

Often when a logical test is done, the objects being tested are of length greater than one. R does not like this and gives a warning that only the first logical element is used. Suppose you want to test whether any element or all elements of a logical object are TRUE. Then, the functions any() and all() are useful. The function any() returns **TRUE** if there are any **TRUE**s in the object, and **FALSE** otherwise. (The function anyNA() also exists.) The all() function returns TRUE if all elements of the object are TRUE, and FALSE otherwise.

For example:

```
> ch17.log=c(
+    TRUE,
+    TRUE,
+    FALSE,
+    TRUE
+ )
> ch17.log
[1]   TRUE   TRUE FALSE   TRUE
> ch17.test = 8
> ch17.test
[1] 8

> if (
+    ch17.log==TRUE
+ ) ch17.test=1
Warning message:
In if (ch17.log == TRUE) ch17.test = 1 :
  the condition has length > 1 and only the first element
  will be used
> ch17.test
[1] 1

> if (
+    any(
+       ch17.log
+    )
+ ) ch17.test=2
> ch17.test
[1] 2

> if (
+    any(
```

```
+      !ch17.log
+    )
+ ) ch17.test=3
> ch17.test
[1] 3

> if (
+    all(
+       ch17.log[1:2]
+    )
+ ) ch17.test=4
> ch17.test
[1] 4
```

Note that in the third test, the test is for **FALSE** because the **!** operator is used to logically negate the **ch17.log** object. In the fourth test, the function all() tests if both of the first two elements of ch17.log are TRUE.

You can find more information about any() and all() by using the Help tab in RStudio or by entering **?any** at the R prompt.

Lists and the Functions list() and c()

Adding to lists can be confusing. Do you use list() or c()? When creating a list, the elements to be entered into the list are separated by commas. But say you want to add some elements. Then, you will usually want to use c() (or append()).

For example:

```
> ch17.list = list(
+    1:4,
+    paste0(
+      "a",
+      1:2
```

```
+   )
+ )
> ch17.list
[[1]]
[1] 1 2 3 4

[[2]]
[1] "a1" "a2"

> list(
+    ch17.list,
+    1:3
+ )
[[1]]
[[1]][[1]]
[1] 1 2 3 4

[[1]][[2]]
[1] "a1" "a2"

[[2]]
[1] 1 2 3

> c(
+    ch17.list,
+    1:3
+ )
[[1]]
[1] 1 2 3 4

[[2]]
[1] "a1" "a2"

[[3]]
[1] 1
```

```
[[4]]
[1] 2

[[5]]
[1] 3

> c(
+    ch17.list,
+    list(
+       1:3
+    )
+ )
[[1]]
[1] 1 2 3 4

[[2]]
[1] "a1" "a2"

[[3]]
[1] 1 2 3
```

The last result is probably what you wanted. (Another method to get the same result is to use append() instead of c() in the preceding expressions.)

Paths and URLs

File paths are character strings giving the path to a file. The file.choose() function allows you to browse to the file to be opened and can be used within a function call in place of a character string giving a file address.

The file.path(), basename(), dirname(), path.expand(), and normalizePath() functions work with character strings containing file names or paths. The file.path() function returns the path, if specified, or the name of the file. The basename() and dirname() functions return the file name and the path to the file, respectively. The path may not be correct. The normalizePath() function returns some or all of the path but is not always correct.

For example:

```
> file.path( "ch11.R" )
[1] "ch11.R"
> basename( "ch11.R" )
[1] "ch11.R"
> dirname( "ch11.R" )
[1] "."
> path.expand( "ch11.R" )
[1] "ch11.R"
> normalizePath( "ch11.R" )
[1] "/Users/margottollefson/Documents/Documents - Margot's
MacBook Air/Apress RQSR ed 3/ch11.R"
```

For the "ch11.R" object, the first two functions return the original string. The dimname() function returns the "." character string giving an address of "./ch11.R". The normalizePath() function returns the address back to the Users folder.

The tilde operator can be used in R to represent the path to a file. The second example uses the "~/ch11.R" character string for the file address:

```
> file.path( "~/ch11.R" )
[1] "~/ch11.R"
> basename( "~/ch11.R" )
[1] "ch11.R"
> dirname( "~/ch11.R" )
[1] "/Users/margottollefson"
> path.expand( "~/ch11.R" )
[1] "/Users/margottollefson/ch11.R"
```

```
> normalizePath( "~/ch11.R" )
[1] "/Users/margottollefson/ch11.R"
Warning message:
In normalizePath("~/ch11.R") :
  path[1]="/Users/margottollefson/ch11.R": No such file or
directory
```

The file.path() function returns the character string as entered. The basename() function returns the file name. The dirname() function returns an incorrect address, as do path.expand() and normalizePath().

For URL addresses and file addresses, the URLencode() function encodes spaces and reserved characters in a character string. The URLdecode() function decodes encoded character strings to the original character string.

For example:

```
> URLencode ( "https://vanward stat.com" )
[1] "https://vanward%20stat.com"
> URLdecode ( "https://vanward%20stat.com" )
[1] "https://vanward stat.com"
```

In the example, the space between vanward and stat is encoded with %20. Then the resulting character string is decoded back to "https://vanward stat.com" by URLdecode().

More information about the functions can be found using the Help tab in RStudio or by entering **?*function.name*** at the R prompt, where *function.name* is the name of the function.

Editing Objects Like Matrices and Data Frames

The functions `data.entry()`, `dataentry()`, and `de()` open an editing table on the computer screen in which objects and/or expressions containing data can be edited. The object(s) and/or expression(s) must be vectors or consist of columns (e.g., matrices or data frames) and/or be a list of such objects or expressions. (For `data.edit()`, the value to be edited should be an object(s), not an expression(s). For `dataentry()`, a single object or expression of the `list` type that consists of vectors or a list of vectors is entered.) The vectors and/or columns must contain data that is of the `integer`, `double`, and/or `character` type(s).

The `data.entry()` function saves the changes to the data object in the original data object if the editing table is closed by clicking on the upper left red box with a diagonal cross. To not save the changes, select the Quit button in the upper right corner of the editing table window.

For the `dataentry()` and `de()` functions, selecting either the red box with the diagonal cross or the Quit button returns a list of the vectors entered into the functions. The changes to the objects(s) and/or expression(s) are included. However, the functions do not change the original object(s) or expression(s).

The `dataentry()` function requires that the modes of the columns be entered. The `data.entry()` and `de()` functions do not, although the modes can be entered. In the three functions, the modes, if entered, must be entered as a list (e.g., list("numeric", "character")). Note that, when entering or changing data in the editing table, the return key must be pressed after the last entered value is entered if the value is to be recorded.

Both `dataentry()` and `de()` accept data frames and return a list. For data frames, `data.entry()` saves any changes that are made in the editing table to the data frame.

More information about the data entry functions can be found by using the Help tab in RStudio or by entering **?dataentry** at the R prompt.

A Bit More

Some new parts of R involve using a pipe to enter the first argument to a function; the c() function removing NULLs unless the only argument to c() is NULL; and c(), when operating on objects or expressions of the factor class, returning an expression of the factor class. Other changes can be found at the R Project website (see https://journal.r-project. org/archive/2021-1/core.pdf for the changes from R 4.0 to R 4.1).

For example:

```
> cbind(
+    1:10,
+    runif( 10 ) + 1:10
+ ) |> cor()
          [,1]        [,2]
[1,] 1.0000000 0.9927491
[2,] 0.9927491 1.0000000

> c(
+    NULL,
+    3:4,
+    NULL,
+    1:2,
+    NULL
+ )
[1] 3 4 1 2
> c(
+    NULL
+ )
NULL
```

```
> attributes(
+   c(
+     factor(
+       sample( 3, 10, replace=TRUE )
+     ),
+     factor(
+       sample( 4:5, 20, replace=TRUE )
+     )
+   )
+ )
$levels
[1] "1" "2" "3" "4" "5"

$class
[1] "factor"
```

Recursive Functions

R functions can be applied recursively. A recursive function is a function that calls itself until a condition is met. We use the series that defines the exponential distribution to illustrate the workings of a recursive function.

Recall that

$$e^x = \sum_{i=0}^{\infty} \frac{x^i}{i!}$$

So we want a function that adds $x^i/i!$ at each step for i equal to **0**, **1**, ..., **n** for some stopping point **n**. Since $x^i/i!$ decreases at each step and gets arbitrarily small, we used the size of $x^i/i!$ to set the stopping point.

The function follows:

```
> ch17.exp = function( x, i=0 ) {
+     if (
+       abs(
+         x^i/factorial( i )
+       ) > 1.0e-8
+     ) {
+       ch17.exp( x, i+1 ) + x^i/factorial( i )
+     }
+     else {
+       0
+     }
+ }
```

At the first step of the recursion, **i** equals zero, so the value of `ch17.exp()` is

$$ch17.\exp(x,1)+\frac{x^0}{0!}$$

At the second step, the value is

$$ch17.\exp(x,2)+\frac{x^1}{1!}+\frac{x^0}{0!}$$

If **i** equal to **n** is the last step before the increment is less than our stopping point of 1.0e-8, then for **i** equal to **n**, the value of `ch17.exp()` equals

$$ch17.\exp(x,n+1)+\sum_{i=0}^{n}\frac{x^i}{i!}$$

but

$$ch17.\exp(x,n+1)=0$$

so the recursion stops. Since the expression in the `if` section of the function is the last statement executed in the function, the function returns the result.

To see how the function works, we let **x** equal one:

```
> ch17.exp( 1 )
[1] 2.718282
> exp( 1 )
[1] 2.718282
```

Note that for **x** equal to one, the function gives the same value as the function `exp()`.

Some Final Comments

R is a great programming language. In this last section, we give some final comments. R takes some determination to use. If you get stuck on a problem and cannot find an answer, do not be afraid to experiment. It is hard to break R. If you are creating functions, remember to try to figure out a way to use indices rather than loops. Take the process in small steps. And remember that data frames are lists, not matrices.

Index

A

anova() function, 518
Assignment operators
    names, 29, 30
    object creation, 31–32
attributes()/attr()
        functions, 486–489

B

base package, 523
    beta and gamma
        functions, 531–533
    built-in constants, 524, 525
    comments, 548–551
    complex numbers, 539–540
    exponential/log
        functions, 529–530
    function descriptions, 548–551
    mathematical
        functions, 534–539
    matrices, arrays, and data
        frames, 540–547
    reserved words, 524
    trigonometric and hyperbolic
        functions, 525–528

C

Character string functions
    casefold() function, 421
    chartr() function, 421
    grep functions
        agrep() and agrepl()
            functions, 410
        charToRaw() function, 413
        gregexpr() function, 417,
            419, 420
        grep() and grepl()
            functions, 409–420
        grepRaw() function, 413
        regexpr() function, 417
        sub() and gsub()
            functions, 416
    substr() and substring()
        functions, 423–427
    tolower() and toupper()
        functions, 420–423
Classes, 93
    array, 103–104
    attributes, 93–94
    data frames, 102, 108–116
    difftime() function, 129
    dimnames() function, 106

© Margot Tollefson 2022
M. Tollefson, *R 4 Quick Syntax Reference*, https://doi.org/10.1007/978-1-4842-7924-3

G, H

S

V, W, X, Y, Z

Printed in the United States
by Baker & Taylor Publisher Services